真金不怕火炼

GOLD FEARS NO FIRE

A Family Saga from China

RALPH TOLIVER

AN OMF BOOK

266
To I

First published ... 1986
Reprinted ... 1986, 1990

OMF BOOKS are distributed by
OMF, 404 South Church Street, Robesonia, PA 19551, USA
OMF, Belmont, The Vine, Sevenoaks, Kent, TN13 3TZ, UK
OMF, P O Box 849, Epping, NSW 2121, Australia
OMF, 1058 Avenue Road, Toronto, Ontario M5N 2C6, Canada
OMF, P O Box 10159 Balmoral, Auckland, New Zealand
OMF, P O Box 41, Kenilworth 7745, South Africa
and other OMF offices.

ISBN 9971-972-47-6

Printed in Singapore
KHL 7K 6/90

Contents

PREFACE

The story of the Lee family, as told in this book, is an attempt to convey in flesh and blood reality the experiences of the past thirty years in China, and especially the toil, testing, tragedy and triumph of the Chinese Church.

My knowledge of China began when my wife and I became missionaries there in 1938. Deported thirteen years later, we were able to return several times after 1981 and at that time spent sixteen months in Hong Kong, following events on the mainland closely and compiling hundreds of pages of information on what was happening behind the Bamboo Curtain, with special reference to the Christians.

Members of the Lee family are entirely fictional, but they gather into their experiences what has happened to many Chinese families during this tumultuous period. I have drawn on personal experience in China and even more heavily on the experiences of many Chinese people. Most (though not all!) of the incidents are based on fact.

The ideal method of depicting Chinese sounds in romanized form has not yet been invented. The present government of China has made a draconian effort to establish such a method in their *pinyin* system. While it has some advantages over former systems, pinyin unfortunately disregards one major element in the Chinese language, that of tones. Here are a few samples of pinyin as used in this book:

X = sh as in *sh*e (Deng Xiaoping)

Q = ch as in *ch*urch (Jiang Qing, Qin Dynasty)

Z = ds in su*ds* (Mao Zedong)

A = *a* as in *father* (Datong)

UI = *way* (Anhui)

OU = o as in b*o*lt (Zhou Enlai)

ZH = j as in *joy* (Zhou Enlai)

AI = ai as in *ai*sle (Shanghai, Hainan, Haikou)

In this system Peking becomes *Beijing*, Chungking *Chongqing*, and Canton *Guangzhou*. The familiar spelling of Chiang Kai-shek has, however, been retained, and the spelling of the family name, Lee, is not pinyin.

It is not possible at this point to say a personal and specific "thank you" to the host of friends and acquaintances, both in and out of China, whose generous sharing of their own stories have made this story possible. Gratitude demands a big "thank you" too to longsuffering Hong Kong friends who have helped by hospitality, friendship and sharing.

I am indebted also to all who have read the manuscript of GOLD FEARS NO FIRE perceptively, including Leslie Lyall and James H. Taylor III. Our five children and their spouses took the initiative in planning our return to China in 1981, and special thanks is due to all of them.

Not least do I owe an unpayable debt to my wife Rebecca, who lived through with me some of the incidents recorded in this book, who has been my patient helper and most astute critic, and who typed the original manuscript.

Ralph Toliver.

PART I

CHONGQING
1948 ~ 1952

1. What the Frogs Told
Summer, 1948

IT WAS A HOT, humid summer afternoon in Chongqing, West China. The sun was almost down, but that brought no relief from the heat of the day, for when the sun goes down the breeze does too, and the rock on which Chongqing is built throws back the heat it has absorbed during the day.

Like the other eight people queuing up for the bus, Noble Heart Lee was hot. The coat of his western-style suit was slung over his left arm. At 35, tall for a Chinese, he was a personable man. Maybe being personable had helped him gain his position as one of the best-known reporters in Chongqing.

Noble Heart was number five in the queue. In front of him was an officer in Chiang Kai-shek's Nationalist army, so short Noble Heart could see over the top of his head. He was in uniform, with revolver in its holster at his side, and he was fingering the carved butt of the revolver nervously. In front of the officer was an elderly woman with her grandson tied on her back.

The bus was crowded. The conductor hopped off, stood in front of the queue and held up three fingers — only three could get on. *That leaves me out*, said Noble Heart to himself.

But the army officer apparently did not feel the same way about it. He elbowed the grandmother, trying to push her to one side. He wanted to get onto that bus! But the old woman disregarded the elbow and started to step up onto the bus. This infuriated the officer and he gave her a push with both hands, sending her and the baby on her back sprawling into the street.

This was too much for Noble Heart. He pushed in front of the officer and, towering above the shorter man, blocked the step up into the bus. "I beg your pardon, sir, but it is not right to..."

But he got no further. The officer whipped out his revolver, held it at Noble Heart's heart and pulled the trigger. "Snap!" the hammer came down on the chamber. But the revolver did not go off.

Maybe he knew it wasn't loaded, flashed through Noble Heart's mind.

Then, as if to shoot one man were not enough, the officer pointed the revolver at the head of the conductor and, again pointblank, pulled the trigger. "Snap!" the hammer came down on the chamber. Again, the revolver did not go off. The conductor collapsed in a heap on the street as if he had been shot dead, lying white and motionless.

Seeing what was happening, the bus driver, scared out of his wits, jumped from the far side of the bus and ran down the street shouting *"Jiu ming! Jiu ming!* Help! Help!"

This was the signal for everybody else to get off the bus as well. So they did — down the steps and out of the windows in a wild scramble. In the melee, Noble Heart ducked around a corner and hopped into a rickshaw. He buried his head in his coat, wanting by all means to avoid further confrontation with an army officer who pulled his revolver on civilians.

Agitation and fear were written across young Bright Victory Lee's face as he pounded on the door.

"Mama! Mama!" he shouted. "Mama! Mama!"

"Here I am, in the back, feeding the pig," his mother called. She dashed to open the door. "What on earth are you so excited about?"

"Mama, I never saw such a sight in my life! I was coming home from school — cutting across the graveyards on South Bank Hill. I saw it. It was awful! awful!"

"Now, calm down, Victory. What was awful?"

Bright Victory stopped talking. His chest heaved, and he

sat down suddenly on the first thing he saw — a long plank bench beside the kitchen table. It wasn't often that Bright Victory collapsed on anything.

"Those frogs, Mama! They were fighting! It was war!"

Jade Moon listened. She made it a point to listen to her twelve-year-old first-born, because what he said was usually worth listening to.

"It was awful!" Bright Victory continued. "These green frogs on one side — brown frogs on the other. The green-uns were coming up the hill like an army. The brown-uns were on top of the big round grave mounds — like soldiers on hill-tops. And they looked straight in each other's eyes. The green-uns didn't stop when they got to the bottom of the mounds. They went straight up. It was awful!"

He stopped again to catch his breath, and went on: "Then when they met on top of the mounds it was like two armies. Except there wasn't a sound. Queer, I call it! They stuck out those long tongues... Then they grabbed each other and began to chew on each other. The brown-uns had longer tongues and the green-uns grabbed their tongues and began swallowing them. Then, suddenly, there were all these little balls — a brown and a green, a brown and a green locked together. Boy! how they chewed on each other! And kicked with their hind legs! Then the blood began to flow...."

"Now, just a minute, Bright Victory," Jade Moon broke in. "Did you *see* all this?"

"I saw it. And, and, old Mrs. Zhou was there, too, and *she* saw it. And you'd never guess what she said!"

"No! What did she say?"

"She said that frogs fighting and killing each other like that happened once in a hundred years, and it always means something..."

Bright Victory's face suddenly turned from pink to greenish yellow. Jade Moon stepped over and put her hand on his shoulder. She was afraid he would faint and fall off the bench onto the dirt floor.

"Hold on, Victory. Here, I'll pour you some hot water out of the thermos."

"No, no, I'm all right, Mama. But what Mrs. Zhou said hit me pretty hard."

Jade Moon sat down beside her first-born, put her arm around him and said softly, "Was that all that Mrs. Zhou said?"

"Well, she said that when frogs fight each other like that it always means something bad. And, and she said that it's specially bad for those who *see* it."

Jade Moon could feel the twelve-year-old's body stiffen under her arm.

"She said something *bad* is going to happen — to the whole country. And maybe to me, too, because I *saw* it! And she said that this is the way that Heaven warns Earth — that this calamity is going to be specially awful."

"Well," said Jade Moon, always of a practical turn of mind, "maybe it wasn't all that bad. Maybe they didn't really *kill* each other."

"Oh, yes they did, Mama!" Bright Victory straightened up, a little hurt at his powers of observation being questioned. "They locked into balls like that and chewed and chewed on each other and kicked and kicked each other until they both died. I stood there and watched them. When it was all over only a few straggled down the mounds again, as if they were drunk, they couldn't hop like frogs are supposed to hop."

"And what did old Mrs. Zhou do?"

"Well, she stayed and watched until it was all over. Then she turned around and started home. She was mumbling to herself. And she walked awfully slowly."

Jade Moon got up. She walked across the kitchen, her step as slow as Mrs. Zhou's had been. She picked up the thermos bottle, took out the wooden stopper with its bit of cloth wrapped around it, and poured hot water into a rice bowl. Then she lifted the wooden cover of the wok and picked up a pancake with a pair of chopsticks.

"Here, Victory," she said, "eat this pancake left over from last night's snack. After a while I want you to run an errand for me. Forget about that crazy idea of Mrs. Zhou's. What do frogs know about the future?"

As Bright Victory finished off the pancake, Jade Moon went into the bedroom, stuck her hand under the sleeping mat and pulled out a soft leather pouch. The drawstring around the top was long enough to circle her neck when she went marketing, and the soft leather always felt good slipping down into her bosom. But of course, inside the house she hid her bit of money under the sleeping mat. Not many robbers, even in robber-infested Chongqing, would dare slip a hand under the head of a sleeping man! She pulled out two bills marked 10,000 dollars each. Like everybody else in China, she was used to "big money, little purchase," as they say.

"Bright Victory, go buy a bowl of bean curd for supper. And pick up a few sprigs of spring onions. That'll give the bean curd some flavor."

Glad to have something normal and comfortable to do, Bright Victory took the bills and shoved them into his pocket. He slid into sandals kicked off automatically when he entered the house.

"Now," Jade Moon wondered half aloud as she settled heavily on the bench Bright Victory had just left, "what can this mean? Of course, I'm not superstitious like the local people, like Mrs. Zhou. I'm a down-river person, not like these superstitious people who live 1400 miles up the river here in Sichuan province. But, who knows? I never heard of a frog war when I was growing up in Shanghai. Maybe there's something about it I don't know... But if calamity does come, we're too far away from our relatives for them to help. Oh, my! Why didn't we go back down river when the Japanese war was over? Why did we let Noble Heart's boss persuade him to stay in Chongqing and work on the news-paper instead of going home! That boss! I wish he weren't so possessive and so pig-hearted! And now, what's going to happen to Bright Victory? And Bright Loyalty? And Lotus Flower?"

Jade Moon's thoughts were shattered by a loud "*Kai men!* Open the door!" As she did so a hearty, "Hi, Mama!" rang through the little house.

Ten-year-old Bright Loyalty was as loud as Bright Victory was quiet. Everybody knew when Loyalty arrived anywhere. He kicked off his sandals, threw his copybook and pencil on the floor, and shouted, "Anything to eat, Mama?"

Behind Bright Loyalty, Lotus Flower, six years old, just managed to keep the door from hitting her in the face. She lived in Loyalty's shadow and sometimes the shadow was rough as the boy himself.

Though only Bright Loyalty had spoken, Jade Moon knew there were two hungry mouths. "There, you two!" she said. "I bought a roasted sweet potato for each of you and kept them hot. Now then! Stay in the house and do your homework until Victory comes back. I'm going out for a few minutes."

"Let me go with you!" from Bright Loyalty.

"Me, too," from Lotus Flower.

"No, not this time, children. I'm busy. More than that, it'll soon be dark and we can't leave the house empty after dark."

Jade Moon grabbed the little leather pouch and slung its cord around her neck. She kicked off house slippers at the door, slid into street slippers, went out of the front door and pulled it firmly shut behind her.

Jade Moon picked her way along the narrow alleys to the shrine of the Goddess of Mercy.

"Please, dear goddess," she prayed "let at least one pair of your arms be extended to help us when this calamity comes."

Then she wound her way on down the alley to the temple of the God of War.

"If what the frogs told us is true," she addressed him,

"then you're the one who can help us. If there is a war we want to be on the right side and you will have to help us win."

Bowl in hand, Bright Victory wound his way along the flag-stone-paved alley, past the tethered ducks and sellers of candied orange peel and dried persimmons. His steps slowed down as his mind relived the Battle of the Green and Brown Frogs. *Were they really telling us something?* he asked himself. *Mrs. Zhou thought so. And what did she mean when she said it was specially bad for those who see it?*

Bright Victory stopped in front of the shop of the vendor of bean curd. "A bowl of that kind," he said, as he pointed to a tray of not-so-white and not-so-light bean curd.

The vendor of bean curd picked up a flat piece of thin aluminum shaped into an extra wide spatula. Like so many tools in West China, it had probably once been part of an airplane shot down during the Second World War. He cut the bean curd into one-and-a-half-inch cubes, then slipped his aluminum spatula under them and deftly slid the jelly-like mass into the boy's bowl.

"Now to get the green onions," Bright Victory said, half aloud. He walked around the corner to the vegetable market, past cabbages, sweet potatoes, carrots, taro and water chestnuts, to the onion stall. He selected a bunch of five, not too small in the bulb, not turned brown in the leaves. Just then a shout went up from the next stall:

"You can't do that! Those are my turnips! If you want them you'll have to pay for them, like everyone else!"

Bright Victory looked over and saw two Nationalist soldiers, one with a gun, the other with two bushel baskets slung on either end of a carrying pole. The latter was picking up large white turnips and filling his basket with them.

"I weigh, you pay!" went on the irate vendor.

"Don't you know who we are?" the soldier with the gun spat out. "We're Chiang Kai-shek's personal bodyguard!"

Bright Victory didn't believe that. And neither did the vendor of turnips, for he kept waving his hands, palm-outward, to say "No! No! No!" The soldier grabbed the barrel of his gun with his right hand, the stock with his left, and pushed the vendor of turnips backwards into his pile of turnips. They rolled in all direction like marbles.

"Don't get in our way again! We've got other places to go!" the soldier growled. And they strode off.

"Wei! Wei!" a cheerful voice boomed in the passageway. "Hello! Open the door!"

Like all the houses in Chongqing, the Lee's door was always bolted on the inside when anyone was at home — which was most of the time. For weren't thieves and robbers good at opening locks on doors?

"Kai men! Open the door!" again the boom.

Bright Loyalty dashed in from the kitchen, where he and Lotus Flower had just finished their sweet potatoes. "I'm coming, Papa!" he shouted.

"Where's your mother?" Noble Heart Lee asked. "And Bright Victory?"

"Victory's gone to the market to buy something for supper," returned Bright Loyalty, "and Mama went out too. She didn't say where she was going but she looked worried."

Noble Heart automatically slipped out of street shoes and western-style suit, and into house-slippers and baggy trousers that tied with a string around the waist.

"Wei! Wei! Open the door! Open the door!" It was Jade Moon this time.

"You'll never believe what I went through on the way home tonight..." began Noble Heart. He was good at mono-polizing the conversation, and always had his say first about the day's happenings. Jade Moon accepted it as a price to be paid for a workable marriage.

After telling his story of the army officer, Noble Heart

gave his judgment: "These Nationalist soldiers are a lousy lot..." His voice trailed off and he caught himself up. "Children! Not a word of this beyond that door!"

"Yes, Papa!" they promised in unison.

"A reckoning day is coming for an army that treats civilians like that! It looks like the Communists are going to take over all China... Children! Not a word beyond that door!"

"Yes, Papa!" the same chorus.

Jade Moon waited until supper was finished — steamed white rice, Sichuan style, plus bean curd topped with chopped onions and dipped in soy sauce and sesame oil. Then she put the children to bed. At 32, she was a thoughtful, far-sighted mother:

"Well," said Noble Heart, "what did you think of Bright Victory's story of the frogs? It must have hit you pretty hard. Hard enough to make you use some of my hard-earned money to buy incense and offer it to the idols!"

"Oh, I didn't tell anybody about that! Did some of the neighbors tell you?"

"No, I saw three sticks of incense burning to the Door God! And then there was that odd stick on the shelf which you hadn't used. That accounts for four. Which means you must have burned six sticks someplace else, because they come in packs of ten!"

"Oh, Noble Heart!" Jade Moon broke out crying. "Don't be so fussy! I didn't spend much! You know I seldom burn incense, even to our own Door God!"

"Here you are supposed to be from Shanghai, and you burn this crazy incense just like the superstitious local people! I thought you knew better than that! And what would my colleagues at the newspaper office say if they knew you were acting like a Sichuanese!"

"Don't talk about the local people like that! It's not kind!"

"Well," Noble Heart relented, "We won't talk about that. Now tell me, who did you burn incense to?"

"The Goddess of Mercy and the God of War."

"Humph!" snorted Noble Heart. "You're betting on both sides at once! The God of War causes destruction and misery, and the Goddess of Mercy is supposed to save you from destruction and misery!"

Jade Moon burst into a flood of tears, dashed into the kitchen, threw a towel over her face and wept into it with her head on the kitchen table. *This is too much!* she told herself between sobs. *Noble Heart should be understanding and kind, after what he went through and after what the frogs told us today!*

2. What the Great Chongqing Fire Told
Summer 1948

NOBLE HEART the enterprising reporter was up before daylight the next morning, and at dawn made his way through the already-busy streets to the house of Mrs. Zhou. The story of the War Between the Green and Brown Frogs was too good to let slide. And a quote from a grown woman carried more weight than the same thing from a twelve-year-old boy, though Noble Heart reckoned that Bright Victory's facts were as straight as the next person's.

Arriving at Mrs. Zhou's house, Noble Heart shouted "*Wei! Wei!*" in the Shanghai fashion.

A sleepy voice, muffled by the heavy boards of the door, came from inside, "Who is it?" Strangers were not casually invited in, any time of day. But this reporter didn't reckon he was a stranger to anybody.

"It's me, Noble Heart Lee of the *Chongqing Chronicle*. I've known the Zhou family for a long time."

Bolts were slowly drawn. The big horizontal bar was lifted from its brackets. Noble Heart could hear the *clunk* as it was deposited, end up, in the corner beside the door. Even so, the door opened only a crack.

"I'm Noble Heart Lee of the *Chongqing Chronicle*," he repeated. He knew that words — no matter what words — were better than silence at this point.

"What do you want?" demanded an old voice.

"Is Mrs. Zhou at home, please? I want to talk with her a few minutes."

By this time the western-style suit had made its intended impression. "Well, Mrs. Zhou is out, but you can sit here and wait for her."

The double door creaked open on wooden pegs that did

duty for hinges, and Noble Heart stepped over the knee-high threshold that old-style compounds boasted. Once inside, he looked around the reception room. It was bare except for three black, severely straight wooden chairs, and a small square table.

The old man took a towel from around his waist and swatted one of the chairs with it. The dust flew in all directions. "Please sit," he said.

Noble Heart obliged, glad enough to sit down after his brisk walk.

The gateman disappeared, returning in a moment with a glass of hot water which he presented to the guest with both hands.

Hm... Noble Heart said to himself, *Mrs. Zhou can't be among Chongqing's poorest, to keep a gateman these days ...* He placed the glass on the table. The water was too hot to drink and, anyway, it would be impolite to drink it at once.

The old man returned again with a besom made of small branches tied tightly together, the twigs forming the action end. He began to sweep away the dust just outside the door.

"Well, nice place you have here," said Noble Heart, conversation-making.

"Hmm," responded the old man.

"Who owns this place?"

"Mrs. Zhou does."

"Does she own any ricelands out in the country?"

"Not all that much. About five acres along the river west of here."

Just then footsteps approached along the lane, and Noble Heart stood up. "Good morning, Mrs. Zhou," he said, as she stepped over the threshold and came in. He noticed she carried four sticks of incense, slung by a straw.

As he anticipated, Mrs. Zhou had little to add to the frog

story. After listening to her he put the critical question, "Do you mind, Mrs. Zhou, if I quote you on this?"

"Why, no, of course not," she replied. "Just don't use my name."

Once outside again, Noble Heart blinked in the bright summer sun and paused to get his bearings. *Hmm...* he thought, *I've gone so far up-river on the South Bank that I might as well walk on up to Haitanggi and take the ferry across the River there.* But as he started walking, he suddenly realized he had not had any breakfast. *Oh, well,* he thought, *I'll take care of that at the ferry pier.*

Arriving at the pier, Noble Heart selected the cleanest-looking vendor of a local breakfast delicacy — rice flour balls the size of your thumb, stuffed with sesame seeds and brown sugar, and served boiling hot in a bowl of lees of rice wine. A good reporter, he pulled pad and pencil from his pocket and made notes on the Frog War story as the ferry chugged across the river.

At the *Chongqing Chronicle* office, he paused to look at the closed doors, thinking it wasn't often he arrived before they were open. He counted the shrapnel holes, fourteen of them, blown into the double doors when a Japanese anti-personnel bomb exploded across the street ten years before. *Glad I was in a cave under the city that day!* he reflected.

"*Kai men*! *Kai men*! Open the door!"

The sound of bolts being drawn and bar lifted came from the other side of the door. Old Bei the watchman had recognized Noble Heart's voice.

"Well, how are you today?" Noble Heart shouted. Old Bei was hard of hearing.

"Good, good. Thank you, sir."

"And how's your son doing?" Noble Heart had never met old Bei's son, but he knew he was his father's pride and delight.

"Very well, thank you. He's junior officer now on a Yangzi steamer. Only we don't like him being away from home in these uncertain times."

Noble Heart settled down to write his story. He was almost finished when Mr. Deng, the editor, came in.

"What do you think of that?" Noble Heart asked, shoving the sheets of hand-written copy toward Mr. Deng. He had just appended his suggested heading to the story, "Fighting Frogs Foretell the Future."

Mr. Deng sat down while he read. After all, when he stood up he had a lot to support. He was fat and fiftyish, and as he sat the folds of fat spilled over themselves, sucked toward the floor by gravity. It was obvious that he enjoyed eating too much, and for too long. His horn-rimmed glasses lent a cherubic touch and accentuated the roundness of his already very round face.

As the editor read, dark eyes behind dark spectacles got darker still. Then he slammed the sheaf of papers on his desk. "It would never get past the censors," he said with finality.

"But...but why? There's nothing about politics there, nothing critical of the government or of the Party..." Noble Heart remonstrated.

"Oh, yes there is! Don't you see it? The government would say that it's a contrived story, an acted-out parable to show that war between Nationalists and Communists is inevitable and that in the frog war everybody is the loser. The government censors would not like *that*. No, it'll never do! And, for now, I want to stay on the right side of Chiang Kai-shek. People say I'm thumbs up for him. Well, be that as it may. At least I know which side of my bread has the butter on it right now."

Just then the editor's wife came in. Like many a Chinese wife she had no official position in the firm, yet when she came in the door everyone from janitor to assistant editor sat up straighter and started to work harder. Maybe they remembered that at the end of the Qing Dynasty in the early 1900's, though the emperor was out in front and gave orders, it was the old Empress Dowager behind the jade screen who whispered to him what orders to give.

"Here!" said Mr. Deng, holding out the frog story to his wife, "Read this! You're always interested in religious things!"

As Mrs. Deng read, her face became more and more serious. "What was Mrs. Zhou's reaction in her own heart?" she asked.

"Well, of course I wrote nothing like that in the story," responded Noble Heart, "but first thing this morning she went out and burned incense to the gods. She didn't tell me, but I saw the left-over incense she brought home with her." *Wa!* he was thinking to himself, *I'm glad she didn't ask that about Jade Moon!*

"It's sad she prayed to those plaster-of-paris gods," said Mrs. Deng, "when she could have prayed to the True God." She rummaged around in the brown wicker basket she was carrying, fished out a small book and handed it to the reporter, saying: "Noble Heart, there are some things in this book you need to know before hard times hit us. Will you read it?"

"Why, yes, of course, Mrs. Deng, if you ask me to."

"To accept what this book offers to you could be the biggest decision in your life."

Noble Heart looked down at the little book in his hand. Red characters on tan cover read, NEW TESTAMENT.

A minute later, Mrs. Deng left the office.

"Why did she give me this book?" Noble Heart asked.

"Well, she's been a Christian, you know, since she was a child," her husband explained. "She never lost her head during the Japanese bombings, and she'll survive the next chapter in the history of China if anybody does."

"'The next chapter,'" Noble Heart picked up the phrase. "What do *you* think about the battle of the frogs? Do you think that is the next chapter in the history of China?"

"I'm not superstitious", said the editor, not knowing he was quoting Noble Heart's own remark, "but I do know hard times are coming." He drew a sheet of paper out of his desk drawer, handed it over and said, "Take a look at this." It was a hand-drawn map of China, the lower half white, the upper half smeared with red ink.

"I wouldn't dare publish the truth, but I listen every night to the BBC on short wave. The Communists have overrun all of North China and much of Central China. They are as far south as the Yangzi River in several places.

"Hmm...," he continued, "that reminds me. It's time something was done about the picture on the wall."

The editor took a picture down from the wall and held it in his hands. A wistful expression came over his face. "He's quite a man! And look at what he wrote!"

To Deng Lihua
in recognition of your faithful
reporting of the bombing of Chongqing
and your service beyond the call of duty.
(signed) Chiang Kai-shek

"I'll have to get rid of this," he said.

"But that's history," Noble Heart interrupted, "Mao Zedong and Chiang Kai-shek were fighting the Japanese together in those days."

"True, but in these days they have forgotten those days!"

The editor picked up the picture of his family — himself, his wife and three children — from his desk, held the two pictures together to compare for size, then called the office boy.

"Han, take this old picture out of the frame and put the family picture in. It's gathering too much dust here on my desk. And destroy the old picture."

Crestfallen, Noble Heart picked up his story, clipped it together with a paper clip and slipped it into the bottom drawer of his desk. How many times, later, he would regret that little action. Even the stillborn sometimes live to haunt us.

At 1 p.m. it was hot and muggy. Noble Heart yawned and stretched his arms, now in shirt sleeves. He wished he were home taking a nap.

Just then a siren wailed at the Fire Department's lookout tower on the hill behind the newspaper office. Noble Heart jumped to the door to count the wails better: "One...two...three...four...five...six." So, the fire was in the Sixth District of the city — that meant down at the Point where the Yangzi and the Jialing Rivers run parallel for a mile, then join together under the high bluffs.

Noble Heart grabbed pad and pencil and was running by the time he reached the pavement in front of the door. No other reporter was going to beat him to the fire! At the top of a rise he could see the Point down below. He stopped in amazement. There was not one fire but several! He counted them, "One, two, three, four, five." *Now, how under the sun could that ever happen, five fires at once!* he thought. *And down at the Point where the shipping companies have their warehouses. Oh my! The oil, gasoline, kerosene, tung oil, paint and lumber that's stored down there! It'll go up in a hurry!*

As he ran toward them, the fires blazed bigger and bigger. Now he could smell the heavy odor of diesel oil and the lighter odor of kerosene. Just then *boom...boom...boom* three gasoline storage tanks blew up, one after the other. Noble Heart slowed down. *What am I doing, running into all this?* he asked himself.

Then the newspaper man in him took over: "The first principle of reporting is, GET THE STORY," he half mumbled to himself. And he knew it was going to be a big story, because it was a big fire. Chongqing's Fire Department was not adequate for even a small blaze, with only a few tank trucks, no hydrants and no water mains! What could they do with five at once — and maybe more, if those tanks of gasoline kept exploding?

Suddenly, Noble Heart found himself between two of the fires, one close at hand on his right, with black smoke billowing out of second-story windows. He almost ran head-on into a man dashing out the door of that building. At first glance Noble Heart thought he was afire, but as he turned to look at the man running crazily down the street, he saw that he was holding a plaited bamboo rope in his hand, like the torches the boatmen use at night, and it was this that was blazing.

Why doesn't he throw it down? was Noble Heart's first reaction. Then, *Why has he got it in his hand anyway? Oh, no!* it hit him like a brickbat, *He set fire to that building! Why would anybody do that? And it looks as if the smoke almost got him too!* He was to retain in his mind for the rest of his days that vignette of a running firebrand of a man.

Noble Heart ran on, as much to get away from that black, billowing smoke as from any compunction to see what was happening farther on down the Point.

Suddenly the streets were seething with human bodies. *A lot of those people were taking a nap when the fires broke out,* Noble Heart thought. Here an old man was pulling at a bamboo bed, trying to force it through the narrow door. There a young mother, fear written across her face, was throwing the long sash across her baby on her back to tie it tight to her body. Two other children pulled on her long blue gown. And, Noble Heart noted, she was about eight months pregnant with a fourth baby. *She'll be lucky if she gets out alive with those children,* he thought. *But* he reprimanded himself, *this is not all that bad a fire — not yet.*

He passed several small-time merchants, busy boarding up the fronts of their shops, as if boards could keep out the fire. A vendor of buttons, thread, needles and shoelaces dumped his wares into two huge baskets and swung them over his shoulder on a carrying pole. Furniture, rickshaws, loads and just plain people were clogging the streets. Some were headed for the steep stairs descending the bluff to the water front. Others were aiming to escape up the neck of the peninsula to the main part of the city.

Suddenly, Noble Heart was aware that the people around him were coughing from the smoke, which now seemed to be coming from all directions. Those coughed worse who were breathing hardest from carrying loads. *Well,* he thought, *I'm lucky not to be carrying much,* and he looked down at his notebook in his left hand, which reminded him that he had a job to do. He spotted a policeman on a corner, trying hopelessly to control the flow of human traffic.

"Excuse me, sir," Noble Heart began, "I'm with the *Chongqing Chronicle.* Do you have any idea how this fire got started?"

"No, I don't know that. But I do know this — you better get out of here while the gettin' good!" And he gave a poke in the reporter's ribs with his night stick.

Hot words welled up in Noble Heart's throat. He wasn't used to being treated like that. Then, on second thought, he muttered "OK."

Just then, some fifty steps ahead of him, came a terrific *Whoosh!* as the roof of a burning building fell in, followed by a wild clatter as thousands of tiles broke into tens of thousands of fragments on the concrete floor below.

That's enough! Guess I had better get out of here! Noble Heart said to himself, and he turned and ran back in the direction he had come from. But going back was not as easy as coming down. Everybody and his dog clogged the street, bent on getting away from the fire. Noble Heart pitied an old woman, struggling under the weight of a wooden chest on her back, and wondered what was inside. Then he almost ran into two old men, both blind and both with canes, but with one holding onto the tail of the other's long blue gown.

Looking down a side street he saw an area with little smoke and turned down the street, only to find after a hundred yards that it was a dead-end with huge brick buildings on all sides. Turning back toward the main street again, he almost ran into the two blind men. Realizing they would be caught with no way out, he grabbed the first by the shoulder, automatically put on his thickest local accent in order not to frighten them with his down-river talk, and shouted above the din and confusion that was worsening by the minute, "You can't get out down there! Here, you'd better follow me!"

At the sound of a friendly voice the blind man in front grabbed Noble Heart's arm and twisted his finger in the end of his shirt sleeve. Now they were three in a row, the reporter first, then the two blind men, all hanging together like elephants in a parade. *I just hope none of my friends see me now!* thought Noble Heart.

With the blind men hanging on behind, he found it slow going. Then the back one stumbled over a pothole in the street and Noble Heart had to pick him up. Now the fires were on all sides. Cries came from inside buildings where people were trapped. Some who did make it to the street were vomiting and collapsing from smoke inhalation. As the three passed a building on the right, the black smoke billowing from the windows suddenly caught fire with a dull *boom*, and the hot blast thrust them bodily across the street. Noble Heart heard a *sss* and felt the hair on the right side of his head singe. He smelled burning cloth and looked down to see holes opening up in his shirt. The two blind men yelped in pain, *Aiya!*

Fortunately for the three, most of the heat from the smoke explosion went upwards. But a young woman and a child she was holding by the hand had been walking nearer the building, and the flames enveloped them. Noble Heart heard the sizzle as their skin fried in the heat and then, suddenly, the terrible odor of burning human flesh filled the air. He kept his eyes forward; he didn't have the stomach to look back.

In a few minutes they were out of the fire area and in a familiar street. Noble Heart turned his feet toward the newspaper office, but as he crossed the threshold he forgot that the blind men were still hooked on behind. When he collapsed onto a bench in the outer office they did the same!

The editor was listening to the local government radio when Noble Heart arrived. Turning to him he said, "They say that the fire was the work of saboteurs... What do you think?"

The vignette of the crazed runner with the firebrand in his hand came to Noble Heart's mind. He thought for a minute, a deadly seriousness written across his face: "No doubt about it. The fire was set, and by a group of people — all at once — in several different places. And with a terrible loss in life and property." He paused, then asked, "But who on earth would set a fire like that?"

"Only two outfits in China today have the men and resources to pull off such a job — Chiang Kai-shek and the Communists," said the editor. "And it wouldn't be Chiang. Chongqing is his capital and he has every reason to protect it. That leaves us with the Communists; they have every reason to destroy it! More than that, when the word gets around it'll strike the fear of hell itself into the common people. It'll destroy their morale. They'll be afraid to be on the wrong side of an enemy as ruthless as that."

Well, Noble Heart mused, *the frogs told us something, and now I guess the great Chongqing fire has told us something, too.*

In the lull after that last remark, great throat-clearing noises came from the other end of the bench.

Noble Heart jumped, and said to himself, *I must have*

thought that they couldn't hear, either! He looked at the editor, and read the same thoughts in his face. Again came the great clearing of throats from the far end of the bench.

"I'm sorry," Noble Heart apologized, and poured them each a mug of hot water from the thermos, using both hands as he offered them "poor man's tea." They were older than he, making up in age what they lacked in position, so he reckoned they deserved the little deference of two hands. Unfortunately, the gesture of respect was lost on unseeing eyes.

Just then the night watchman came in. "I heard on the street about you rescuing two gentlemen from the fire..." he began.

"Oh! No!" exclaimed Noble Heart. "I suppose I won't be able to keep *that* story from going the rounds! 'Once a word is out, a four-horse chariot can't overtake it', as the old saying goes. They'll be talking about the Parade of the Three Blind Men!"

A knowing grin spread across the night watchman's face, all the wider because he knew the blind men could not see it. He said, "And now that you have rescued them, what are you going to do for them next?"

"What do you mean, 'next'?"

"Well, being from down river, you may not know our local customs," the watchman said with all the respect he could muster, yet with the grin getting broader and broader.

"What do you mean, 'local customs'?" Irritation edged Noble Heart's voice. More than that, he didn't like that grin.

"The old folks always taught us that if you save a person's life once, you have to keep on saving him from then on! You saved the blind men from the fire. If they had died in the fire that would have been their fate. But now they are alive, through your action, so you have taken onto your shoulders the responsibility of fate."

"Let's just leave theory alone. What are you trying to say — in practical terms?"

"First thing — look at their clothes," pointed out the watchman. "They're practically burned off them — they need new clothes. And look at those burned spots around their ears and cheeks and arms — they need some medicine. And they'll need food tonight and somewhere to sleep! You see, you take a lot on you when you interrupt nature and stop the wheel of fate!"

"Are you saying I would have done better to let them die in the fire?" Noble Heart's hackles were rising.

"*Hmmp! Hmmp! Hmmp!*" louder this time. The subjects of this discussion apparently didn't relish being thought of as spots on the dice of fate. But then, in unison, as if by pre-arranged signal, each blind man's right hand hand went to blistered ear and cheek and left hand felt the length of scorched pant leg.

"Yes, it's true," their leader said. "What's going to happen to us next?"

Noble Heart was glad to see Mrs. Deng appear in the doorway at this critical moment.

"I've just come by the church and talked with the pastor," she anounced. "We've decided to open up the church building for refugees from the fire. You can run that in the paper, please, and I'll call the radio station and get them to broadcast it..."

"Will you be able to feed them?" asked the editor.

"Yes, we have some relief supplies stored up, and some clothes, too."

"Great! That'll let me off the hook!" Noble Heart shouted. "When will they start taking them in?"

"They've already started," replied Mrs. Deng.

"Come on, let's go!" Noble Heart called to his two blind followers. The first blind man screwed his fingers into Noble Heart's sleeve and the second grabbed hold of the tail of the first one's blue gown, and they set off down the street again three in a row.

For the moment, the relief of finding a solution to his problem drove from Noble Heart's mind the fact that this second traipse across the city could only add juicy details to the Parade of the Three Blind Men.

3. What the Frogs Told Comes to Pass
Autumn 1949

"THERE'S SOME OMINOUS news today, Noble Heart." Editor Deng lowered his voice. He had closed the door to his inner office quietly after giving a sharp glance outside to check for would-be eavesdroppers. "The head government censor called me. He said we must not in any way let this news get out, no matter where we hear it from."

"What news?" Noble Heart asked.

"All prisoners were released today from both the federal penitentiary and the city jail."

"What's so hush-hush about that?"

"Don't you see, Noble Heart? It's not the action itself, but the motive behind it."

The reporter sat upright in his chair. "Right! I've got you now! It reveals something they don't want revealed..."

"Correct," the editor interrupted him. "By releasing the prisoners they admit they have no hope of defending the city against the Communists. And all these hundreds of criminals on the loose will be just that much more of a headache for the new government. Also," and the editor's voice took on a softer note, "it's a very humane thing to do. Those poor guys in jail could easily die of thirst and starvation before the new government got around to taking care of people at the bottom of the totem pole. You'll have to admit there are some very humane things about Chiang Kai-shek. It's just too bad that the Old Man hasn't had the clout to stop graft and corruption. Why, just yesterday I saw some of his soldiers begging on the street, lying flat on the sidewalk with their pants all bloody from dysentery. And I know for a fact that the doctors in the military hospital took case after case of sulfaguanidine given by America, sold them on the black market and pocketed the money.

"But, look, the reason I called you in is this: if the prisoners are being released, things are in a bad way. Generalissimo Chiang Kai-shek just may not be around here much longer. After all, he fled from Nanjing to Chongqing to escape the Communists. Now, where will he flee next? To Tibet and out to India? Hardly, because India is not China. To Chengdu in the western part of Sichuan? That would only put off the evil day. My guess is Taipei, the capital of Taiwan Province, because he has a neat little moat a hundred miles wide between Taiwan and China mainland, patrolled by the United States Navy. Now here's what I want you to do; find Chiang and interview him — as if you have no idea things are as tense as they are. Do you have the brass to try?"

"'Brass' do you call it?" asked Noble Heart. "I'll just take it as an assignment."

The reporter hopped onto a rickshaw and headed for the Generalissimo's office. Little did he realize it, but this was to be his last rickshaw ride ever. His press card let him past the sentry at the main gate, and once inside he looked for a familiar face, like the good newsman he was. In a minute he spotted an acquaintance who said the Generalissimo had left for the airport. *Well, he might have a few minutes to give me an interview*, Noble Heart figured.

The sun was going down by now. In one of his few financial flings, Noble Heart hailed a taxi — one of only three in the whole city — and told the driver, "Airport!" To his surprise, the taxi arrived just ahead of the Generalissimo's cavalcade with its two outriders on motorcycles. Noble Heart jumped out and ran ahead along the only sidewalk leading toward the departure area. Then he nonchalantly slumped down in a chair at an open-air noodles stand, picked up a newspaper lying on the table and pretended to be reading, all the time looking carefully at each person getting out of the three official cars. To his amazement, one officer in army uniform was none other than the man who had drawn the revolver on him more than a year before. *He must have come up in the world since that little incident,* thought Noble Heart. Slumping down in his seat, he pushed the newspaper up almost to eye level. He did not want to be recognized by the gentleman-of-the-revolver.

But now the Generalissimo himself was getting out of the limousine. He was dressed in civilian clothes, and looked far more subdued and vulnerable than in his military uniform with the rows of medals parading across the chest. His head was bent low as he walked along the sidewalk toward Noble Heart, and he was dabbing a white handkerchief at his nose.

As he passed, Noble Heart heard him mutter to himself, pathetically, "Nobody fights for me anymore." The great man was crying.

Electrified, Noble Heart repeated the words to himself, "Nobody fights for me anymore." *Why!* he thought, *the Old Man has given up! And he's not here to meet anyone: he's here to leave! But leave for where? I've got to find out!*

Noble Heart sat quietly behind his newspaper, figuring out his next move. *Hmm... It's not what you know but who you know that's important. Let's see, who do I know around here?* And he searched every face in sight, though the failing twilight was making that difficult.

A Chinese Airforce jeep pulled up to the curb and an air-force officer got out, carrying a briefcase and an unusually large suitcase. *Hey, that's Captain Chen, my old classmate from Shanghai!* Noble Heart realized. *He must be flying out someplace tonight!* He put down his paper, stood up and was having a good stretch when Captain Chen came up. "Hi, Meng!" Noble Heart said, "How's everything?"

"Good," Captain Chen returned. In a rather short way, Noble Heart thought.

Half under his breath, the captain continued, "But everything'll be much better if you do just as I say. Take this briefcase with the airforce insignia and walk with me direct to the plane. We're talking airforce talk from here on. Understand?"

"OK," replied Noble Heart. He took Captain Chen's briefcase and fell in step beside him.

"No," Captain Chen said, as if answering a question from the man walking beside him, "I've never flown an F–86 Sabre jet, but I want to get my hands on one the first chance I have."

The two men walked briskly across to a B–24 transport plane sitting on the tarmac without lights. The sentry on duty saluted, and Captain Chen and Noble Heart returned the salute. Then the captain climbed directly into the plane and went forward to the cockpit, and Noble Heart followed him, as if he had made the same moves every day of his life.

Closing the cockpit door and locking it, Captain Chen settled into the pilot's seat, motioned Noble Heart into the co-pilot's seat, and then said, "How would you like to stay in that seat until we arrive in Taiwan?"

For once, Noble Heart's aplomb deserted him. "What... what do you mean by that?"

"Well, here's the story. I'm under orders to fly Generalissimo Chiang Kai-shek and Madame Chiang out of here tonight to Kunming and then Canton. And eventually Taiwan. My co-pilot doubles as navigator, so there's a vacant seat here in the cockpit. And, to be frank, I wouldn't object to the company of an old friend, because this flight is a one-way deal..."

"What? What? You mean *me* — go to Taiwan?" Noble Heart was dumbfounded.

"Yes, that's right. And you'd be a lucky man, too. And so would your wife and children..."

"My wife and children! You hit it on the head, Meng. If it weren't for them I'd be sure to go with you. But I can't leave them behind!"

"Why can't you?" his friend returned. "That's exactly what I'm doing. It's better to have a live husband than a dead one, even if the live one is a thousand miles away. And in my position I wouldn't last long if the Communists come in. No, I mean *when* they come in."

"Yes, of course, you're an officer in the airforce. You'd have a rough time..."

"Don't kid yourself, Noble Heart. You're a high profile man yourself. You won't last long either. I'd say a month at the outside...then..." Captain Chen's voice trailed off.

Noble Heart realized, instinctively, that one of the biggest decisions in his life was staring him in the face. The tumult inside him was in strange contrast to the quietness around the soft semi-darkness of the cockpit, the comfortable seat, the even tones of Chen Meng's voice, familiar from so many years ago.

"I...I..." he stuttered. "I can't make up my mind just like this, just sitting here!"

"No rush, Noble Heart. We can't take off until Madame Chiang arrives. You just go back into the passenger section and think it over."

Relieved to do something, even if it were only getting out of the seat and walking, he did as Meng suggested. As he stepped into the cavernous interior of the plane, darker than the cockpit because the curtains were all drawn, Noble Heart thought to himself, *There's no light for me here! Where is there light on this question? I wish I knew how to pray — but who can I pray to? I don't know anything about the gods. What...what was it Mrs. Deng said about the "True God"? I don't know anything about Him, either. But maybe I'll try...* "True God, if you're out there somewhere, please, this is Noble Heart speaking. If you don't mind.. if you could give me a minute, just speak to me right now!"

His eyes becoming accustomed to the darkness, he saw a seat and plopped down into it, heavily. Suddenly, he realized that perspiration had broken out on his forehead and was running down into his eyes.

"To go to Taiwan..." He was talking aloud now, "and to get away from what Meng calls 'certain....'" He could not push himself to say the word "death". He took out a handkerchief and scrubbed his forehead, as if getting rid of the sweat might also get rid of the problem.

"And to stay *alive*! I could get a job in Taiwan and send for Jade Moon and the children later...But how can I leave Jade Moon and the children without talking it over with them? For one thing, she would be worried sick if I didn't come home tonight. And there's all this business of the big changeover and maybe a battle just in front of us..."

All of a sudden, a voice spoke out, loud and clear, "Fasten your seat belts. Stay in your seats until..." As suddenly as it had begun, the voice stopped.

Noble Heart jumped. *Is that the way the True God sounds? And He said, "Stay in your seats until..." Until when? Why did He stop just then?* Then he slumped back into his seat, realizing it was only Chen Meng testing out the recording system. But he kept on thinking. *I'm not very acquainted with the way the True God talks to people. Maybe He does use a loudspeaker sometimes. What was that He said, again, "Stay until..." Well, I can't leave Jade Moon and the kids like this, as much as I want freedom.*

Noble Heart got up and strode forward to the cockpit. He thanked Meng for his kind offer, said "No, not this time" (wondering if there would ever be another time), said goodnight and climbed down the ladder to the tarmac.

As before, the sentry saluted Noble Heart and he returned the salute. A rumble of rolling wheels greeted him as he turned to face the airport building. They were rolling out the stairs for passengers to board the plane. His plane or rather, the plane that could have been his plane.

There was the Generalissimo in his plain suit. And

Madame Chiang in a shiny silk dress buttoned high at the neck. And the whole retinue of the Generalissimo's body-guard, aides-de-camp and advisers and their families and — at the end — the co-pilot. But, and Noble Heart sub-consciously made a note of this, not the officer who had drawn the revolver on him at the bus stop. *Quite a load for that plane*, Noble Heart thought. *And there goes my interview*, the newspaper man in him said.

He watched the plane disappear into the darkness, bound eventually for Taiwan and a known future. Then he turned his back on the airport and in the darkness took a bus into the city, and into an unknown future.

Noble Heart never told Jade Moon about Chen Meng and his offer. He reckoned there were some things a husband did better not to tell his wife.

The silence was eerie. None of the usual night noises. No beggars, no noodle vendors, no clatter of mahjong tiles.

"What *can* we do? Where *shall* we go? Who *can* take care of us?" Jade Moon's voice was getting tenser and tenser.

"Now, Jade Moon, we can't answer all those questions at once. It's hard to be in the middle of a war, but there are some things we should be grateful for. The newspaper office is closed until further notice, and you and I and the kids are all home. Whatever we face, we face together." Noble Heart's voice was consoling. At least, he meant it to be.

"If we just knew which direction they were coming from, that's where the fighting will be, and we could go to the other side of the city," Jade Moon proposed.

"Well, we don't know, do we? And think what a mess it would be if all the people moved across the city. Then someone *would* get hurt! We'd better stay at home."

"And we can pile up tables and chairs against the door to keep the soldiers out," suggested Bright Loyalty the activist.

"And I could help," chimed in Lotus Flower.

The first half of the night was an anticlimax. There had never been such a quiet night in Chongqing. Then, about midnight, *Crrump! Crrump! Crrump!* heavy artillery shells began to explode.

"Those may be *our* shells." Again, Noble Heart was the consoling husband and father.

But the action was coming closer. A bullet zingged over the house. Another hit a tile on the roof and shattered it. The fragments fell into the pig pen. Suddenly, Noble Heart realized that the whole family was near windows. Belatedly, and with the bullets more frequent now, they all moved into the kitchen, as far from the street windows as possible. And they lay on the floor, as far from those flying bullets as possible.

There was a rush of feet in the lane outside. Then a shout, rough, with a northern accent. Then silence. Whoever "they" were, "they" had passed on to another part of the city.

Next day the newspaper man in Noble Heart took over. He *had* to see what had happened during the night.

"No! No! You can't go out on the street today! You might get shot," remonstrated Jade Moon.

"Oh, well, if I see any Communist soldiers around, they're just Chinese like me. They are out for Chiang Kai-shek's hide — and he's gone already. They have no reason to hate me."

Noble Heart dressed in the leisure clothes he usually wore around the house. No western clothes this morning. He didn't know it, but he would never wear that western suit again. On his walk he saw no soldiers, only an old man with long bamboo tongs picking up dog manure to sell as fertilizer, and an old woman with her chamber pot heading for the public toilet. *Maybe they're so deaf they didn't hear the bullets last night,* he mused.

He was almost ready to turn around and return home,

when he heard a hiss. Looking in the direction of the hiss, he saw the doorway to Mrs. Zhou's compound was cracked ever so slightly.

"Come in, Mr. Lee. Mrs. Zhou wants to see you." Noble Heart recognized the old gateman, more by voice than by sight.

"Me?"

"Yes, please come in."

Noble Heart stepped inside. The old man closed the gate carefully and barred it.

Mrs. Zhou had heard their voices and came dashing into the gatehouse, wringing her hands. The words came tumbling out, "I don't want him here! I can't keep him here! But I can't turn him out like he is, can I?"

"Now, just a minute. First, who is 'he'?"

"Oh, of course. Excuse me. You didn't know. It's this soldier who broke into the compound last night. He said they were going to kill him. And he had already been shot once..."

"Let me see him, would you please?"

"Why, yes, come this way."

The soldier, whose green uniform proclaimed him one of Chiang Kai-shek's men, was lying on a sleeping mat on the floor, his left leg bloody from a wound in the thigh. Noble Heart took his pocket knife and cut the cloth away from the wound. He saw that the bullet had made a small hole on the back of the thigh, but a large, ugly hole on the front where it had come out. Blood was oozing from the open wound in front. The man groaned as Noble Heart slowly moved his leg to be sure the bone had not been hit.

"I can't keep him here..." Mrs. Zhou began.

"Right. He should go to the hospital," said Noble Heart. "But first could you give him some rice gruel and some meat? He'll need strength for the trip to the hospital."

After the soldier had eaten, Noble Heart took the uniform

off him and wound a towel around his thigh as a makeshift bandage. Then he dressed him in some old clothes of the gateman's. As the two hobbled out the door, the wounded man leaning on Noble Heart's right shoulder, Noble Heart little realized under what bitter circumstances he would recall this scene.

He said to the injured man, "It's the best part of a mile to the mission hospital. Can you make it?"

"Yes, sir, I'll try."

Less than halfway a rough voice challenged them, "Halt! Who goes there?"

Noble Heart looked up to see for the first time in his life the mustard-colored uniform of the People's Liberation Army, complete with rifle and bayonet. The bayonet pointed straight at his own stomach.

"Civilians, sir."

"Where are you going?"

"Hospital, sir."

"Why?"

"My friend was in a fight last night and got stabbed in the thigh. Just look at that blood!"

"Pass!"

Well, we got by him all right, mused Noble Heart. *What am I going to say next time?*

Arriving at the mission hospital, Noble Heart registered the injured man, who slumped down on a slat bench to await his turn. A hundred people were ahead of him, many of them still wearing the green uniform of Chiang Kai-shek's forces. The missionary doctor was having a very busy morning.

4. The Meaning of "Liberation"
Spring, 1951

"PAPA, WHY DO THEY call it 'Liberation' when we are not liberated from anything?" asked Bright Victory, now fourteen years old. "Is it 'Liberation' because they told us to not eat with chopsticks anymore but to eat with spoons like the Russians?" He disdainfully held up for inspection the table-spoon with which he was eating his rice and pickled cabbage.

"And there's more you *can't* do than you can," Bright Loyalty took up the lament. "Can't visit your friends outside the city, can't play on the street at night, can't buy meat..."

"And can't buy any pretty clothes," Lotus joined in, "only those baggy old pants and jackets that make everybody look alike."

"And all the stuff we do in school these days," added Bright Victory, "slogans, songs about Mao Zedong and all those dances to that same beat of *Dah-dah, dah-dah-dah*. It drives me crazy!"

"You're right, children," Noble Heart said, "to think about these things. That's what you have minds for. But we'll all admit some things are better than before Liberation."

"'Liberation'! Papa, have you got to use that word?" asked Bright Victory.

"Yes, son, we've *got* to use it, if we want to keep our heads on our bodies. That's the fashion in the New China. Now, be honest," he continued, "you'll admit some things are better." He paused to be sure that he himself was honest. "Soldiers don't take vegetables by force anymore, prices are stable and there's no inflation, beggars are gone. And as Chairman Mao says, China is standing up among the nations."

Bright Victory got back to a more personal thing: "Papa,

why do you have to go to those meetings every night of the week?"

"Well, son, it takes a while to learn the new ways, and the new words and what they mean. We have to be flexible, to adjust, otherwise we will not survive."

Lotus Flower came out with a question her eight-year-old brain had been struggling with: "Mama, why do you have to work in that old factory? I liked it better when you were home like you used to be."

"I don't mind work," Jade Moon replied, "except for leaving you children. But I don't like the job they assigned me to, making bullets at the armament factory. Why are they making so many bullets?" ... Her voice trailed off and she gave a little shudder.

"Yes, sir," Bright Victory said to the army sergeant at the desk in the police precinct, "my name is Bright Victory Lee and I live on Liberation Lane, No 97. I want a permit, please, to spend the night across the river with my friend Deng Shun."

"What's your father's name?"

"Noble Heart Lee, sir."

"Wait."

The sergeant went over to the wall, which was entirely covered with bookshelves and books. Finally he found the book he was looking for. Like all the rest, it was the thickness of a man's finger and bound with blue cotton cloth wrapped around cardboard.

The sergeant leafed through the book for a minute, then turned to Bright Victory: "We cannot issue you a permit. Your father is not on the right list."

He returned to the desk and looked down at the fourteen-year-old. Something in the boy's face must have touched the soldier's heart, and he said, "But you are a good boy. Here! Have you seen your family's book?"

"No," replied Bright Victory. He almost said, "I didn't know we had a book," but stopped himself in time. He remembered his father's caution, "Answer what you're asked but don't volunteer information."

"Here it is," said the sergeant. "Have a look."

Bright Victory thumbed through the book. To his surprise, it *was* about his family — one page for his father, one page for his mother, one each for the children, then several blank pages headed "Visitors" and more pages headed "Comments." He surreptitiously looked back at his father's page, and with a quick glance took in the words, written in red ink, "Suspected of being a counter-revolutionary and anti-Communist." Then he closed the book, handed it back to the sergeant and said, "Thank you."

Bright Victory paused on the pavement outside the precinct door, his head reeling. He mumbled to himself, "What does that mean, 'Suspected of being a counter-revolutionary and anti-Communist'?"

The nightly meetings that Bright Victory complained about were growing more intense. Now Jade Moon had to attend as well as Noble Heart, and before long the loss of sleep after the long hours in the factory began to tell on her. She lost weight, dark bags formed under her eyes, and she looked ten years older than her 34 years. But it was Noble Heart who bore the brunt of tension in those nightly meetings.

Noble Heart often thought back to the very first of those meetings, almost a year ago now. The head of every family in the neighborhood had been summoned with a mimeographed sheet: "You must voluntarily attend a neighborhood meeting tonight at 7 o'clock in the courtyard of the Seventh Elementary School."

What do they mean, "must" and "voluntarily" in the same sentence? he had asked himself. *But the new world is full of double talk. Say nothing about it!* And he clipped his teeth tight together, as if that would help.

The heads of houses had all gathered in the courtyard of the Seventh Elementary School. But no one in uniform had arrived, and there was no leader for the meeting. Like everyone else, Noble Heart felt his tension building up. Then the police sergeant strode in, followed by another man in mustard-colored uniform, and they stopped under the one electric bulb high on its pole beside the speaker's table. Noble Heart almost fell off his bench. The man in uniform was none other than the Nationalist army officer who had pulled the trigger on him at the bus stop, two years before!

"A double-crosser!" Noble Heart mumbled to himself. "He must have been spying for the Communists all that time!" But he said nothing, and in the semi-darkness of the courtyard no one had noticed the startled look on his face. Nor could they hear his heart pounding at twice its usual rate.

"This is Comrade Chang," the sergeant had said. "He will be leading your discussions every night. He is an outstanding member of the Communist Party, a man you may emulate."

So, a Communist Party member! If that is true, Noble Heart thought, *he must have been one when he pulled the trigger on me at the bus stop, since they have received no new members into the party since liberation... Just hope he never recognizes me!*

From learning new ways, new words and new meanings for old words, the nightly meetings progressed to the applying of all the "new" things. One after another of the neighborhood residents was told to bring his own self-examination statement. To his horror Noble Heart realized that these were confessions, and that if the confession was not strong enough and self-accusing enough it had to be doctored to bring it up to standard. Much of the actual meeting time was now taken up with the constant revising of confessions. And since Noble Heart, the newspaper man, knew more about writing than anyone else in the group, it fell to him to "improve" the confessions. That part could hardly be expected from Lieut. Chang who, it developed, had only had primary education.

This artificial "improving" of confessions threw Noble Heart into a dilemma. After what Bright Victory told him concerning the family dossier in the police station, he knew he was a marked man. But it galled his soul to write the self-accusing tripe that he knew pleased Lieut. Chang. He knew his time was coming, and he suspected that Chang was awaiting that day like a cat waiting to pounce on a mouse. The neighbors constantly turned their questions to Noble Heart rather than to Chang, and this the lieutenant could not tolerate. More serious still, did Chang recognize Noble Heart as the man who had confronted him at the bus stop? If he did there was never a flicker of an eyelid or a motion of a finger to drop a hint in that direction. At those nightly meetings the cat and the mouse were in the same cage together. The mouse recognized the cat: did the cat recognize the mouse?

From accusing oneself it was only a short step to accusing other people. And for most of the populace this was a welcome relief, for it is always more comfortable to accuse others than to accuse oneself. With the change, however, came a sinister shift: the relatively innocuous discussion meeting was deftly changed to kangaroo court. The accused were arrested and brought in to face their accusers.

One night Mrs. Zhou was brought in by a People's Liberation Army soldier, her hands tied behind her back with a rope. Her shoulders twitched and she leaned wearily against the post that held the one electric bulb. Noble Heart and Jade Moon were shocked to see her, but they would have been even more shocked if they had known what was to transpire that night.

"What is your name?" demanded Lieut. Chang.

"Zhou Meilin, sir."

"You don't need to 'sir' me!" snorted the lieutenant. "Don't you know that today in China everybody is equal? Don't you know we have no class distinction now?"

"Yes, sir," answered Mrs. Zhou.

The subdued titter that ran through the crowd seemed to irritate the lieutenant, as if they were laughing at him. After all, humor is no virtue under a communist regime.

"Zhou Meilin, you are brought before the people today as an enemy of the people. You own five acres of rice land, and anybody who owns that much land is automatically an enemy of the people."

"But I treat my tenants well..." began Mrs. Zhou.

"That's not the question. The Great Leader Chairman Mao says that anybody who owns more than two acres of rice land is an enemy of the people. The rice land your family has used to exploit the people hereby reverts to the people!"

With that declaration, almost a shout, Lieut. Chang pulled a legal-looking paper out of his pocket and slammed it down dramatically on the table. Everyone was wide awake, wondering what was coming next.

"Here are the deeds to your rice lands," the lieutenant continued. "That is, what you used to called *your* rice lands. But the Great Leader says that all rice lands revert to the people." Loud clapping broke out at the four corners of the gathering. The people glanced around nervously then, catching the cue, all began to clap. Finally, the lieutenant waved for them to stop.

"Zhou Meilin, do you know what is going to happen to your deeds?"

"No, sir."

Again, a subdued titter. Again, a scowl from the lieutenant.

"To let you and all the people know that your rice land has reverted to the people..."

He did not finish the sentence, but took a box of matches out of his pocket, struck one, held the deeds by one corner and lit the other corner. As the flames consumed the paper, a stifled gasp flitted across the crowd.

Again, from the four corners of the crowd, clapping. Again, from the crowd, clapping. After it died down the lieutenant spoke again: "We are not through with you, Zhou Meilin! You do not own any land anymore. But you are a landlord by class, and all in that class are enemies of the people and must be punished. There are people here today to accuse you. They will make you confess your sins and your oppression of the people."

Then, facing the crowd, "Comrade Lao!"

"Present!" responded an old man on the front row.

"Comrade Lao, do you live on the land formerly owned by Zhou Meilin?"

"Yes..." The "sir" almost came out but was stifled.

"Tell the people how much rice Zhou Meilin demanded from you every year."

"She took half the rice I produced."

"What kind of a person is Zhou Meilin to take half the rice Comrade Lao produces?"

"She's an enemy of the people!" several people shouted in unison.

Noble Heart could not bring himself to shout these cliches along with the crowd. Rather, he was saying to himself, *Only half? Most landlords demand sixty percent or even two-thirds. Mrs. Zhou has been kind to her tenants.*

Old Mr. Lao still stood facing Lieut. Chang; he was nervously fingering his cap, a bemused expression on his face.

"Sit down," the lieutenant said, and shouted for the second witness: "Comrade Wang!"

"Present," responded a middle-aged man on the front row.

"Comrade Wang, do you live next door to Zhou Meilin?"

"Yes."

"Did you see anything unusual at her house the morning of the first day of the liberation of Chongqing?"

"Yes, I did."

"Tell the people what you saw!"

Comrade Wang cleared his throat in an unaccustomed-as-I-am-to-public-speaking manner, and began, "Zhou Meilin took in a soldier of that traitor Chiang Kai-shek, fed him and clothed him, then got a nephew to take him to the hospital."

Noble Heart cringed when he heard those words, and was glad that in the semi-darkness no one noticed his face. *But what about Mrs. Zhou*, he wondered, *how will she react? Will she look at me?*

Mrs. Zhou, however, was playing her part well. She was no longer leaning against the lamp post but standing erect, and in spite of her hands being tied behind her back she was now calm and self-possessed.

"Did you hear the witness of Comrade Wang?" Lieut. Chang shouted at the crowd.

"Yes! Yes! Yes!" the crowd yelled.

"Sit down," the lieutenant said to Mr. Wang.

Then the third witness was called. "Comrade Peng!" shouted the lieutenant.

"Present." To Noble Heart's surprise, Mrs. Zhou's old gatekeeper stood up. He was shaking like a leaf in a typhoon.

"Comrade Peng, what is your occupation?"

"I am Mrs. Zhou's gatekeeper."

"Don't say 'Mrs. Zhou'! Say 'Zhou Meilin'!" the lieutenant stormed. Then, in a more coaxing tone: "You have been called here today to reveal to the people how tyrannical and wicked Zhou Meilin has been to you. Tell them!"

"Well...well..." the old gatekeeper stuttered, shaking worse than ever.

"You know what to say. Go ahead!"

"Well, there's one thing I can say. When her husband died, she gave me his leather shoes. They were too small for me and I couldn't wear them."

A voice came from back in the crowd, "See? She deliberately made them too small in order to embarrass you and oppress you!"

"Yes! Yes! Yes!" the crowd chimed in.

Lieut. Chang stood up. "Comrades," he said, "you have heard the evidence. Zhou Meilin is a lackey of the traitor Chiang Kai-shek. She gave refuge to one of his soldiers. She has mistreated her tenants and her servants. Worst of all, she is a landlord. All landlords must be eliminated. What is the verdict of the people?"

Silence. This was something new to the South Bank people.

Again, louder this time: "What is the verdict of the people?"

A single voice responded, "Kill her!" Then, as if by prearranged signal, a bedlam of voices, "Kill her! Kill her! Kill her!"

Noble Heart and Jade Moon gasped and clung to each other. They saw Mrs. Zhou reel, turn half around, and collapse. The soldier standing beside her grabbed her and held her upright, all except her head which lay crazily on her left shoulder as if she were already half decapitated.

"Hah! she's playing tricks on us!" shouted the lieutenant. "I'll teach you to do that to me!"

With that threat he whipped off his heavy leather belt with its ponderous brass buckle. At the same time the soldier supporting Mrs. Zhou pushed her limp body up against the light pole and used the ends of the ropes around her wrists to tie her arms high up on the pole. He wrenched her hands upwards so suddenly that Noble Heart and Jade Moon heard the shoulder bones pop out of joint. The sudden pain brought Mrs. Zhou out of her swoon. A cry of anguish escaped from her lips and her head straightened up on her shoulders. Fear and unbelief were written across her face. Noble Heart read her thoughts: *How could this ever happen to me?*

"I'll teach you a thing or two, you bloated capitalist!" shouted the lieutenant, with an oath.

The people on the front benches had stood up and leaned forward — a few had even taken a step forward — mesmerized by the tragedy that was unfolding before their eyes.

"Stand back!" the lieutenant shouted savagely, and punctuated the command with a swing of his belt. The crowd fell back, aghast.

"I'll teach you a thing or two!" hissed the lieutenant again, this time from a red face and through teeth clenched almost shut. Holding the belt by the end away from the buckle, he swung it around his head and landed the buckle on Mrs. Zhou's body. Noble Heart and Jade Moon heard a "snap" as a rib broke with the impact. Then another swing around to pick up speed and the buckle struck her face. A gash opened up across her cheek and the blood flowed down her face and off her chin.

At this point, mercifully Mrs. Zhou fainted for the second time. Again and again the officer struck. Revolted and overcome by the tragedy he could do nothing about, Noble Heart's gaze was yet fixed like a magnet on the defenseless body tied to the lamp post. The reporter in him unconsciously came to the top and he was counting the blows: "One, two, three, four....thirty-eight, thirty-nine, forty."

Noble Heart was still going to work every day at the newspaper, now renamed *Liberation Daily*. Like every other worker in the city, he was frozen in his job by government decree. It was even comforting to see the fourteen shrapnel holes in the front door, for they reminded Noble Heart of the brave days when Chongqing and its people had stood up to the merciless bombing of the Japanese war planes. Inside, his desk was the same, and the clatter of the press from far inside was also the same. But there were changes. A government spy checked on things — and people — in the editorial room, and another did the same in the pressroom.

The worst thing to endure, though, was seeing Mr. Deng walking around with a broom and a dustpan, shamelessly demoted from editor to janitor.

"The only reason they keep him around is to keep tabs on him," Noble Heart explained to Jade Moon. "He's virtually under house arrest. It doesn't look good for the future."

At Mr. Deng's desk as editor sat Comrade Huang. He knew nothing about newspapers but he was politically reliable and a member of the Communist Party. *In all honesty,* Noble Heart thought to himself, *we don't need an editor now, with all this canned propaganda coming out of Beijing. And we don't need a reporter, either. This isn't a newspaper anymore, it's just a paper.*

China had stepped into the Korean War on North Korea's side, and the paper's daily cartoon rang the changes on the theme of China defeating America. A favorite picture was of Uncle Sam being pierced by darts thrown by Chinese children, with red ink flowing from his side. One picture supplied by Beijing was from Chicago, USA; it showed a shop with a big sign, "HORSE MEAT FOR SALE." The caption explained that the American people were so poverty-stricken that they were reduced to eating horse meat. It did not explain that the horse meat was for the American pets.

One day the new editor called Noble Heart in. "I want you to write an article," he said, "on how well off the beggars are now as compared to before liberation." He wrote out an address and handed it to the reporter. It was a shelter where former beggars were housed.

Relieved to have an assignment that took him outside the office, Noble Heart decided to walk to the shelter. Actually, he had little option. Rickshaws were no more — they displayed too much class distinction between rider and puller and so had been eliminated. The three taxis which the city once boasted had long since been commandeered by the military. And the buses were as crowded as ever.

The main gate from the street into the ex-beggars shelter opened onto the exercise yard. What should Noble Heart see as he entered the gate but a familiar sight — two blind men, one with his fingers twined into the shirt tail of the other, walking round and round inside the yard.

Why, there are my two friends from the day of the great fire! said Noble Heart to himself. *And they still have on the pants and shirts the church people gave them!*

"*Wei!* Hello!" he said as he walked up to them.

"Oi! Mr. Lee! it's you!" said the two almost in unison. "How did you find us?"

"Well, to be honest, I wasn't exactly looking for you," answered Noble Heart. "I came here on an assignment from my newspaper to find out how you all are in this shelter."

"Great! You see, we are keeping fit, doing our exercises," said the front man. "And there is good news just today. They are going to start giving us vitamins — they call them 'happy pills' — and they're to send us to work in the fertilizer factory."

After a few pleasantries Noble Heart said goodbye and headed across the exercise field toward the office. He turned around and looked back at the two blind men. The one behind had his fingers twined around the shirt tail of the one in front. There was a smile on each face.

Hmm, said Noble Heart to himself. *What does that mean, 'happy pills' and 'fertilizer factory'?*

5. Another Struggle
Spring 1951

"I DON'T LIKE this a bit. Not one bit," Noble Heart said to Jade Moon. "Look at this."

Jade Moon read the note:

"You are hereby summoned to a struggle meeting at 4 p.m. May 12, 1951, at the Headquarters of the Chongqing Garrison in the City of Chongqing.

Signed, Garrison Commander"

"The trouble with these 'struggle' meetings," said Noble Heart, "is that they always struggle *against* someone. It's another name for a kangaroo court. But the truth is, it's not a court. And I'm sure that kangaroos have more sense than is displayed at these meetings."

"Oh, Noble Heart!" A wild and terrified look came into Jade Moon's eyes. "Are..." she clutched at her throat. "Are they going to struggle against *you*?" As she spoke a tear rolled down each cheek.

"No, my dear, I don't think so. The present regime is very methodical, and they struggle against a man in his own precinct. It's for effect on his friends and neighbors. So if they were aiming at me, it would be here on the South Bank."

"But, Noble Heart, don't you see? It might be because you are connected with the newspaper, and that's only a few blocks from the Garrison Headquarters!" The tears were rolling faster now.

Noble Heart comforted her as best he could but warned her he might not make the last ferry across the Yangzi. "The meeting starts at 4 p.m. and may go on to midnight. And the trouble is, I have received this summons!"

He looked down again at the piece of rough paper. Then

he rolled it into a twirl and twisted it viciously, as if to wring the poison out of the paper. He unrolled it and tore it into a hundred pieces, then took the bits in his double hands and dumped them on the fire under the wok where their supper rice was steaming.

The following morning at the office Noble Heart was surprised to see broom and dustpan leaning against the cupboard door where the cleaning equipment was stored, but ex-editor-now-janitor Deng was not to be seen. Noble Heart enquired quietly of the old employees, careful to be out of earshot of Editor Huang and the two government spies. No one knew anything about Mr. Deng or why he had not come to work.

Promptly at 4 p.m. Noble Heart stepped into the compound of the Garrison Commander. Looking around he saw a dozen employees of the newspaper, all from former years like Old Bei the watchman. Editor Huang and the two spies were there as well.

A few minutes later there was a flurry of activity in the section where the jail was located. A small knot of men moved toward the drill ground, where a table, chairs and several electric bulbs hanging from poles proclaimed the location of the struggle meeting. To his horror, Noble Heart saw in the middle of the knot of men his old boss, Editor Deng, his hands tied behind his back. "Oh, no!" he exclaimed under his breath. "That's why he wasn't at work today. He's been arrested! And they're to have his trial right now!"

The newspaper man in Noble Heart surfaced even at this sinister moment. He walked over to an officer in uniform and casually enquired, "Is he guilty of something?"

"Of course he is!" the officer snapped. "If he were not guilty we wouldn't arrest him, would we?"

Noble Heart had no answer to that one. He sought refuge among a group of onlookers whom he did not know — and whom he hoped did not know him. *Let me remain anony-*

mous — that's all I want right now, he said to himself.

"Comrade Tai!" Captain Tang, the officer in charge, shouted. A hush fell over the crowd. They knew by experience the deadly seriousness of such a struggle meeting.

Noble Heart recognised the electrician from the press-room, a chronic troublemaker.

"Comrade Tai, how long have you known Deng Lihua?"

"For thirteen years."

"How did Deng Lihua treat you?"

"Terrible!"

"Give the people an example of how he treated you," and Captain Tang waved to the crowd as if they were to be the arbiters of Editor Deng's fate.

"His tips at Chinese New Year were always small."

"Well, Noble Heart said to himself, *he didn't get a cent this year under Editor Huang!*

"Next witness. Comrade Tao!"

When Comrade Tao came up, Noble Heart detected a shift in tactics. Here was a man who had been coached in what to say.

"How long did you work for Deng Lihua?"

"For thirteen years."

"Was there anything you observed Deng Lihua doing that was injurious to the people?"

"Yes."

"What was that?"

"He was the stooge and pet dog of that traitor, Chiang Kai-shek."

"Give an example."

"One time during the Japanese War I saw him stick both thumbs up and say, 'Chiang Kai-shek is a great guy'."

A murmur flitted over the crowd. This accusation was serious.

"Do you have anything else to say?"

"Yes. At one time Chiang Kai-shek gave him an autographed picture. He put it on the wall in his office. It's still there."

Noble Heart gasped. This testimony was touching the quick. *But surely,* he said to himself, *that's a lie about the picture still being on the wall. I saw him take it down myself. And he told the office boy to destroy it.*

"Now, are you sure of what you are saying?" Captain Tang was continuing to question Comrade Tao. "Are you sure that picture is on the wall now?"

"I'm sure. I saw it there myself yesterday."

How... how could that be? Noble Heart thought. *If that is true, the noose is closing around him.*

"Enough!" shouted Captain Tang. "If that picture is on the wall now in the newspaper office, we have all the evidence we need to deal with Deng Lihua. And now," he continued, "we shall adjourn to the newspaper office. Every person here will accompany me. We shall proceed! This meeting is adjourned!"

Noble Heart stumbled along the street. He wanted above all else on earth to get close to his friend the editor, to take him by the hand, to put his arm around his shoulder, to say a word of sympathy... But these were hopeless thoughts. He knew it would be suicide to show the slightest sympathy for the accused.

However, he did the best he could; as the crowd moved toward the newspaper office, he edged up close to the editor, hoping he would notice him in the crowd. As he got nearer, he was disgusted to see the soldier in charge ruthlessly pushing the editor along. He was stumbling into potholes and panting from this unusual physical exercise for his overweight body.

Arriving at the newspaper office, Noble Heart stationed himself where he could see the fateful picture on the wall. *Hey, wait a minute,* he said to himself, *that's the picture of the editor's family, just like it's been for months.* Sure enough, there was the picture of husband, wife and three children, looking serenely down on the seething, sweating mob crowded into the office.

"Come to order!" shouted Captain Tang.

Silence spread through the office and overflowed onto the street.

"Comrade Tao!"

"Present."

"Now Comrade Tao, show the people the picture you spoke of." Captain Tang gave a magnanimous flourish toward the crowd.

"There it is on the wall."

"I see that picture. But it is of a man, a woman and three children."

It flashed through Noble Heart's mind. *He's play-acting. He's doing his part well.*

"Yes," replied Comrade Tao. "But you haven't seen what's *behind* that picture."

"Oh," replied Captain Tang, feigning surprise. "Is there something behind that picture?"

"Yes, there *is* something behind it."

"Well, you'll have to prove it to the people." Again that magnanimous gesture toward the crowd.

Captain Tang flicked his finger toward the picture. Comrade Tao stepped over to the wall, removed the picture from its hook and began tearing into the back of it with his finger nails. In a minute he had the first layer of cardboard off. Then from the middle, between the family picture in front and what had been the cardboard backing, he triumphantly pulled out a picture of Chiang Kai-shek.

Oh, no! exclaimed Noble Heart to himself. *It is that picture!* And he repeated from memory the telltale legend:

"To Deng Lihua
in recognition of your faithful
reporting of the bombing of Chongqing

and your service beyond the call of duty

                         (signed) Chiang Kai-shek"

A gasp of astonishment and disbelief swept outwards from those close enough to see the picture of the Generalissimo.

"Let me have that picture!" Captain Tang commanded.

Comrade Tao dutifully handed over the picture. Captain Tang took it into his hands disdainfully, as if he were handling a snake — but a dead one.

"Deng Lihua, is this your picture?"

Editor Deng did not reply.

"What can you say for yourself, you lackey, you pet dog of Chiang Kai-shek?" Captain Tang's voice was rising. Noble Heart immediately recognized the tone; it was the beginning of the end for Editor Deng.

Now Captain Tang was holding the picture with two hands, the face outward toward the crowd. He stepped over to Editor Deng and thrust the picture into his face. "There's your friend! See if he can help you now!"

From Editor Deng, silence. Noble Heart knew there was no point in the editor replying, and admired his apparent composure. But he could see beads of sweat on his forehead and face and knew what terrible pressure he must be under. That pressure was increasing by the minute. The eyes of all were glued on the editor. Noble Heart said to himself, *that could be me — and that's what a lot of other people around me are thinking, too.*

"Ha! You were a friend of the snake Chiang Kai-shek, were you?" the captain was taunting him now. His face was getting redder and redder and his voice was a screech.

"Ha! You held up both thumbs, did you, and said that Chiang Kai-shek was a good guy, did you?"

Noble Heart knew the climax would soon come, at this rate.

"Comrade Tai!"

"Present,"

Noble Heart wondered what this could mean, calling up the electrician again. His testimony had been too weak to condemn anyone.

"Comrade Tai, you are an electrician."

"Yes."

"On this newspaper?"

"Yes."

"You know where all the wires are on the press back there?"

"Yes."

"Well, you go back there and rip out two wires, heavy ones, each a meter long. And bring a hammer and a screwdriver with you when you come back."

What in the world does this mean? Noble Heart gasped inwardly.

The Captain nonchalantly took the picture over to the wall and hung it up again. But he had removed the family picture and had thrust that of Chiang Kai-shek into its place. Soon Comrade Tai was back, depositing wire, hammer and screwdriver on the table in front of Comrade Tang, reverently, as if he were making an offering to a god.

"Take the hammer and the screwdriver and knock two holes through the wall just above the lintel of the door into Deng Lihua's office. I mean, what used to be his office. Put them a half-meter apart."

Captain Tang sat down, a satisfied smirk on his face, like a fox with a dying chicken in his paws.

Comrade Tai jumped to do as he was told, pushing a bench under the door so he could reach the lintel.

I'm mystified, thought Noble Heart. *But this can't mean anything good.*

Wham! Wham! Wham! In a couple of minutes Comrade Tai got down from the bench, and placed hammer and screwdriver on the table in front of the captain again. Captain Tang climbed onto the bench with the meter-long wires in his hands. He pushed one end of a wire through a hole above the door and tied the end back around the wire securely, leaving the other end dangling. Then he did the same with the second wire.

Back on the floor, the captain stood directly in front of the editor and bellowed: "Get up on that bench in the doorway! Face the picture of Chiang Kai-shek! Hold both thumbs high. I'll show you what happens to a man who is thumbs-up for Chiang Kai-shek!"

His chest heaving, the editor moved over to the bench. He put one foot on the bench, then collapsed in a heap on the floor. Whether he fainted or whether with his huge weight he lost balance, Noble Heart could not tell. Three soldiers grabbed the editor and lifted him onto the bench. As they held him upright, the captain jumped onto the bench as well. Then, to Noble Heart's horror, he saw the captain take a dangling wire and wrap it around the editor's right thumb, pulling it so tight that the skin broke and blood spurted, and tying a knot to hold it.

"*Aiya!*" groaned the editor between clenched teeth and from a face white as a sheet of paper.

The captain then took the other wire and wrapped it around the editor's left thumb. Again, he pulled tight and the blood spurted. Again, he tied a knot to hold it.

"Back off!" the captain commanded the soldiers.

With one kick, the captain kicked the bench out from under the editor. His body lurched against the wires, quivered for a moment, then swung suspended with the toes just touching the floor. A terrifying groan escaped his lips.

Noble Heart fainted with the horror of it, and did not hear the "Meeting dismissed" from the captain. A minute later he came to his senses and found himself collapsed against the door with the fourteen shrapnel holes. Half the crowd had left, and others were still going and coming. In the confusion Noble Heart slipped inside, past the suspended body of the editor, and back to the corner where that morning he had seen broom and dustpan leaning against closet door. No one appeared to notice him, so he slipped inside, closing the door gently after him.

For a long time Noble Heart lay on the closet floor, an ear to the crack under the door. Gradually the commotion in the newspaper office died down. Perhaps it was two hours later that he heard the sound he was waiting for — the *chunk* of the heavy crossbar being dropped in place behind the front door. That sound signaled that only Old Bei, the watchman, was inside and that everyone else had gone.

Everyone, that is, except Editor Deng. Noble Heart knew it was the practice of the communist executioners to leave their victims where they fell for the relatives to pick up. He hoped against hope that there was still life in the editor's body. When he dashed out into the office, there was Old Bei examining the editor's body with a what-can-I-do? look on his face. That look changed to hope as he saw Noble Heart. The two of them pulled three benches under the editor. And Noble Heart dashed to the pressroom and returned with a pair of pliers. He quickly cut the two wires and, as gently as they could, they lowered the editor onto the makeshift bed. Noble Heart grabbed the editor's wrist to feel for a pulse. There was none. Then he ripped open his shirt and placed his ear on the chest. There was no sound.

Disheartened and defeated, Noble Heart began the delicate job of removing the wires from the editor's thumbs. This was not easy because thumbs and hands had swollen and the thumbs had turned black. That finally accomplished, they massaged arms and heart and applied cold cloths to the face. But to no avail. The editor had already been dead for some time.

"*Kai men! Kai men!* Open the door! Open the door!"

"Who is it?" an aged female voice asked from inside.

"It's Noble Heart and Jade Moon Lee. Is Mrs. Deng at home, please?"

"Wait a minute," the voice answered.

There came the grating sound of wood against wood as the great bar was removed from the double doors, and the *chunk!* as it was deposited upright in a corner.

"Come in! Come in!" It was the voice of Mrs. Deng herself.

Once they were inside and the old servant had closed and barred the doors behind them, Noble Heart began, "We are so sorry for what happened and we want to express our sympathy." His voice tightened and his words stopped.

"Thank you. It is kind of you to come," answered Mrs. Deng. "But I should tell you right out that I was prepared for this. Two weeks ago I was praying and asked God for a sign of what to expect. It seemed that I heard a voice saying to me, 'Read in the New Testament, Second Timothy chapter three verse twelve'. I had no idea what that verse could be, but when I opened my Bible, it almost jumped off the page:

'All that will live godly in Christ Jesus
Shall suffer persecution.'

"And I knew my husband was an obvious man around town for them to take their vengence on, because he *was* an admirer of Chiang Kai-shek..."

With that, Mrs. Deng lowered her voice and looked over her shoulder as if she expected to see an eavesdropper behind the curtain. Her shoulders twitched ever so slightly as she turned back to Noble Heart and Jade Moon.

At that instant the old servant came in and said, "Excuse me, ma'am, but there's a man at the door. Sounds like a boy, really. Says his name is Fang Han and that he worked for Mr. Deng."

Noble Heart and Jade Moon exchanged glances. It was the

office boy from the newspaper, the one who was told to destroy the picture of Chiang Kai-shek.

"Ask him to come in," Mrs. Deng said.

Han burst into the room. Without the usual conventional greetings he fell on his knees in front of Mrs. Deng and moaned rather than said, "Oh! Mrs. Deng! Please forgive me! Please forgive me!"

Then, as if kneeling was not enough, he prostrated himself full length on the floor and moaned again, "Oh! Mrs. Deng, please forgive me!"

Mrs. Deng took him by the hand to raise him up. Catching the cue, Noble Heart picked him up by the armpits and deposited him in a chair. There he slumped in a shapeless heap, still moaning.

"Pour some tea from the thermos," said Mrs. Deng to the old woman.

A few sips of hot tea seemed to bring Han to reality. "Mrs. Deng," he began, "I was so terribly shocked when I heard what happened to Mr. Deng — and all because of me. I started to hang myself, with a sheet all twisted up like a rope. But my father found me before I jumped. He said I should see you. Clear the family name, he said. Because I didn't do it on purpose. No, I didn't!" And Han burst out in tears.

"Here, just drink some more of this tea," encouraged Noble Heart. He was anxious for Han to talk, not cry. Han obeyed, apparently glad for anything in the physical world to hold onto, even a cup.

"Now, Han, tell us what happened," Noble Heart said.

"Well, it was that picture. Mr. Deng told me to destroy it, and I wish to heaven I *had* destroyed it, like he said. But I just threw it into the trash can for the time being. Then I tried to fit the picture of you, ma'am, and the family," (this with a nod to Mrs. Deng)" into the frame. And it was too loose. So I went to the trash can to look for some padding. And here was this sheet that just fitted into the frame and took up the slack. It was that awful picture!" And Han broke into tears again.

"But didn't Mr. Deng say to *destroy* it?" demanded Noble Heart.

Jade Moon stepped on his toe with a do-be-patient message, and he fell silent.

"I guess by then 'destroy' was watered down in my mind to 'get rid of '. And so I did get rid of it. Behind the family picture. Just for packing. But that turncoat Tao must have seen me put it there."

"Then he used that knowledge to get himself in well with the new authorities and to rub their fur the right way," Noble Heart completed the thought.

Han stood up resolutely. "Now, please excuse me ma'am. I'm going home to hang myself. It's the least that I can do." He turned and started toward the door. But Mrs. Deng stood up and bodily blocked the way to the courtyard.

"You'll do nothing of the kind, Han!" she said. "One death is enough. We'll not have two. More than that, I've got something important to say to you. You came here today to ask my forgiveness and I want you to know that you *have* my forgiveness, full and free. I'm a Christian. Jesus Christ has forgiven me my sins and he says I must forgive others as he has forgiven me."

"You, you mean," Han gulped. "You mean you *really* forgive me?" This was talk he had never heard before.

"Yes, I do, Han. And if I forgive you, then you must forgive yourself, too."

"You mean, I don't have to..." he shuffled his feet nervously, "to commit suicide?"

"No, Han, you don't have to commit suicide. That would only make matters worse."

"Well, I thank you, ma'am. And I'll tell my father you've forgiven me. That'll make him feel better!"

While this was going on, Noble Heart and Jade Moon

stood, transfixed by what they heard and what they saw written on the two faces in front of them.

When Han had gone and they heard the big doors across the courtyard shut again, Noble Heart turned to Mrs. Deng:

"Mrs. Deng, we want to know how we, too, can get this amazing love of yours. Why, you forgave the very person who was responsible for your husband's death! It's like, in that little book you gave me, when Jesus said, 'Father, forgive them,' and those were the very rascals who were killing him!"

"Now, in the first place, don't over-rate Han's part. They were out to get my husband and they would have done so sooner or later, picture or no picture. It was just a handy thing for them to latch onto. And it would be sad if a young man died due to my husband's death. He did not mean to harm anyone."

"Well, it beats me..." began Noble Heart.

"And me, too," said Jade Moon. "How long have you been a Christian?"

"Since I was a child. My parents were leaders in the church in Suzhou, down-river." The conversation went on a long time.

Back home, Noble Heart called Bright Victory, Bright Loyalty and Lotus Flower together. They knew something important was coming up, for their parents called such a conclave only once in a great while. It had been six months since the last one.

"Children," said Noble Heart, "my boss and good friend Mr. Deng is dead and buried. He died due to no fault of his own. He was a kind and good man.

"Now we have to realize that things are going to be very different from now on. A new age has begun in our country. I told you about the great Chongqing fire — maybe life is going to be like living through a fire. Fire is dangerous. It can kill people and cause them terrible suffering. But fire can also do good. It can refine and purify. As the proverb says, 'True gold does not fear the purifying fire.'

"Children, I have learned something recently that I should have known when I was your age: that there is a great God in heaven and that He looks after those who trust in Him. I believe that He will let us live and not die, and will use the fire to refine us.

"In the end we will find peace. But it will not be the peace of Marx and Mao standing on top of our graves. Our peace will come from living according to our own conscience and from knowing that we have put God first in our lives, before man."

6. Noble Heart Evens The Score
Summer, 1951

CROSSING THE FERRY one morning on his way to work, Noble Heart was hanging over the rail pretending to study the eddies and whirls in the muddy water of the Yangzi. But he was thinking rather of the eddies and whirls of the new society in the turbulent river that was the New China. And of the unending series of changes that boggled even a trained mind — liberation, land reform, oppose-America-save-Korea, purge of the capitalists and landowners, redistribution of the land, nationalization of all industry, business, schools, transportation, hospitals, and banks, confiscation of all private property, the endless instruction classes night after night, and now the accusation meetings...

He gave an involuntary sigh and, as if to divest himself of the eddies and whirls in his mind, he stood up, threw his shoulders back and took a deep breath. As he did so his eyes fell on a familiar building high on the bluff on the city side of the river — the beggars' shelter where the two blind men were housed. That reminded him of those two expressions they had used: "happy pills" and "fertilizer factory".

More concerned now than ever for the two blind men, Noble Heart went direct to the beggars' shelter before going to the newspaper office. As he stepped onto the exercise field, he was relieved to see his two friends still walking round and round, in spite of the heat, and with the fingers of the man at the back entwined in the shirt tail of the man in front.

"We may go to the fertilizer factory any day now," they said quite cheerfully. "But they haven't started giving us the happy pills yet."

"Sit down over here in the shade. I want to talk with you a minute," said Noble Heart.

Once seated on the ground, he asked the men, "Where is your old home?"

"We come from Peng Mountain County just south of Chengdu," they told him. "We are both named Peng. We are first cousins."

"Is there anyone in Peng Mountain who will take care of you?"

"Why, yes, those are our own people."

Noble Heart plunged into the reason for his visit. "How would you like to visit home before you go to work at the fertilizer factory?"

"Would we!" they responded in unison. "How we would like to go home! But we don't have any money for train and bus tickets."

"I'll see that your tickets are paid for. But you'll have to ask for travel permits yourselves. Will you do exactly as I say?"

"Yes, sir! Yes, sir!" in unison.

"OK. Here is the plan. Say you want to go home before you are assigned to new work. Now listen: say you want to go to 'Peng County'. Do not say 'Peng Mountain County'. You won't be telling a lie. After all, you have to pass through Peng County on the way to Peng Mountain County. Just say exactly what I've said to you. Don't mention my name. If they ask who will guide you on the way, say you made your way from home to Chongqing and that you can make your own way back again. Understand?"

"Yes, sir! Yes, sir!" in unison.

"All right. You apply for the travel permit today. In fact, right now."

"Yes, sir! Yes, sir!" in unison.

Noble Heart's next hurdle was to convince Editor Huang that he needed to go to Peng Mountain County in the western part of the province, two days' trip from Chongqing. After all, Peng Mountain County was a very small place with little going for it.

"I've got a good idea, a really hot one," he told him. "The government is going to spend a million dollars to develop a park at Mt Omei in West Sichuan. In the old days mostly religious people visited the mountain but now the government is opening it up for everybody, so that this most famous mountain in West China can be enjoyed by all the people."

Noble Heart rolled out the magic phrase, "the people", holding it as long as he dared. It was Editor Huang's favorite.

It was harder to convince Jade Moon.

"What's this about their applying for 'Peng County' when they are really from 'Peng Mountain County'?" she demanded.

"You'll have to leave that to me," answered Noble Heart. "If I tell you, you'll have a piece of information you may have to answer for. As the saying goes, 'Ignorance is bliss'."

"But even if you take them to Peng Mountain, you yourself have no permit for that place..."

Noble Heart unrolled his map of the province. "Here, we take the train to Chengdu. From there we take a bus to Peng Mountain. Their tickets will read 'Peng Mountain'. Mine will read 'Luo Mountain'. That's near Mt Omei. Just look at the map. The highway from Chengdu to Luo Mountain passes through Peng Mountain. When we arrive there they get off the bus and I continue on to Luo Mountain. No problem at all!"

"You always say 'no problem', yet you always get yourself into all sorts of problems!"

Noble Heart was quiet. He didn't have an answer for that one.

"And," continued Jade Moon, "you don't really believe what the nightwatchman said about having to keep on saving the blind men, do you?"

"Well, from his standpoint there's no doubt something to

it. But I've got something else in mind. We've seen two of our friends killed, Mrs. Zhou and Editor Deng. Now I'd like to even the score by saving two other people. If they stay in Chongqing, the blind men will not live long. I'm very suspicious about that 'fertilizer factory.'"

"But, Noble Heart, the risk!"

"Oh, yes. But what was that part in the Bible that Mrs. Deng gave us, about 'We ought to lay down our lives for the brethren'? Anyway, I've always wanted to see Mt Omei!"

Ten days later Noble Heart was back from his trip to Mt Omei. He asked Jade Moon to ask for some flowers from the neighbors, and on Sunday afternoon he wrapped the flowers in newspaper and tied them with a piece of straw from the market, leaving a loop to carry them by. To anyone who was suspicious about what he carried, it would look like a purchase from the market. A growing problem was that spies — both paid and unpaid — were more and more nosey about peoples' parcels.

Late in the afternoon when the fierce Sichuan sun was hanging low in the west, Noble Heart started up the steep lane that climbed the hill back of South Bank. He climbed higher and higher, and finally stopped before a new-made grave. He stood for a moment and looked down the slope to the river, to the city on the far bank and to the great ball of fire sinking into the earth beyond the city. Then he turned to the grave, dug a small hole with his fingers in the soft earth, pushed the stems of the flowers into the hole and pressed the earth around them so they would stand up straight.

"Editor," Noble Heart addressed the man in the grave, "I wanted to save you but I could not. The fire was too hot. But I've come today to tell you that if I could not save you and Mrs. Zhou, at least I have saved two other lives. Maybe that's evened the score a bit.

"And," he continued, "thank you, Editor, for all you

taught me about words. I used one little word to help save those two lives. There was no problem in changing the travel permits made out for 'Peng County'. I just added the little character for 'mountain', only three small strokes of the pen, and made the permits read 'Peng Mountain County'. So now the fertilizer people can look for them all over 'Peng County' and they will not find them. Good night, Editor."

Noble Heart retraced his steps down the hill in the gathering dusk, carrying the rolled up newspaper suspended from his finger by the piece of straw.

7. Lightning And Storm
Winter 1951–2

"THIS IS IT! They have finally nailed me down to a struggle meeting!" Noble Heart spoke in matter-of-fact tones, yet with a quiet tenseness heavy with foreboding. "Take a look at this," he went on, handing the slip of rough, off-white paper to Jade Moon. She read:

"You are hereby summoned to a struggle meeting at 6 p.m. Friday, Feb 23, 1952, at the Seventh Elementary School. If you do not voluntarily appear at 6 p.m. you will be escorted by comrades at 6.30 p.m.

Take due note and act accordingly.

Signed, Garrison Commander
City of Chongqing"

"They are threatening arrest. As the saying goes, 'Don't argue against force'." Noble Heart's voice was somber, more so than Jade Moon had noticed since Editor Deng's murder. "It sounds like a replay of Mrs. Zhou. Same place, same time. But she was a landlord, and owned a house in town and some gold and jewels. I have no land, no wealth, no executive position on the newspaper. But I am a college graduate and was connected with Editor Deng. And I am a Christian. Those things are enough to condemn a man."

The next day another summons came, this time for Jade Moon, Bright Victory, Bright Loyalty and Lotus Flower.

"This is serious," said Noble Heart. "It means that you and the children may be called on to take the witness stand against me."

"*Aiya!* Noble Heart!" wailed Jade Moon. "If only we could get aboard one of those steamers I see on the river every day! Within a week we would be in Shanghai!"

"But no captain would allow us aboard his ship without travel permits, and it's already six months since we applied for them. Anyway, Jade Moon, are you sure we would have enough money to buy tickets? After all, there are five of us."

"We have fifty silver dollars hidden under a board in the pigsty, plus twenty dollars in People's Money in a hole in the wall back of the clothes cupboard. That will be enough."

"Hmm. You know, the government is encouraging the last of the Japanese War refugees to return down-river, if they can get enough money together to buy a ticket. So, why don't they let us go? That dossier that Victory saw, calling me 'Suspected of being a counter-revolutionary and anti-Communist' — could that be the holdup, I wonder? There's not much we can do about that. But there is *one* thing. We can ask Mrs. Deng and the other Christians to pray for us. Maybe God will send a miracle. We could make good use of one right now."

Friday, Feb 23, dawned cold, dark and dreary, even more miserable than the average miserable day of a Chongqing winter. Noble Heart had asked for time off so, unusually for him, he was at home to see the children off for school. There were no smiles on their faces as they said good-bye that morning.

"Just in case," he said to Jade Moon, once the children had left, "I'll go and check our applications for travel. This will be trip number eleven! But it won't hurt to ask this one last time before the struggle meeting tonight. Who knows? God may give us a miracle."

Noble Heart took the usual ferry across the river. As he set foot on the boat the strange feeling came over him that this would be his last trip into the city on the familiar ferry. Was it a premonition, or the reflection in his troubled mind of the dull and threatening heavens above?

He entered the huge door marked "Public Security Bureau",

and walked across a courtyard to a smaller door labeled "Foreign Affairs Section". Now that there were almost no aliens in West China except Russians, the Foreign Affairs Section had little else to do and dealt with applications for travel to the coast.

As Noble Heart crossed the threshold he saw a nineteen-year-old girl sitting at her desk on the opposite side of the room, and it flashed through his mind what a remarkable government this was, that a girl so young could head such an important office. Ping Lian was the daughter of a Presbyterian pastor in Shandong Province; she had risen rapidly in the ranks after taking the witness stand against her own father, at a struggle meeting when he was exiled to Xinjiang in Central Asia. Ping Lian was capable, cynical and would have been beautiful, Noble Heart thought, if she were dressed like a woman instead of in the ubiquitous baggy pants and Mao jacket.

As she saw Noble Heart enter, Ping Lian's lower lip curled ever so slightly. Then, in the curt, unsmiling language standard to the new regime, she spat out, "You think you're lucky, don't you? Here are your five permits. Sign for them in this book."

After signing, Noble Heart could not resist the temptation to revert to the old, pre-revolution courtesy. He said a simple, "Thank you."

"You know better than to thank me! I'm only doing my duty. Don't ever say 'Thank you' to me again!"

"Yes," replied Noble Heart, with a meekness that surprised him. He turned and started out of the office, clutching the permits to his fast-pounding heart. But as he stepped out into the courtyard the cold, threatening sky hit him like a blow from a cruel fist, and he thought, *Nature and man are both against me. What good will these permits do if I am condemned by the kangaroo court tonight?*

Still, that fateful session was hours away and there were

practical things to be done before then. *As of this moment,* he thought, *I am still a free man.*

First he went by the Transportation Information Center. Hundreds of people were milling about. *How many of these want to go to Shanghai?* he wondered, *And how many have a struggle meeting against them tonight?*

High on a blackboard Noble Heart saw the news: "*S. S. Min Jiang* loading Friday to sail at dawn Saturday for Shanghai."

Next, he went to the newspaper office. Not for sentimental reasons; he would be glad to forget that place of tragedy. But he wanted to see Old Bei the night watchman, and he knew that he often pottered around outside. Sure enough, there he was, polishing the brass on the door in the time-honored way.

Noble Heart beckoned Old Bei from a distance. "Come over to my house after your daytime duty. Get your assistant to take your turn for tonight," he said to the old man. "And bring your carrying pole along."

Without questions, Old Bei nodded and said, "Yes, Mr. Lee." Somehow, his relationship with Noble Heart had always given him a comfortable, proper-and-in-place feeling.

As he turned his back on the newspaper office and headed home, Noble Heart did not know how felicitous this arrangement with Old Bei would prove to be.

Back home, Jade Moon burst into tears when she saw the five travel permits. Any other day they would have brought her joy and laughter in anticipation of returning to her old home and family. But today they brought only sorrow, with the struggle meeting a few hours away.

"Jade Moon," said Noble Heart, "let's pray about this."

Side by side they knelt at the wooden bench in the kitchen, the room farthest away from curious ears on the lane outside.

"Lord," prayed Noble Heart, "here we are. Thank you for the permits. But we don't understand why they came the same day as the struggle meeting against me. Lord, I can't believe you have brought us to this point to let me die in front of a mob like Mrs. Zhou did. We'll just leave this up to you to work out as you see best. Amen."

On their feet again, Noble Heart was the man of action. "We will pack what we can carry, and that's all we'll take. Except our bedding, and Old Bei will carry that on a carrying pole. We'll eat the ship's food; no problem there. And you'll be responsible for the money..."

"Noble Heart! You talk as if you were going on the *S. S. Min Jiang*, too, but... but that awful struggle meeting at six o'clock!"

"Jade Moon, we will do what we can do. And we'll leave the rest with God. You did ask Mrs. Deng and the other Christians to pray, didn't you?"

"I most certainly did," replied Jade Moon, a little hurt that Noble Heart would even entertain the idea that she had failed to ask them to pray.

"I want you to go into the city to the ticket office," continued Noble Heart. "I don't think it would be good for me to be seen there. And you should wear a Mao jacket and baggy pants so you will look as inconspicuous as possible."

In spite of the day of dread that had come upon them, Jade Moon allowed herself an inward glow. She was proud of her reporter husband and the way he thought things through.

"The problem is," he went on, "the government insists that everybody traveling buys his ticket at the ticket office, not on the boat. I suppose this is so they have their names and addresses beforehand. It's just a tiny segment of their overall philosophy. They must control everything. They can't tolerate what they cannot control."

Jade Moon took the money and left. In a minute, however, she was pounding on the door and yelling "*Wei! Wei!* Hello! Hello!"

"It's so dark and heavy outside," she explained. "I should take my umbrella, in case it rains."

On the ferry, she could see lightning in the southwest, with faint rumblings of distant thunder. She noticed that the crewmen on the ferry had dropped their usual bantering and went about their duties a little nervously. *After all*, she thought, *thunder and lightning in February is unusual.*

"We have only deck passage left and you're lucky to get that," the ticket seller told her. "Some people who came to buy tickets left when they saw the storm coming up. I guess they didn't like the idea of deck passage in bad weather."

Jade Moon showed her five travel permits, gave their names and address, and was counting her change when the phone rang on the ticket seller's desk. When he put down the receiver he turned back to Jade Moon. "I'm sorry, ma'am," he began, unconsciously slipping back into old-fashioned courtesy, "but Operations just called and said they are moving the *S. S. Min Jiang* across to the South Bank due to the weather. You'll have to cross on the ferry to board the ship over there."

Jade Moon thanked him. Then, silently, she said, *Thank you, dear Lord.*

Back at home, the children arrived in from school at 4.30, and quick smiles came to their faces when they saw the travel permits and steamer tickets. But the smiles vanished as they remembered the struggle meeting at six o'clock at Seventh Elementary School. Then Bright Victory put into words the questions that had been in their parents' minds most of the day, questions that they subconsciously felt would go away if not voiced. "How did you get those permits if there is a struggle meeting announced against you for tonight? And how could Mama buy tickets today?"

"Shush...Not so loud," cautioned Noble Heart, and led them back to the space between kitchen and pigsty.

"You're right, Victory, that's the way things usually operate nowadays. Once a person is up for a struggle meeting, he and his family are blacklisted. No travel permits. It was obvious that Ping Lian at the travel permit section didn't know about tonight's meeting, and neither did the ticket seller. We'll pray to God that the list will not arrive at either office this afternoon. It looks as if the bureaucrats dropped the ball on this one. Let's pray they won't pick it up, at least not until tomorrow!"

At 5.30 Old Bei arrived. Noble Heart quickly outlined to him his part — that he was to carry the family bedding to the *S. S. Min Jiang* and that, for old time's sake, he was to come back to the house later and take the family pig home as a gift. "And here is a key to the front door, for fear I forget it later."

"I'll go alone to the meeting," Noble Heart told his family. "You must all appear, but it would be better if you are not seen with me. But, before you leave the house, be sure your things are all packed and in one place, because we are going aboard the *S. S. Min Jiang* tonight — or, at least, you four are."

For the first time the possibility of a tragic end to the struggle meeting had been put into words, and this opened flood-gates of tears. The children clasped their father around knees and waist, and Jade Moon curled her arms around his shoulders. They all wept unashamedly, even in front of Old Bei. For his part, Old Bei could only look on with a what-can-I-do-about-it? expression on his face. But in a minute the tears began to trickle down even his leathery old cheeks.

At exactly six o'clock, Noble Heart walked into the playground of the Seventh Elementary School. He was alone. At least, he appeared to be alone. Old Bei had followed him fifty yards behind, and a minute later Jade Moon and the children came in. All were dressed in baggy trousers and high-neck Mao jackets of inconspicuous dark blue. Not many people were there; the casual and the merely curious had been discouraged by the black clouds forming in the west.

The same light pole to which Mrs. Zhou had been tied stood in the same spot, its one dim bulb casting uncertain shadows on the table and chair below. Now and then a vicious gust of wind blew the bulb at odd angles, and the shadows contorted into new and strange shapes. Though he was dressed in his warmest wadded garments, Noble Heart shivered in the wind.

He noticed a commotion over at the wing of the school building that the military had taken over, and then a little knot of men in uniform straggled over to center stage, around the table and chair. When the group parted a bit, Noble Heart saw to his horror that the man who had seated himself in the chair was none other than Lieutenant Chang.

The man who beat Mrs. Zhou to death. Numbness descended on mind and body, but thoughts still chased each other through Noble Heart's head. *The man I confronted at the bus stop. The man who pulled the trigger on me! It doesn't look good. But the big question is, does he know I am the man of the bus-stop incident? The mouse recognizes the cat, but does the cat recognize the mouse?*

"The meeting comes to order!" shouted Lieutenant Chang. "The following people have been informed that they must voluntarily attend this meeting. As their names are read they will say 'Present'. Noble Heart Lee."

"Present."

The lieutenant continued through the names of Jade Moon, Bright Victory, Bright Loyalty and Lotus Flower. To each name the same response, "Present."

"Noble Heart Lee will now step forward and kneel before the people."

Noble Heart stepped forward and went down on both knees, as he knew the requirement was, in front of the lieutenant.

"No! I said 'before the people'!" Chang made a vicious half-circle with his hand. Relieved to turn his back on Lieutenant Chang, Noble Heart swung around, still on his knees, and faced "the people". He was glad that not nearly as many had shown up as for Mrs. Zhou's trial. *If I am to die in public*, he thought, *the smaller the crowd the better.*

"First witness! Sergeant Lin from the police precinct!"

The sergeant stepped forward, carrying in his hand a thin book, bound with blue cloth.

"What is that book in your hand, Sergeant?" Chang asked.

Play-acting, murmured Noble Heart to himself, shifting his knees slightly to relieve the discomfort of kneeling.

"The dossier of the Lee family, which is filed in the precinct office."

"Is anything recorded of the Lee family that is critical?"

"Yes, there is."

"What is it?"

"Concerning Noble Heart Lee, it is recorded in red ink, 'Suspected of being a counter-revolutionary and anti-Communist!'"

"Did you record that yourself?"

"No. It was written in the book before I came to work in the office."

The lieutenant appeared a little crestfallen because he could not follow up this lead. He dismissed Sergeant Lin and called, "Next witness. Comrade Tai!"

To Noble Heart's surprise, Electrician Tai from the newspaper office made his way to the front.

"Comrade Tai, what is your work?"

"Electrician on *Liberation Daily*"

"How long have you known the accused, Noble Heart Lee?"

"For thirteen years."

"What are the political sympathies of Noble Heart Lee?"

"He is pro-Chiang Kai-shek."

"How do you know?"

"After former Editor Deng was hung by the people, Noble Heart Lee cut him down and tried to save his life."

How did he know that? Noble Heart was startled. But his

face showed no reaction.

"Comrade Tai, what else do you know about the accused?"

"He often wrote articles critical of the Communist Party and of the People's Liberation Army."

"Can you give an example?"

Comrade Tai reached into the inside pocket of his Mao Zedong jacket and pulled out a sheaf of papers. "Here is a story he wrote with his own pen belittling the People's Liberation Army. He compared it to an army of frogs."

"Witness dismissed," Lieut. Chang declared, and then shouted, "The third witness against Noble Heart Lee is none other than I myself!"

Aiya! This is it. The cat has cornered the mouse! The realization hit Noble Heart like a stab in the chest. Though he tried to control his body, he swayed on his knees.

Suiting action to his newly-adopted stance as a witness, Lieut. Chang got to his feet and stepped over to the witness stand, if it could be called that, immediately under the single electric bulb, which was by now swinging wildly in the wind. Since there was no one to question the prosecutor-cum-witness, the lieutenant delivered a monologue:

"I have known the accused since before Liberation. In fact, we had a near-tragic confrontation in the summer of 1948. That was while I was an undercover agent for the Communist Party, of which I am a member."

The lieutenant paused a long ten seconds to let the last statement sink in. Then he continued, "I was masquerading as an officer in the army of that traitor, Chiang Kai-shek. In fact, I was one of his bodyguards."

At that revelation, the lieutenant laughed. But, Noble Heart noted, no one laughed with him. The crowd's reception of this information was as cold as the wind that was whipping across the assembly.

"I was queuing up for a bus. I was number five in the queue and the accused was number four, right in front of me."

He got the facts reversed, Noble Heart said to himself.

"And," continued the lieutenant, "the conductor would allow only three people aboard from our queue. But the accused insisted on boarding the bus. He even took an old woman who was ahead of him in the queue, with a child tied on her back, and threw the two of them onto the street. I was shocked at such treatment of the common people by a bourgeois and I challenged him. Face to face."

How terrible! Noble Heart fumed under his breath, *He's deliberately turned the whole story around!*

"The accused was infuriated that I should challenge him. He took a pistol from his pocket, aimed pointblank at my head and pulled the trigger."

The liar! Noble Heart gritted through clenched teeth. Involuntarily, he began to get up from his kneeling position, growling, "I'll shake those lies out of his mouth!" However, by this time his knees had gone to sleep from kneeling on the ground, and for a long moment he struggled to get up but could not.

Just in that instant, lightning struck the wing of the school building where the barracks were located. Then as if loath to return to heaven before fulfilling heaven's mandate, balls of fire shot across the school yard from the barracks. One ball struck the lamp post, knocked out the electric bulb and in a split second traveled down the post and jumped to the head of Lieutenant Chang. There was a loud sizzle as his hair caught fire.

Still on his knees when the lightning struck, Noble Heart was not touched. By the time he had struggled to his feet it was gone. By the light of the flashes of lightning farther away, he saw Lieutenant Chang writhing and jerking on the ground. The soldiers paid no attention to either accused or accuser but were running towards the barracks, which were now aflame and billowing smoke.

Noble Heart realized he was not hurt, and with the effort

of standing his knees were coming back to life. "Where's Jade Moon? And the children? And Old Bei?" he asked aloud. Without waiting for an answer, he ran towards the main gate as fast as sore legs could carry him. Then straight for Liberation Lane, not minding the rain which was now peppering down.

Sure enough, Jade Moon, the children and Old Bei were there before him. "Thank God! You're all here. And I'm free, at least for now! Jade Moon, have you got the permits, the tickets and the money?"

"Yes, they're in my leather pouch around my neck, and they've been there all evening!"

"All right, everybody grab his own pieces, and let's go!"

"But, Papa it's storming outside," objected Lotus Flower.

"God sent the lightning and God sent the storm, my dear, all to protect us. Nobody will venture out to look for the Lee family in this storm."

With that, Noble Heart stepped out into Liberation Lane with a hearty "Let's go!" He was followed by Jade Moon, Bright Victory, Bright Loyalty and Lotus Flower in that order. Old Bei brought up the rear with a bundle of bedding dangling from each end of his carrying pole. Far-sighted Jade Moon had wrapped the bedding in oilskins to keep it dry.

"Let's go the back way," Noble Heart said. "We want to miss the front gate of the Seventh Elementary School!" As they made their way through back lanes and alleys a strange glow filled the sky and lit their path before them.

"I'm sorry for the children who will have no school tomorrow," Jade Moon said.

"And for the soldiers who have no beds tonight," added Noble Heart.

PART II

SHANGHAI
1952 ~ 1957

8. Afloat
Winter 1951–2

Fifteen minutes after leaving home the Lee family were at South Bank Wharf. Sure enough, there was the *S. S. Min Jiang*, with one end of a wet gangplank resting invitingly on the boards of the old scow which was the floating wharf. The family paused at the foot of the gangplank to wait for Old Bei. He puffed for a minute from his exertion, then said, "You wait here. I'll go on and see the captain first."

A few minutes later Old Bei came back down the gangplank with a man half his age. Without a word the younger man picked up the bedding from one end of Old Bei's load and carried it aboard. The other roll of bedding in his hand, Old Bei followed with a cheery, "All aboard!"

Once on board the younger man led them to the bridge. Noble Heart felt it strange; their tickets called for deck passage, not Captain's quarters!

"I've told the Captain who you are," said Old Bei, once they were on the bridge, "and that you have permits and tickets. But I have told him to remove your names from the passenger list, as if you did not make the ship before it sailed. Oh! I'm sorry," he continued. "I failed to introduce you. This is Captain Bei. My son."

Noble Heart grabbed the Captain's hand in his own wet one and pumped it up and down a dozen times. "It's a pleasure to meet a friend after meeting others tonight who are not friends."

"I know," returned the captain simply. "Welcome aboard the *S. S. Min Jiang!*"

"Now that you're all safely on board, I'll leave," said Old Bei, picking up his carrying pole. "I'll need this to carry the pig home with." Without further ado, he walked down the gangplank and disappeared into the darkness and driving rain.

"The first thing is to get you and your family out of sight," Captain Bei said. "I'll put you in my chart room." He stepped over to the wall on the aft side of the bridge. The entire wall was panelled with oak and beautifully polished. The captain pressed a knot in the wood; a door opened inwards on hidden hinges. He invited, "Please step inside. Bring your things with you."

The family stepped into what appeared to be an oversized closet. The captain shut the door and flicked a switch, and the light revealed a side of the wall set with shelves.

"This ship was originally the *S S Argyle*," he explained. "Owned by Jardine Matheson and registered in Hong Kong. The new government confiscated it. It was for the China Coast trade; that's the reason for this large chart cabin. But we don't use it now. Our charts are all in the minds of the old river pilots, who know the river like the back of their hand. So you can stay here until we get to Shanghai. Oh, yes, it has a door to my private bathroom..." He turned a brass knob and opened a small door. "Use this while you are my guests," he said.

Their eyes wide, Bright Victory, Bright Loyalty and Lotus Flower rushed to stick their heads through the little door.

"Wa!" exclaimed Victory, "Is that what they call a 'flush toilet'?"

The next morning, at first hint of dawn, the *S. S. Min Jiang* quietly turned her nose into the current of the Yangzi. She was quickly turned around, the last hawser was thrown off the stern, and she headed downstream, 150 feet of white paint and steel on her way to Shanghai.

After they were well under way, there was a knock on the inner door, and Captain Bei himself brought in a large tray with cups of hot tea and cookies. "My cousin is a steward on the ship," he told them. "He will bring your breakfast by and by. Through the bathroom."

Now that it was daylight, Noble Heart and Jade Moon looked around at their private cabin. It was about eight by eight feet, apart from the shelves for charts. The shelves themselves were festooned with their wet clothes; their bags and bundles were mostly perched on the top shelf, and their bedding occupied all the floor space. Opposite the shelves was a single porthole, covered by a curtain.

"Just look at that!" exclaimed Jade Moon as she drew the curtain aside and tied it back. "Bamboo, pine trees! How beautiful! Oh, look, Noble Heart, the sun is coming up clear and bright. That storm must have cleared the air. I wonder if *your* storm is over, my dear." She brushed a tear from her cheek. "I thought last night that..." And she broke into tears, in spite of the cheerful sunshine streaming in through the porthole.

"...that Lieutenant Chang would be the end of me, like he was of Mrs. Zhou," Noble Heart completed her sentence for her. "I know, my dear, you couldn't help but think that. And Lieut. Chang had a lot more against me personally than he had against Mrs. Zhou. Why, he didn't even know her... I wonder if he died last night when the lightning hit him. Maybe we'll never know."

By this time Bright Victory, Bright Loyalty and Lotus Flower were awake. They downed the cookies in no time, and when the tea was finished Noble Heart said, "The big thing right now is to praise God for our deliverance. And look, we are the personal guests of the captain of this ship. Who could ever have dreamed that one up? God has been better to us than our fears, and He has given us more than we could have asked. Let's each one pray and thank God for His mercies."

The last "Amen" said, they all leaned back against the shelves, their lower bodies luxuriating in the comfort of warm bedding, when a knock came on the bathroom door.

"I'm Old Bei. Not the one you know, but his cousin. The captain sent this for breakfast."

Old Bei shoved the tray through the door and Noble Heart took it. The children's eyes widened at what was on the tray. Rice congee with black beans floating in it, sliced salted eggs, a dish of mixed pickles, peanuts, tiny salted fish fried to a crisp so you could eat bones and all, and a half dozen other enticing dishes.

"Wow!" yelled Bright Loyalty, "what a breakfast!"

Tears filled Jade Moon's eyes. It was a real Shanghai breakfast, like she had as a child.

Upper Yangzi steamers do not travel at night, due to the treacherous currents and shifting shoals. So, at four o'clock at Wanxian, the largest city in Sichuan east of Chongqing, the *S. S. Min Jiang* swung around in the middle of the river and then, bow facing into the current, nudged up to the floating wharf.

"There may be questions about you in Wanxian," Captain Bei had warned the Lee family. "After they recovered from the shock of lightning and fire, the soldiers no doubt went to your house to arrest you. They would have traced you through the Foreign Affairs Office and then the ticket office, and would have connected the *S. S. Min Jiang* with your disappearance. And the telegraph and telephone wires are open to Wanxian."

Sure enough, as soon as the steamer docked four officers in uniform came aboard. They went direct to the bridge to see the captain, and handed him an official order, signed and sealed with red ink.

Captain Bei read the order out loud, loud enough for Noble Heart, his ear pressed against the door, to hear clearly:

"Comrade Captain, *S. S. Min Jiang*,

You are hereby ordered to identify and deliver to the bearers of this order the following fugitive from justice:

Noble Heart Lee

You are also ordered to deliver to the bearers of this order the wife and three children of the fugitive, as material witnesses.

(signed) Garrison Commander
Wanxian, Sichuan"

"Well, now, who is this Noble Heart Lee?" Captain Bei asked innocently.

"According to Chongqing, he is a passenger on this ship. And his entire family. Here, give me your passenger manifest."

"Why, of course, here it is," Captain Bei answered.

Noble Heart, Jade Moon and the children waited tensely. There was a long silence during which the officer looked through the passenger list. Noble Heart thought he could hear the heartbeat of his wife and children, but maybe it was only his own heart pounding his ribs.

Finally, from the bridge, "Hmmp! No name like that here."

"Of course, you understand that the list compiled by the ticket seller and the list made up by my purser as passengers come aboard are seldom identical — people get sick at the last minute, or change their minds, or just don't make the sailing time."

"Hmmp! There's nothing for it but to check the papers of every passenger aboard. Tell your purser to take us around. We'll start with deck passage; that's the kind of ticket Noble Heart Lee bought."

An hour and a half later there was the clatter of table and chairs being set up on the bridge. Still later, the voice of Captain Bei could be heard. "I'm sorry, Lieutenant. You and your men have gone to much trouble, and you have not had your supper. Please sit down and take a little light refreshment."

On the other side of the panel, Noble Heart was listening carefully. He heard the usual remonstrance, the usual urging and finally, the scraping of chairs as the four men and Captain Bei sat down together.

Just then there was a quiet knock on the bathroom door. The five Lees, startled, all jumped. Noble Heart motioned them to sit down, and then he stepped over, turned the brass knob ever so slowly and opened the door a crack. Then he laughed and threw the door open. There was Old Bei the Second, as they had dubbed him, with a huge tray and a half dozen covered dishes.

"The captain invited the men to a meal," Old Bei said with a twinkle in his eye. "He ordered the chef to bring out shark fin soup, crab, squid and shrimp — the best stuff we brought from Shanghai. And you are having the same menu. Ha!" he chuckled quietly."You are eating the same food but you're on this side of the partition and they're on that!"

The following morning at daylight the four men were helped ashore, and halfway up the stone steps that mounted to Wanxian's main street the lieutenant sat down and went to sleep. He did not see the S. S. Min Jiang turn her nose into the current, swing around and begin the day's voyage downstream.

A little later Captain Bei came through the bathroom and paid the Lee family a visit.

"Yes, your menu was the same as theirs," chuckled the captain, "except for two items, Tsingtao beer and maotai wine. They drank so much that they had a very pleasant night's sleep.

"The river is rising with all the run-off from the storm night before last," he continued. "We'll make extra good time today and should anchor in Hubei Province tonight. Once we are out of Sichuan you have nothing to fear. Even if you were a convicted criminal they wouldn't pursue you beyond the provincial border. I guess the officials in Hubei have enough trouble on their hands already without borrowing more from Sichuan, and Hubei officials resent being ordered around by Sichuan officials. So, just let your hearts down. Everything is going to be okay."

The last ten miles up the Huangpu River to Shanghai was the slowest leg of the voyage. The *S. S. Min Jiang* had skimmed along the oceanward flow of the mighty river Yangzi, the third largest on earth, but now, on turning into the Huangpu, the ship seemed to dig deeper into the muddy water as it fought not only the current but also the outgoing tide. The confluence of the Yangzi and the Huangpu is only a few miles from where the Yangzi empties into the East China Sea; tides are strong therefore on the Huangpu.

The Lees were standing on top deck, above the bridge, the vantage point from which they had viewed the magnificent Yangzi Gorges as well as the Great Central Plain from Yichang eastward. Their faces were tanned by the wind and by the unusual week of winter sun all across Central China. As the ship swung hard to port to enter the Huangpu, however, a cloud came across the sun and the temperature dropped. So did Jade Moon's face, which had been cheerful and smiling in anticipation of arriving home.

"Oh, the sun is gone!" she exclaimed. "I was hoping we would arrive home on a sunny day, and you know how cold Shanghai can be in March. Especially if it rains."

The *S. S. Min Jiang* tied up at the Shanghai Port Passengers' Quay on the west bank of the Huangpu just short of the mouth of Suzhou Creek.

"Oh, good!" exulted Jade Moon, as the ship nudged itself snugly into the dock, "Now we can see the entire Bund as we ride along in rickshaws!"

Noble Heart and Jade Moon went ashore first, she with her suitcase and odds-and-ends and Noble Heart with one of the two bedding bundles. The three children stayed on the ship guarding their things and the second bedding bundle. Once on the quay, Noble Heart said, "Okay, Jade Moon, you look after these things and I'll make another trip for the bedding."

In the end he made three trips off the ship carrying their things, then yet another back to thank Captain Bei for his kindness in virtually saving their lives. They had all been so excited about arriving home in Shanghai that for the moment they forgot the man who brought them there.

"Noble Heart," said Jade Moon, when with the hundreds of other passengers they were finally collected on the quay and ready to start across the city, "I still haven't seen any rickshaws."

"Of course! Why didn't I think of it! There may not *be* any rickshaws now, any more than there are in Chongqing. I'll go up to the street and see."

In a few minutes, he was back, reporting, "No rickshaws. But I've hired a three-wheeled pedicab to take our things. We'll do the same as before and make three trips."

Finally, with all their things piled into the box-like body over the rear axle of the pedicab, and with the driver-motorman mounted on the bicycle seat and ready to pedal, Noble Heart asked him, "Where are the pedicabs for people?"

"Oh," replied the pedicab man, "There are almost none. You're lucky to get me to haul your things. But, look, there's room for the little girl on top of the baggage."

Noble Heart hoisted ten-year old Lotus Flower high on top of a bedding bundle, where she first laughed and then cried. But in the end she decided that riding atop a bundle of bedding was better than walking across Shanghai. By this time the four older Lees were resigned to doing just that.

"But... where are the taxis?" asked Noble Heart.

"Hmmp!" snorted the pedicab man. "You *could* get a taxi

all right — if you were a big cadre, or a Russian. Even then, you might wait an hour for one. But for ordinary Shanghai people-of-the-hundred-surnames like us, we don't ride taxis."

Noble Heart and Jade Moon were pleased to hear themselves classed as "ordinary Shanghai people-of-the-hundred-surnames". They had automatically slipped into the Shanghai dialect in talking with the pedicab man, leaving the liquid Sichuan dialect behind in the distant province itself.

"Well, how are things with you?" asked Noble Heart, making conversation.

"Hmmp! Before, it was the British who told us what to do. Then the Japanese. Now it's the Northerners who came in with the army. Why don't they let us Shanghai people run our own city?"

The pedicab man stopped talking. At that point he had to concentrate all his strength, standing on the pedals, to climb the incline going up to the bridge across Suzhou Creek. Puffing, blowing and perspiring, he made it to the level roadway of the bridge itself, then eased down again onto his narrow seat and continued the steady pumping up and down that drove his low-geared vehicle forward.

By this time the jingle of bicycle bells, the shouting of the pullers of carts and the jangle of trolley bells mounted to such a cacophony of sounds as to drown out further talk. Noble Heart was just as happy. The open street was no place for conversation, though as he walked alongside the pedicab he was bursting with a thousand questions he wanted to ask the old man.

More than that, the eyes, ears and noses of the Lee family were testing the sights, sounds and smells of Shanghai. To Noble Heart and Jade Moon, the milieu engulfing them was familiar yet strange, now bringing a wave of nostalgia, now convincing them they were in a strange city they had never known before. The Garden Bridge had not changed. The towering Shanghai Mansions Hotel to their right looked the same as before, its tan face only a little more dirty. And what was that smell wafting up from the Suzhou Creek below? Unmistakably, it was the fragrance of human ordure being ferried out of the city in vat-like boats to fertilize the vegetable fields that surround Shanghai. But there was something about the scene that brought a strange uneasiness to Noble Heart. *What is it that is so different from before?* he asked himself. Later, in the middle of the night, he awoke and realized what it was — everybody wore a blank face and nobody talked to anybody else.

Across the bridge, on their right loomed up an impressive double gate. Noble Heart remembered the sign that used to hang there, "British Consulate General"; he had seen it last in 1937, when he and Jade Moon and baby Bright Victory passed that gate on their way to board a steamer and flee to West China, before the advancing Japanese army reached Shanghai. Now there were a half dozen signs, white planks with black characters, each hung vertically and each reading from top to bottom, "Shanghai Municipal This" and "Shanghai Municipal That". No sign in the English language. There were, however, a few signs in Russian, which Noble Heart could not read.

Now they were on the Bund proper where the great trans-Pacific passenger liners, *Empress of Japan* and *Empress of Asia*, used to disgorge their passengers. Noble Heart looked for the old familiar sign "Hong Kong and Shanghai Banking Corporation." He saw the building and he saw where the sign had been chipped away, still leaving the shadow of its former self in both Chinese and English. He saw the Cathay Hotel but on closer look found that a new sign proclaimed "Peace Hotel."

"Oh! It's beginning to rain!" shouted Jade Moon, above the din of traffic. They stopped for her to pull five umbrellas out of their baggage. The rain hastened the darkness. Soon they were away from the Bund, which Noble Heart noted was now called "Zhongshan Road East" after the given name of Sun Yat-sen. They took a short-cut along narrow streets to what used to be the French Concession, for it was there that Jade Moon had been brought up and where she hoped to see her parents in the familiar big old house.

"I wonder if the house is going to be the same?" she mused aloud. "And the yard? You know, they haven't mentioned the house for two years now. I wonder why... I wish it hadn't started to rain," she continued. "And it's so dark, all of a sudden. That's a bad omen. Except that now I'm a Christian and don't believe in omens anymore."

Noble Heart wondered why her voice dropped. That last bit about not believing in omens anymore was not very convincing.

There were few street lights on the back streets and now daylight had almost completely faded from the sky. The pedicab man, panting for breath, still found enough of it to curse the rain and the road. He was swinging left and right to avoid potholes and in so doing was slowing down the speed of the little party. The rain was peppering down now and the unpaved street was muddy. Water and mud erupted in cascades as a foot hit a pothole instead of solid ground.

"In Chongqing at least we had stone to walk on," stated Bright Victory, "not mud like Shanghai."

Finally they came out on a larger street. Jade Moon and Noble Heart recognized it even in the dark as the street where she was born and grew up, and saw by a dim street light that it now had a new name, "Long March Road". They turned right, and in a moment Jade Moon stood before the house in which she was born. *Are my parents home? Will they somehow know we are coming?* Questions tumbled over themselves in Jade Moon's mind.

In spite of the darkness, she noticed the piles of debris — bricks, plaster, stone and dirt — heaped up meaninglessly.

Moss covered the walkway leading to the house, and shutters hung limply askew. The place was unkempt and unkept; she had never seen it like this before.

Treading gingerly on the moss, now wet and slippery, they approached the big double door.

"*Wei! Wei!* Hello! Hello!"

No answer.

"*Wei! Wei!*" Noble Heart shouted again.

Still no answer.

After four more shouts, a shutter near the door creaked open. "Who are you?" asked a female voice out of an unlit room.

"I'm Jade Moon Song," Jade Moon spoke up, giving her maiden name. "Are any of the Song family at home?"

"Song family?" asked the voice. "No one of that name lives here. Why are you looking for them?"

"I'm Jade Moon Song," repeated Jade Moon. "I was born in this house and grew up here." She was fighting back the tears by this time, tears at not finding her loved ones but only a callous, unidentified voice speaking out of the darkness.

"Hmmph! You were, were you? You must be bourgeoisie. *We* are the people now."

With that the shutter closed and there was silence, a silence broken only by the patter of rain on umbrellas.

"Sir!" The voice came from out in the yard. It was the pedicab man, standing there in the rain. "I must go now and get out of this wet. I'll put your things under the eaves."

Noble Heart fumbled for some money to pay him, and he disappeared, pedaling into the wet, enfolding darkness.

"Please, please, it's raining and it's cold." Jade Moon's voice was higher now. "Can't you just open the door and let us in out of the rain?"

The shutter did not open again, but a muffled voice came from inside, "Go away! Go to the police station if you want help. That's where you should have gone in the first place!"

"Please, can't you just let us into the hallway out of the rain?"

"There's no place for you here! Go away now!"

Jade Moon turned to Noble Heart. The questions tumbled out: "Where *are* my parents? Who *is* this woman? What *can* we do? Where *can* we go?"

As if to add insistence to her pleas, the rain suddenly came down harder.

Just then a light shined from the street, picking out each face, mercilessly.

"This is the police. What are you doing, standing there? You must be off the street by nine o'clock!" With that, light and voice disappeared into the darkness.

Jade Moon bit her lip. But that did not stop the tears flowing down her cheeks. By this time Lotus Flower was sobbing uncontrollably. All five were clutching their umbrellas to their hearts as if they were the last things on earth they could cling to.

9. Home In Shanghai
Winter 1951–2

"NOW, LOOK HERE," Noble Heart spoke up, breaking the silence the policeman had left behind. "It's no good being sorry for ourselves. God saved us the night we left Chongqing, didn't He? Can't God save us now? We'll pray and ask His help. Oh, God!" he began, "It's raining here in Shanghai and we need help. Please get us inside someplace out of this rain."

As Noble Heart opened his eyes he looked up. Maybe he was expecting God to open a window in heaven. What he saw was not a window in heaven but a window — a shutter, to be exact — opened upstairs, immediately above the window that had opened and then closed with such finality.

Outside the window burned a candle, and holding the candle was a gray-haired woman.

"Just a minute," the old woman said, so quietly that Noble Heart would not have heard her if he had not been looking straight at her.

A minute later the door opened, slowly and softly. The same soft voice said, "Please come in."

Eagerly the five Lees grabbed their things and went into the house. Following the old woman's example, they mumbled "Thank you" under their breath quietly, and silently followed her upstairs. Two more trips sufficed for Noble Heart to bring the bedding bundles. On the last trip he quietly — very quietly — closed the double doors. He noticed that when he took the candle downstairs for the bedding, the room above was left in total darkness. Apparently the old woman had only one candle.

"I'm a little hard of hearing," said the old woman, "but The Demon down below was talking so loud I heard her. And from the tone of her voice I knew someone must be in trouble. Please speak softly. If she hears us she'll come up here and demand to know why I asked you to come in."

She had not yet asked their names. Apparently that was not important to her.

She turned to Noble Heart and asked, "Do you have papers saying your being in Shanghai is legal? If so, you had better report to the police tonight. You can give them this address, 331–5 Long March Road."

She told Noble Heart the turns to make to reach the police station. After he had gone, shown downstairs by Bright Victory and the one candle, the old woman said to Jade Moon, "Now I'll make some rice congee for you and the children before you stretch out for the night. And I have a little pickled cabbage to go with it."

Jade Moon noticed that she left the candle with them when she went over to the far side of the room to boil the rice on the single hot plate resting in the bottom of what was once an earthenware pot. She seemed to cook by feel, her fingers lightly touching here and there.

When Noble Heart returned, the congee was set out, five bowls in all, with spoons and chopsticks. After they were well on their way to being satisfied by the hot, almost liquid rice, the old woman said, "You should know that you are my special guests tonight. In a way, I was expecting you, or something else as remarkable, because I prayed this morning that I would be able to help someone special today. And here you are."

"You prayed!" gasped Jade Moon. "Who did you pray to?"

"Oh, I prayed to my Father. You see, I am a Christian."

Before she could add more, Jade Moon grabbed her hand and kissed it, and her tears flowed down and over it.

Noble Heart cleared his throat with difficulty. "I'm not surprised," he said. "We had just finished praying to your Father when I looked up and saw you and the candle in the window."

The next morning when Jade Moon opened her eyes the sun was already streaming into the room that had been so dark the night before. She looked around; the five Lees had taken up all the floor space in the room. She chuckled when she realized the whole family was lying in the same positions and taking up exactly the same space as in the chart room on the *S. S. Min Jiang*.

Well, God does provide us enough space to stretch out in, Jade Moon said to herself, *but not an inch more!* Sitting up in bed, she ran her eyes over the room: their wet shoes propped against the wall to dry, their wet stockings hung over the backs of three straight chairs, the narrow wooden bed of their hostess, the hot plate nested in its cracked earthenware pot, the rickety wooden table with the stub of last night's candle, a few nails in the wall with sundry bags, a shawl, a blue jacket and a pair of dark blue pants draped over them.

Then it suddenly came to Jade Moon, *I was born in this room! Exactly the room to spend our first night in Shanghai!* But then she wondered, *Where is the old lady, our hostess?*

Just then the old woman came in, backing through the door and holding a basket of bowls, chopsticks and spoons in her two hands as if it were too heavy for her.

"We have a common kitchen for the six households. It's downstairs. Next to the common bathroom. Only those two rooms have running water in them."

Hmm. I know, responded Jade Moon to herself. *Our kitchen. Our bathroom!*

By now Noble Heart was up and stretching himself in the morning sun. Dressing was no problem. Like the others, he had slept in his clothes. "Let's see, could I have a jug, please?" he was saying. "I'll go out and get some hot soy bean milk and dough strips for breakfast."

After he had gone, Jade Moon turned to her hostess: "I owe you an apology. Last night we were so excited we failed even to ask you your name. How remiss of us!"

The older woman laughed. "Think nothing of it! Just call me *Jie Jie*, Big Sister. That's what the Christian brothers and sisters call me."

Now they were alone, with the children still asleep, Jade Moon plunged straight into the question nearest her heart: Do you know anything about my parents? The Song family. They own this house. At least, they used to, and I thought they still did. They never wrote to tell me that they had left the house. I don't know where they are now..."

Suddenly Jade Moon realized she was running on and on with questions and not giving Big Sister a chance to answer any of them.

"I know what you're talking about," the older woman began slowly. "I had to attend a meeting, a 'struggle'..."

Jade Moon gasped. She had never heard this about her parents, nor even dreamed of it.

"And what happened?"

"In the mercy of God they were not killed, nor even sent to prison. But they were forced to leave this house and..." Big Sister hesitated, "and move to another place."

"Do you know where?"

"Yes, I know where. We were given a sheet of paper with their — what do you call it? Confessions? — printed out. That gave their — what shall I say — assignment, maybe. And address. I'll get it for you."

Big Sister went over to a plastic satchel hanging on the wall. She felt around inside the bag for some minutes, then pulled out a folded sheet of paper and handed it to Jade Moon.

"Is this it?" she asked.

Jade Moon glanced hurriedly through the document. It was the usual stock-in-trade confession, replete with "capitalist," "imperialist," "feudalistic," "reactionary," "counter-revolutionary," "fascist," and so on. Down near the bottom Jade Moon found what she was looking for:

Sichuan Road, Lane 41, No 17½

"Oh, yes, that's over near Hongkou Park. My parents used to take me there to watch the ducks in the lake." Jade Moon read on below the address: "'To clean, maintain and protect said premises until further notice.' Well, at least my parents have a place to stay."

Big Sister made no reply.

Jade Moon suddenly remembered she had asked Big Sister nothing about herself.

"Big Sister, how long have you been in Shanghai and when did you move here?"

"I'm a retired Bible woman. I was born in Shanghai and I was living back of the Maranatha Church until the Shanghai Opera Company took over the property. Then I was assigned to come here."

"And did they assign the other people to live here also in our...." something caught in Jade Moon's throat, "yes, our house?"

"They did, including..."

Big Sister felt her way to the door. She gave it a shove, though it was closed tight already. "Including The Demon down below. She is a spy for the police and reports everything."

"Excuse me for asking, Big Sister. But I notice you use your hands a lot when you move around the room. Do you have poor eyesight?"

"Oh, haven't you noticed?" Big Sister replied. "I'm blind. Completely blind."

After breakfast of hot soy bean milk and dough strips boiled in deep fat and sprinkled with brown sugar, the Lees set out to walk across Shanghai. Trolleys were going their way; they tried twice to board one but both times were ruthlessly thrust aside by other people boarding. So, there was nothing for it but to walk.

"This is great," declared Bright Victory. "Now we can

really see Shanghai as we walk along."

"Noble Heart, what does the 'half' of '17½' mean in my parents' address?" Jade Moon enquired. "How can they live at 'half'?"

"I asked Big Sister. She didn't know."

The Lee family were walking along Jiangxi Road now, in downtown Shanghai.

"Oh! There's the bank building where my father used to work!" exclaimed Jade Moon. "I wonder what it is now ... and why are all the lower windows boarded up?"

Opposite the main door of the bank building they stopped and looked at the big sign in the Russian language; beside it Chinese characters explained, "Sino-Russian Friendship Association — Downtown Branch."

They turned into Sichuan Road, crossed the bridge over Suzhou Creek, and began counting the lanes that led off, right and left. Some were dirty, muddy, unkept, and piled high with half-rotted rubbish and debris; others were clean and neat with a few trees hanging over ancient walls, including here and there a fresh evergreen contrasting sharply with the otherwise gray drabness of the city.

Suddenly they ran into a roadblock. Policemen motioned them curtly to squeeze themselves onto the narrow sidewalk.

"Wa! It's a military parade! And it's forming right here! exclaimed Bright Victory.

Looking up, they read banners written in red characters on lengths of white cloth: "Down with America! Oppose America, Aid Korea! Kill the Paper Tiger! Drive America out of Korea!"

Like the other pedestrians, the Lee family made their way slowly along the crowded sidewalk. This gave them the chance to satisfy their curiosity as to the tanks, weapon carriers, jeeps, artillery pieces, self-propelled guns, mortars, ambulances and trucks lined up for the parade. They had never seen such a display of military might in Chongqing. A feeling of national pride welled up in Noble Heart's heart and lodged in a lump in his throat:

"This is the Chinese Army," he said, more to himself than to anyone else. "It's got a punch to it. Like the Chairman says, China is standing up among the nations now."

Victory and Loyalty were wide-eyed. Noble Heart wondered what they were thinking.

Beyond the parade they walked out in the street again, and then Bright Victory spoke up: "Papa, did you ever see so many tanks and guns and things?"

"No, son, I never did. And they wouldn't show them now except that they want to drum up support for the Peoples' Volunteers fighting the Americans in Korea."

Victory continued: "Papa, did you notice where all those things were made? About one-third were Russian, another third was American and the rest were made by our Chinese people. But Papa, where was the Japanese stuff? Didn't we capture a lot of stuff from the Japanese? Where is it now?"

"Son, you'd better ask those questions in private."

Finally they came to Lane 41. It ran along a canal, which had obviously seen better days. Now there were a few night soil boats tied up here and there, and the smell of human manure permeated the narrow lane that clung to the bank of the canal.

As they walked along Lane 41, Jade Moon eagerly read off the numbers on the doors, "one...three...five...seven."

She was so intent on counting that she almost ran into an old woman carrying two wooden buckets. The old woman set her buckets down to regain her balance. "Excuse me," she said.

"Mama!" shouted Jade Moon, and grabbed her up and hugged her.

Without the voice she would never have recognized as her

mother the aged woman standing before her in dirty pants and jacket and straw sandals. And the smell... It certainly was not her mother's smell.

"Mama!" shouted Jade Moon again. "It's you! It's you! We're here. You know Noble Heart. And this is Bright Victory. And Bright Loyalty. And Lotus Flower... Where do you live? Where is Papa? Is he all right? How is your rheumatism?"

Mrs. Song laughed: "You're just the same as ever! More questions in a minute than I can answer all day long. Now, which question do you want answered first?"

Jade Moon blushed a little, then asked again, "Where is Papa?"

"He's off on a boat. That's his assignment."

"At his age? He's sixty-five now."

"Oh, he stays healthy. Always out in the open air."

"And how is your rheumatism?"

"Well, to be honest, not so good. The place where I live is damp all the time."

"Why do you say 'I' and not 'we'?" Jade Moon demanded. "Have they separated you and Papa?"

"Why, yes and no."

"Now, tell me, where do you live? Would there be room for us to move in?"

Now it was Mrs. Song who blushed. "I'm afraid you'll have to see my house first." She dropped her head, then lifted it again and said in a barely audible whisper, "There it is."

Mrs. Song pointed to a low concrete building, half of which extended out over the canal and rested on concrete stilts coming up out of the water. There was a government sign on the front: No. 17½. Shanghai Municipal Toilet No. 113.

Tears came into Jade Moon's eyes. Finally she asked:

"Do ....do you *live* here?"

"Oh, yes. There's a bench just inside the door. I sleep

there. Besides cleaning up, I hand out paper to the women as they come in."

"And... and does Papa live here, too?"

"This is his address. But he works on an ordure boat. He eats and sleeps on the boat."

10. "We've Been Manipulated!"
Autumn 1952

"ONE, TWO, THREE, FOUR! One, two, three, four! One, two, three, four!" The counting and shouting went on and on interminably.

"Why does that man shout like that? And he never says anything else, always, 'one, two, three, four!'" The complainer was Lotus Flower. It was early in the morning, just after daybreak, and the alarm clock of "one, two, three, four" had jangled her unwillingly awake.

"It's nothing very special, Lotus Flower. You come to the window and look." Her mother opened the shutter and Lotus Flower stuck her head out. There was the shouter standing in the yard below, his back to the house and his face towards a dozen old men and women, who were all dressed alike and all jerking their arms simultaneously to the beat of "one, two, three, four."

"They're taking their morning exercise," Jade Moon explained. "And the leader is a soldier — I can tell by his cap with the red star on it. Only a soldier wears a red star cap."

As they were talking about the red star cap, suddenly the soldier pulled it off and slammed it down on the ground. The exercise must be warming him up. Jade Moon then noticed a strange thing about him — he was perfectly bald, with unusual red lines crossing his head where the hair used to be.

Lotus Flower noticed the red lines, too. She tittered: "Mama, he's got a map on his head! Look at the rivers and lakes!"

Jade Moon would have good reason, later, to remember that bald head and its map.

"But why do they have to wake me up doing their exercises?" Lotus Flower still wanted to know.

"Well, that's the custom," her mother told her. "It's the popular thing to do. But you don't *have* to do your exercises in a group. Lots of people prefer to do shadow boxing on their own. See those people across the street? All those slow, funny contortions they get into is called shadow boxing."

The Lee family had been able to sleep in Big Sister's room for several nights, then for a while they visited relatives, all of whom were crammed into one or two rooms and none of whom had space to take them in on a permanent basis. Even old Grandpa Lee had been squeezed into one room of his formerly spacious house. But Big Sister had promised to pray for accommodation and one day, sure enough, two rooms fell vacant right across the hall from her. Now Victory and Loyalty slept on the floor in the living room, and Noble Heart, Jade Moon and Lotus Flower slept in the other room, with a curtain made from two old sheets hung across the middle. The family rice, salt and other food was stored in this room. Of course, the kitchen and bathroom downstairs were shared with the other five households.

A little later that morning, the family sat down to breakfast of rice gruel. The only other dish on the table was a saucer of coarse ocean salt to flavor the gruel and help it down.

Bright Loyalty spoke up: "I'm not complaining about the food, Mama, but when we were in Chongqing you always told us about the wonderful meat and fish and fruit you had in Shanghai when you were a girl. Did you ever have only rice gruel and salt for breakfast?"

"No, of course not, Loyalty. The trouble is that not just here in Shanghai but in many places there are floods, and in others drought, so food is scarce now. In fact, many people are dying of hunger." Jade Moon waved her hand, palm outward, the sign of the silent negative. "But not a word of this beyond that door!"

"Yes, Mama" the children all replied together.

With solemn faces they ate their rice gruel and salt.

In good time for the new term, Bright Victory applied to attend high school. But his father's background was investigated and, in the end, he was not even allowed to take the entrance examination. Instead the municipal authorities assigned him to work in a factory making starter motors for tractors, as Assistant Cleaner. His work every day was the same: sweeping, mopping, cleaning.

One day when he was sitting on the ground in the shade of the main building eating his lunch, Victory noticed another young man seated not far away. Had he really prayed before eating, or was he only scratching his forehead? Determined to find out whether or not the other fellow was saying thanks for his food, Bright Victory strolled over to him and opened the conversation:

"Excuse me, but may I ask you a question?"

"Certainly," the other responded.

"I see you are about my age; have you recently been assigned to work here?"

"Why, yes, I tried to take the entrance examination for high school. For the second year straight. But I wasn't even allowed to take the examination."

"Do you know why?" Bright Victory asked, his suspicion growing stronger.

"They never told me. But I think I know the reason."

"Would you mind telling me what you think is the reason?"

"Why, no, not at all. Perhaps it's because I come from a Christian family," said his new friend quietly.

"Now, *that's* the real question I wanted to ask you. I'm a Christian, too!" Victory shot out his hand and the other grabbed it. They shook vigorously.

So began a warm friendship between Bright Victory and Strong Hero. He also had the exalted title of Assistant Cleaner. They often worked on jobs together, ate together, and attended the after-work political meetings together. Though they were not paid overtime for attending, they had no option about it. Strong Hero's friendship was particularly helpful to Victory, since he usually had to work on Sundays. The staggered off-days at the factory meant he could attend church only once in seven or eight weeks.

One day the foreman came to Bright Victory. He was holding a piece of paper in his hand and there was a quizzical, uncertain look on his face. "Comrade Lee," he said, "I want a word with you, privately."

When the two were alone, behind some unused machinery, the foreman blurted out: "I never thought religion would have anything to do with running a plant! But here it is. Just look at that!" He shoved the sheet of paper into Bright Victory's hand. It read:

"Plant Superintendent, Sunrise Starter Motor Company, Shanghai:

You are hereby requested to release from after-hours political study, each Tuesday for the next four Tuesdays, the following workers at your factory:

Bright Victory Lee

Strong Hero Liang

They are to attend a rally each Tuesday for four Tuesdays at Gabbart Memorial Church. Inform accordingly.

(signed) Three-Self Reform Church"

"I never heard of the 'Three-Self Reform Church' but they are using stationery of the Religious Affairs Bureau. So if it's a bureau that this letter comes from, that's it."

The foreman took the letter back from Bright Victory and started to walk away. Then he turned and asked: "Do you know Strong Hero Liang?"

"Yes, sir."

"Then tell him the two of you are excused from political classes each Tuesday for four Tuesdays."

"Right!"

After work the following Tuesday, Victory and Hero made their way to the Gabbart Memorial Church. They were surprised to find its main auditorium filled to capacity with young people like themselves. Most of those attending seemed somewhat nervous and uncertain of themselves.

Bright Victory decided he would learn as much as possible about the others before the meeting started. So he went up to an open-faced young man of about twenty years of age and said politely, "Excuse me, but may I ask if you usually attend this church?"

"Why, no. Do you?"

"No, I've never been inside this building before. Do you know why we are here?"

"I haven't the slightest idea."

At that point the meeting was called to order by a man who stood up and said: "My name is Fu Yubang. I am a cadre of the Three-Self Reform Church. We work under the Religious Affairs Bureau and in close cooperation with the Party."

Bright Victory noted that this was not a church meeting at all. At least, it had none of the marks of a church meeting — no hymn singing, no prayers, no music. Instead, there were the same terms regularly used at the after-work political indoctrination classes: "Aid Korea, oppose America... American imperialism... counter-revolutionary... rotten elements... reactionaries ... love the country, love the Party...."

At the close of his speech Mr. Fu revealed the reason for the meeting: "On Tuesday afternoon, September 10, you will be a part of a huge rally at the Love Country Stadium. We will arrange for each of you to be excused from your work that afternoon. For the next two Tuesdays, you will come here for further instruction."

The next two Tuesdays brought more speeches from Mr. Fu, with special emphasis on how the missionaries from abroad were spies working for the American government and how they were agents of cultural imperialism. *That* was a new term for Bright Victory!

After his speech each Tuesday, Mr. Fu instructed the group as to how they were to act at the great rally at Love Country Stadium.

Bright Victory later remarked to Strong Hero: "He told us how we were to 'act'. That's about the size of it. We are to put on an 'act'. Didn't he strike you as a stage director rehearsing his 'act'? And we are the 'actors'!"

On the great day, the two boys arrived at Gate 3 of the Love Country Stadium at exactly one o'clock. To their amazement, they were stopped in the wide open space in front of the stadium and lined up in rows. Young women in uniform of the People's Liberation Army walked back and forth, calling out names. Finally Bright Victory heard his name called. He raised his hand and shouted "Here!" and he read with amazement the identification card the girl handed him.

"Bright Victory Lee

Gabbart Memorial Church"

He whispered to Strong Hero: "They've got me down as a *member* of Gabbart Memorial Church!"

"And look," said Hero, "there must be a dozen other groups as large as ours at all the different gates!"

"Well," returned Bright Victory, "this is a bigger deal than I imagined. What a job to organize a meeting like this!"

Strong Hero pulled out his hankerchief and mopped his face: "I just wish they would let us inside. This heat is about to finish me!"

Sharp at two o'clock the Gabbart Memorial Church delegation marched into the Love Country Stadium. What a relief it was to be under a roof and out of the sun!

Again, young women in military uniform ushered them to their seats. Strong Hero exclaimed: "There's Mr. Fu! He's with the delegation. So, he's not going to be a speaker."

It developed that at least some people on the platform were far bigger fish in the Shanghai pond than Mr. Fu. There was a rattle of drums, and when quiet had settled over the huge assembly a young woman announcer stepped up to the microphone and shouted into it, like they do in the theater, "Comrade Jia Bifang, Vice-Mayor of Shanghai!"

Mr. Fu jumped to his feet and clapped loudly. This was their cue — Victory and Hero clapped loudly too, and so did the rest of the delegation.

The Vice-Mayor's speech was purely political. He lashed out at America, "the great paper tiger", and his final climactic sentence was: "We shall rip the paper tiger to shreds!"

The announcer stepped forward to her microphone again: "Comrade Feng Yuliao, Vice-President of the Three-Self Reform Church!"

Again, loud clapping led by Mr. Fu and a dozen others like him.

Bright Victory and Strong Hero later decided this was the most important speech of the day. Comrade Feng said, among other things:

"Chairman Mao has declared that today China is lifting her head high among the nations. I declare to you that today the Christian Church is lifting her head high among the Chinese people... For the first time in history, the Premier of China has called a delegation of Christian leaders to the capital and honored them with three days of his precious time... He told us that the American concept of separation of church and state is a Johnny-come-lately idea, and that he accepted the thousand-year-old European concept that church and state are one... He told us that we are cleaning house in China and that when you clean house you don't want any guests around; therefore the missionaries must go and it's up to you to see that they go."

The Vice-Chairman paused here and there, each time Mr. Fu jumped to his feet and clapped loudly. And so did Bright Victory and Strong Hero and the rest of their delegation.

Now the announcer stepped to her microphone again:

"Miss Liang Saimei, editor of *The Christian Home*.

"Missionary Agnes Johnson came from Guelph, Ontario, Canada," proclaimed Miss Liang, "but she was educated in New York State, USA, and was an agent of American cultural imperialism. She often said, 'in America we do it *this* way.' She constantly belittled our great Chinese culture and the great Chinese people. If she were here today, I'd say 'Put her in jail for a hundred years!'"

Great clapping by Mr. Fu and his delegation.

"More than that," continued Miss Liang, "I have with my own eyes seen missionaries physically attack and mistreat the common people of China. In Guizhou Province I knew a missionary named Joel Fisher from Freemantle, Australia. One day I saw him argue with a Chinese who had come onto the missionary's property to gather firewood. The Chinese said that the land was China, and that he was Chinese and had a right to gather firewood there. The missionary disagreed and physically took hold of him and shoved him down a bank. Then he threw his baskets and carrying pole after him. If Joel Fisher were here today I would throw him down a hundred banks and then cut off his two hands!"

Thunderous applause from all, including Victory and Hero.

Six more speakers followed. They attacked not only the missionaries but also the Chinese Christians who had been friendly with them. The longer the speeches went on the more vehement and vituperative they became.

A Mr. Sun, who had been introduced as pastor of a Shanghai church, demanded: "Let's ferret out the pet dogs of the foreigners — those who have been willingly led around on a leash — and let's tie them to the flagpole in the British Consulate on the Bund and whip them until they die!"

Mr. Fu jumped up extra fast this time, and the clapping was thunderous throughout the stadium. Bright Victory looked at Strong Hero's hands. Hero looked at Victory's hands. Both were going through the motions of clapping. Neither was making a sound.

The rally closed at six o'clock. Hot and tired, Bright Victory and Strong Hero walked across the city toward home. At the corner where their ways parted they stopped and looked each other in the eye. Bright Victory voiced what each was thinking: "We've been manipulated."

11. Life In Shanghai
Autumn 1952

LIKE ALL OTHER MARRIED WOMEN, Jade Moon was assigned a job. Had not the directive come down from Beijing that everyone must become "productive", sex and age notwithstanding? To her relief, she was not assigned to a factory, with its monotonous mechanical movements, but to a Vegetable Distribution Center. The crates and baskets of vegetables were heavy, but at least there was variety in the work. What was more, she always had her scissors and plastic bag handy and could go to the rubbish heap and snip off usable bits to take home.

One day when Jade Moon returned home from work she encountered The Demon standing at the door like a sentry on duty. Her words were sharp as a bayonet: "What's that in your bag?"

"Oh, some sweet potatoes and *bak-choy*," answered Jade Moon disarmingly, opening the bag for The Demon to look inside.

"And I see the mailman brought you a letter this morning from Chongqing — from a Mrs. Deng. Do you know her?"

"Yes, I've known Mrs. Deng for many years ..."

Jade Moon slipped quickly past The Demon and ran upstairs, hoping to be out of earshot of the next question. Later, she recounted the incident to Big Sister.

"Oh, my," Big Sister groaned. "Pastor Bao, who's just been let out of prison, is coming this afternoon for a prayer time. I hope he gets in without her seeing him ... You must come over and join us, too."

Shortly afterwards Pastor Bao called quietly at Big Sister's door, *"Wei! Wei!* Hello! Hello!" and was gladly let in.

"Yes," Pastor Bao was relating to Jade Moon some time later, "many Shanghai pastors have been 'struggled', including myself. But God has ways of keeping His own. The one thing I feared most in a 'struggle' was to be forced to kneel before my accusers. For years I have not been able to kneel. It's too painful for my knees. So, when I pray I sit, or walk around the room.

"Sure enough, when my time came I was ordered to kneel down. I had excruciating visions of the pain ahead of me, but you do not reason with your tormentors. With a silent prayer to my Heavenly Father I went down on my knees. I was amazed! Instead of the pain I expected, my knees immediately went numb, and stayed numb the whole three hours I was forced to kneel. They sent me to jail for eighteen months, and I was released last week."

"And now that you are out of jail, what is the thing you most want to do?" Jade Moon asked.

"Most of all, I want to sing!" exclaimed Pastor Bao. "For eighteen months I have sung silently to myself but now I want to sing with God's people — together. What shall we sing?" The old pastor enthusiastically launched out:

"When I survey the wondrous cross
On which the Prince of Glory died,
My richest gain I count but loss,
And pour contempt on all my pride."

They had just finished the first verse when the door burst open. There in the doorway, arms akimbo, stood The Demon.

"Aha! What's that singing I hear? An illegal meeting, is it? I'm going to report you to the police!"

One morning ten-year-old Lotus Flower arrived at her new school to find an air of excitement in the classroom. The children were gathered in little knots, their attention riveted on something. Not one to be left out, Lotus Flower pushed her way into one group and there she saw what the excitement was about. A boy was proudly holding up a new red neckerchief and saying, more to himself than to those around him:

"Now I'm a Young Pioneer!"

"Where did you get that?" Lotus exploded.

"Teacher's giving them out."

Lotus Flower whirled around. Sure enough, children were lined up and the teacher was handing out red neckerchiefs, complete with rings to holds them tight. Without waiting to ask questions, Lotus lined up too.

"Name?" the teacher asked.

"Lotus Flower Lee."

"Hmm. Lotus Flower Lee," the teacher repeated to herself as she thumbed through a stack of 3" × 5" cards.

"'Lee' did you say? 'Lotus Flower Lee'?"

"Yes, Comrade Teacher."

"You do not get a neckerchief, Lotus Flower."

"Why not, Comrade Teacher?"

"Your father's name on your registration card has a black mark beside it. There must be something wrong with your father."

Drooping, Lotus made her way to her seat and sat down.

"Must be something wrong with your father." What did she mean by that?

At noon, Lotus Flower reached in her desk and pulled out bamboo chopsticks and aluminum lunch box. It was a beautiful autumn day. Lotus and her three special friends liked to eat outside on days like this. With luck, they might even hear a bird sing in one of the trees surrounding the school yard.

All four girls wore dark blue pants and dark blue jackets buttoned up to the neck. The younger children wore bright pants and jackets — red, yellow, purple or green — but by the time they reached Lotus's age the bright clothes had to be put aside, and each child assumed the standard peasant pants and Mao jacket which she would wear through the rest of her life.

There was some variety, however. Each little girl was allowed to tie her pigtail with her own size and color of ribbon. The look in each face was different, too. Chinghua, for instance, had a spark of mischief in her eye that proclaimed, "I'm going to do things different, even though we are all supposed to do everything alike!"

As they arrived under their favorite tree and all four sat down on the grass, Chinghua's spark-in-the-eye began to flash. She lifted one corner of the lunch box lid and peered inside. Then she snapped the lid shut again. "Oh, guess what's in my lunch box today — crab meat!"

Lotus too, lifted the corner of her lunch box lid, smelled the fragrance from inside, and snapped the lid shut again

"Guess what's in *my* lunch box today — pork chops!"

Then it was Yulin's turn. She lifted one corner of her lunch box lid, gave a deep sigh as she smelled the delicious food inside and said: "Guess what's in *my* lunch box — jumbo shrimp!"

Finally, Liwen lifted one corner of her lunch box lid. She rolled her eyes and smacked her lips, then said: "Guess what's in my lunch box — oysters fried in sesame oil!"

The four girls laughed merrily. Each took off her lunch box lid, fitted it neatly underneath the box and with great gusto began to eat her cold rice and pickled cabbage.

After arriving in Shanghai Noble Heart and Jade Moon had enquired about the different churches and pastors, and had decided to attend Grace Church, not far from where they lived.

One Sunday morning they stayed behind to ask Pastor Huang about having a house meeting in their home. Although they wanted to do this they were afraid of asking other believers to come to a building where there was a spy like The Demon. As they were discussing this with Pastor Huang and three of the elders, there was a commotion in the back of the building, and they looked up to see a number of men in the uniform of the Peoples' Liberation Army. As the four men approached Noble Heart noted that, as usual, there was no insignia of rank; but the quality of cloth of their uniforms showed they were officers. Even in a classless society those with class will, it seems, find a way to show it.

"We are looking for Pastor Huang," the man in front said, interrupting Noble Heart in the middle of a sentence.

The pastor spoke up: "I am Pastor Huang."

"We are from the Shanghai municipal government. We hear that you have a large hall here ..."

Noble Heart wondered what the officer was working up to.

"But in this large hall, where there are public meetings for the citizens of Shanghai, you do not have even one picture of Chairman Mao. Now, why is that? Don't you love your country?"

Noble Heart detected an edginess in the voice that hinted at difficulties to come.

"It's true, Comrade, that we do not have a picture of Chairman Mao in our hall," replied Pastor Huang. "This hall is dedicated to the worship of God through Jesus Christ. Please look around the walls. We do not even have a picture of Jesus Christ on the walls. How can we put up a picture of Chairman Mao?"

"Hmmp! So that is your answer! You will have to be responsible for that!"

The four officers turned their backs on the little knot of Christians and, without saying goodbye, marched out of the building.

Pastor Huang turned to Noble Heart: "I have been expecting this. When the Japanese were in control of Shanghai, they came here and insisted I put up a picture of Emperor Hirohito. I gave them the same answer. The Japanese were gentlemen enough not to push the matter further. I do not expect the same from the officers who were here just now."

When the Lees arrived for church service the following Sunday they heard that Pastor Huang had been arrested on Tuesday and was being held incommunicado, no one knew where. More than that, the building was being taken over by the municipal government; today was the last service.

"This will be a hard service for Elder Dai to take," whispered Noble Heart to his wife. But the practical Jade Moon had other questions in her mind. As the choir marched in to the tune of "Onward Christian Soldiers", "What will they do with the choir robes?" she whispered to Noble Heart. During the special number, she whispered again, "What's going to happen to the piano?"

Since this was the last time the building would be used for a service, Noble Heart thought it particularly appropriate that the Lord's Supper was observed. But even then, Jade Moon whispered, "Who will take care of the communion set?"

Elder Dai's sermon concluded: "This is a sad occasion. Our church is being merged with the Milton Memorial Church, so we were informed by the Three-Self Reform Church." He paused, as if unwilling to go on. "The building itself will be converted into a match factory so that it will become productive and help the livelihood of the people. Our pastor is not with us today. He is at a distance. One final thing: Keep your heads bowed and your eyes closed. It is appropriate that we close this service in prayer for the church in Shanghai and throughout China."

Elder Dai began to pray, and almost instantaneously everyone present joined together in the Chinese fashion of "united-sound-prayer." But today the united prayer reached such a crescendo that the roof could hardly contain the volume of sound. After some ten minutes, Elder Dai's prayer became virtually a shout, overriding the rest, and this was the signal for others to taper off. Then Elder Dai himself quietly coasted downhill to an ordinary volume of prayer. When it came time for his "Amen", he was the only person praying.

He had started the prayer; it was his responsibility to close it. But, in response to his single "Amen," every mouth in the hall thundered back a united "Amen". The service was officially concluded.

But there was a surprise in store for the worshipers. When they straightened up they saw that while they were praying, Elder Dai had taken a thick writing brush and written in characters a foot high across the wall in back of the pulpit:

"The gates of hell shall not

prevail against God's church."

Weeping, the people silently filed out of the building.

12. "Let The Hundred Flowers Bloom" — And Fade
Summer 1956 — Winter 1956–7

"WE ARE PREPARING a commemorative issue of the *Great Wall Daily*," Editor Lin told his staff. "It will commemorate the liberation of Shanghai and will be twice the usual size of the paper." Although a Cantonese, Editor Lin always addressed his staff in precise Mandarin, in a deliberate effort to give the lie to the derogatory saying: "Fear nothing on earth or in heaven, fear only a Cantonese speaking Mandarin."

"Chairman Mao has generously proposed, 'let the hundred flowers bloom'," he continued. "He feels that the party and the government have been too hard on the intellectuals and suppressed their creativity and initiative to the detriment of the nation. He wants to rally the intellectuals to the Communist Party, and to do this he has promised them liberal treatment. The most important thing, in the Chairman's words is to 'let the hundred flowers bloom.' He means, let people with ideas and creativity come out frankly and speak their piece. At the same time the Chairman has launched a 'Party rectification' movement to get rid of sectarianism, bureaucratism and subjectivism through criticism and self-criticism.

"This means that you, comrades, can really write what is on your heart and mind. And we will publish it in the *Great Wall Daily*, instead of using only the material from Beijing."

Editor Lin always spoke of the Beijing propaganda line as "material." He was too honest to call it "news" as many in his profession euphemistically did.

Editor Lin then turned to Noble Heart: "Comrade Lee, you were assigned to our paper shortly after you arrived from Chongqing, and you have never yet had an opportunity to try your wings as a reporter here — in anything creative, that is. I want you, Comrade Lee, to write something in a lighter vein. Humor has no place in a Communist society, apparently. Maybe we can rescue it from the trash heap and restore it to its rightful place in the newspaper world. So, Comrade Lee, write an article on the lighter side connected with the liberation of Shanghai by the People's Liberation Army!"

Noble Heart was making his way to the *Great Wall Daily* office earlier than usual today. He wanted to get Editor Lin's ear before the rest of the staff arrived. Turning off Nanjing Road, he picked his way along the lane, climbing over piles of debris made up of the mortar, plaster and bricks that had fallen from the face of the old buildings. At least by walking on the debris, he kept out of the mud-and-water potholes that pitted the lane like pockmarks on the face of a smallpox victim. He wondered how much of the debris had been knocked off the walls when the People's Liberation Army took Shanghai seven years before.

Noble Heart entered the main door of the paper's offices and turned right down the central hallway. Again he had to climb over or circumnavigate piles of debris from the building and piles of new materials brought in to replace the old. Finally he turned into Editor Lin's office. A single electric bulb hanging by a cord from the ceiling tried in vain to dispel the darkness of the windowless room. Sheaves of articles, letters and directives mounted along each wall and spilled over onto the floor like congealed lava from a volcano. Cobwebs filled the corners and festooned the ceiling. And in the middle of the floor stood a young woman in peasant pants and Mao jacket with a sheaf of papers in her hand. Noble Heart asked her: "Comrade, is Comrade Editor in?"

"Yes. Be seated. Comrade Editor will be back in a minute."

Noble Heart looked around. Be seated? There wasn't a single chair in the room apart from that behind the editor's desk.

"Here, Comrade Editor, is the article in the lighter vein that you asked me to write."

Noble Heart handed the article to Editor Lin, who read it through on the spot:

"When the People's Liberation Army came into Shanghai they were in for plenty of surprises. Most of them were Northerners and many, due to the repressive ways of the regime of that traitor Chiang Kai-shek, had never been to school and therefore never learned to read. Some aspects of Western civilization, as they ran into them in Shanghai, were fearful and wonderful and entirely incomprehensible to them.

"After the liberation of Shanghai a certain platoon was billeted on Nanjing Road in what had formerly been the office of a British firm. As with any army, the People's Liberation Army moves on its stomach. That is, it must be fed. This particular platoon had its own rice but they could not locate a place in this former British office to wash their rice. Finally one of the men found just the thing: a porcelain crock attached to the floor and standing high enough so that a comrade could kneel and wash the rice. There was water in the crock already.

"Everything went well and the rice was being washed. Another comrade, however, was curious about a chain that hung from a tank on the wall behind the porcelain crock. He gave it a hard pull. With that, water gushed into the porcelain crock and carried the rice away in an instant.

"The unfortunate comrades went hungry that night. That was the last of their rice ration for the day."

"Ha, ha, ha!" laughed Editor Lin, slapping his knee with delight. "Good enough for them!" Always the Cantonese, he seldom missed a joke when it was at the expense of Northerners.

Then he quietened down, held his jaw in his left hand, thought for a minute, and said, "It's exactly the kind of thing I asked you to write. But ... I think we'll have to save this for a better day. The time isn't ripe for this kind of humor. I'll put it aside for future use."

Little did either editor or reporter realize just what "future use" might mean. All they knew was that Editor Lin tossed the article on top of a pile of papers in the corner of his office. Like the Frog War story in Chongqing, Noble Heart would live to rue the day when he put on paper the Story of the Porcelain Crock.

"This is our fifth winter back in Shanghai," Jade Moon grumbled a few months later. "In Chongqing I used to hanker for Shanghai, especially when it was so cloudy and dark day after day in the winter time. But I guess I forgot how downright cold it can be in Shanghai." She held out her hands: "Just look at my chilblains! And they hurt so much when they crack open. I wear gloves, even in the house, but it doesn't help much."

"Yes, it's especially hard on people like you with poor circulation," answered Noble Heart understandingly.

"Couldn't we buy a little charcoal for a hand brazier?"

"I thought about that, Jade Moon, when I saw your hands red and bleeding the other day. I went to the charcoal shop, but they asked me for coupons. So I went to the district municipal office, and they said no coupons were being issued for charcoal for braziers."

"No coupons! How come?"

"Well, they showed me the official ruling from Beijing. It said: 'North of the Yangzi is cold; south of the Yangzi is warm. Coupons for fuel for house-heating will therefore be issued north but not south of the Yangzi'. It's just too bad that we live ten miles south of the Yangzi River!"

"So we can't have even a little heat in the house? I get so tired of wearing quilted jacket and pants! I look like a balloon!"

Noble Heart saw that Jade Moon was on the verge of tears, and knew he must shift the topic of conversation quickly. "Yes, I've been noticing Lotus Flower lately. She's really getting to be a young lady. And only fourteen. If only she could wear something besides those floppy pants and that floppy jacket!

"Jade Moon, you know I've dreamed of us being transferred to a warmer climate. It would be so much better for you. Say, Canton. Or even Hainan Island. That's south of Hong Kong, you know. I hear they grow bananas and pineapples and coconuts all year round on Hainan Island."

"Noble Heart, don't even mention Hainan Island! It's bad luck even to talk about it! That's where the emperors used to exile their political prisoners in the old days."

Editor Lin was talking to Noble Heart after office hours. "Comrade Lee, I had high hopes last year when the Chairman told us to 'let the hundred flowers bloom.' I thought it was an honest response to the problems of writers, artists, doctors, teachers, lawyers — in short, the intellectuals. And now it looks as if the whole thing has backfired. Why? I can't help wondering if it could have been a ploy by the government and the Party to give the intellectuals enough rope to hang themselves with." He automatically looked around to see if anyone was listening.

Noble Heart's mind was full of thoughts of the other editor he had known so well, Mr. Deng of Chongqing. But it was not the occasion to speak of him now. Rather, he said: "Well, I do hope this new turn of national events will not affect you. I have a real respect for you."

The editor cut him short: "It's too late. I've been given notice to prepare my confession. Just look at what was delivered this afternoon — it's the beginning of the end for me." Silently, he handed a sheet of paper to Noble Heart.

Noble Heart read it through quickly. He soon realized the second paragraph had the sting in it:

"1. In the *Great Wall Daily* you encouraged rightist, Fascist, feudalistic and counter-revolutionary thought.

2. You failed to publish news from Beijing even though you were urged to do so by loyal cadres.

3. Instead, you took the capitalist road and published articles written in Shanghai.

4. Specifically, you encouraged articles critical of the Great People's Liberation Army.

You are required to write your confession and appear with it at the Shanghai Municipal Government headquarters on February 1, 1957, at 10 a.m."

February 1 dawned wet, cold and windy. It was Shanghai at its worst, as if Heaven had sent a bitter wind and Earth had replied with sticky cold slush. Noble Heart and the other reporters, sub-editors and copy readers all had official notice to attend Editor Lin's confession meeting.

A fellow reporter whispered to Noble Heart: "It's the old, old way — 'kill the goose for the duck to see.' It's a warning to the rest of us."

Noble Heart was relieved to find that the hearing was scheduled for an inside hall. An open-air session today might bring pneumonia on more than one.

The editor was required to stand and read his confession. Having had experience "improving" confessions in Chongqing, Noble Heart soon sensed that something was wrong. The editor was paying lip service to the government and the Communist Party. He acknowledged his sins and short-comings, and that the accusations laid against him were true.

Yet there was a missing element. What was it?

Oh, yes, he's not mouthing all the in-jargon. He's not using the terms they want him to use. He's being too restrained. He is keeping his self-respect, but he may lose his life!

Up to this point, Noble Heart's eyes had been fixed on Editor Lin. He had merely noted that the men sitting at the table were in military uniform and that one of them was perfectly bald with unusual red streaks where his hair used to be.

After Editor Lin had finished reading his confession, the men at the table conferred together in low tones for several minutes. Then a subaltern announced: "The verdict will be read by Colonel Chang."

When the Colonel — the man with the bald head — began to read, Noble Heart's eyes almost jumped out of their sockets. He hardly heard the verdict — three years of correctional labor in the forests of Heilongjiang, northern Manchuria — because he had recognized the voice of the man reading the verdict. Colonel Chang was none other than Lieutenant Chang, from whom he had escaped in Chongqing five years before.

At home that night Jade Moon asked: "Didn't you recognize Lieutenant Chang when you saw him?"

"I was more concerned about Editor Lin than about the other men up front. And how was I to know who the bald-headed officer was? You remember, we thought maybe Lieutenant Chang was killed by the lightning. And that was 1,400 miles away and five years ago!"

"Well, anyway, you should have left the hearing at once!"

"Jade Moon, I couldn't have left that accusation meeting if I had tried. They checked off our names coming in the door. We were *there*. Just about prisoners."

"Do you think he recognized you?"

"Well ..."

"Oh, Noble Heart! I just thought of something! What did you say his head looked like?"

"Perfectly bald. With strange red lines, almost like a map."

Jade Moon suddenly turned white as a sheet, and began to sway uncertainly back and forth. Noble Heart grabbed her before she fell and helped her to a chair.

"I'm all right," she said.

"What's the problem? What gave you that funny turn?"

"Just give me a drink of water ... Thank you. I never mentioned it to you," she went on, "but Lotus Flower and I saw that man right here in our front yard. Leading exercises. In army uniform with a red-star cap. He took his cap off and threw it down, and we saw his bald head and those red lines. Lotus Flower said they looked like a map. Could that have been where the lightning struck him?"

"How long back was that?"

"Years ago. We had been in Shanghai only a few months. Do you think he was on your trail even then?"

"Hardly likely. It must have been a coincidence, or somebody else."

"Noble Heart, something tells me that the man Lotus Flower and I saw was Lieutenant Chang. He's had a knife up his sleeve for years, a knife with your name on it. He's just biding his time to stick it in your back." Jade Moon shuddered involuntarily.

A week later Noble Heart, now Acting Editor of the *Great Wall Daily*, was in the office. A soldier walked in and handed an order to Noble Heart's secretary.

She motioned him to wait, saying: "Just a minute. I'll see if I can find what you want."

She searched through the stacks of papers and articles piled along the walls and in the corners, and finally came up with a sheaf clipped together with paper clips. Handing it to the soldier she asked: "Is this what you are looking for?"

The soldier examined it a minute and said, "Yes, this is it." Then he folded the sheaf of papers carefully, shoved them into the inside pocket of his jacket, buttoned the jacket up and left.

The secretary turned to Noble Heart: "Excuse me, sir. Perhaps I should have consulted you about that. But you know how it is when the government wants something."

"What did he want?" asked Noble Heart.

"Oh, that funny story about the soldiers and the porcelain crock. We never ran it in the paper, did we? I wonder how the government even knew there was such a story."

This time it was Noble Heart's turn to shudder.

"Name?"

"Noble Heart Lee."

"Age?"

"Forty-three."

"Occupation?"

"Acting Editor, *Great Wall Daily*."

"Remain standing. Face the inner door."

Noble Heart was relieved to be able to face the inner door. This meant his back was turned to his fellow-reporters and others from the *Great Wall Daily*, unwilling attenders at his trial. He knew he could not look into their faces and keep control of his own.

His inquisitors had not yet appeared. Would *he* be one of them — Colonel Chang, the Lieutenant Chang of Chongqing days who had condemned Editor Lin four weeks ago in this very room?

With a start, Noble Heart realized that he was standing within two feet of the very spot where Editor Lin had stood. *If Jade Moon were here she would say that is a bad omen...*

but I'm glad she's not here. No good for her to go through this again like she did in Chongqing.

Noble Heart stood for fifteen minutes before the door finally opened. The first man to step through was bald headed with strange red lines where his hair used to be. Noble Heart exclaimed under his breath, "Colonel Chang!"

The four officers took their seats behind the table. The spokesman was Colonel Chang: "Comrade Sergeant, read the accusation."

The seageant read: "Noble Heart Lee is arrested and brought to trial on the following charges:

1. He is a fugitive from justice, having fled from Chongqing in 1952 before his hearing was completed.
2. In Chongqing he was known to be pro-Chiang Kai-shek.
3. He oppressed and mistreated the people.
4. He has consistently made fun of the great People's Liberation Army. Examples are the so-called Frog War story in Chongqing and the Porcelain Crock story in Shanghai."

The sergeant folded the paper and sat down. Colonel Chang got to his feet.

"Noble Heart Lee," he said acrimoniously, "you thought you were getting away from me, didn't you? Yeah, that's right — you were running from me, weren't you? But I've known every move you've made for five years. Ha! Ha!

"And I know you run with those superstitious people who call themselves Christians. So, you hide behind a facade of a foreign religion, do you? But the days of Christians are numbered in China! Christians are the tools — and fools — of Imperialist America. For the record, I am going to read to this court what you wrote about the great People's Liberation Army."

Colonel Chang proceeded to read the two stories word for word as Noble Heart had written them. Then he summarized:

"You see, comrades, how Noble Heart Lee compares our Red Army soldiers to most despicable creatures — to frogs, no less. And how he laughs at Red Army soldiers as ignorant country bumpkins."

The Colonel turned to Noble Heart:

"You thought your God delivered you from me in Chongqing, didn't you? I heard it — that was the story going around. But we'll see if your God can deliver you this time. You should be shot. One shot in the back of the head by a gun from the hand of the Red Army soldier you laugh at. But times have changed. You are lucky to survive to the present, when the Great Chairman is lenient toward people like you who call yourselves 'Christians' and 'intellectuals'."

Pronouncing those words had a strange effect on Colonel Chang. His voice suddenly rose, his face flushed red and the red raced through the lines on his bald head, turning them scarlet.

Noble Heart gasped, "He's going to have a stroke!"

Shaking, the colonel sat down. The sergeant stood up and announced officiously: "The court will now confer on the punishment for Noble Heart Lee."

The officers seated at the table whispered together for several minutes. Noble Heart could sense his colleagues behind him growing more and more tense. Finally Colonel Chang, who by now had collected himself, scribbled something on a piece of paper. He handed it to the sergeant.

The sergeant stood up and saluted Colonel Chang then, for some reason Noble Heart could not understand, he turned and saluted the prisoner. After that he read:

"Noble Heart Lee is hereby condemned to be transported to Hainan Island, Guangdong Province. There under the tutelage of the peasants he will for three years accept Reform through Labor on the state-operated rubber plantation."

PART III

HAINAN ISLAND
1957 ~ 1958

13. Reform Through Labor
Summer 1957

"BANG!... BANG!... BANG!... BANG!"

A length of old railway rail suspended from a rafter sprang to life when struck with a hammer. The clamor reverberated through the dormitory. It was 5.30 a.m. at Happy Days Nationalized Rubber Plantation, Hainan Island, South China.

Jarred awake were sixty men. A few jumped quickly off the three-tier bamboo slat bunks, twenty sets of which occupied a dirt floor 40 by 24 feet. There were three windows on each of two sides of the room, a blank wall on the third side and a single door on the fourth. A guard, who occupied an iron cot beside the door, had clanged the rising bell.

For every man who had jumped at the sound, ten others groaned and moaned and wished the night could go on for another hour. Among these was Noble Heart Lee. He had just dreamed a most delightful dream — that he was at home with his family seated around the table eating huge fresh-water crabs. In his dream, he was poking out the sweet white meat of a claw with the butt end of a chopstick, and eating it without salt or condiment in order to relish the flavor of the crab itself.

Hmm ... What are we going to have for breakfast this morning, fresh-water crab? he said to himself ironically.

At 5.45 came line-up for roll call. This morning there were three absentees. As usual, they were found still on their bunks, ill. Real? Or pretended? Never mind, the barefoot doctor will soon be along, whose treatment is usually worse than the disease; pretenders will be at work before the morning is half gone. Minus their breakfast.

Noble Heart soon learned what was for breakfast: rice

gruel and pickled cabbage, ladled into the enamelware bowl each man washed for himself and brought back for the next meal, and eaten with his own chopsticks.

At 6.30 names were called again, and knife and bucket were issued to each man. He carried the two into the rubber plantation, the *raison d'etre* for his being assigned to Hainan. For on Hainan Island there is no frost, and rubber trees thrive.

Noble Heart liked this early morning walk. For one thing, they were not marched out to work herded by soldiers with fixed bayonets as was true in other labor camps. Often he walked with Hou Helang, a former Certified Public Accountant in Shanghai, now also on the receiving end of "reform through labor" and "learn from the peasants." Actually their straw boss was not a peasant at all, nor even a farmer; he was a city man from Canton, put in charge of the sixty men due not to his knowledge of how to grow rubber but to his political dependability. He was a member of the Communist Party, a fact he seldom allowed anyone to forget.

Noble Heart walked a little faster to catch up with Hou Helang, and said to him: "Repeat John chapter three again today. You left out part of it yesterday."

So Helang began: "There was a man of the Pharisees, named Nicodemus ..."

The next day it would be Helang's turn to drill Noble Heart. They liked each other not only because they were both Christians but because they were both from Shanghai, and could talk their native Shanghai dialect together.

In case of a disagreement over the memory work, the two men would later hide behind a rubber tree and consult the text itself. Noble Heart always kept his New Testament with him, but not always strapped to his thigh as it had been on the day of his trial back in Shanghai and the long days of the sea voyage to Hainan Island.

The day's work began: take the 24–hours-worth of drippings — about one ounce — that had collected in the bowl suspended to the rubber tree, and pour the virgin latex into the bucket. Slash a slanted sliver of bark from the lower end of the denuded area. Attach the bowl to catch another 24 hours-worth of drippings. Every so often, when the bucket filled up, it had to be carried to the tank cart, where a thin bamboo slat was issued for each bucket delivered. At the end of the day each tapper surrendered his bamboo slats as proof of quota filled for the day.

The man at the latex tank also handed out the aluminum lunch boxes at noon. Today lunch was cold rice with a little salt. Noble Heart especially liked the coarse ocean salt, folded in a piece of newspaper, and was careful to eat every grain of it. Supper sometimes brought a surprise — a bit of fresh squash or leafy vegetable added to the standard fare of rice-and-soup, and maybe twice a month a bit of pork floating in the soup.

The day ended with political instruction from 7 to 9.30 p.m., lights out at 10. As Noble Heart stretched out on his bamboo bunk that night, he rethought the day. The one thing different from any other day was his conversation on the way back with Mr. Lu, a fellow-detainee.

Mr. Lu had overtaken him on the path and asked in a friendly way: "I understand your sentence is 'Reform through Labor'. What are you being corrected for?"

"For several things," Noble Heart had replied. "The most serious was two articles I wrote which didn't give proper respect to the Red Army. I'm truly sorry now I ever wrote those articles."

"Don't you hate their very gizzards for sending you to a place like this?"

"Why, no. I've never thought of hating them. You see, I'm a Christian, and in the Christian faith it is more important to love than to hate. In fact, the Bible says, 'If a man says, I love God, and hates his brother, he is a liar: for he who does not love his brother whom he has seen, cannot love God whom he has not seen!'"

Then Mr. Lu took another approach: "I'd like to see Chiang Kai-shek come back to the mainland and drive these lousy guys back to the caves of Yanan, wouldn't you?"

"Why, no," Noble Heart said again. "I've never thought about that. You know, the Bible says that the powers that be are ordained of God."

Then Mr. Lu switched again: "If I had a chance, I'd escape to Hong Kong. What about you?"

"My wife and children are in China," replied Noble Heart. "I have no interest in going to Hong Kong."

As Noble Heart lay on his slats that night, he asked himself, *What have I done? I've shared my Christian convictions with a casual acquaintance. Does that make me a better Christian? Or was I foolish? Termites survive by staying in the dark. But who wants to be a termite?*

One morning, three weeks later, Noble Heart noticed that Mr. Lu's bunk was empty. He did not appear for roll call and, strangest of all, his name was not called that morning.

On their way to work, Helang asked: "Did you notice that Mr. Lu has gone? I'm not surprised."

"Why not?"

"Well, you know I've had this impacted molar and yesterday I went to Haikou to have it seen to. After the dentist worked on me I had an hour before catching the bus back here, and just for kicks I went around to the steamship ticket office to see if they offered passage to Shanghai — not that I'm going, mind you! While I was looking over the schedules on the wall, who should walk up to the ticket counter but Mr. Lu! He apparently knew the man behind the counter, for they talked in the Hankou dialect, and he said to him, 'I'm glad this assignment is over, and I can get onto that ship for Canton!'"

Then Helang voiced what both of them were thinking: "Was Mr. Lu a plant?"

14. The Great Leap Forward
Autumn 1958

"THEY SENT ME to you because you understand words and you know Mandarin. Could you please explain this to me?"

Noble Heart took the sheaf of printed papers proffered by Commune Leader Tao, head of Daybreak Commune No 19. He was surprised that the head of a commune of ten thousand people should seek out a prisoner in a labor camp, and was even more surprised to hear Commune Leader Tao use that bourgeois word, "please", a word outlawed from the vocabulary of Communist China.

"No problem. I'll do what I can to help you, except that I'm leaving for the rubber grove in five minutes ..." Noble Heart showed his visitor his bucket and knife.

"Oh, I've cleared it with the camp commander," answered Commune Leader Tao. "He suggested your name."

Noble Heart looked at the title on the top of the first page:

"Detailed Instructions on How to Construct and Operate a Small-Scale Blast Furnace."

Comrade Tao went on: "There are so many technical terms, no one in our commune understands it, so I came over here to see you."

Noble Heart glanced through the paper. As he read, a dozen questions bombarded his mind: *How does anyone in Beijing expect a farm commune on Hainan Island to make pig iron? ...Where will the iron ore come from? ... And the coal? ... And why have they roped me into this impossible situation?* Aloud he said, "I'm sorry, but this will take some study. Could you come back tomorrow at this time?"

Disappointment written across his face, Commune Leader Tao turned away.

Noble Heart went immediately to Camp Commander

Chen and showed him the paper. The Camp Commander swore: "No, no time off! You must keep up your quota. Let the ..... go to ....! Their problems are their problems, not mine!"

Noble Heart took the sheaf of papers with him to the rubber grove. He worked extra fast for an hour then sat down on the ground and read the papers. While eating his lunch of cold rice and salt he did the same. By the end of the afternoon he had read all twenty pages and had made notes on the margins — in as simple language as possible — of the procedure the commune would have to follow and the equipment and materials needed.

While Noble Heart was finishing off his soup at supper someone tapped him on the shoulder. He turned to see Commune Leader Tao, whose voice had steel in it! "Comrade Camp Commander will excuse you from political instruction. I must know tonight what's in those twenty pages."

Noble Heart replied: "Excuse me while I finish eating."

Commune Leader Tao retreated from the mess hall, and as he disappeared Noble Heart jumped up and headed in the opposite direction. He said to himself: *What Tao says Chen said and what Chen really said might be two different things. There's bad blood between the two of them and I don't want to stir it up any further.*

Fortunately, he found the camp commander without delay, and asked: "Comrade Chen, may I be excused from class tonight to help Comrade Tao with his problem?"

"Why doesn't he mind his own business...?" After more of the same tirade, the camp commander's voice tapered off. Finally he said, "Okay, then, but lights out at ten!"

There was a coloring to that last sentence which said to Noble Heart, "Of course, I told Commune Leader Tao you could have the time. But I don't like him fooling around my unit!"

The commune leader was still waiting at the mess hall. Noble Heart asked him: "Why must you know the contents of this paper tonight?"

Commune Leader Taò replied: "There was a covering letter with this paper, over the signature of the Great Helmsman himself. He said that because there is iron ore in the mountains of Hainan we must be an example to the rest of Guangdong Province in the Great Leap Forward. He says we must complete the Five Year Plan in one year!"

Noble Heart noticed that Comrade Tao's voice was shaking, and so was his right hand holding the papers. Himself shaken by the whole business, Noble Heart poured out the questions that had tormented him all day long. "Who is going to mine the iron ore? Will it be in sufficient quantities? Where is the coal coming from? Who will burn it into coke? And where? Where is your equipment coming from? Who will be in charge of this operation?"

To the final question alone did Commune Leader Tao have the answer: "I am in charge, full-time. But I am also in charge, full-time, of the commune ..."

At ten o'clock Comrade Tao left. His face was flushed and he walked unsteadily, like a man who has been drinking too much. He was mumbling to himself, "Great Leap Forward, Great Leap Forward...."

"Today Production Team Number One cleans the banana plantation and cuts the bunches ready to harvest ... Number Two empties the latrines and carries out the nightsoil to the cabbage fields ... Number Three hoes out the pineapple field ... Number Four goes out to search again for coal ... Number Five sends a group with the commune truck into Haikou for equipment for the Pig Iron Blast Furnace Project ..."

Noble Heart didn't listen to the orders for the other production teams. He was thinking of the ride into the city of Haikou, which he had not visited since first arriving on

Hainan Island eighteen months before. And to ride in the front seat of a truck — what a treat!

After much unwinding of red tape and two heated confrontations with Camp Commander Chen, Commune Leader Tao had finally wangled a temporary transfer for Noble Heart to Daybreak Commune No 19. On paper he was "Advisor to Pig Iron Blast Furnace Project." *De facto*, he was in charge of the project. The shift was quite a jolt for him — from his one-job-only work as rubber tapper to being in charge of the complicated project of back-yard pig iron blast furnace, a job neither he nor anyone else on Hainan Island had the slightest clue about. That is, apart from those twenty pages of complicated and jumbled instructions, which Noble Heart pored over daily.

"No 15, Bubbling Well Road, Haikou."

Noble Heart turned the slip of paper over and looked at it again, though he had memorized the address before they left the commune. He asked the truck driver: "Do you know where No 15 Bubbling Well Road is?"

"Not got a clue. I'm from the mainland."

"Do you speak Hainanese?"

"Wouldn't stoop to learn the stuff. Cantonese is the original Chinese. Everybody should learn Cantonese."

"Well, stop the truck then." Noble Heart jumped out and spoke to the men riding in the rear: "Any of you men know where Bubbling Well Road is?"

They looked at each other. One after another shook his head.

"How many speak Hainanese?"

One timid hand went up.

"Okay. You ride up in the cab."

The streets of Haikou, largest town on Hainan Island, were clogged with pedestrians and hand-drawn carts. There were few bicycles, fewer trucks, no private cars. After much enquiry they finally found Bubbling Well Road. When they located No 15, Noble Heart stifled an exclamation of surprise. It was a church building! He could make out the faint outlines of the characters, "Haikou Gospel Hall", once chiseled into the stone lintel above the big double gate. Whoever had erased them had not gone deep enough into the stone to remove the original words completely.

Did the stone mason leave them that way on purpose? Noble Heart mused.

Another sign, new, on a plank eight inches across by six feet long, hung vertically beside the same gate. The characters, black-on-white, read from top to bottom: "People's Republic of China, Guangdong Province, Haikou County Government Warehouse." An ancient gatekeeper was snoozing in his chair just inside the gate. Not even the sound of the truck arriving had awakened him. Noble Heart shook him and asked: "Where's the man responsible for the warehouse?"

"He stepped out. Said he'd be back in thirty minutes."

The property seemed to extend back away from the street through several courtyards. Suddenly an idea struck Noble Heart: there might still be some Christians living on the place! He said to the driver: "I'm going to have a look around. Call me when the cadre comes back."

Noble Heart sauntered through the first archway, casually, slowly, as if at the moment killing time was his sole purpose in life. His sharp reporter's eyes identified the first rooms as having at one time been a school — a Christian school, no doubt. Now they were living quarters. He strolled through two more archways. The last remnants of paint here and whitewash there were flaking off and lying in sad little patches on the ground. Bits of scraggly shrubs and what had once been flower beds spoke of the beauty and color that had once enlivened the compound. But there was no color now; a drab grayness had settled down over everything like a shroud.

Noble Heart had just turned to retrace his steps when he heard a throat-clearing sound. Instinctively he looked around, and there in a doorway stood a white-haired old lady. She was large-boned and large-bodied; dignity and peace shone out from her broad face.

"Excuse me," she said, "are you looking for someone?"

"Yes, thank you, I am. To be frank, I was wondering if there are still any Christians around here."

"Why, yes, there are. You are looking at one right now. And may I ask if you are a Christian yourself?"

"I most certainly am. My name is Noble Heart Lee and I am from Shanghai."

"My name is Ba Yudeng, for many years Bible Woman at this church."

"Are any churches open in Haikou now? I'm anxious to know. I've had no news of the Lord's work for a year and a half."

"This church was closed last year. There are no more Christian services in the city, nor on the entire island so far as I know. Only brothers and sisters in the Lord meet for prayer in their homes."

At that moment a voice came from the front of the compound: "Comrade Lee! Where are you? The cadre is back."

Noble Heart was in no hurry to leave. "And you... how is it that you are still in the church compound?"

Miss Ba laughed. "Well, I'm so old they didn't think I could cause any trouble. I'm eighty now, so they just left me here."

Noble Heart gave her an old-fashioned bow. He said, "I hope we'll meet again."

"Thank you," she returned "We shall meet again."

"You're from Shanghai, aren't you?"

The questioner was the driver. Fire bricks, blowers, air ducts, cement and other materials were bouncing along with them over the dusty, mud-rutted trail that was the main road from the city to the commune. Noble Heart and the driver were alone in the cab.

"Right. I'm from Shanghai," Noble Heart almost shouted to be heard above the noise of engine, load and road. "And you're from Guangzhou, since you speak Cantonese."

"Correct. But my wife is from Hainan Island. We settled here after we married. Are you married?"

"Yes, and I have three children."

"You're lucky your wife is not here!"

Noble Heart was surprised at the vehemence with which the driver spoke. Quietly, he responded: "I don't know what you mean. I wish she were here."

"Oh, no, you don't! It's like hell having your wife so near you see her every day. But she might as well not be your wife..."

"I don't get you," replied Noble Heart, puzzled.

"I mean with this damnable commune system. I get a glimpse of my wife every day, that's true. But she's detailed to the communal kitchen team. She sleeps in the women's dormitory and I in the men's." The driver was sputtering with anger.

"Oh yes, I see," said Noble Heart thoughtfully.

"And I'm with my wife privately once every two weeks," the driver went on, "for thirty minutes. There's a bed there, yes. But we just sit on the edge of the bed and my wife cries for thirty minutes. Then that hag in charge of the room yells 'Time's up! Get out! It's time for the next couple!'"

"I'm sorry about that," Noble Heart murmured.

"And there that woman sits with her ball pen and note-book, keeping a record of every couple. I could wring her neck! You'd better be glad your wife's a thousand miles away!"

Noble Heart tried to tactfully shift the subject: "Do you have any children?"

"Oh yes, a boy and a girl. But they're in the nursery and we see them once a week. For thirty minutes. They're so brainwashed with singing and dancing they don't even know who their parents are. What's the point in having children?"

"Well, things will get better. We must have patience."

"Patience! Besides family problems, I've now got a hungry stomach, thanks to Mao Zedong and Company! Do you know they reduced our rice ration by one-third yesterday?"

"Why did they do that?"

"They said it was because of drought in the North. But I know better. Northerners don't eat rice anyway. There may be calamities that are heaven-sent, but ours on Hainan Island are man-made."

"Hush, not so loud," Noble Heart warned.

The driver went on, as loud as ever: "They drained the swamp to increase production, so they said. But the canals they cut through to the ocean let salt water back up into the irrigation channels at flood tide and ruined a lot of riceland ... And now these teams looking for coal scrape off the top soil of upland fields and leave nothing but clay and stone where good soil used to be..." He went on and on. Noble Heart was glad there was so much noise that the men in the back could not hear. One never knew who might be a spy.

He tried to quieten the driver by a more positive suggestion: "But there are all these vegetables and fruits the commune grows ..."

"Yeah! Don't I know! See that pineapple field over there? Every pineapple in that field will go to Hong Kong or Macau for the sake of foreign money. I haven't tasted a pineapple or a banana for six months!"

Still Noble Heart remonstrated: "But don't you have a plot of ground you tend for your own use?"

"Not now. The commune has swallowed up everything. Three months ago I had to give up the deeds of my land. That was the land the rich people used to own. It was cut up and the pieces handed out during Land-Reform in the early fifties. But now the land has been re-reformed and I have nothing!"

A sudden fright struck the driver, making him almost run off the road. "Say, Comrade Lee, you won't tell anybody I told you these things, will you? Everybody knows. But if you open the front of your head to talk about them you'll get a bullet through the back of it."

At that, the driver stuck his right hand back of his head, the thumb pointed like the barrel of a gun, and made a loud cluck with his tongue to imitate a shot being fired.

Noble Heart was beginning to discover what an anomalous position his was — a labor camp prisoner and thereby at the bottom of the pecking order; and at the same time in charge of one of the most daring schemes ever witnessed on Hainan Island, the Pig Iron Blast Furnace Project, and thereby suddenly elevated in the pecking order. Just how thin a line he was walking he was soon to find out.

One problem was the bad feeling between Labor Camp Commander Chen, who legally had charge of Noble Heart, and Commune Leader Tao, to whom he had been seconded by action of the Guangdong Provincial Government. But therein lay the seed of trouble; the transfer was for three months only.

One day Commune Leader Tao came to Noble Heart: "Comrade Lee, can't you get a move on and at least fire up the furnace. We've got to show *something* to the higher ups."

"The basic problem is right there, when you say, 'Fire up',," Noble Heart told him. "On Hainan Island we have iron ore and limestone. But we don't have coal. I put in a requisition for coal to the provincial authorities in Guangzhou, but they haven't even answered my letter. I sent a telegram; they haven't even acknowledged it."

"Well," returned Tao, "Chairman Mao himself ordered us to set the pace and become the example for all Back Yard

Furnaces in the province. If we don't do just that, I'm going to lose face. And you — you're going to lose more than face!"

Noble Heart was between the devil and the deep blue sea. If he did not return to the rubber plantation at the end of three months, he would incur the wrath of Camp Commander Chen and all those above him who held that "Reform through Labor" was the only way to deal with China's intellectuals. On the other hand, if he left the Pig Iron Furnace Project now it would collapse from lack of leadership, and he would raise the ire of Commune Leader Tao and all those above him who believed this was the way to advance China industrially and attain the Five Year Plan in one year. As the fateful three-month deadline approached, he prayed for special wisdom.

The dread date arrived. At the end of the day's work, Noble Heart went to his bunk, folded his personal belongings and laid them onto his square carrying cloth. This he tied corner to corner and hung it from one end of a bamboo carrying pole. With his bedding roll slung from the other end and his straw hat pushed down over his eyes, he quietly slipped out of Daybreak Commune No 19. The last thing he wanted to do was to say goodbye to Commune Leader Tao. It would only mean an explosion.

Threading his way through the fields at dusk, half-trotting coolie fashion under his load, Noble Heart could have passed for any one of a million other labourers on Hainan Island.

On arriving at the camp, Noble Heart went direct to his old bunk. He knocked off the dust and cobwebs of three months, thinking that at least nobody else had occupied it and brought his particular breed of bedbugs.

At the evening meal he made brief, surreptitious eye contact with the other detainees. Only Hou Helang, the other Christian in the camp, was brave enough to shake hands and verbalize what all felt — that they were glad to see him again, and in good health.

During the three months Noble Heart had been away the rice ration had been cut in half. Helang told him that half of their staple diet was now hard bread made from rice bran and "extended" with sawdust and ground rice stalks. Each man's portion was now weighed out by steelyard as he waited in line.

Noble Heart turned over his assignment order to the guard, whose duty it was to report his arrival to the commanding officer. He duly took the paper and left the room.

Tired from his trek across the fields, Noble Heart stretched out on his bunk. His assignment at the commune did not end officially until midnight; there was no obligation for him to attend the indoctrination class tonight like the other prisoners....

Suddenly he heard a noise outside. He opened his eyes, realizing he had dropped off to sleep. As he lay there, strange patterns of light flashed back and forth through the windows looking away toward the back of the camp.

All at once, torches burst into the dormitory, and men boiled in behind them. More noise came, not so much a shout as a mumble and growl of suppressed anger. Noble Heart sat upright in his bunk, amazed. Here was something out of control in a land where everything was controlled, even man's inmost thoughts.

"What's up? What's happening?" he asked. But there was no reply.

Just inside the room the crowd stopped, torches held high above their heads. The glare filled the room, but Noble Heart could not make out the faces, only that the torches were the woven bamboo ones commonly used at night for walking outside.

Then one of the men dipped his torch and knocked off the charred portion against the floor. In that instant Noble Heart recognized the face of Commune Leader Tao.

What on earth is he doing here? flashed through Noble Heart's mind, *and with all this mob?*

He did not have long to wait for an answer. Commune Leader Tao sprang forward. With a curse he grabbed Noble Heart by the shoulders and shook him. His face was red and his breath was coming in gasps.

"You ....! What do you mean, leaving me like that? Not even telling me you were going! ....! I'll teach you a thing or two! Do you want the whole project to collapse? And ruin me and my whole commune?"

With another oath he flung Noble Heart back onto the bunk. Then he stood up, breathing hard from anger and exertion.

The attack surprised and angered Noble Heart. But with effort he controlled himself and, trying to pour oil on troubled waters, he said: "Yes, I realize I should have said goodbye to you. I apologize. Only, you knew that today was my last day. I had no alternative but to leave ...."

"No alternative!" Tao stormed. "And what alternative do *we* have if you walk out on us!" To Noble Heart's astonishment, he took a pair of handcuffs out of his hip pocket. He grabbed Noble Heart's right wrist. Snap! Then his left wrist. Snap!

"What do you mean by doing that?" demanded Noble Heart. Being treated like a common criminal made him really angry now.

"You'll see what I mean! Put on your shoes! Quick!"

Noble Heart did just that. He had no option but to obey. As he was tying the shoestrings of his cloth shoes, he wondered where the guard was and how the mob got into the camp without being stopped. Maybe the clump of bamboos between the dormitory and mess hall blocked out the view ...

His reflections were cut short as Tao grabbed him and set him on his feet. "Now march!" he ordered.

Something was pushed into his back. Noble Heart wondered, *could it be a gun?* Within seconds they were outside the camp the back way and retracing the path Noble Heart had traveled only an hour before.

Well, this is a queer turn of events, mused Noble Heart. *But at least these handcuffs are in front of me and not behind my back. And I'm glad I have my shoes and my pants on!*

15. Death at the Window
Autumn 1958

VERY FEW THINGS in the camp could be done in secret. A cook's assistant was back of the mess hall scrubbing a pot with ashes from the kitchen fire when the mob broke into the dormitory. It struck him as unusual — maybe something to be reported. He looked for someone higher up the chain of command to report to, and saw a guard in uniform strolling across the yard in the half-light from the mess hall where the meeting was in progress.

"There's something going on here," he told the guard. "All those flares. They went into the dormitory, and in a couple of minutes came out again. Then they left the back way."

"What direction were they headed?"

"Toward the commune, Comrade."

"Got any idea who they were?"

"No, Comrade."

"Or what they were up to?"

"No, Comrade."

When Camp Commander Chen heard the guard's report, with the further information that Noble Heart Lee was missing, he immediately jumped to a conclusion: "It's that ... Commune Leader Tao. He's determined to have his own ... way, orders or no orders!"

Chen rounded up the four guards plus their rifles, added a couple of cooks armed with meat cleavers from the kitchen, strapped on his own service revolver, lit torches and marched out as if he were Hannibal heading for the Alps.

More than an hour had lapsed from the sounding of the alarm until the expedition moved off. Then the unfamiliar and unmarked paths between the fields caused them to lose their way several times. It was past ten o'clock when they arrived at Daybreak Commune No 19. All was quiet. Lights were out.

When the armed and well-lit band arrived at the main gate of the commune, the guard on duty beat a strategic retreat. Camp Commander Chen pushed straight for the central group of two-story buildings. Sure enough, a sign beside the largest door of the largest building proclaimed, "Daybreak Commune No 19, Headquarters Division."

Chen jerked his revolver out of its holster and, holding it by the barrel, beat on the door with the butt, at the same time yelling: "*Kai men! Kai men!* Open the door! Open the door!"

No answer.

Again, the same.

No answer.

This time Chen shouted: "Open the door! I want this door opened or I'll break it down!"

A woman's face looked out of an upstairs window, lit by a candle. She asked: "What do you want?"

"I want to see Commune Leader Tao! I want to see him right now!"

The face and the candle withdrew. Two minutes later both returned, and the woman said: "Commune Leader Tao is not in now."

Chen was pacing back and forth in front of the door, fingering the trigger of his revolver. He shouted: "You open this door in one minute or I'll break it down!"

There came the sounds of bolts drawn and bar lifted on the other side of the door. Finally the door cracked open. More impatient by the minute, Chen unceremoniously kicked it with his shoe. It flew open, banged the side of the house and almost shut on the rebound. Chen gave another kick, more vicious than the first, accompanied by a mouthful of obscene language.

This time someone inside grabbed the door and held it open. Chen strode over the threshold, and the others followed. He demanded: "Where is that man named Tao? I want to see him right now!"

The same woman who had answered from the window, now revealed as portly and middle-aged, responded: "I'll see if I can get him for you. Please wait here."

In her agitation, she unconsciously reverted to the pre-liberation word, "please".

"Get on! I can't wait!" answered Chen curtly.

The men milled around the reception hall of the commune. Chen strode up and down, still holding his revolver in his right hand and muttering under his breath.

The fat woman returned in a moment. "Please sit down," she said.

"Don't try that 'please' business on me. I want to see that man named Tao right now!"

The fat woman disappeared through the inner door. When it opened again a very meek Tao stepped into the room. Behind him, the fat woman. Tao's gaze was glued onto the revolver. As Chen brandished it, still walking back and forth, Tao's eyes followed it.

"Yes, sir! Yes, sir! What can I do for you, sir?"

"None of that 'sir' stuff! I want one thing and one thing only!"

"Yes, sir! And what is that, sir?"

"Show me where Noble Heart Lee is! Right now!"

"Yes, sir. But won't you sit down? Let's talk about this matter. The whole future of my commune is at stake. We must make progress with the Pig Iron Furnace ...."

Tao was regaining something of his aplomb. His eyes had moved from the revolver to the tip of Chen's right shoulder. But his attempt at reasoning infuriated Chen. He brought the pistol down out of the air and pointed it at Tao's belly, and yelled: "I don't want talk! I want action! Now! What do you mean, kidnapping a man from my unit?"

At the rising tones of Chen's voice, Tao's eyes went back to the gun, now shaking a bit in Chen's shaking hand. Tao thought he saw Chen's index finger tighten on the trigger.

"Yes, yes. Of course." he said hurriedly. "Come this way."

He led the way across the road and around the corner of an old building, and pushed open a door. As it opened, the smell of welding burst on the night air. Tao motioned Chen inside. The floor was cluttered with pieces of sheet iron, a half-constructed blower with the motor attached, bags of sand and cement, piles of fire brick, tools ....

"There he is," said Tao, motioning to a bunk at the far end. Noble Heart lay sound asleep, exhausted by his two trips across the fields and by the stress and strain of the day.

"Get up!" ordered Chen "You're going back where you belong! Right now!"

Noble Heart half opened his eyes and groaned, "Ughh?"

"Get up! Out of that bed!"

Chen grabbed Noble Heart by the shoulders and sat him up in bed. Noble Heart could not believe his eyes — Camp Commander Chen here — in this place — ordering him around? But he was awake now; it wasn't a dream after all.

"Get your shoes on! Quick!"

Noble Heart said to himself: *I've heard that order before — and just a few hours ago.* He looked past Chen and saw Tao, a quieter and meeker man now than when he gave that same order.

As Noble Heart stood up, Chen grabbed some rope off the floor and deftly tied his hand behind him.

Oh — oh! A criminal again! he thought. *But behind my back this time. If Jade Moon were here she'd take that for a bad omen — that things are getting worse.*

With his revolver, Chen motioned Noble Heart toward the door. As before, there was no option but to obey. Once outside the building, he saw that the guards and cooks from the camp were lighting new torches from their old ones; that meant they were headed back to the camp at once. They rounded the corner of the building.

The fat woman was standing at the upstairs window again, only minus her candle. Apparently curiosity had the better of caution; she wanted to see what was happening.

They passed the still-open door of the commune office. Tao slunk inside and closed the door quickly after him.

Noble Heart said to himself: *I hope I've seen the last of you for a while, Mr. Tao.* He had no way of knowing how soon and how tragically he would see him again.

Arriving at the main gate of the commune, Chen ordered the band to halt. He retied the ropes on Noble Heart's wrists, pulling them so tight he winced with pain. Then he ordered: "March!"

He had just uttered the word when a shot rang out. The bullet zingged by overhead, too close for comfort. Chen and his men dashed for cover, extinguishing their torches as they ran. No point in being the obvious target for the next shot! In the light of the fading torches Noble Heart spotted a ditch beside the main gate. Hands still tied behind him, he half fell, half dove into the ditch. Anything was better than standing up in the open with bullets flying around.

But as he hit the ditch he heard something crack, like a dry stick being snapped in two for kindling. At the same time he realized he had landed on something soft. A cry of pain came from beneath him. Someone was lying in the ditch!

"I'm sorry," began Noble Heart. "I didn't know you were here."

Only a groan came back at first. Then the words, "You broke my arm!"

"I can't help you," went on Noble Heart. "My hands are tied behind my back."

In the meantime, Chen's men had reached cover of sorts. In the darkness they fired back toward the commune headquarters, for the first bullet had come from that direction.

Noble Heart asked the man he had landed on top of: "Who's that firing at us?"

"That's the commune platoon of militia. I'm one of them. We were ordered to ambush you here at the gate and not let you take Comrade Lee back to the camp."

Rifle cracks continued — heavier cracks from Chen's men, lighter cracks from the lighter rifles of the militia. Then the heavier cracks receded as Chen and his men withdrew from the scene of battle.

Noble Heart felt more like talking now: "I'm Comrade Lee. That's why my hands are tied behind my back. I'm sorry to be on top of you, but I can't move..."

After what seemed an age but must have been only fifteen minutes, Noble Heart wriggled and squirmed along the ditch, which fortunately had no water in it, and finally removed himself from on top of the man beneath. The procedure was slow because he was trying to avoid hurting the man, whose moans and groans and shouts of "*Aiya!*" punctuated every move.

Once Noble Heart was off him, the man had little problem climbing out of the ditch despite his broken arm. Then with his good arm he helped Noble Heart climb out.

"Here! Untie my hands, won't you?" Noble Heart pled.

But the militiaman's mind was on his own problems: "I've got to find a doctor for my broken arm." With that he disappeared into the darkness.

Noble Heart had little alternative but to head for the commune office. Once faced in that direction, he saw lights and heard footfalls of men running here and there. *What can the commotion be now?* he wondered.

As he drew nearer he saw that the commune office was lit up with candles, and hoped there would be someone there who could untie his hands.

But as Noble Heart stepped over the threshold into the office, no one paid any attention to him. Rather, all eyes were focused on the woman stretched out on the large table that occupied the center of the reception room. Noble Heart recognized Mrs. Tao, the portly wife of the commune leader. The doctor was working over her feverishly, trying to massage her heart, feeling her pulse, listening with his stethoscope. Finally he straightened up, beads of sweat glistening on his face. "I'm sorry, Comrade Tao, but she's gone."

"Gone! How can that be? She's so strong and healthy!"

"That's not the question, Comrade Tao. The bullet hit her in the chest as she was standing in the window. It must have gone straight into her heart."

"Where's the bullet now?"

"It entered the front, and there's no evidence of it coming out the back. So it must still be in her body, maybe lodged in bony structure in the posterior section of the chest cavity."

"I want that bullet out! We'll use it as evidence against Chen for murdering my wife!" Tao said almost hysterically.

"Well, I can take the bullet out all right," the doctor agreed. "We'll need a stretcher and a couple of men to take her over to the clinic."

As the doctor stood waiting for a stretcher, Noble Heart approached him: "Comrade Doctor, do you have a scalpel in your bag? Would you mind cutting this rope off my wrist?"

As the doctor was cutting the rope, he said: "Hmm. Bad laceration. Some bleeding. Rope burn. You'd better come with me to the clinic and I'll dress your wrists for you. Come on. We'll not wait for the stretcher."

As they walked along, the doctor remarked, "Take care of the living before the dead, that's my policy."

He had just finished wrapping Noble Heart's wrists with bandages when the body of Mrs Tao arrived. Glad enough to sit down, Noble Heart slumped into a chair. Though physically tired he was mentally alert, and followed the doctor's work in exploring the wound and tracing the course of the bullet. Finally the long-handled forceps got hold of the bullet and brought it out. *Pop*, it sounded coming through the skin; a suction had been created as the bullet was drawn through layers of fat.

Always the reporter, Noble Heart jumped up and looked at the fatal bullet. "What kind of a bullet is it, doctor?"

The doctor looked at it a minute, then slowly replied: "Hmm. It's a small caliber bullet, like those used by our militia... That's strange. It seems the commune leader's wife was not killed by Commander Chen's men but by a bullet from our own militia."

"The hearing will now come to order!" announced a non-commissioned officer.

The scene was all too familiar to Noble Heart: Five officers of the People's Liberation Army sitting around a table in Garrison Commander's Headquarters. Two secretaries taking down every detail. The announcer. No lawyers, since such a bourgeois profession had been wiped out by the People's Republic of China.

One thing, however, was different from previous trials Noble Heart had witnessed and experienced; usually it was quite obvious who the defendant was, but today Noble Heart could not figure this out. Camp Commander Chen and the six other men in the raiding party — were they the defendants? Or Commune Leader Tao and his militiamen who had opened fire — were they the defendants?

Others as well had been subpoenaed — he himself, the doctor, even the two who had carried the stretcher. Where did they all fit into the picture? *Well, I'll sort it out soon enough*, he said to himself.

Someone had prepared a brief of the incident, and the announcer read it. As the reading droned on, Noble Heart's reporter instincts surfaced. *Why, they are not accusing Chen at all for his high-handed action. And not a word of blame for Tao for kidnapping me ... And all this sob stuff about Mrs. Tao being shot — but not a word about that bullet and who fired it....*

Finally the doctor was called to the stand. He was told to give an account of his efforts to save Mrs. Tao's life and for what reasons he certified her dead. But there was no questioning about the bullet that killed her. Noble Heart began to feel uneasy. And this feeling increased when he was not called on to give testimony. *And yet they subpoenaed me ... What's the point?* he murmured under his breath.

The sergeant who read the account folded the paper, handed it to the officer in charge, and sat down. The officer got up, cleared his throat and asked, "Does anyone in the room have anything to add to the account as read?"

No one dared either question or add to a document which had already stated the government's case. There was silence.

The announcer arose: "The officers will now consider the disposition of this case."

The officers put their heads together and talked in whispers. Finally, as the whispering died down, one of them took a sheet of paper out of his briefcase. This was passed around among the officers, who one by one nodded their heads. The officer in charge motioned to the announcer, who proclaimed: "The officer in charge will now read the verdict of the People's Court."

Then the officer began to read the document which had just been circulated around the table:

"From the statement of the case of Happy Days Nationalized Rubber Plantation versus Daybreak Commune No 19, and from other information gathered by the examining panel, the following is deduced:

"That both Commune Leader Tao and Camp Commander Chen are members in good standing of the Communist Party of the People's Republic of China and that therefore it is beyond the realm of reasonable possibility that either of them could have acted in any illegal or unworthy way in the incident in question.

"That the untimely death by accident of Mrs. Tao, wife of Commune Leader Tao, is to be deeply deplored.

"That in the investigation by the panel, it has been determined that the basic cause for said incident is none other than Noble Heart Lee, detainee for Reform through Labor at Happy Days Nationalized Rubber Plantation. Lee is the *causa sine qua non*. Without the person and actions of said Lee, the aforesaid incident would not and could not have occurred.

"The defendant, Noble Heart Lee, is therefore convicted by the panel on the following charges:

1. Guilty of words and actions leading to said lamented incident; and
2. Guilty of maliciously attacking and breaking the arm of Su Defa, militiaman of Daybreak People's Commune No 19; and
3. Guilty of manslaughter in the death of Tao Aideng, wife of Commune Leader Tao."

The officer folded the paper and handed it to a secretary. Then he said a thing unusual for such a hearing: "Is there any comment on the aforesaid findings?"

The blood had rushed to Noble Heart's face as he heard the verdict, and his hair stood straight on end. Only the officer in charge and two others on the panel saw his reaction, for everyone else in the room was looking straight ahead or keeping his eyes lowered. But Noble Heart could feel their inner eyes fixed on him, and the unspoken words of either accusation or commiseration.

Then Noble Heart regained control of himself, and said: "Comrade Officer, I have a comment, if I may be allowed to make it."

The officer blinked twice. Obviously he had not expected

anyone to speak, certainly not the man now revealed as the defendant. But rather to Noble Heart's surprise, he answered: "I have asked for comments. What I have said I have said. Speak."

Noble Heart began: "Comrade Officer, I request a re-opening of the case and a hearing of testimonies by the persons involved. I request a re-examination of the verdict. You have pronounced me guilty without even putting me on the witness stand.

"Sir, I am not the defendant. I am the victim. During the first part of the said incident I was handcuffed with my hands in front of me. During the second part of the said incident my hands were tied behind my back. I was not inciting mob action; I was the victim of mob action. As to the broken arm, which I regret, it was broken when I jumped into a ditch to escape flying bullets. As to Mrs. Tao's death, have you enquired as to whose bullet killed her?"

A strange quietness had settled over the courtroom, until Mrs. Tao was mentioned. At that point Commune Leader Tao exploded: "You'll bring my wife's name into this, will you? I'll teach you!"

With a mouthful of obscene language he lunged at Noble Heart and struck out with his fist at Noble Heart's face. He ducked and avoided the blow. Before Tao could come at him again, the sergeant grabbed him from behind and pinned his elbows to his side.

"Order! Order!" shouted the officer in charge, pounding his fist on the table.

In a moment the only sound that could be heard was Tao's heavy breathing. He was still in the sergeant's grasp.

The officer in charge shouted: "The case is closed! Clear the courtroom!"

Along with the others present, Noble Heart started to walk out of the room. One of the officers on the panel pushed over and grabbed him, saying "You wait here!"

As at so many times in the past, Noble Heart had no alternative but to obey orders. He noticed that the sergeant escorted Tao to the door, then closed and locked it behind him. He looked around and realized he was the only one left in the room, apart from the military men who had already taken their places again at the table.

The officer in charge nodded to the announcer. In tones suitable for addressing a thousand people instead of one, he shouted: "The hearing will come to order! The officer in charge will read the sentence."

The officer rose from his seat and — as if nothing had happened since the reading of the verdict — read the sentence, which had also been written out beforehand: "By order of this court, Noble Heart Lee is hereby sentenced to an additional three years of hard labor at Happy Days Nationalized Rubber Plantation, the sentence to begin after his present sentence is completed."

It was a quiet morning on the rubber plantation. For the first time in months Noble Heart was on his way out to tap rubber, carrying his rubber-tapper knife and bucket with him.

Halfway along the road Hou Helang overtook him, squeezed his hand and said: "Congratulations, Noble Heart for standing up for the truth, even in a kangaroo court."

"Thank you, Helang!"

After they had walked quietly in step for a few minutes, Noble Heart asked: "Say, Helang! You know the Bible better than I do. Could you tell me if there is a verse like this in the Bible: 'Blessed are the scapegoats, for they shall outbutt their enemies in the end'?"

PART IV

SHANGHAI AND NORTH CHINA

1957 ~ 1968

16. Enter The Russians
Autumn 1957 — Winter 1958

"YOU'RE MY PRECIOUS FLOWER, my only little flower," Jade Moon said as she combed Lotus Flower's long pigtails. "If they don't allow you to attend high school they'll send you to work in a factory like your brothers." She cradled the long black hair in her left hand as she combed with her right so as not to pull out a single strand. "And just think, today you start your last year in elementary school. It will be your last year in school, ever, unless the Lord does something unusual for you."

There was a catch in Jade Moon's voice. A tear formed in Lotus Flower's right eye, rolled down her cheek and hit the floor with a plop. Lotus brushed the dampness from her cheek with the back of her right hand, felt in the pocket of her blouse to be sure that her Identity Card was there, and skipped out of the house on the way to school. Neither she nor her mother dreamed what the day would bring forth.

Late in the morning two tall white men in military uniform drove up to the school in a jeep. Complete with ribbons and medals, their uniforms were resplendent compared to the monotonous green uniforms of the Chinese army without insignia and without identification. After a perfunctory call on the school principal they strode into Lotus Flower's classroom, the principal tagging along behind like a postscript.

"Is this the brightest group of your graduating class?" the taller of the two demanded, addressing himself to the teacher in Russian. To Lotus Flower it sounded a rough and uncouth language. An interpreter who, like a shadow, had followed the two officers from the jeep, translated his words into Chinese.

"Why, yes, it is," replied the teacher, surprised at the direct-question-without-introduction approach of the abrupt foreigner.

The officer continued: "We have come to your school to select twelve students to train as interpreters for the new Sino-Russian Friendship Association Center on North Shaanxi Road."

The principal wormed his way in front of the two officers, holding the written order they had just presented to him in his office. He was waving it around and around, as if it were a magic wand. He sputtered: "Yes, yes, of course, if that is what you want. Of course. Of course. But *who* is selected must be at the option of school authorities!"

He tried to make that last declaration sound final. But its finality was lost on the Russians. The tall man went on, disregarding the principal: "We will use our own language aptitude test. It is scientific. Everything we do is done scientifically. We will pass out the test papers to your students now."

The following week the results were announced. Lotus was second highest of the twelve who placed. She wondered intuitively why there were no boys among the twelve.

When Jade Moon heard the results she sat for a minute with her hands folded in her lap: "Maybe *this* is your chance to go on for more education," she said thoughtfully. "You are fifteen now. You would have finished elementary school, but you lost time at liberation and again when we moved to Shanghai... I wish your father were here to ..."

"I'm sorry, Mama," interrupted Lotus Flower, "but it wouldn't make any difference. Here's the order for me to transfer to the Russian school at once."

Startled, Jade Moon said: "Let me see. Whose order is it?"

Lotus Flower handed over a piece of paper, and Jade Moon read in amazement:

"To Jade Moon Lee:

Your daughter, Lotus Flower Lee, 15, is hereby transferred to the Russian Interpreters' School of the Sino-Russian
Friendship Association, the transfer to take effect
immediately.

(signed) Shanghai Municipal Dept of Education"

"Hmm," said Jade Moon. "The Chinese issue the orders,
but the Russians make the decisions. What kind of new
imperialism is this?"

The next morning, twelve teenage girls stood awkwardly
around the classroom, nervous and uncertain of themselves.

Two teachers, one in front and one behind, escorted the
twelve girls through Shanghai streets to Yenan Road. They
stopped in front of a four-story building. The wall around
the compound had been doubled in height to some twenty
feet; broken glass stuck in the top of the wall sparkled in the
sun. But the barbed wire stretched above the glass did not
sparkle; it was glum and sullen.

A Chinese soldier with green cap and red star stood sentry
duty outside the huge wooden gate. It was huge even by
Shanghai standards since it, too, stood twenty feet high, high
enough to do double duty as a drawbridge. But there was no
moat that needed a drawbridge. It just stood there, incon-
gruously, twenty feet in the air.

The sentry read the order that the teacher handed him.
Then he rapped a code signal on the wooden gate, and the
door swung open a few inches. Lotus Flower could see the
uniform of a Russian soldier on the other side. She whispered
to the girl next to her, "Why do they have two sentries, one
Chinese and one Russian?"

There were one hundred Chinese girls in the school behind
Russian walls, gate and sentry — the cream of students from
several schools. But all girls. There was not a boy among them.

The girls soon discovered that it was a "specialty" school:
Russian history, Russian geography, Russian literature, but

mostly the Russian language, hour after hour after hour. Gone was Chinese school with subjects in the Chinese language Lotus Flower loved. She now found herself face to face with an adult world, with Russian instructors using the "direct method" to cram more and more into her mind. Lotus Flower studied so hard and tried to remember so much that at night she wept into her pillow and silently sobbed herself to sleep.

One day an instructor told them — in Russian — of how the French feed ducks by forcing the food down their throats with a chopstick to make their livers grow bigger and bigger.

Lotus Flower remarked to a classmate: "That's me. I'm a duck. They are force-feeding me with a chopstick. But why do they want my liver to grow bigger?"

Lotus Flower had heard all about "big nose". "Big nose" was always the American, the villain in short story, novel, drama and movie. Now she saw "big noses" at first hand, but they were not Americans; they were Russians. However, they all looked alike to her. Americans or Russians, she could not tell which was which. Except that the Americans were always villains, the Russians were always heroes.

But Lotus was learning fast about Russians. One day in class a hornet flew in the open window. A Chinese teacher would have remained still while the hornet buzzed around. Not the Russian. He grabbed a newspaper off his desk and chased the hornet, spitting out epithets in Russian that the girls had not learned yet. For five minutes the instructor chased the hornet around the room, growing more and more red in the face with exertion and exasperation.

Finally the hornet flew out the same window he had flown in. The girls lowered their eyes; they had seen a display of temper beneath the dignity of even a Chinese farmer.

As autumn crept toward a Shanghai winter, the season of

cultural exchanges opened with concerts, ballets and operas presented by the Cultural Affairs Office of the Russian Consulate General. The opening concert was given by Russian artists in magnificent costumes, performing splendidly against a backdrop more gorgeous than the Chinese who attended had ever seen before. When they saw the splendor of the Russian stage, a few Chinese muttered "revisionists" and "capitalist-roaders". Most, however, just gulped, held their tongues and were swept away by the overpowering display.

For Lotus Flower, as she sat on the tenth row from the orchestra in a choice seat near the center of the theater, it was an evening of splendor that transported her into a world she had never dreamed of.

Strangely enough, in that crowded theater, there was one seat still not occupied, the seat on Lotus Flower's left. So she was not surprised when, well after the concert was under way, a man came in and plopped himself down in the seat next to her. He was a Russian, wearing a heavy overcoat. She was surprised to see such a coat at that time of year.

As the Russian sat down, his overcoat flew open and the right-hand pocket swung toward Lotus like a pendulum. Something hard in the pocket hit, *Whack*, on her left arm. Instinctively she moved away, though she could not move far in the opera seat.

The man murmured in Russian: "I'm sorry."

As he sat down, Lotus smelled alcohol, and it flashed through her mind, *I'd better find another seat.* But looking around, she could see none. The only alternative to sitting beside the Russian was to leave the theater, and *that* she did not want to do. She was enjoying the performance too much to leave.

"Has Madame Petrovich appeared yet?"

With a start, Lotus realized the question was addressed to

her. She thought: *What shall I do? If I answer him it will start a conversation.*

"I said, 'Has Madame Petrovich appeared yet?'" There was a steel-like insistence in his tone this time.

Suddenly, Lotus felt cold inside. She drew as far away from the man as she could without getting out of her seat. "No... no... she hasn't appeared yet," she managed to answer.

At the moment an older man with a great shock of white hair was singing an aria from *La Traviata*. Lotus glanced at the program and saw Madame Petrovich was next. She held it up and pointed to the name, "Madame Petrovich".

"Good!" muttered the Russian. "I...I...am Mr. Petrovich. Madame Petrovich is my wife. She has been unfaithful to me. She has been sleeping with that swine, Colonel Borodin. I'm going to kill her!"

With that, the Russian pulled a revolver from the right-hand pocket of his overcoat. Lock, stock and barrel, the pistol gleamed with chrome. He caressed the trigger with his forefinger. Then, irrationally, he asked Lotus: "Do you think I should shoot her?"

Lotus gripped the arms of her seat hard. In the most explicit Russian she could muster, she said: "*Nyet!* Don't!"

The Russian asked, surprised: "Why not?"

"Because you would ruin the concert."

"Oh," responded the Russian. He lowered the pistol to his lap.

The old man with the great shock of white hair was just completing his aria. To ample applause, he bowed himself off the stage. The announcer, over at the end of the stage, was proclaiming in affected falsetto: "We present you: Madame Petrovich!"

Madame Petrovich floated onto the stage from the left wing. The long skirts of her deep orange dress undulated like autumn leaves in the breeze as she tripped across the stage in the focus of spotlights which moved with her steps. The enraptured audience broke out in spontaneous applause. Lotus Flower thought she had never seen anything so beautiful in her life.

Aiya! she thought to herself in sudden horror, *She's blinded by the spotlights! She can't see her husband in the crowd. And certainly not that pistol!*

Madame Petrovich had reached the center of the stage and was bowing in acknowledgement of the continued applause.

The two spotlights faded and with them the applause. Madame Petrovich launched into a soprano solo with a burst of power and vigor that must have been the envy of every woman in the theater.

The man beside Lotus slowly raised his revolver.

"Please, sir, don't!"

Lotus's voice was husky with tension. He lowered the pistol far enough to look over at her.

"And why not? She's been sleeping with that .... swine!"

"Please, sir! You can't!"

"Why can't I?"

The question had a peculiar innocence about it.

"Because this is so beautiful. You can't destroy the beauty." Lotus was surprised at how easily the words came out in the strange language.

Again the Russian raised his pistol.

By now Madame Petrovich's eyes had adjusted to the light. Perhaps she caught the glint of the chrome. Fear and horror flashed across the beautiful face, and in the middle of a word the beautiful voice stopped. The orange skirts whirled, and she ran to the back of the stage and disappeared.

The man next to Lotus stood up. It flashed through her mind: *He's going to follow her*! and she grabbed the tail of the overcoat. "Stop! They'll arrest you!"

The Russian tried to shove the pistol back into his overcoat pocket. But he missed, and it fell, *klump*, to the floor.

Lotus saw her opportunity in that split second and deftly gave a flick with the toe of her left shoe. The pistol landed two rows of seats forward.

The Russian knelt down and felt around the floor for the gun, all the time cursing under his breath.

Lotus Flower sat back in her seat. Outwardly she appeared indifferent and relaxed, but inwardly her heart was racing and her mind was asking a thousand questions.

"Mama, this will be my last night home for a while."

"Why, Lotus?"

"Because Major Malinovsky, our director, says the new dormitories are ready now and they want us in a Russian atmosphere twenty-four hours a day."

"Why do they want dormitories? I just don't understand this Russian school business at all."

"They feed us well, Mama. And if I'm there day and night you won't have to provide food for me. That'll make things easier for you."

"Don't you think about that, Lotus. As long as there is one grain of rice in the house it's yours. And with your brothers staying in the dormitories at their factories it's not hard for me to support you as well as myself."

A more serious tone crept into Jade Moon's voice as she went on: "I'm concerned about your being at that school. I've asked Big Sister to pray specially for you. And I know God hears her prayers. But what about Sundays? Will you have Sundays at home?"

"I guess I'll be coming home only once every few weeks, Mama."

"Then what about church?"

"The Russians never say anything about church. Maybe they don't *know* anything about church."

"Today you young women start a new class, called Russian

Culture. You will learn relationships between men and women. You will learn the importance of the Russian male..."

Major Malinovsky paused a long moment for this to sink in. A cold chill ran up and down Lotus Flower's backbone. Instinctively she felt a similar response from the other girls.

The director continued: ".... How to entertain a Russian male, to make him feel at ease and thoroughly relaxed. What he likes and what he doesn't like. How you can make him happy ...."

Lotus Flower felt a blush stealing up her neck and suffusing her face.

".... In short, and I make this announcement now for your future benefit, you are to learn how to be consorts to Russian army officers."

Major Malinovsky himself taught the Russian Culture class. Lotus Flower was surprised — and sometimes horrified — at what he said.

"We have chosen you girls as young as you are, from fourteen to sixteen, to Russianize you as young as possible ...

"We are feeding you well because we want you to be chubby and chunky, not skinny like Chinese girls are ...

"We will need more girls like you to be consorts for Russian army officers, because in the future there will be more in China. In fact, before long the top command of the Chinese army will be taken over by Russian officers."

Some of Major Malinovksy's ideas were beyond Lotus Flower's grasp, especially since he always spoke in Russian.

"Chinese," he said one day, "is a language I do not care to learn."

On her next visit home, Lotus Flower's big question to her mother was: "Mama, what does it mean to be a 'consort'?"

A month had elapsed since Lotus Flower had a day at home. She was weary, both physically and spiritually. She decided to attempt what none of the other girls had successfully done — to ask for a day off. Specifically, the following Sunday. More than anything else, she wanted to attend church and worship God together with His people.

"Don't make such a request," warned a classmate. "You're asking for trouble. It's even dangerous to approach Major Malinovsky in his office."

Deciding there was little to lose and possibly something to be gained, Lotus went to the director's office. She asked the secretary in the outer office — a heavy-set Russian woman in uniform with the stripes of a sergeant on her sleeve — if she could see the director.

"Do you really want to see the director?" the sergeant asked, raising her eyebrows. "Just let me have your message and I'll take it in for you."

"No, I have a personal request. I want to see the director myself, please."

"Oh, is that the way it is? I hope you know what you're doing!"

Without explaining what she meant, the sergeant turned, opened the door to the inner office and went in. A minute later she came out and said: "You may go in."

Lotus could not understand the disturbed look on the sergeant's face and the tightness of her voice. However, she did not stop to ask but entered the door the sergeant held open. She noticed it was left open.

Once inside, Lotus stood facing Major Malinovsky across a wide expanse of desk. She had never been inside the office before, and suddenly she felt uneasy.

"So. You have chosen to come to see me. You are a wise girl. I'm glad you have come on your own initiative."

"Excuse me, sir. I have a request. May I go home next Sunday?"

"Yes, yes," the director said. But it was not in answer to Lotus Flower's question. He got up from behind the desk and rubbed his hands together. He walked over and closed the door, then took a key out of his pocket and locked it. Going back to the desk and sitting on the front of it, almost touching Lotus, he asked: "And how long have you been thinking of coming to see me?"

"Well, I ... I .. I guess only today, sir."

"But I have been thinking of you a long time. I noticed you when you first came. You are well-developed for — what is your age? Sixteen, is it? And you are mentally and emotionally developed as well. Yes, yes. You and I — we can do well together!"

Keeping her face to the director, Lotus Flower backed over to the door and twisted the knob. The door did not budge.

She pled: "Let me out! Let me out! Please! I want to go now!"

"Aha! Putting up a show of resisting, are you? Good! I like a woman with some spirit to her!"

The director took a step towards her, and she backed up a step. Lotus could hear him breathe now. Short, hard breaths, closer and closer together. *I've never heard a man breathe like that,* she thought. *Are all men like that?*

Having backed up several steps, she found herself in a corner of the room. There was nowhere else to go. She started to slap the big face towering above her. But something told her that would only make matters worse. So she straightened herself up as tall as she could in the corner and yelled: "Help! Help!"

In her heart she prayed, *Oh, Lord! Help me!*

The director hissed: "You pussy cat! No one can help you! Not even God Himself. I've got you."

Lotus could only plead: "Please! Please let me out of the room!"

"Yes, but why did you come into the room if you didn't

want to submit to me?" He hissed again: "I'll show you, you pussy cat!"

He grabbed her right wrist, twisted her arm and turned it behind her back. She cried out with pain.

Still holding her wrist, he pushed her over to the wide desk, and with right hand holding her wrist, used his left hand to push her body back onto it.

He said: "And now, my little pussy cat, do you take your clothes off yourself? Or do I take them off for you?"

Lotus Flower's only answer was another scream: "Help! Help!"

The director's big hand slapped her mouth. He hissed: "No more of that!"

She struggled to free herself from his grip. But he pushed her relentlessly onto the desk, his big face closer and closer to her face.

Lotus thought she was going to faint. She prayed, *Oh Lord! Don't let me faint!*

At that moment there was a knock at the door. Not any ordinary knock, more like the sound of heavy wood striking the door on the far side. At the same time there was a shout:

"*Kai men! Kai men!* Open the door! In the name of the People's Republic of China!"

The voice was Chinese.

The director cursed. But he did not move, and his face was still close to Lotus Flower's.

Again came the voice outside: "Open the door! If you don't, we'll break it down!"

Still the director did not move.

Suddenly there was quiet outside the door, and he turned his attention again to Lotus: "Aha! They've gone away. And now, my little pussy cat ...."

But he did not finish the sentence.

With a terrible crash the door burst open and fell flat onto the floor. On top of the door landed the secretary's desk. It was an effective battering ram. Effective, that is, in the hands of four Chinese soldiers, who tumbled into the room after it. Following them were four more Chinese soldiers with rifles and fixed bayonets, and finally an officer with a sheet of paper in his hand.

The officer did not notice Lotus lying on her back on the table. He was too busy reading at the top of his voice from the paper in his hand:

"To the Director

Major Malinovsky

Russian Language School, Shanghai

You are hereby ordered to close down and desist operation of the Russian Language School, Shanghai, as of today. You yourself must leave China within forty-eight hours of receiving this notice. You are hereby declared *persona non grata*.

(signed) Mao Zedong

People's Republic of China, Beijing"

Lotus sat up on the table and shook her hair out of her eyes. She felt her mouth where the director struck her, and realized her lip was bleeding. She wiped the blood off on her blouse.

By now the director, dumbfounded, was standing up. In front of the drawn bayonets he began to retreat, a step at a time. In a moment he was in the same corner Lotus had so recently occupied.

Then Lotus felt a strong arm circle her shoulders, and heard a voice say in Russian, "My dear, my dear! I'm so sorry. I was afraid this would happen."

Lotus Flower looked up. It was the sergeant from the outer office. She held her up and helped her out of the room. Once in the outer office, Lotus turned to the older woman, laid her head on her broad shoulder and wept and wept.

That afternoon the Chinese officer who had served notice

on Major Malinovsky gathered the girls together in the school dining room and explained: "For a long time the Russian advisers whom we invited to China have become increasingly overbearing and obnoxious. There was the rumor that the Russian army, through its officers already in China, would pull off a coup and take over China. But we were not prepared for what did happen. The other day Chairman Mao Zedong received a letter from Nikita Khrushchev, Premier of the Soviet Union, with the formal request that Russian officers take command of China's armed forces.

"Chairman Mao flew into a rage, and it is only a question of time now until all Russian military advisers will be sent back to Russia.

"Chinese intelligence has known for quite a while that the school for interpreters in Shanghai was a front for something far different from interpreting one language into another. Chairman Mao is showing his displeasure with the Russians by disbanding the school. So you may all go home, today."

On arriving home that afternoon, the first thing Lotus Flower did was to find Big Sister and thank her for her prayers.

17. Bright Victory's Problems
Summer 1960

"To the old rugged cross I will ever be true,
  Its shame and reproach gladly bear;
Then He'll call me some day
To my home far away,
  Where His glory forever I'll share."

THE WORDS MELTED AWAY into the darkness beyond the light of the single unfrosted bulb hanging from the ceiling by a twisted cord.

They had learned to sing quietly, these believers who met to worship God together. Since the government-organized Three-Self Patriotic Movement had closed down their church — "merge" was the official term — these seven had met together to sing, read and pray. Pastor and Mrs Bao, Big Sister, Jade Moon, Bright Victory, Bright Loyalty and Lotus Flower. The meetings were at night — now and then Sunday night. But since Sunday was a work day for most units and since time allowed away from one's own unit was rare, the meetings at Pastor Bao's place were irregular. But the very irregularity was a help in keeping them low-key and secret.

"This hymn means a great deal to me," Pastor Bao was saying. "While I was in prison it went through my head thousands of times. Sometimes as a solo, sometimes like a great choir singing, but always with music and always with an uplifting of my spirit."

Before he could finish the sentence a knock at the door interrupted him. Then a pounding. Then a shout: "Open up! In the name of the police!"

Pastor Bao walked across the room and opened the door.

Three men in uniform entered, and one of them demanded: "Are you people all relatives?"

"No, not according to the flesh," answered Pastor Bao."

"What do you mean, 'not according to the flesh'?"

"We are brothers and sisters in the spirit."

"Hmmp! You can leave that 'spirit' hogwash out of this! I want to know if you are relatives or not!"

"No, we are not all blood relatives."

"In that case, you are seven individuals. That means you are having an illegal, unauthorized meeting. Here! Write down your name, age, address and unit!" The officer handed a piece of paper to each person.

In a minute he collected them again and said: "You're lucky we didn't arrest all of you on the spot. We'll inform your different units and let them deal with you. In the meantime, if you have any thought for your own good, you'll stop this kind of nonsense. Hmmm! 'Brothers and sisters in the spirit!' Hogwash!"

"Strong Hero, have some more watermelon seeds. And may I pour you another cup of tea?"

Strong Hero Liang took the aluminum lid off his mug, and extended the mug with both hands in the old-fashioned gesture of courtesy. Lotus Flower did not fail to notice the two hands. The slightest of smiles played around the corners of her mouth.

Lotus poured the tea from an old teapot the family had brought from Chongqing eight years before. That teapot appeared only on special occasions. And today was a very special occasion, Bright Victory's 24th birthday. To celebrate, he had asked Hero home with him. Many weeks before, the two had applied for the day off.

With Jade Moon home from work and the four of them sitting on the bed and on the two straight chairs in the Lees' main room, it was a more relaxed occasion than they could remember for a long time.

Lotus took the teapot downstairs to add hot water. Jade Moon went into the inner room to fetch more watermelon seeds. Hero leaned over to Victory and whispered, "Your sister is a very pretty girl."

A few days later the foreman at the tractor starter factory sent Bright Victory a chit, calling him to his office.

Before he went, Victory looked up Hero and showed him the chit. "What do you make of this?" he asked.

Strong Hero, never a man with a quick answer, rubbed the lobe of his left ear between thumb and forefinger. That signaled he was thinking.

"Victory," he said after a while, "you have just had a birthday, and a promotion is long past due. Could it be a promotion you are getting?"

"Well," returned Bright Victory, "I'd be just as happy to throw my broom away. I've worn out dozens. But I'm afraid it has more to do with the visit of the police the other night to Pastor Bao's house ..."

Foreman Kong was sitting behind his desk when Bright Victory came in. Great piles of papers on the desk and crumpled pieces on the floor bespoke a not-too-efficient administrator. Victory's hands itched to get his broom and sweep up the floor. But the office was off limits to cleaners.

"I believe you wanted to see me," he said, presenting the chit.

"Yes, yes, Comrade Lee." The foreman shuffled some papers on the top of a pile and came up, apparently, with the desired sheet. He looked at it a moment. Then: "You had a birthday last week — right? Twenty-four years old now. You have worked here almost eight years as Assistant Cleaner. I must tell you that you are a model worker, Comrade Lee. You should be in line for promotion."

The foreman paused, and hope welled up in Victory's heart.

Then Foreman Kong continued: "There are two things I want to question you about. First, a report has come from the police that you were caught in an illegal unauthorized gathering. That is counter-revolutionary and a grave offense. Second, it is reported from our own mess hall that you have a peculiar habit of bowing your head and closing your eyes before you take the first bite of rice. Why do you do that?"

The blood rushed to Victory's face and he blushed, not so much from shame as from anger. He muttered to himself, *Those filthy spies — they are everywhere!*

At his hesitation the foreman raised his voice and demanded: "I said, 'Why do you do that?'"

Victory stood up straight and squared his shoulders: "I'll be frank, Comrade Foreman. I am saying 'Thank you' to God for my food."

"Hmmp! When you say 'God' like that it means you are a Christian. Is that true?"

"Yes, Comrade Foreman. It is true."

"And now this other matter: The police inform me that you were caught attending an illegal meeting in a private house. Is that true?"

"The constitution of our country guarantees me the right of believing ..."

"Just cut out that 'constitution' bit. You know you were attending an illegal meeting. Right?"

"That's what the police said, but..."

The foreman interrupted: "Well, I am a member of the Communist Party. Therefore an atheist. And I would advise you to get on the bandwagon and forget this religion stuff. That is, *if* you want to be promoted!"

There was a pause.

Victory asked: "Is that all, Comrade Foreman?"

"Yes, that's all."

Three days later another chit came. Again Victory shared it with Strong Hero, and again Hero rubbed the lobe of his left ear between thumb and forefinger. But he offered no prognosis. He just said: "I'll be praying for you."

As before, Foreman Kong was sitting behind his desk. Bright Victory presented the chit and said: "I believe you wanted to see me, Comrade Foreman."

"Yes, yes, Comrade Lee." He shuffled his papers, then went on. "It's been a long time since you have had a vacation, Comrade Lee. The management of the starter factory commune have decided to give you a change."

There was something about the foreman's face and in the tone of his voice that kept Victory from saying "Thank you." Instinctively, he knew this was not a happy moment.

The foreman continued: "There is a small room back of the boiler room, which has a cot, a table and a chair, and connects to a small latrine. You will stay in that room while you write your autobiography. You will be assigned a companion to help you do so."

Then he added his personal postscript: "We'll not have any of that religious stuff around here!"

"You'll have to rewrite this autobiography. Don't you know that when they say 'autobiography' they really mean 'confession'?"

Inquisitor, as Victory dubbed him secretly, was a young man only slightly older than himself. He had a good position in the office and had learned to cross his "t"s and dot his "i"s in the accepted style of the Communist Party.

He went on: "Now, I don't want you to get into trouble. If you do as I tell you you won't be here very long, and you'll get a promotion. You're not a dumb bunny like most of those broom pushers. But you'll never escape from that job if you don't improve this paper."

With that, Inquisitor left the room, locking the door

behind him. Bright Victory sat down on the wooden cot, and by the light of one high barred window he surveyed his surroundings for what must have been the hundredth time: the dirt floor that needed sweeping; the cot he sat on, too short and too narrow, with his own padding he had brought with him stretched over the boards; the table and straight chair, "provided for your writing"; his own bowl and chopsticks on the table; a bottle of water, and the open doorway leading to the tiny latrine, which was just a hole in the ground.

The two things hardest for Victory to bear were the stench from the latrine, and the constant throbbing of the engines in the boiler room through the wall.

He tried to think through Inquisitor's attitude. In the three days he had been imprisoned, Inquisitor had shifted from a conciliatory attitude to an instructive pitch — "I'll show you a thing or two!" At that point Victory could hardly foresee the other phases Inquisitor would pass through: irritation, condemnation and finally threats.

"Oh! It's you, Strong Hero. Please come in."

Jade Moon opened the door and Hero stepped inside. He was out of breath.

"Is there something wrong, Strong Hero? Are you sick? Here, sit down and I'll bring you a cup of hot water."

"No, no. I'm all right. But I'll sit down a minute."

Jade Moon poured a mug of hot water from the thermos on the table.

"I've missed supper," Hero went on, "and I have to get back for political instruction. I can make it if I walk fast. I... I have some news for you. It's about Victory. He has some problems."

"*Aiya!*" said Jade Moon. It was almost a moan. Her hands went to her head. It was her turn to look unwell.

Hero continued: "I haven't seen him for three days, and I think the commune is holding him somewhere. I don't know where, and I'm not sure why. But I think it's because he gives thanks for his food. You'll ask the believers to pray for him, won't you?"

With that, Hero said a hurried goodbye. But not without looking around the room first. He didn't see anyone else.

Bright Victory rewrote the "autobiography". That is, he did the writing but Inquisitor virtually dictated it. He insisted: "Put down everything you can remember from age six."

Victory wrote the names of relatives, friends, neighbors, their occupations, religion, political views. Church connections in Chongqing and Shanghai. Elders, deacons, pastors. His parents — their background, education, political persuasion, present whereabouts.

Inquisitor pounded him with questions: "Why was your father a reporter? How much did he earn? Why didn't your mother work? Did your parents own property? What Americans did your father know? Was he a member of the Kuomintang? Did he ever talk with Chiang Kai-shek or H. H. Kung? Why did your family stay in Chongqing after the Japanese War? What was the connection of your father's boss with Chiang Kai-shek?"

Then the questions moved into Victory's personal life: "How far did you go in school? Where do you attend church? Who do you know there? Who are your friends in the factory? Do you have a girl friend? Were you ever a member of the Youth Corps? What is your view of the Communist Party? Are there other Christians in the factory besides you? Why do you promulgate your religion by praying in public?"

Another day Inquisitor illuminated Victory with grue-some stories of spy-missionaries and spy-pastors:

"Don't you know the reason missionaries opened hospitals all over China was to gouge out the eyes of Chinese children to make medicine with? Look what palatial, western-style houses the missionaries lived in; do you think they ever went hungry? They were all very well paid by their governments in Washington and London, and they were here to seduce and oppress our people and spy on us."

The missionaries seemed quite remote, all of them having left China and gone beyond the power of the Communists to help or harm. But when the vilification zeroed in on Victory's own father it was hard to endure: "Your father was twice brought up before a Peoples' Court and he was justly condemned to 'Reform through Labor' on Hainan Island. He is a classic example of an Enemy of the People."

At this, Victory boiled inside. He wanted to get up and punch Inquisitor's face and throw him into the latrine. But he knew that this could only make matters worse. So instead he breathed a short and silent prayer: *Lord, show me what to say!*

Then, to Inquisitor: "May I ask if you ever met my father?"

Inquisitor sputtered: "Why, why ...no. But why do you ask?"

"If you knew my father you would take him for what he is, a gentleman and a patriotic Chinese citizen."

With visible effort Inquisitor disregarded this remark. He struck his conciliatory stance again: "But don't you see, Comrade, that a man in your position must distance himself from anyone who had been found guilty before, even if it is his own father?"

"You are asking me to do something you would not do yourself."

Inquisitor was taken aback for a moment. Then he rallied with the party line: "If you are to get anywhere in China today you will have to denounce your father."

"Can I, a Chinese, do that and keep my self-respect?"

Inquisitor did not choose to answer but went on: "You will have to declare in writing that he is no longer your father."

"No real Chinese could ever do that. Could you?"

Inquisitor flushed red to the roots of his hair, angry at having the ball put in his court. Again he did not answer but pursued his set lines: "And you will have to praise the government and the Party for exiling him to Hainan Island."

Victory replied simply: "That I could never do."

Inquisitor got up and strode angrily out of the cell.

That night Victory found it difficult to eat. He pushed the bowl of cold rice and stringy sweet potatoes back to the center of the table and looked at it, thinking, *That's my problem. I can't swallow all this stuff Inquisitor is saying any more than I can swallow cold rice and stringy sweet potatoes.*

The following day Inquisitor came into the cell with a decisiveness in his stride and a hardness in his voice that Victory had not seen before.

He came immediately to the point:

"China is a communistic, atheistic country. Belief in God is superstition. Why do you insist on praying before you eat your rice, and that in public?"

"Because God provides us with food and I thank Him for it."

"God does not provide us with food. The labor of the people provides us with food."

"I know what you mean, and I am grateful to the farmers for their hard work. But how could they produce food unless God sent the sun and the rain?"

"Well, let's get to the point of your being...er... detained in this room: you must deny that you believe in God. Of course, you are crazy for ever believing in God in the first place."

"I could deny God with my lips but I would still believe in my heart," Victory said firmly.

Inquisitor chose not to debate that point but went on:

"And you must declare in writing that you are not a Christian now."

"Is that all?"

"And you must thank your fellow-workers for calling your attention to your error in praying before meals and taking part in an illegal meeting."

Inquisitor's voice grew harder and more threatening: "If you don't put all that down in writing before tomorrow morning, your public trial will be held July 10th. And I have been authorized to tell you that the trial will not be held in this work unit, but before a military court of officers of the People's Liberation Army!"

Inquisitor had whipped himself up to a frenzy. He spun on his heel and stamped out of the cell. As he did so, something fell from his pocket onto the dirt floor. He locked the door and strode off into the night.

Victory bent down and picked up Inquisitor's ball pen. He read the characters printed on it: "Liberation Brand".

"Hmm," he murmured. "'Liberation' is what we often hear about but have not yet seen!"

July 10th, 1960, dawned hot and muggy in Shanghai. Bright Victory awoke with the thought, "This is it!" He was under no illusion about a trial in the People's Republic of China. He remembered that his father had been told, "We would never bring you to trial if you were not guilty."

Victory knelt on the dirt floor beside the wooden cot and prayed: "Dear God, help me to be a good soldier of Jesus Christ today! Save me from self-pity. And please, I'd like to survive. For Jesus' sake. Amen."

Breakfast arrived, thin rice gruel and pickled cabbage. The gruel was cold and tasteless but Bright Victory forced himself to swallow it. He was chewing the last tough bit of pickled cabbage when he heard a scratching sound high on the wall opposite him. Expecting to see a bird at the window, he looked up.

It was not a bird but the familiar face of Strong Hero Liang.

Hero said: "Hi, Victory! You okay?"

"Yes, I'm okay."

"Victory, I can't stay. I'm standing on some crates. I just want you to know we are praying for you."

The face disappeared.

Bright Victory was overjoyed not only to see his friend but to hear that "we". "So", he said aloud, "God's people know, and they are remembering me." He sat down on the wooden cot and the tears streamed down his face.

It was hot and stuffy in the courtroom. Surrounded though he was by a crowd of people, Bright Victory had never felt so lonely in his life. Was it the fact that twenty feet separated him from the nearest person and that he was an island in a sea of faces? Or was it the look of apathy, of don't-involve-me-in-this, on those faces? But then as his eyes traveled from face to face, his heart jumped for joy; in a far corner stood Hero, and with him Jade Moon and Lotus.

My brave mother, he thought. *I hope she won't get a heart attack*! He remembered that night when he and his mother and brother and sister had been forced to attend his father's trial at the schoolhouse in Chongqing. But times had changed; Jade Moon and Lotus Flower were here today voluntarily.

How much Victory wished he could say something to them! To tell them he loved them, to tell them not to worry, whatever happened today ...His reverie was cut short by a strident voice announcing: "The court will come to order!" and then: "The defendant, Bright Victory Lee, will step forward!"

Bright Victory stepped forward two paces. Only then did he look carefully at the men sitting at the table in front of him. Six men, all in military uniform, two with pads and ball-point pens — the secretaries — and four older, more pon-derous men, obviously officers though no insignia on uniform distinguished them as such.

The strident voice came again: "The court presents Colonel Chang, who will read the charge and question the defendant."

Colonel Chang! Victory gasped when he heard the name. *Could it be the same Colonel Chang who twice tried my father? The very man who sentenced him to exile?* He was horrified at the thought. But he tried to keep an impassive face, as if the name meant nothing to him.

On the far side of the courtroom, Jade Moon too heard the name with dread and dismay. If this were *the* Colonel Chang, Victory could only expect the worst.

The heavy man at the head of the table, apparently as hot as everyone else in the courtroom, removed his red-star cap. Crimson lines stood out all over his bald head, like a map. When Jade Moon saw the bald head with the crimson lines, she reeled, suddenly feeling she was dreaming an old night-mare again.

Lotus pinched her arm, hard, and whispered in her mother's ear: "Brace up, Mama! It'll never do to faint now!"

The bald-headed man rose to his feet, shuffled papers on the desk in front of him, and began his questions: "So! You are Bright Victory Lee! Let me get you straight. Your dossier lists you as the son of Noble Heart Lee, from Chongqing. Is that correct?"

"Yes, that is correct."

"Hmmm! Then we have met before. In a schoolyard on the South Bank, Chongqing."

Victory did not answer. His head was whirling. The turn of events was almost too much for him.

Colonel Chang continued: "And your father is now serving a double term of Reform through Labor on Hainan

Island. Hmm! Like father like son. But," he went on, "you will be judged for your own crimes, not those of your father. The charges against you are: insubordination and counter-revolutionary activities, specifically the public promulgation of superstition and attending illegal gatherings."

Back in his corner, Hero rubbed the lobe of his ear between thumb and forefinger. He whispered to Jade Moon: "All that! Against the best worker in the factory!"

Colonel Chang continued to read: "After the defendant was caught publicly promulgating superstition in the commune mess hall he was duly cautioned and exhorted by faithful members of the Communist Party. But he was recalcitrant, refused to be admonished and continued to promulgate superstition publicly.

"And you must realize, comrades" — here Colonel Chang addressed the crowd — "that China is a progressive country crusading against feudalistic superstition, especially superstition masquerading under the false face of religion. Today we must strike a blow for science, progress and the illumination of the Chinese people!

"For a long time Shanghai has needed an example of punishment to such a counter-revolutionary who is at once a participator in illegal gatherings and a promulgator of superstition. Today is our opportunity of showing such an example to this great city!"

Applause broke out from the crowd.

Colonel Chang returned to his written indictment: "The defendant was given a week off from work to write his autobiography. In spite of the help of a faithful member of the Communist Party he refused to admit his guilt. I present to you Gong Xilin, the man who most patiently tried to show Bright Victory Lee the error of his ways."

Inquisitor stepped forward, and began his speech formally: "Colonel Chang, fellow members of the Communist Party and comrades. For one week I endeavoured to show Bright

Victory Lee his irrationality and recalcitrance but to no good effect. He remained untaught and unteachable. Our only recourse is to sentence him to correction by the people!"

Again, applause.

Colonel Chang stood up and asked: "Are there further accusations against the accused?"

Silence.

"Is there anything to be said in his defence?"

Again, silence.

"Harr---ump!" Colonel Chang cleared his throat. "It is obvious that the extreme penalty should be meted out to the defendant, not only for his own correction but as an example to the people of Shanghai. But the Chinese people, government and party are lenient and long-suffering; a light sentence will be given the defendant."

Still there was silence from the crowd.

Colonel Chang sat down again and conferred with the others on the panel. Victory knew this was only play-acting and that the sentence had been written down before the trial began.

Again came the strident voice: "The punishment will be announced by the court!"

Colonel Chang arose and said: "This court finds Bright Victory Lee guilty of the crimes as charged. He is therefore sentenced to five years of Reform through Labor in the coal mines of Shanxi Province, North China."

At this seeming finale, the people crowding the courtroom began to move toward the door. But Colonel Chang struck the table with his gavel and made a sign to the Person-with-the-Strident-Voice, who shouted: "Order in the courtroom!"

All became quiet again, and Colonel Chang said: "As a special mark of leniency to Bright Victory Lee, this court will allow him to travel without escort from Shanghai to Shanxi. This court will also give him the special opportunity of showing his repentant spirit and his loyalty to the government

by purchasing his own railway ticket from Shanghai to
Shanxi. You are dismissed."

18. Learning to Mine Coal
Datong, Shanxi, Summer 1960

CENTRAL CHINA is hot in July. In the "hard seat" section of the train, Bright Victory tried to sleep by propping his feet up on his bedding bundle. His rattan suitcase was jammed onto the luggage rack above. These were the two pieces the police allowed him to bring.

As long as the train was moving, a breeze came through the open windows and brought some relief from the heat. But when the train made one of its interminable stops at the mud brick stations, the air was stifling.

Late in the night Victory sensed that the train was slowing down and that the steam locomotive up front was laboring to climb a long grade. He realized this must be the watershed between the Yangzi on the south and the Yellow River on the north. *In the morning I'll get my first look at North China,* he thought. *I'll be well acquainted with it by the time I've been here five years!*

Before daylight the train picked up speed. Victory could feel the brakes alternately applied and released on the downhill grade. *Now we are heading for the Yellow River basin,* he thought. Thoroughly awake by this time, he looked around him. The "hard seat" car was so crowded that some people were sitting on their bedding rolls in the aisles, while others were leaning against door facing or seat arms to relieve their feet. If the snoring were any indication, most were sound asleep. Even those standing up seemed more asleep than awake. They swayed back and forth with the motion of the car, only just catching themselves before falling onto the floor.

Looking them over one by one, Bright Victory said, almost aloud: *I wonder how many of these people are going north voluntarily and how many are under orders like mine. You can't tell a man's destination by looking at his face.*

The great cauldron sitting in the middle of the car, into which kettle after kettle of boiling water had been poured the day before and from which the water in tea mugs had been unendingly replenished, was now cold and unattended, its only contribution at this hour being a resounding slosh now and then as the train jerked on through the night.

Twenty-six hours later, having changed trains at Zhengzhou in Henan Province, Bright Victory watched the sun rise over the Tainang Mountains which separated Shanxi on the west from Hebei on the east. As far as the eye could see stretched the yellow loess soil of North China. Victory gazed unbelievingly at the dry and barren landscape.

Is this China? he asked himself. *It's not only like another country, it's like another world. Until now I've looked at green all my life! What would a northerner think, to go to the Yangzi Valley and see something besides yellow?*

Fellow passengers told Victory that the drought this summer was the worst in years, so that the usually precarious livelihood of the country people had degenerated to near-starvation level. Many were subsisting on roots and barks, and some were even eating white clay to fill their stomachs and assuage the pangs of hunger.

Even so, he was not prepared for what he saw at the first station after daylight.

The station platform and building looked like a hundred others — the same signs, attendants, buildings of mud brick. What made this station different was the huge crowd of people. As the train drew into the station and stopped, the people on the platform rose like a swarm of bees and ran toward the train. At first Victory thought they were passengers anxious to board it, but instead of making for the doors they ran towards the windows along the length of the cars.

Maybe they're peddlers trying to sell something, Victory surmised. Then, to his horror, he realized they were all beggars. Every single person was holding out an empty tin can or broken mug. And, as if by prearrangement, they were all shouting the same thing: "Give me money! Give me money!" The only exceptions were a few women in the crowd, some with babies tied on their backs. Their shout was: "Give me the scraps from your lunch for my baby!"

Victory was amazed, dumbfounded. *Is this China, where the government looks after the people like a father looks after his children?* he asked himself.

Without consciously realizing what he was doing, he drew back from the windows facing the platform. But when he looked out on the other side where there was no platform, only more tracks, he saw people were converging on the train there too, with the same pitiful appeal: "Give me money! Give me money!"

Again, involuntarily, Victory turned back to the platform side of the coach. Now he saw there were many children in the beehive of beggars. And every child was naked.

Some of the passengers were reaching into their pockets and pulling out coins and bills of small value. As they threw them into the crowd there was a mad scramble, fighting and cursing.

Victory, too, reached into his pocket and pulled out some money. As he threw it out of the window his eye followed it, and he saw three children hold out their hands to catch it. No, they were not children. They were teenage girls in the first stage of puberty. And they were naked.

For the third time since he left Shanghai, Bright Victory sat up all night, this time in the station waiting room in Taiyuan, capital of Shanxi Province. Before daybreak he boarded the local train and headed north again for Datong, center of the coal-mining industry at the upper tip of Shanxi.

He wanted to arrive in Datong by daylight, so as to see as much as he could of the city and surroundings. Once inside the mining area, he might not be able to leave it — dismal prospect — until his sentence was completed five years hence.

As the train pulled into the Datong station, Victory saw a big sign with an arrow, "To Yungang Caves," *Some tourist attraction, I suppose,* he thought. *Not for me, though.*

But, as he crowded his way off the train and onto the platform, the thought struck him: *Why not for me? No one in sight knows that I am headed for the mines, to be a prisoner. Why not head for the caves and be a tourist? And then disappear in the other direction after I've looked at them?*

Bright Victory put down his suitcase and bedding bundle in the middle of the crowd, took off his cap and prayed, "Lord, give me wisdom just now."

As he finished praying, a vision of his mother came up before him. It struck him like a slap on the face: *She is a hostage! If I disappear, they'll take her to jail! No, I'm not a tourist. But one thing I do want to look at — the locomotive that pulls this train.*

Like most passengers, Victory had boarded his assigned car without ever seeing the locomotive up front. Now he worked his way along the platform to the great steam engine. Opposite it he put down his bedding bundle and suitcase, and with a thrill took in the sheer massiveness of the brute, its fenders painted shiny black, its drivewheels accented by bright red paint, its cowling high in front like belligerent shoulders ever thrusting forward. He was intrigued by the steady "chuff, chuff" of the panting monster, with white smoke puffing out of the smokestack, like a mighty charger champing at the bit and anxious to stretch on to Mongolia and Siberia beyond.

Suddenly he was jarred back into reality by a sharp jab on his lower spine. He turned to see a soldier in uniform, who barked: "No loitering here! Move on! The exit is down yonder!"

Inside the station, Victory handed in his papers at the police counter and was told to wait for an escort to the mines. He strolled over to the window and looked out, seeing the pall of smoke and dust hanging over streets and buildings. *Is this what I'll be breathing for five years?* he wondered.

After what seemed an age, an officer tapped him on the shoulder, and said, "Let's go." He started for the door, and Victory grabbed bedding roll in one hand, rattan suitcase in the other, and followed him out. The street itself looked paved with coal dust. The buildings around seemed to be in a contest, the native yellow brick fighting to retain its own color against the deposit of coal dust and smoke that gradually smudged everything to dreary, sooty black.

A mule cart stood waiting. By the grim look of driver, cart and mule, Victory guessed that the rig had just delivered coal to the railway yard and, now empty on its way back to the mines, had been pressed into service as his private taxi.

Bright Victory threw his baggage onto the cart and climbed up after it. The soldier-escort plopped himself down on the bedding, as the softest option. Victory had second choice and sat on his rattan suitcase. The driver had no choice at all and sat on the forward end of the cart. He whacked the mule over the back and off they started.

Meeting them along the road in an endless stream were lorries and mule carts headed for the railway yards, each loaded with coal. Running alongside each vehicle were one or two hopefuls with sack or basket, picking up lumps of coal that jostled out at every pothole, of which there were plenty.

What they could not pick up was the coal dust, which constantly sifted down from cart and lorry and added a new sprinkling to dust-covered road. Then the hot, dry July wind picked it up again, swirled and eddied, and deposited it generously and without discrimination on people, buildings, yards and fields.

What a place! thought Victory. *As different from Shanghai as night from day! No wonder they put Reform through Labor people here to mine coal. Who else would want to live in this God-forsaken place?*

"I'll never get through this day alive! I wish I'd never been born!"

The speaker was Wang Yuan, a young man Bright Victory's age, who always saw the dark side. And there was plenty of the dark side down in the bowels of the earth.

"If I just had a shovel! How can human beings load coal with their hands?" This time Yuan voiced what the crew of ten men felt. But Victory knew it did no good to say it. He dug in with both hands, fingers extended and facing each other, and scooped up as many lumps of coal as double hands could hold. These he used to level off his bucket, then emptied the bucket into the wagon, murmuring: "One more bucket toward my quota for today."

"Why *don't* they give us shovels to use? Pastor Ling, you know all the answers. Tell us." It was Yuan again.

"Well, I don't know any more than you do, Yuan," Pastor Ling replied. "Maybe it's because shovels could be used as weapons, and they're afraid of an uprising in the camp."

"If that's so, why do they give us picks?"

"True. But they don't allow any crew more than three picks, and those must be checked in the first thing when we get back topside." Pastor Ling went on, "And as to shovels, we do use our buckets to scoop up the stuff."

"Well, I don't see how you can be so easy going. It sounds as if you are defending the system! Don't you ever blow your top about the way they treat us? No tools, no freedom, not enough food and what there is as miserable as pig food. Don't you ever react against all this?"

"Yuan, I don't like it any more than you do. And I know you were framed or you wouldn't be here. But you are here and I am here, and there's no use bucking the system. If you rebel — well, they have the guns, handcuffs, leg irons and whips. Better keep what energy you have and use it to survive rather than blow it and die young."

At this point Straw Boss Liu spoke up: "Here, you guys! Cut the chatter! If you don't meet your quota by noon you won't have any lunch!"

Yuan bridled: "Lunch! What lunch? Do you call a bowl of water with a few vegetable peelings and roots floating in it 'lunch'?"

Pastor Ling continued in his balanced, soothing tones: "Well, things could be worse. Like in the past when they whipped all of us for what one man did. I learned years ago that if you chew peelings and roots well before you swallow them, you might get *some* nourishment out of them."

"*Wah!* You Christians! You always try to make things sound better than they are. Are you sure you're not a stooge or spy working for the Communist Party?"

Pastor Ling laughed. A laugh was so unusual in the Datong mines that the whole gang stopped work and looked at him.

"What are *you* laughing at?" came a sarcastic voice out of the semi-darkness.

"Well, if I *am* a spy," the pastor answered, "my only reward has been to spend ten years underground. I came here when some of you were still drinking milk! And I've got eight years yet to go. No, I guess spies are better paid than that."

"Come on now!" shouted the straw boss. "Cut it out and get to work! Hard. Or none of us will get a bite to eat the rest of the day!"

The work day ended at 6 p.m., exactly twelve hours after the three thousand men in Mine No 3 had entered the earth that morning. Exhausted, back aching from working all day in a tunnel three feet high, hands bleeding from scooping up raw coal hour after hour, knees bleeding from constant kneeling on bits of coal, Bright Victory stumbled out into daylight. He took a deep breath of relatively fresh air and examined new lacerations of hands and knees.

He did not go to a clinic to treat his cuts and bruises; there was no clinic, no doctor, no nurse. He did the only thing he could — wash his wounds in cold water. Then he turned his attention to the rest of his body and washed and washed and washed. But with no soap he could not get himself clean. After only two weeks in the camp, the coal dust had already ground deep into his skin. To no one in particular he said: "I'm so black already that my mother wouldn't know me!"

After supper of hard corn bread with neither meat nor vegetable nor fat to help it down, Victory walked slowly toward the barracks. Pastor Ling caught up with him and took him by the arm. Victory knew the old pastor did this in order to get closer to his ear, but even so the touch of a fellow human being felt good, and he unconsciously pressed the hand close against his side.

The pastor began: "Victory, you have been here only two weeks now and you're doing okay. But there's one thing you should know about Yuan. He's a member of the Octopus Gang ..."

"Whatever's that?" Bright Victory interrupted.

"That's one of four different gangs, all named after fish. The others are the Black Eel, the Golden Carp and the Dolphins. They are like societies within a society. Each appeals to a different kind of man and represents a particular point of view on our incarceration. The Octopus Gang are the collaborators. That makes me hang a question mark over what Yuan said to you today. You're new. Maybe he was playing out a length of rope so you could hang yourself with it... Well, yes, I have children at home, two boys and a girl, but they are grown now."

They had just passed two lounging guards, and Pastor Ling had automatically shifted gears, subject-wise, for their benefit.

"Good night," Pastor Ling said, as he turned into his barracks. Bright Victory walked on slowly, musing, *So, there are wheels within wheels. Just so I don't get crushed between two of them!*

The one respite from the constant grime and grind was the day set aside for political instruction every two weeks. That day no coal was mined; it was completely given over to lectures, discussion — and accusation. Bright Victory looked forward to that day, thinking it would bring relief from the pit below. As it turned out, however, after his first "study session" he would rather have spent the day mining coal.

The men from Victory's dormitory gathered in the mess hall after breakfast to hear a harangue by the Deputy Camp Commandant. His theme was: "The Leniency of the Government in Giving you the Chance of Self-Reformation in the Mines". Then the group broke up into teams. The same team that mined coal together now set out to mine the nuggets of wisdom of Marxism, Leninism and — especially — Mao Zedong Thought.

On this particular day, however, Bright Victory's team-mates had a different assignment. Instead of a lecture from the greats of Communism, the class was set, as it were, for a laboratory session on how Communism works in practice. A guinea pig was to be dissected — the newcomer, Bright Victory Lee.

The straw boss in the pit was suddenly the instructor in the laboratory, and his instrument for dissecting the guinea pig was Bright Victory's dossier, lifted from the files in the office for the occasion.

Straw Boss Liu opened the blue cloth covers of the dossier with a flourish. Victory noticed that he virtually licked his chops with delight. However, it was only when he began to read that Victory realized it was *his* dossier, and that therefore he was in trouble. Only later did he learn it was standard procedure to harass every newcomer with a public recounting of all his sins, crimes and shortcomings.

Straw Boss Liu began: "We have in our midst a shining example of the extremes to which superstition can drive a man. No doubt about it — if it weren't for Bright Victory Lee's religious superstition he would not be here mining coal."

"Right! Right! Right!" a handful of men shouted, as if touched off by some prearranged signal.

Hearing such concerted criticism from his workmates, Victory stiffened. After all, weren't they all in the same boat together? Weren't they all alike in being punished for real or supposed crimes? Why should they single him out for condemnation?

Pastor Ling, who was sitting beside him, sensed his reaction, and gave him the slightest touch with his elbow, as if to say: "Take it easy! Don't react!"

Straw Boss Liu continued: "I read here that Bright Victory Lee was convicted for counter-revolutionary activities."

A voice from the rear shouted: "Down with the counter-revolutionary!" and others took up the shout: "Down with the counter-revolutionary!"

Straw Boss Liu waved his hand for quiet: "No need to express your opinions now. Just wait and I'll call on each of you to have his say about Bright Victory Lee. No one will be exempt, not even Bright Victory Lee himself."

Victory's head reeled. "*Me? What am I going to say about myself? This is all new to me!*

Liu went on: "And be careful what you say, because every

word you utter will be put down in your dossier and will be a mark for or against you."

It was only then that Victory realized this little meeting was dignified by having a secretary to take minutes. Wang Yuan was writing like crazy, taking down everything that was said.

Liu's voice droned on: "Bright Victory Lee's counter-revolutionary activities are most heinous and most dangerous to the State. He is guilty not only of holding religious super-stition but of publicly promulgating the same. Moreover, he was caught in the act of attending illegal and unauthorized meetings."

Again came that united denunciation: "Down with Bright Victory Lee! Down with Bright Victory Lee!" Victory flinched as if he had been hit.

Straw Boss Liu read the entire transcript of Bright Victory's trial. Then he called on one man after another to comment. And they all denounced him, praised the Party and the Government, mouthed slogans and extolled the merits of Chairman Mao.

Finally it was Pastor Ling's turn. He stood up and began: "There is none righteous, no not one. Bright Victory Lee has gone out of the right way. In fact, we all have gone out of the right way, and I include myself there alongside Bright Victory Lee. There is much that Bright Victory Lee must learn in this time of correction and instruction. I hope he will learn well. Thank you." He sat down.

Straw Boss Liu spoke again: "All right, Bright Victory Lee. What do you have to say for yourself?"

Victory began: "I make no defense for my actions. It is true that I prayed to God in public to thank him for my food. But it is also true that the constitution of the People's Republic of China guarantees freedom of religion to every citizen. If you do not believe in God but accept atheism, that is your right. But if you believe in God, it is also your right to believe in God. So says the constitution of our country. I have not stepped beyond the bounds of that constitution. Thank you."

Straw Boss Liu opened his mouth to speak but was interrupted by the gong for the noon meal. At the thought of food, suddenly any idea of further confrontation was driven from their minds and the men hurried off to their cornbread and watery soup.

When the afternoon session opened a half hour later, Straw Boss Liu chose to forget that Victory's defense had been left hanging in mid air with no rebuttal. Instead he opened the meeting on an entirely different tack: "It is our duty this afternoon to peruse recent copies of the *People's Daily*." Then he made a magnanimous proposal: "What do you want to look at first?"

A back-bencher responded: "Can't you find something interesting in the paper to read to us?"

Liu was taken aback. He knew, and the men knew, that the *People's Daily* made no attempt at being a newspaper in the usual sense. Rather, it was purely and simply an instrument of State propaganda. But to openly infer that it was not interesting was close to heresy.

Liu soon had hold of himself: "I'll look and see what I can find."

The men sat patiently, hoping Liu would come up with something juicy. Finally, he held up the back page, on which were the only two pictures in that issue of the paper.

He said: "I'll pass this around for you to see. I've heard that the American people are oppressed by their leaders and that their life is hard. Here are two pictures from Chicago, USA, proving that the common people are reduced to eating dog meat."

The paper finally came to Bright Victory. Sure enough,

there it was, two pictures of a shop in Chicago with a big sign across the front: "HOT DOGS."

By the end of three months, Bright Victory felt as if he had mined coal all his life. Not that he had grown to enjoy it — rather, that twelve hours a day, seven days a week, wears a man down and makes him into an automaton.

In the mines, the only chance a man had to stand up straight and stretch, the only respite from that tyrannical daily quota, was to go to the latrine and relieve himself. One afternoon Victory noticed someone following him to the latrine. Without looking up he said, "Seems to be a bit damper down here than usual."

"Hadn't noticed it," came the response. It was the voice of Wang Yuan.

Then Yuan's tone turned from casual to intense: "Victory, I'm going to escape tonight! I can work you in on it, too, if you'll do exactly as I say. What about it?"

Victory remembered Pastor Ling's warning about Yuan. But on the other hand, he had inherited a good portion of his father's curiosity. So he said: "You tell *me* about it. What's your plan?"

"I've bought two government identification cards from the man who drives the ordure cart for our barracks. They're real. People died and the relatives never reported it, so they could use their ration cards. The driver will bring his tank in empty, pretend to fill it but put us inside instead. A mile away from the mines we get out and walk away. It's as simple as that. And we have the proper identification cards to start a new life outside. I had old Pang lined up to go with me, but he's so sick at his stomach this afternoon he can't stand up straight. So, it's your opportunity for a free life if you want it."

With that, Yuan pulled out two official identification cards. They were indeed the real thing, the kind of card

Victory had surrendered when he arrived at the mines. A wave of excitement swept over him. What a chance to get away from this hellhole of ceaseless work and endless pain! "Thanks, Yuan. It's awfully good of you to make the offer. But ... but I'm a Christian and I'll have to pray about it first."

Yuan's face suddenly changed. He swore viciously at Bright Victory, turned and strode away in anger.

Well, I guess that settles it, Victory said to himself. He returned to the gang and began loading coal again as if nothing had happened.

Everything inside the camp was done on clockwork precision, even the collecting of nightsoil at exactly 9 p.m.

Knowing that the old man and his mule cart with the tank on it would arrive on the dot, Bright Victory got out of his bunk a few minutes before nine and headed for the door. Again, his curiosity was operating. As he opened the door, a gust of wind blew in a few flakes of snow.

"*Aiya!*" exclaimed Victory in surprise. "The first snow of winter and here it is only November."

He buttoned his jacket up tight and strolled out into the darkness. No street lights had been wasted on the camp, but reflection from the powerful searchlights around the perimeter fence cast an uncertain glow over the area. By that light, he saw on his right a figure in dark clothes and cap, with scarf around his neck, slinking behind the toilet toward the cesspit at the rear.

To Victory's left stood the nearest guard, with rifle and fixed bayonet. Victory recognized him as Old Fatso, the most garrulous of the guards. Pretending to pass him by, he remarked: "Certainly strange to see snow in November."

It was against the rules for guards to fraternize with prisoners, but he guessed correctly that Old Fatso would rise to the bait: "Oh, no! We often get snow like this in November.

You're from the South and don't know our Northern weather!"

"Yes, I guess you're right. We don't have snow much in Shanghai. Haven't seen it, even, for a couple of years." Victory was as casual as if to talk with Old Fatso were his daily habit.

The Northerner was happy, having put the Southerner right. And the Southerner was happy, having seen out of the corner of his eye a figure disappearing feet-first into an ordure tank on a mule cart.

The next morning prisoners in Mine No 3 opened the door of their barracks to step out into a white fairyland. Scarcely powdering the level, it was piled into drifts by a violent wind whipping down from the Gobi Desert.

The men finished their breakfast of millet gruel and were glad to disappear into the earth and away from the vicious clawing of the north wind. Down in the mine the temperature stood at a constant 57 degrees Fahrenheit, summer and winter.

Entering their tunnel, Pastor Ling whispered to Bright Victory: "Today is Sunday. Maybe we'll have a few minutes to pray together and worship the Lord."

"Good," returned Victory. "I hope so."

That afternoon the gang hit a rich pocket of coal that mined more easily than usual; by 5 p.m., their quota for the day was filled. Glad of a let-up, most of the gang sat on the ground, smoking and swapping yarns. Victory and Pastor Ling went off to one side.

After they had prayed together, Victory asked: "I don't understand it. Pastor. Why would Yuan, an Octopus and therefore a collaborator, want to escape?"

"Son, I don't have all the answers," replied the pastor, "but maybe being an octopus was a red herring — ha! ha! excuse my fishy joke! — to keep the cadres in charge from suspecting his plan to escape. Anyway, he has had a rough time in this blizzard. Few local people would risk taking in an escapee and giving him shelter."

On Tuesday morning, as the prisoners were going to work, the camp grapevine buzzed with the news that a farmer had found Yuan's frozen body in the corner of a field. A detail of guards had gone out and brought the body back in a burlap sack.

At supper that night the loudspeakers blared: "Members of all production units will assemble on the drill ground at 7.30 p.m."

The announcement was repeated twice. Men stole glances at each other silently, inquiringly.

At 7.20 the men began to filter onto the drill ground. No one wanted to be last to leave the barracks. To be caught inside at 7.30 could mean ten lashes with the whip.

Arriving at the drill ground, the men were surprised to see that a wooden platform had been thrown up at one end. It was bathed in the glare of four floodlights. What occupied them most, however, was not curiosity about the platform but the unseasonable chill that needled their thinly-clad bodies. They stamped their feet and clapped their hands to increase circulation and fight off the cold.

At exactly 7.30 a bugler mounted the platform and blew a few bars. Quietness settled over the three thousand men. The only sound was the moan of the north wind through the pine trees.

Two guards swung a burlap bag up onto the platform followed by a rifle, after which the two of them climbed up. Finally, several cadres also climbed up.

There was no ceremony about what the cadre said. He yelled into the microphone: "You men know that not one single man has ever escaped from Number Three Mine and lived to tell the tale. Wang Yuan tried it Saturday night, and a farmer found his dead body Tuesday morning. For your education we will now do for Wang Yuan, dead, exactly what we would have done for Wang Yuan if he had been captured alive."

The cadre waved his hand toward the burlap bag. The two guards picked up one end and shook it, and out rolled a human body. A faint gasp rippled across the concourse, not at seeing the body but because it was stark naked. Somebody, somewhere along the line, had stolen the clothes off the corpse. And a corpse without coffin and without clothes is the ultimate disgrace.

At least, they thought this was the ultimate disgrace. But more followed. And quickly.

The officer yelled again into the microphone: "Set him up!"

The two guards, with some difficulty, pulled and pushed legs and arms and finally set the corpse up in the semblance of a sitting position.

Again the yell: "Proceed as instructed!"

One of the guards picked up the rifle, slammed a bullet into the magazine, aimed at the back of the corpse's head and pulled the trigger. With the impact, the body slumped onto the platform. The men nearest the platform recoiled as bits of the brain splattered on them. A ripple of horror and unbelief ran across the crowd.

Again, a yell into the microphone: "Take him to the crematorium!"

As Bright Victory stumbled back to the barracks, the question kept running through his mind: *What has China come to? This place hasn't got a clinic but it has got a crematorium. And for burning twice-killed bodies at that.*

Then a prayer took precedence over the question: "Thank you, dear God, that there were not two bodies on that platform tonight. The second one, mine."

Interlude
Shanghai and Hainan, Autumn 1962

"AI....DAH, DAH, AI...DAH, DAH." Jade Moon suddenly stopped humming and burst out laughing. For the first time in years she had been humming a popular tune, and a Russian one at that, "The Volga Boatmen."

Then the laugh gave way to a shiver that ran up and down her backbone. Doubts stormed her mind: "Will they really give me a pass for the trip to Hainan? Can I get a ticket on a steamer? Will I be able to see him even if I get to Hainan?"

She took out Noble Heart's last letter and read it for the twentieth time:

"I don't see any reason why you can't visit me if you want to and can get time off from your unit. You will have to change ships in Guangzhou. When you reach Haikou, look up Ba Yudeng, No 15 Bubbling Well Road. She will put you up overnight ..."

Jade Moon lined up on the table the things to take to Noble Heart: A new shirt, a suit of underwear, a pair of cloth shoes she had made herself, a jar of lard with a lid that could be screwed down tight, a half-kilo cake of brown sugar, six hard-boiled eggs.

She addressed the little row of gifts as if they had ears and could hear: "I've really had to scrimp and save on coupons and money to get you all together. But if I can only get you to Hainan it will be worth it!"

It was a bright sunny morning when Jade Moon boarded the bus at Haikou for the trip to the rubber plantation. Her lap held her zip bag; inside were the precious items from Shanghai plus three big round crisp pancakes she had bought that morning from a street vendor.

In the bag were also her overnight things, in case it might be possible to spend the night at the plantation.

Well, mused Jade Moon to herself, *this is my fifth day travelling — three days on the ship to Guangzhou, one from Guangzhou to Haikou, and now this bus. I wonder what Noble Heart will look like after all these years ...*

For the umpteenth time she checked the date on her fingers. Yes, this was the date Noble Heart had written that he had a day off and could receive a visitor.

Finally Jade Moon arrived at the gate with its sign:

HAPPY DAYS NATIONALIZED RUBBER PLANTATION

The guard at the gate did not waste words: "Give me your ID card. Wait here." He walked over to a building which Jade Moon presumed was the office.

She stood on the dirt floor and looked blankly at the reception area, open on three sides to the weather, with a small black table and two black chairs backed up against the one wall.

Eventually the guard returned and gave her a blank form with two dozen or so spaces to be filled in. Once Jade Moon had filled it in, the guard took the paper without a word. In a few minutes he was back, and motioned to her to sit down.

After what seemed an age, an older man walked across from the office. He was gaunt, stooped; his face was brown and furrowed. But his walk was familiar...

Jade Moon spoke first: "Noble Heart!"

The reply was in a familiar voice that had not changed: "Jade Moon!"

Just then the guard appeared from the recesses of his room. He stood in the doorway, hands on hips, and listened to every word. With an effort Jade Moon controlled her voice and repeated what she had gone over and over in her mind on the bus: "Bright Loyalty and Lotus Flower send their love. They said how much they want to see you."

"How are they, Jade Moon?"

"They are well. They both work hard at their factories and are glad they can contribute to our ancestral country. Victory is working hard, too, to reconstruct China."

Jade Moon hated herself for mouthing stock phrases when she was seeing her husband for the first time in so many years. But her sixth sense told her that the guard was making a mental note of everything they said.

Noble Heart changed the subject: "Thank you for coming all this distance to see me. You are looking so well..."

Jade Moon wished she could say the same of him. Aloud she said: "You have never told me when you plan to come home."

Noble Heart moved his body just enough to turn his back to the guard, so that the guard could not see him close his right eye halfway, as if to say: *Careful! Dangerous ground!* "Oh, didn't I write you? he said innocently. "I will soon be a 'free worker'. I would like to go home, but the plantation needs more workers and the government has assigned me here. Maybe some day I can visit you in Shanghai, when I can save some money."

Jade Moon then brought up a question very close to her heart: "Is there a place here where I can spend the night?"

The guard interrupted curtly: "No! It's against the rules."

Jade Moon tried to keep the disappointment from showing on her face. But that was hard to do: her face had always been a mirror to her thoughts. She thought it safest to change the subject: "I've brought some things for you."

She took the shirt, underwear and shoes out of her bag, holding them up carefully so the guard could see them. Piece by piece Noble Heart took them and placed them on the table. Then she pulled out the jar of lard, the brown sugar and the six hard-boiled eggs and placed them on the table.

Again the guard spoke up at once: "Visitors are not allowed to give food. To accept food is the same as saying that what the government provides is not sufficient. Take it back with you." He took the butt end of his rifle and nudged the food back toward Jade Moon, as if to say: *I have a gun; guns enforce regulations.*

Dejectedly, Jade Moon put the food back in her bag. Again, she knew that her feelings were showing on her face.

The guard spoke again: "Time's up. You've been here thirty minutes."

"But I came all the way from Shanghai..." Jade Moon blurted out. Again Noble Heart signaled her, with both eyes this time. For years she had depended on Noble Heart's judgement; she knew that somehow he must be right now.

The guard said: "Oh, the government is very lenient with 'free workers'. You can come again when he is a 'free worker'."

Jade Moon bit her lip. She could hardly keep back the tears. Noble Heart rushed to fill the gap: "Since I'll soon be a 'free worker', I'm permitted to walk fifty paces from the gate with a guest."

He looked at the guard as if his corroboration of this was of utmost importance. The guard dutifully nodded a "Yes". Noble Heart stepped through the gate and down the path, and Jade Moon followed reluctantly.

When they were out of earshot of the guard, she whispered: "Noble Heart, are you still going to be a prisoner!"

"Well, yes ... And no. We have a saying here, 'Once a prisoner, always a prisoner'. There is nothing I can do about it. But, Jade Moon, God will reunite us someday. I believe that, don't you? Remember the little chorus we used to sing?

'God is still on the throne

And He will remember his own'."

"Oh, Noble Heart! I need you so much. Can't you come home?"

The tears began to flow down Jade Moon's cheeks. She brushed them away, though what she wanted to do was to let them flow and flow — on Noble Heart's shoulder.

But that was not to be.

"Fifty paces!" came the voice of the guard, shouting out the regulations.

"Here!" Jade Moon said. "The guard didn't say you couldn't have these! I remember how you used to buy them on the street in Chongqing on your way home from work."

As she spoke she unbuttoned Noble Heart's shirt and shoved the three pancakes inside, flat against his chest. Then she buttoned his shirt up again. "I love you," she said. Then she turned and walked away.

"Oh, you're back earlier than I thought you would be," Ba Yudeng said as she held the door open for Jade Moon.

"The guard gave us only thirty minutes," Jade Moon replied. "Imagine! Only thirty minutes after a five-day trip from Shanghai!"

That thought, verbalized to a person with listening ears and a warm heart, opened the floodgates. The tears she had not been able to shed on Noble Heart's shoulder now flowed onto the comforting shoulder of Ba Yudeng.

Jade Moon wept and wept. It was as if the pent-up tears of over five years flowed that afternoon in Haikou. Yudeng stood there and held Jade Moon and let her weep. She knew that after her experience of the morning she needed a good cry, and now was the best time for it.

Finally, exhausted from her trip and her emotions, Jade Moon collapsed into a chair. Yudeng said: "You wait a minute and I'll make us some tea." As she expected, she found Jade Moon more composed when she returned with the pot of tea.

"Oh, I'm so glad you're here," Jade Moon said. "I don't know what I'd do without a friend right now!"

"Yes," replied Yudeng, "I know what it is to have brothers and sisters in the Lord..."

Now that she was sipping the hot, clear tea, Jade Moon seemed in a listening mood, so Yudeng went on: "You know,

I have been a 'non-person' ever since Liberation. When they first classified everybody, I wrote on the form 'Bible woman'. They told me that in the new China there was no such occupation, but I said that God had called me to be a Christian worker and that I could not change until I got new orders from Him.

"'If that's it, you will not get any coupons for food and clothing', they told me. So, these thirteen years since Liberation I have never had ration coupons, nor have I accepted one penny from the government handout.'"

Sitting straight up on the chair now, Jade Moon asked: "Well, how in the world have you lived?"

Yudeng laughed. "A lot of the time, without my asking for it, I have eaten government rice. In jail, that is. I've been in and out of jail so many times I've lost count."

"Where was that?"

"Oh, all over Hainan Island and many other places in Guangdong Province where I've preached. But the last food I had in jail was so bad you wouldn't feed it to a pig. I was so ill I thought I was going to die. But God answered the prayers of the believers. After 194 days they let me out and I gradually came back to health again."

"By the way," said Jade Moon, "I want to leave with you the things they wouldn't let me give Noble Heart."

She took out of her zip bag the jar of lard, the cake of brown sugar and the six hard-boiled eggs and placed them on Yudeng's table. Yudeng remonstrated and began to put the things back into the bag. Jade Moon smiled to herself at seeing the old-fashioned courtesy. But she insisted, and in the end Yudeng accepted.

Jade Moon sat back in the chair, alone with her thoughts a few minutes. Then she began: "I...I want to share something with you, Older Sister ...."

"What's that?"

"Noble Heart ...he.." Jade Moon paused and shifted her

feet uneasily. Should she be frank about Noble Heart or not? Then she plucked up courage and plunged on. "He looked so old! I only recognized him by his walk and his voice! I was so ashamed not to recognize him. But he has changed so much. I ...I almost wish I hadn't come! To see him look like that!"

Jade Moon broke out crying again, but it did not last as long this time. When she had control of herself again she asked: "Older Sister, wouldn't it be better to remember him as he was — free and in good health and so nice looking — than to remember him like ...like I saw him today?"

Yudeng thought for a minute, then said: "When you talk like that you are saying that you'll never see him again. But you will, and in Shanghai. I know about this so-called 'free-worker' business, when in reality they are still prisoners. But our God is bigger than any human government, even the government of China. There's a little chorus that goes

'God is still on the throne

And He will remember His own'."

"Yes," said Jade Moon, "God *is* still on the throne. And, strange as it may seem, those were the last words that Noble Heart said to me today."

19. Bright Victory Is Free And Yet Not Free

Datong, Shanxi, Summer 1965

THE DAY DAWNED bright and warm. It was summer but not yet hot. Bright Victory breathed deeply of the fragrance of flowers that filled the air, and thanked God he was alive. It was his last day in the mines — he had arrived at Datong five years ago tomorrow.

As he entered the mines that morning he prayed: "Lord, please let me have a little time with Pastor Ling today. I may not see him again ..."

God answered that prayer. The work gang's quota was filled early, and while the others smoked, the two Christians prayed. Afterwards Victory said: "Pastor, I want to share something."

"Good. Go ahead, Victory."

Bright Victory began: "As you know, I've been concerned that there is no medical help whatever for the men in Mine Number Three. A month ago I wrote Cadre Commandant and asked if they would at least put in a 'barefoot doctor', with basic medicines to dispense to the men. Do you think it was wrong to make that suggestion?"

Pastor Ling's gaze was not on Bright Victory. He had a faraway look in his eyes, as if he were seeing far down the road. Then he said slowly: "Victory, some day our beloved China will come to its senses and treat people like people. Maybe it will be the responsibility of the Christian church to help China do that. And we must begin now, by doing what we can. No, you were not wrong. But you did run a risk ..."

It was a bitter-sweet time for the two friends. Sweet, because Victory was to be released. Bitter, because Pastor

Ling still had three years in the mines. The old pastor held up three stubby, gnarled fingers and said, "Three years yet."

Looking at his fingers, Victory commented: "You bear the marks of the sufferings of Christ on your hands. I hope you won't mind my saying so, but I don't think you have a single whole finger left."

Pastor Ling grinned. He opened both hands and held out what was left of all ten fingers. "Yes, Victory, I could tell you how each one of those fingers was cut off, bruised, crushed or just worn down loading coal. But when I begin to feel sorry for myself I think of Jesus up in heaven, still with the scars in His hands, and then I forget my hands ...."

That night at supper Victory received a chit: "Report at the office at 8 a.m. tomorrow." *Well, that's it*, he said to himself. *Better get my things packed.*

"Yes, sir, my suitcase is packed and my bedding is tied up." Bright Victory was speaking to Cadre Commandant of Mine Number Three.

The commandant said: "You have completed your alloted five years of Reform through Labor. You have been a model worker. I notice you have also taken to heart the needs of all the workers here."

The commandant picked up a sheet of paper from his desk, and with excitement Victory saw that it was his letter about medical help. His heart beat faster.

The commandant went on: "You are now a free man. But you are only free to accept job placement by the People. And since the Party represents the People, this means that you are assigned work by the Party and the Government.

"You have suggested a 'barefoot doctor' for Mine Number Three. You yourself are the answer to this need. You have been assigned to take a six-week course in medical practice and disease diagnosis. After that you will return to Mine Number Three as 'barefoot doctor'."

"Uh, uh ... you mean..." the new turn of events threw Bright Victory off balance, and he could not put his words together. "You mean...I'm not going home?"

The commandant stormed: "Whoever said you were going home? Don't you know that in China today everybody is *assigned* work? You are *assigned* to Mine Number Three. Here is your pass to the Datong Municipal Health Center. Now, go and learn to be a barefoot doctor!"

Bright Victory stepped out into the public road in front of the main gate of Mine Number Three. He was free. And yet he was not free. With a carrying pole swung over his shoulder, bedding bundle suspended from one end and rattan suitcase from the other, he walked away from the gate and into a new life. Within two hundred yards, however, his shoulder began to object to the unaccustomed weight concentrated on a few square inches of bone and skin. Victory lowered his load to the ground and looked around. Could there possibly be a ride?

A mule cart plodded along, loaded with coal and headed for town. Victory yelled up at the driver: "Hey! What about a ride into town? I'll pay you if you'll just take my bundles."

"Hmmp!" returned the driver. "No ex-convict'll get a ride from me!" Then to the mule: "Giddap!" Mule and cart pulled away and left Victory and his baggage beside the road.

That label, "ex-convict", took him aback. *But*, he thought, *maybe that's just an especially cantankerous driver*. He hailed the next cart, with the same response. And the next. Finally he slumped down on his bedding bundle. Inside, his spirit slumped, too, and a wave of despondency swept over him. He bore the stigma of a convicted criminal!

Just then from a clump of bushes beside the road came the clear, beautiful song of a bird. Bright Victory sat up straight and listened. A word from the Bible about birds came to his mind: "God does not forget a single sparrow." As he sat on his bedding bundle and listened to the bird, a smile crept slowly across his face and a load lifted from his heart.

Then from somewhere above where the heavenly songster was perched, another message came as clear and sweet as the song of the bird itself: "Speak to the next driver."

Another cart filled with coal was heaving into sight. Victory waved it down. "Hey! Could you take these two pieces of baggage and carry them into town?"

The cart stopped. The driver, an older man, looked at Victory quizzically, then said: "Hmmp! Not used to carrying things with a carrying pole, eh? But your hands look as if you've done a lot of dirty work. From the mines, are you?"

"Yes, I am," Victory admitted.

The old man said: "Toss 'em up, son! And you can climb up yourself if you want to."

Surprised at the offer, Victory did just that.

"Giddap!" said the driver, and off the cart started.

The driver turned to Victory: "Where're you going?"

"Into town."

"Where in town?"

"To the Municipal Health Center."

"Hmmp! You don't look sick."

"No, thank God, I'm not sick. I've been assigned to study a little medicine."

With that, Victory took the order from the commandant out of his pocket and handed it to the driver. But he handed it back absent-mindedly without looking at it. Something else was evidently on his mind. Eventually he asked: "Did I hear right? Did you say 'Thank God'? Only a Christian says that. Are you a Christian?"

"Why, yes, I am."

Bright Victory thought back about the bird, and the message to speak to the next driver. Suddenly the whole thing fell in place. He exclaimed: "And you must be a Christian, too!"

"That I am, young man, and I'm glad you are! Giddap!" and he whacked the mule over the back.

"Here, have another piece of steamed bread!" Mrs. Huang lifted the lid from the two-tiered bamboo steamer basket. A cloud of steam rose to the bare gray underside of the roof tiles.

Bright Victory smiled. It was his first time in five years to see the homey sight of steaming bread. As Mrs. Huang brought over the bamboo basket, his mouth watered. What beautiful chunks of luscious food! He reached out his chopsticks and politely took the smallest piece. As it emitted steam and fragrance, he held it up in front of him to let it cool off a bit before taking a bite.

"I'll heat up your soup," said Mrs. Huang. She dipped a ladleful of hot soup from the wok, careful to fish out four of the five remaining little chunks of fat pork.

Again Bright Victory's mouth watered. At the mines they tasted meat only twice a month, and here in this one ladle was a month's ration of meat! He spoke with difficulty; somehow a lump in his throat got in his way: "Mr. Huang, I can't tell you how much I appreciate you bringing me home with you. Just... just... to be inside a home again is worth a million dollars! And, Mrs. Huang, this soup! And this steamed bread! What a feast!"

Mrs. Huang spoke for the two of them: "Think nothing of it. Jesus said the foxes have holes but that He didn't have anywhere to lay his head. Well, He's not here, but we're glad to welcome you instead."

Mrs. Huang knew more of the Bible than her husband did. Bright Victory suspected that she could read but he could not.

"How many do you have in your family, Mr. Huang?"

"Well, there's our son. He drives a mule cart like I do. Then we have a daughter, True Virtue. She's twenty years old and works at the Municipal Health Center. By the way, that's where you're headed this afternoon, isn't it?"

Just then a full, merry laugh broke into the conversation from outside the door. The owner of the laugh burst into the room: "Oh, Mama! I just saw the funniest ..."

She stopped suddenly, suspended in mid-air. True Virtue had just spotted Bright Victory.

As for Victory, he thought he had never seen anything so entrancing in his life — this buxom, healthy young woman with her mouth still open at the last word she had said. And speechless because she had seen him!

He laughed. But he wasn't quite sure why; it could have been because he was nervous or embarrassed, or just from happiness.

"Oh! Excuse me, please!" True Virtue said. Then, to her mother: "I didn't know we had a guest." She came down to earth, as it were, and put on her for-company-in-the-house face.

That's a shame, said Victory to himself. *She's much prettier when she laughs.*

Bright Victory eased his load down in front of the black-on-white vertical sign which read from top to bottom:

DATONG MUNICIPAL HEALTH CENTER

Mr Huang had brought him in the mule cart to within two blocks of the main entrance. He explained to Bright Victory that fewer questions would be asked if he carried his things the last two blocks.

Going in, Bright Victory saw a door immediately to the right of the main gate, and on it a sign which said:

INFORMATION

Behind a table just inside the door sat a woman of about thirty, with a sharp, you-can't-put-anything-over-on-me look on her face. Victory approached, carrying his bedding in his left hand and his suitcase in his right. He reckoned this was more dignified than to bring in his baggage suspended from a carrying pole like a coolie carrying for hire.

He began: "Good afternoon," and set his baggage down outside the door.

Miss Information responded: "Good afternoon." Then, somewhat grudgingly he thought, "Come in."

Silence as Bright Victory fished out the official letter from Mine Number Three, which he presented with two-hands courtesy. Disregarding the gesture of politeness, Miss Information took the letter with one hand and gave Victory a "don't-try-old-fashioned-things-on-me" look.

"Hmmm," she said, talking to herself more than to him. "I'll have to check this out." She went, on talking to herself: "Camp Commandant, Mine No. Three .. Of the twenty-four ranks, that's uh... which level?" Her voice trailed off as she flipped through a loose-leaf notebook on the table. "Here it is, Rank No 16. That's pretty high. He has a lot of clout compared to No 20 for my boss ..."

Turning to Bright Victory she went on: "Wait a minute. I'll take this in to Director Tang." Five minutes later she returned and said: "Director says to come in."

Again carrying a piece of baggage in each hand, Victory followed Miss Information inside.

Without conventionalities, the Director began: "Hmmp! So you were sent by Camp Commandant of Mine No. Three ... Very irregular... I'll have to check this out ... Rank No 16, is he?"

A strange feeling crept over Bright Victory. Who was the winner and who was the loser in this numbers game? A class-less society — with 24 classes — How could that be?

Director Tang continued: "So you are Bright Victory Lee and you want to be a barefoot doctor, eh?"

"Yes, Comrade Director, that's true."

"Well, we run such courses only in the spring and fall — twice a year for six weeks each. But since the Camp

Commandant has sent you, we have no alternative but to accept you. Harrump! We accept you for on-the-job-training."

With that, Director tinkled a hand bell on his desk, and Miss Information appeared at the door.

Director ordered: "Call Comrade Huang."

At the name, Victory's heart skipped a beat. Could it be ...?

He had little time to wonder. The door opened again and *the* Miss Huang came in. Her face and demeanor were all businesslike, and she gave no intimation that she had ever seen Victory before.

Director Tang said: "Take Comrade Lee and show him the quarters for students." He raised his eyebrows ever so slightly in the direction of the door, and Victory knew he was dismissed. Without even a glance at Bright Victory, True Virtue picked up the rattan suitcase and walked out.

Bright Victory grabbed bedding bundle and carrying pole and followed her through the door. He was glad enough to exchange the Director's company for that of True Virtue Huang.

True Virtue and Bright Victory approached a drab yellow building topped with gray tiles. By now they were out of sight of Miss Information. Virtue said: "It's nice seeing you again."

Victory was overcome. For the first time in five years he was alone with a young woman, and she was speaking to him with kindness. Morever, she was nice looking. Tears came to his eyes. He was ashamed to wipe them away, so he blew his nose violently, hoping this would carry him through the crisis. He dared not say a word in reply, knowing his voice would crack if he tried as much as, "Nice seeing you, too." Which is what he was thinking, over and over.

But instead he put his bedding bundle down on the ground and continued to blow his nose noisily.

True Virtue set the rattan suitcase down and asked: "Do you have a cold?"

"No...no ..." The words came out muffled. "I'm ... I'm sorry. Something just struck me."

"Do you get these spells often?" True Virtue asked.

"Well, no. I haven't had one for a while."

"It's too bad to have a problem like that," she commiserated. There was an awkward silence punctuated by more nose blowing.

"I have a cousin whose little boy has fits, too," Virtue went on. "They give him asafetida, a few drops on a lump of sugar, and he holds it in his mouth until the sugar melts ... Maybe I could borrow a few drops from her. You wouldn't mind the taste and it might help you."

The prospect of asafetida-and-sugar treatment was enough to overcome Victory's reluctance to wipe his eyes; he pulled out a grimy, gray handkerchief and began to dab each eye in turn.

This sparked new concern on True Virtue's part: "Oh! The fits must have affected your eyes, too. That's like Papa. He gets his eye drops here at the Center. Just wait a minute and I'll see if I can get some for you." She turned to leave.

This was a shock treatment Victory needed. He stood up straight, took a deep breath and said: "No, no! Thank you. I'm all right now." To prove he was all right, he returned the handkerchief to his pocket and picked up the bedding bundle. With masculine fortitude he refused to notice one tear that had just slid down his cheek and was now poised on the tip of his chin, ready to drip into space.

But True Virtue noticed it. She whipped out a handkerchief and handed it to Bright Victory. How white it was compared to the dingy gray of his! As he obediently put it to his chin to wipe the recalcitrant teardrop, a gush of fragrance engulfed him, the fragrance of dried rose petals in which the handkerchief had been kept.

The feminine touch of rose-petal-fragrance was more than Bright Victory could stand, and the tears began to flow again. He dabbed his eyes dry with the fragrant handkerchief. Then with a supreme masculine effort he stood tall, took a deep breath and returned the handkerchief to True Virtue.

On her part, Virtue kept her aplomb, as if she saw males acting like this every day in the week. She took the handkerchief and stuck it in her pants pocket. Then from another pocket she pulled out a huge ring of keys and, selecting one, opened the door of the yellow building.

"I'm responsible for the inventory of furniture, equipment and supplies," she explained. "That's why I have the keys." Setting the rattan suitcase down outside the door, she went on: "Select your bed and use whatever furniture you like. It's all yours for right now. Here's a key. Supper is at 5 p.m. in the mess hall. Goodbye."

But Victory wanted to prolong the conversation; he pulled a question out of thin air: "Excuse me for asking, but what is the name of the Information lady?"

"Oh, she is Orchid Qiu. Treat her nicely — she has a lot to do with the way things are run around here."

With that, True Virtue turned and left.

Bright Victory gazed after her until she rounded the corner of a building. Then he said to himself: *A businesslike young woman. And very pretty.*

Bright Victory stepped along briskly on his first country trip as an apprentice paramedic, or "barefoot doctor". He was carrying their equipment on a shoulder pole; from one end was suspended Dr. Hua's black bag, while from the other end hung an assorted load including two thermoses of hot water, two mugs, two lunches, assorted towels and bandages and, heaviest of all, Dr. Hua's personal stool. He insisted on taking his stool on trips because, he said, "When you sit on their stools or their beds you never know what you're going to bring home with you."

Walking along a quiet country road with no one in earshot, Victory decided to ask a question that had been on his mind for some time: "Dr. Hua, I hope you won't object to me asking you, but I hear that you are a Christian ..." He let the sentence trail off. He didn't want to push. But he did want to know.

"You're right, Bright Victory," the doctor replied. "Except, change the 'are' to 'was'. I *was* a Christian before the revolution. But there's no point in being a Christian today."

"Why do you say that?"

"Don't you know the old proverb, 'when the wind blows the bamboo bows'? Well, the wind has been blowing for fifteen years now. There's no point in trying to hold your head up against the wind. I would never have landed the number two slot at Datong Health Center if I had listed myself as a Christian."

"But," pursued Victory, "I hear that you attended Christian schools in the old days ..."

"Oh, yes, I did. And I graduated from Peking Union Medical College, the outstanding Christian college for doctors, but I've got enough sense to know which side of my bread has the butter on it now."

Just then a knot of travellers overtook them, and for fear of being overheard Victory did not reply.

In a few minutes they topped a hill, and Victory's mouth dropped at the sight before him. The whole hillside looked as if it were on fire. Smoke was rising here and there from the surface of the ground, but with neither fire nor people in sight.

"What in the world!" he exclaimed, "Where ... where's the smoke coming from?"

Dr. Hua laughed. "From fires in the homes, of course."

Victory was dumbfounded: "Homes? I don't see any homes!"

The doctor laughed again. "They're all under the hill, in

caves. We'll walk across the top of the caves, then go down to the entrance on the far side of the hill."

In a few minutes they stood in front of the door to a cave house. The door itself was made of cornstalks cleverly bound together with vines. Victory lowered his fragile load carefully to the ground.

Dr. Hua shouted: "*Kai men lai!* Come, open the door."

Before the door was opened, Dr. Hua explained to his apprentice: "This family has chronic trachoma. It's an infection, but it's aggravated by the smoke inside the cave."

Someone peeked through the cracks around the door. Then, having determined who the visitors were, they began to push the door aside.

A voice from inside called: "Come in, please."

The doctor answered: "No, you come outside. The light's better out here." Then quietly to Victory: "You can't see their eyes very well inside the cave."

There seemed some hesitation inside the cave. In the meantime, Dr. Hua parked himself on his stool and opened his black bag on the ground before him, taking out bottles and arranging them on the ground in a semi-circle as if he were opening a stall at a country market.

Finally a teenage boy stepped out through the corn-stalk door. Victory was horrified to see that the large, otherwise healthy-looking boy had both eyes inflamed and swollen almost shut.

Dr. Hua said: "Victory, pull his right eye open."

Victory obeyed. He pulled the lower lid down and the upper lid up, being as careful as he could not to touch the infected areas. Dr. Hua put two drops of sulfadiazine in the right eye, then two drops in the left eye.

The boy blinked several times, then blew his nose with his thumb pressing first on one side of his nose then on the other.

"Tell the next person to come out," ordered the doctor.

After a few minutes an older man came through the corn-stalk door. Symptoms, the same. Treatment, the same.

Again, after some delay inside, an older woman appeared. Symptoms, the same. Treatment, the same.

After treating six people the doctor shouted: "Anybody else inside?"

"No, nobody," came the answer.

"Here, Victory," said the doctor, "wet this towel with a little rubbing alcohol and wipe your hands. You touched their skin. Maybe you noticed I did not."

After wiping his hands, Victory took notebook and penc.. out of his pocket and wrote down "Symptoms: such and such. Treatment: so and so." Then, as he collected the paraphernalia, he asked: "There's one thing I didn't understand; why didn't they all come out at once to be treated? Why this one-by-one business?"

"Oh, you noticed that. And did you notice that when the boy went back inside it was a couple of minutes before the next person came out?"

"Why, yes, I did notice that."

"Well, Victory, it's like this: These people are so poor they have only one presentable pair of pants in the family, so they took turns wearing the pants when they came out to be treated. They wasted our time but they saved their self-respect."

As the day wore on, Dr. Hua treated many cases of trachoma but also tuberculosis, syphilis, a broken leg, rheumatism, strep throat, all at no charge except for the medicine used and that was only a few bits of paper money. The whole operation, Victory learned, was highly subsidized by the government.

The old man with the broken leg could not come outside to be treated, so for the first time that day the doctor and Victory went inside. As they entered there was a scurry of bodies disappearing into the inner room of the cave. Victory's eyes had not adjusted to the semi-darkness, and he sensed rather than saw that they were people, people who apparently wanted to get away from the two strangers. He was surprised at this, since people are always curious about how a doctor treats a patient, and there is no privacy about doctor-patient relationships. Why should there be, when illness is not only a personal but a family affair?

The cast had already been removed from the old man's leg, but he was complaining of pain. This time the doctor did touch the patient, first pushing the trouser leg up beyond the point of fracture. As he did so, Victory noticed that the cloth gave way under the doctor's touch, quietly, without the sound of tearing, as if the garment had already perished on the wearer and was just falling apart.

After leaving the cave, Victory asked Dr. Hua: "Why was it, when we first went in, that the family disappeared into the back of the cave?"

"Son, you've got a lot to learn. Those people were ashamed of the way they were dressed. Just about the only things they had on were sacks and burlap bags."

Bright Victory applied for and got a Sunday off, so he sent word by True Virtue to her parents that the day was free. How pleased he was when word came back, "Come over and spend the day with us."

Sunday dawned hot, as hot as only an August day in North China can be. Victory had been given six brown eggs by a patient's grateful family, and these he placed in the center of his best handkerchief, carefully tying the opposite corners together to make a handy carrier for the precious eggs. With these as a gift for the Huang family, he set out with a lighter heart than he had known for five years.

As he walked he looked down at his hands and breathed: "Thank you, dear Lord, that I can wash my hands with soap and that the blackness and sores are disappearing."

Then with a pang he thought of his friends in Mine

Number Three — especially Pastor Ling — who still had no soap to wash their hands with.

The day with the Huangs was joyous. Victory even had the luxury of a nap after lunch in the shade of the grape arbor in the Huang's tiny yard. The only incompleteness about the day was that Virtue was on duty at the Health Department and did not arrive home until 6 p.m. That was in good time, however, for a leisurely evening meal. How contented Victory was just to sit beside her at the table!

The big event of the day was the church service in the evening. It was more private in the evening, Mr. Huang explained, now that their old church building had been converted into a pencil factory. Also, not many people could get time from their jobs for a daytime meeting.

For the first time in five years Victory was going to church! But the Huangs were cautious about how they arrived at the meeting place. It would not do for as many as four people to arrive together, so Mrs. Huang walked with True Virtue, and her husband and Victory followed two hundred yards behind.

The meeting place was a private house built around a courtyard. When the Huangs and Victory arrived, one of the men was teaching a hymn. He had neither instrument nor hymnbook; he would sing a line of the hymn, then all would follow and sing the line together. After going over the hymn three times in this way they sang the entire stanza.

Bright Victory looked around at the courtyard packed with people. There were no chairs or benches; everybody stood. Many fanned themselves vigorously, as the courtyard was close and airless in the evening heat.

After a few minutes the leader called the meeting to order. The only Bible seemed to be in the hands of the leader, who read by the light of a candle. During the prayer time everyone prayed aloud. It was the same order-in-seeming-chaos that Victory was familiar with from Shanghai. In closing the leader gave a mighty "Amen!" and in response everyone in the congregation joined together in a still more mighty "Amen!" For his part, Victory finished his prayer before those around him were halfway through. Perhaps his curiosity got the better of his piety — he wanted to know what these fellow-believers in North China were praying about. He heard several pray: "Lord, be with us tonight. Keep our meeting from being interrupted."

The text of the sermon was, "We ought to obey God rather than men." The speaker declared that the closing of the downtown church was "of and by men", even though done by the Three-Self Patriotic Movement, the state-recognized church, in the name of God.

"On the contrary," the speaker continued, "our meeting in this place is of and by God. The fires of persecution cannot consume the church of God."

In closing, the speaker quoted an old Chinese proverb: "in no prairie fire do the seeds perish; see, their new blades shoot forth amid the spring breezes."

20. Earthquake!
Summer 1965

ONE MORNING, before dawn, Bright Victory was awakened by his bed shaking. He thought someone was trying to wake him, and asked sleepily: "Hello! What do you want?"

No one answered, but the shaking continued. He flicked on his flashlight to see a crazy sight — all the beds in the dormitory were moving back and forth. Then he heard the rattling of the beds and creaking of the rafters.

"Earthquake!" he shouted. There was no one to hear, of course. But that did not keep him from shouting again: "Earthquake!" He ran out of the building, taking with him only the flashlight to show the way. But by the time he reached the outside, the tremor had stopped. He looked at the roofs of the buildings. All were intact.

"No great deal," Victory said to himself. "The epicenter must have been somewhere else." As he went back to bed, little did he know how much that earthquake had shaken his life and changed the course of it.

Early that afternoon Victory was helping Dr. Hua in the outpatients' department when Orchid Qiu came with a note handwritten by Director Tang himself: "Come to the office at once. Do not delay."

"What's up?" Victory asked Orchid.

"How am I to know? Go and find out," she responded.

Arriving at the Director's office, Victory found him busily consulting the loose-leaf notebook that spelled out the "numbers game." He left Victory's arrival unacknowledged, unless a twitch of the eyebrow could mean, "Okay. You're here." He was too busy talking to himself: "Let's see.

'Administrator of Emergencies, Main Office, Bureau of Public Health, Beijing.' Now, what's his rank? Oh, here it is! Number 13. That's two higher than Camp Commandant of Mine Number Three. So I'll be safe in sending Lee off...."

With that, Director slammed the notebook shut and turned to Victory: "I have received an order to release one person to join a medical team to help the earthquake victims in southwest Hebei Province. The team forms tomorrow at Handan and leaves for the epicenter of the earthquake area day after tomorrow. I called the railway station to reserve a hard-sleeper berth on the night train to Taiyuan. Go to Information and pick up your papers and travel money."

Bright Victory asked: "Is that all, Comrade Director?"

"That's all." With the raising of one eyebrow, Director ushered him out.

Once outside the door, he paused, trying to take in the turn of events. He shook his head sharply, as if to clear cobwebs away from before his eyes, and then prayed in his heart: *"Lord, give me wisdom, I don't want to make a mistake right now!"*

Orchid Qiu was extraordinarily helpful: "Come back in twenty minutes. I'll have your papers and money ready."

Next Victory dashed back to the outpatients' department and told Dr. Hua what had happened. To his surprise, the old man said quietly: "God bless you, son."

Then Victory went to True Virtue Huang's office. No one else was around. To his great surprise she walked over, said "Goodbye", and then added, putting her hand lightly on his arm: "I'll see you again."

Among the chits ready for him at Information was one to the Police Precinct, authorizing them to surrender his residence certificate "in view of indefinite absence on official business."

Back in the dormitory Victory threw everything he owned into his rattan suitcase, rolled up his bedding, and left by the back door of the compound.

At the Police Precinct the sergeant looked at Victory's orders: "Hmmp! 'Indefinite absence on official business' is it?" Then I'd better give you all the papers I have here."

With that, he handed over both Victory's local residence certificate and — much to his surprise — his Shanghai residence certificate which he had not had in his possession for five years!

On the boarding platform at the station, Victory looked down the tracks at the rusty old car marked "Hard Seats", the class he had arrived on five years before, and compared it with the quite respectable car he had a ticket for, marked "Hard Sleeper."

He said to himself: *I arrived Third Class and I'm leaving Second Class. Make me worthy, Lord, of your hitching me up a peg.*

Late the following afternoon Bright Victory's train approached Handan. He could see more and more destruction from the earthquake, and the train itself was running slowly because of emergency repairs to the track. When they finally drew into Handan, he was shocked to see the station building a mass of bricks, rafters and tiles with workers salvaging the wreckage piece by piece. Confronting him was a sign hastily written in large characters: "Rescue personnel from outlying areas report at south end of platform."

That night Victory, along with dozens of doctors, nurses, paramedics and other workers, bunked down on the floor of a school building. The following morning the eight members of his team gathered, ready to set out for the Chang Family Village ten miles west of Handan. All eight — two doctors, two nurses, two carriers, a woman they called "housekeeper", and himself — were loaded with medicines, bandages, wash basins, towels, soap, stethoscopes, splints and food, beside their own clothes and bedding.

"Where's our truck?" Victory asked Dr. Hei, the doctor in charge.

"There is no truck," he replied. "The bridges have all collapsed and no truck can get through. We're walking."

Victory looked at his load and was glad for the practice of the last two months, carrying Dr. Hua's medicines and stool around the Datong countryside. But ten miles! Could he make it? Then he looked at the two doctors, one of them a woman, with backpacks almost as heavy as his own load, and he felt a little ashamed of his self-pity.

Weary of body and blistered of foot, the eight arrived at Chang Family Village at 3 p.m., having seen such devastation along the way as Bright Victory had never imagined. Many times people pled with them to stop and give medical aid, but the doctor-leader was adamant: "Another team has been assigned to your place."

They found that the elementary school in Chang Family Village was not occupied, except by rubble of collapsed roof and crushed desks and benches. "Clear a space now for your bedding," ordered the leader. "You'll be dead tired when you finally get to bed tonight."

Victory chose a place up against the one remaining wall of the building, a thick wall of tamped earth which looked solid. He reckoned that this would give him some privacy for prayer, and congratulated himself on being able to make his own decision about where to sleep. He stretched out on his bedding for a few minutes before Dr. Hei called for all to go out on their first mercy mission.

Victory noticed that the woman called "Housekeeper" stayed behind. He asked the leader: "Why is Housekeeper not coming with us?"

"Oh," responded Dr. Hei, "that's the way these teams are set up. One person stays behind, looks after our things and cooks the meals for us."

Bright Victory nodded: "That makes sense.."

Chang Family Village was near the epicenter of the earthquake, and the destruction and casualties were unbelievable. Every building in the village had been flattened. Broken tiles lay everywhere. Timbers stuck up at strange angles. The people were still digging dead bodies out of the ruins, while householders rummaged through what had once been their homes, to salvage what they could. Every family that was still alive was camping in the streets, which blocked traffic and reduced the able-bodied almost to immobility.

The injured lay in the streets on makeshift stretchers and pallets, some with head wounds from collapsing roofs, others with cuts, bruises or broken bones. The doctors took the more serious patients, leaving the nurses and Victory to give first aid to those less badly hurt.

Darkness fell before they had worked a hundred yards along the main street of the village. By flashlight they picked their way wearily back to the school building.

Walking beside Victory, Dr. Hei remarked: "It's fortunate the center of the quake was a rural area. If it had been a city like Beijing, millions could have died ... And even here we must be prepared for aftershocks. They can be about as bad as the original quake."

Victory could not know it then, but some ten years later he was to see even greater destruction in a heavily-populated city, Tangshan in northeast Hebei Province, where three-quarters of a million people died in a cataclysmic earthquake such as human history had perhaps never recorded up to that time.

Arriving dead tired at the camp, Victory went direct to his pallet to rest before supper. That is, he went to the place where he had laid out his pallet. To his surprise, it was not there. Exhausted, he was in no mood to start looking for stolen bedding. The woman called "Housekeeper" was in the middle of dishing up stir-fried vegetables from the wok, and had a "don't-bother-me-now" look on her face. But Victory was intent on finding his bedding, and here was the one person who should know about it. So he blurted out: "Can you tell me where my bedding is?"

Housekeeper replied: "Don't bother me now! Can't you see I'm busy? I'll tell you later."

Hot words rose to Victory's lips: "Just tell me, can't you? You were the only person around and you're supposed to..."

Waving the wrought iron vegetable turner menacingly, Housekeeper shouted back: "I told you I'm busy! Get out of my way or I'll sock you one with this!"

The woman doctor, hearing the commotion, ran over and pushed herself between the two. Sensing that Housekeeper was higher in the pecking order than a mere paramedic, she turned on Victory and said: "Just let her alone. Let her get the food on the table. You can talk with her later about your problem."

Abashed at being thwarted by two women, Victory turned away from them and stalked angrily out into the darkness. The two women let him go. They were tired and frustrated, too, but he didn't think of that. His dominant thought at this point was that he had lost face — and before two women! For the moment the loss of face drove from his mind the loss of his bedding.

Bang! Bang! Bang! Bang! The beating of a wooden spoon on an aluminum pot broke into Victory's thoughts. At the prospect of food, other matters receded somewhat into the background, and he rather sheepishly started back toward the circle of light. In doing so he caught his foot on something and, looking down, saw it was none other than his lost bedding bundle, thrown down carelessly near the bedding of the others in the team.

After supper Victory sought out Housekeeper. He felt half abject, half resentful, and started off by apologizing: "Comrade, I'm sorry I spoke to you inappropriately." But then his anger took over and he went on: "But I do want my bed back by that wall!"

Housekeeper was ready to vent her pent-up feelings, too: "You bare-foot doctors! You are neither bare-foot nor doctor! You are too proud for words! It got under my skin when I saw your pallet off to one side and not with the rest of us — why are you so proud?"

"If you had asked me I could have told you why I made my bed over by the wall..."

"I didn't ask you then and I'm not going to ask you now! You ought to know that I'm in charge of living arrangements here. I put your bed with the crowd and it's going to stay with the crowd! Do you hear me?"

With that, Housekeeper turned on her heel and stalked off in a huff. Victory stood there, nonplussed. The same anger that had welled up in his heart a half-hour earlier was boiling again, only worse. He, too, spun around and walked away, in the opposite direction. He still had enough sense to put physical distance between himself and the object of his anger.

The night air cooled him down a bit. But what really cooled him down was suddenly recalling some parts of the Bible that old Pastor Ling was fond of reading aloud down in the bowels of the earth at Mine Number Three. Victory could hear the old man's intonation: "Why do you not rather take wrong? ....Whosoever shall smite you on the right cheek, turn the other side....If it be possible, as much as lies in you, live peaceably with all men."

The memory of those words and the expression on Pastor Ling's face as he read them did something to Victory. He bowed his head and said: "Dear God, I'm sorry. I've made a fool of myself. I'll try not to do it again."

By this time his heart had stopped beating so fast. He turned around, rolled out his bedding in the place Housekeeper had put it, and stretched out on it. Before long he was sound asleep.

About midnight the earth began to shake violently. Victory sat up abruptly, grabbed his flashlight, and just happened to have it spotted on the one remaining wall of the school building when with a mighty roar it crashed inward. Dirt, tiles and bits of wood landed among the team. The floor where he had stretched out his bedding a few hours before was completely crushed, and was now covered by an awesome pile of dirt and debris.

A humbled and chastened Bright Victory bowed his head and said: "Thank you, Lord. You saved me in spite of myself."

The following morning the team began again to work its way down the main street of the village. As it did so, Victory noticed that internal tensions were not the sole prerogative of the medical team, but were also surfacing among the local people. The team had hardly begun work when a commotion broke out down the street.

Dr. Hei ordered Victory: "Go down there and find out what the trouble is."

It did not take long. A young woman dashed up to him with tears running down her face, and she yelled hysterically, almost in his ear: "I'm bringing my baby up here. He's bad. He can't wait. You've got to take care of him now!"

Before Victory could answer, however, another woman stepped up, grabbed the young woman by the shoulders and pushed her backwards. She hissed: "Get back in your place! Don't try to butt in before us!"

Then a middle-aged woman tugged Victory's sleeve and pled: "Come over here and treat my mother! She's about to die!"

Victory saw at once that keeping order among the injured — or rather among the relatives of the injured — was going to be a major problem. It was a raw and elementary human equation: everyone wanted his own family attended to first and no one wanted to wait while someone else's family was cared for.

Dr. Hei appealed to the local chief of police to maintain order. But as the morning wore on tensions increased, and by noon the hot sun had exacerbated the situation. Patience was in short supply, tempers became more and more inflamed.

One particularly belligerent man grabbed Dr. Hei's arm and shouted: "You've got to go down there and see my little boy right now!"

The doctor shook him off: "I can only do one thing at a time. You'll have to wait your turn!"

In the class-conscious countryside, such a word from a person as high up the scale as a doctor would normally put a man in his place. But in Chang Family Village that morning circumstances were not normal.

Wild-eyed, the man looked quickly around and spied a meat cleaver that someone had salvaged from their kitchen. It was hanging on a pole supporting a makeshift tent. He grabbed the meat cleaver, lifted it high over his head, and lunged forward. The doctor had turned his back and was bending over a patient, oblivious to the danger.

Nearby, Bright Victory had just straightened up to take a breath of fresh air when he saw the man hurtling toward Dr. Hei, cleaver held high. With a leap, he jumped over the patient he was attending to and landed beside the doctor and in front of the attacker.

Shouting "*Wei!*" to attract Dr. Hei's attention, Victory thrust up his hand and grabbed the man's wrist, striking it with such force that the cleaver flew from the man's hand. Unfortunately, it flew straight up into the air then, like a thick arrow, straight down again. Its sharp point descended toward Victory as if guided by some malignant spirit, and struck him just below the knee, slicing through his trousers and into the flesh of his leg. He doubled up with the sudden pain and collapsed on the ground, inadvertently sitting on the cleaver itself.

Angered still more by being foiled in his attack on the doctor, the man looked around for his weapon, and of course could not see it. But he did see Victory on the ground, now defenceless, and began kicking him in the stomach and chest. A number of villagers closed in on the man and overpowered him. In a minute a policeman, shouting "Make way! Make way!" pushed through the crowd, put handcuffs on the man and took him away.

Bright Victory tried to stagger to his feet, then collapsed in a heap again with pain and loss of blood.

Dr. Hei acted quickly. He stretched Victory out on the ground, slit his trouser leg open, grabbed several absorbent pads from his box and slapped them on the wound. Then he pressed down firmly on the pads and tied them in place with a bandage around the leg. In a few minutes both pads and bandage were red with blood, so he added more pads on the top of these already saturated and tied the bandage tight again. With a jacket borrowed from a villager and folded over several times he made a pillow for Victory's head. Then he took a bench and elevated the leg. Finally, he had a villager readjust a bedspread, doing duty as a temporary tent, so as to keep the sun off Victory.

By this time Victory had lost a fair amount of blood. He was also thirsty, and a villager brought boiled water for him to drink. The doctor gave him four aspirin to relieve the pain.

After making Victory as comfortable as possible, Dr. Hei ordered a couple of bystanders to fetch the leader of the commune of which the village was a part. Before long the leader appeared, distress and fear written across his face. The messengers had told him what had happened, and he feared what power the doctor — straight from Beijing — might wield in this obscure village.

The doctor recounted what happened, then went on: "Look here! One of my team is seriously wounded, and I myself might have been killed. I want you to gather your work brigade foremen together and tell them that if your people continue to be disorderly — and especially if *this* happens again — we will pack up and leave your village at once!"

The commune leader literally shook. This ultimatum could mean not only the loss of medical help during the emergency, but the loss of his job and rank as well. With the latter possibility uppermost in his mind, perhaps, he hastily assembled all work brigade foremen and laid down strict orders: "Every one of you must keep his people under control. No more getting out of line. Wait until the medicos arrive to treat your sick and injured."

For Victory the price paid was high, but his injury did insure orderly and effective work by the medical team from that point on. He remembered the Old Testament stories about the sacrificial lamb, and concluded: "Well, at this time and place I guess I'm the sacrificial lamb."

One result of the meat-cleaver incident was to immobilize Bright Victory and keep him at camp. Ironically this meant that, while the team was at work, he and Housekeeper were constant companions. And Housekeeper was the one person in the team he had had a falling out with.

This did not bother Victory, however, and the next morning the others had hardly left camp when he said to Housekeeper: "I hate having nothing to do. If I could chop up some vegetables for you, just let me have them."

"Hmmp! You mean you want to help me? After the hard time I gave you the other day?"

He laughed out loud: "Well, it's a good thing you won that argument. I could have won the argument but lost my life. Of the two, I think I would rather lose the argument."

It was Housekeeper's turn to laugh, and Victory joined in. He felt that to bring their difference out into the open and talk about it was like opening a door and letting the sun shine into a dark room.

When she stopped laughing, Housekeeper turned quite serious. With arms akimbo she said: "I hope you don't mind my saying so, but you are almost acting like a Christian."

Victory laughed again. "Thank you for the compliment. As a matter of fact, I am a Christian."

Housekeeper continued in a serious mood: "You know, the Christians have suffered a lot. Some of my neighbors are Christians. They have suffered, but somehow they don't complain about it."

There was a lull in the conversation.

Then Victory said: "Please hand me the vegetables and I'll get busy chopping them up."

Bright Victory's leg healed up quickly. Dr. Hei gave him penicillin tablets to head off infection and an injection to prevent tetanus. However, the place where he had been kicked in the side was more and more painful. "The trouble is," the doctor analyzed it, "that guy who kicked you was wearing a pair of old Japanese army boots. They're heavy and tough, not like the straw sandals most peasants wear. You may have a cracked rib."

When after two days the pain in his side continued to get worse, Dr. Hei became worried. "You may have internal injuries," he said, "I'm going to send you to Beijing for X-rays and treatment. After all, I'll never be able to repay you for saving my life."

The big problem was how to cover the ten miles to the railway station at Handan. Dr. Hei detailed one of the carriers to go with Victory and carry his rattan suitcase and bedding roll. By slow walking and frequent resting they made it to the point where the bridges had been repaired and the buses were running.

At the ticket counter in the train station, Victory opened the envelope Dr. Hei had given him with travel money, letter of introduction and travel pass. To his surprise, he also found a note:

"As a token of my gratitude to you, I have enclosed not only your official travel money for a 'Hard Berth' to Beijing but also enough extra from my personal funds for a 'Soft Berth' ticket. Have a comfortable trip."

Later that afternoon the train for Beijing puffed into Handan station. Victory looked down the train at the "Hard Seat" cars, then at the "Hard Berth" cars. His companion carried his baggage aboard the "Soft Berth" car and helped him find his berth. Victory stretched out luxuriously, and breathed a prayer: "I arrived here Second Class and I'm leaving First Class. Thank you, Lord, for hitching me up another peg."

At 8 o'clock the following morning the train pulled sedately into the main Beijing Railway Station. Bright Victory was so excited at arriving in the great northern capital, redolent of China's long history and the 24 emperors who had ruled from there, that he almost forgot the pain in his side. When he lifted his suitcase, however, a jab of pain jarred him into the present. He was glad enough to surrender his baggage to a porter.

Victory stood in line for a motor tricycle taxi, and in the Beijing dialect which he had picked up at Mine Number Three told the driver to take him to the Sixth Municipal Hospital. His Shanghai dialect had been forced into cold storage ever since he set foot in North China.

After some waiting for an additional passenger going to the same section of the city, they started off. Now Victory suffered not only from the pain of plunging and jerking along the streets in the three-wheeled vehicle, but also from the claustrophobia induced by the completely enclosed sides.

Arriving at the hospital, Victory was amazed and delighted at the "open sesame" his letter of introduction proved to be. The doctor who took over his case knew the introducer personally — and such relationship can spell the difference between life and death, even in ostensibly egalitarian Communist China. He received almost VIP treatment. But deflation came with the X-ray report: "A rib is broken and has punctured the right lung."

21. Enter The Red Guards
Shanghai, Summer 1966

"LONG LIVE THE GREAT CULTURAL REVOLUTION!"

Marching students shouted the slogan. Clenched fists raised to the sky punctuated each shout with a vehement exclamation mark.

Then, in unison, they switched to other slogans: "To rebel is right! Bombard the headquarters! Down with the Four Olds!"

Bright Loyalty Lee and his fellow-worker Mighty Tower Gou stood poker-faced on Nanjing Road, watching students march past eight abreast and listening to the slogans. The thousands of marchers were flooding the whole street — downtown Shanghai's main artery. Traffic had been diverted to other streets.

As Bright Loyalty and Mighty Tower walked back to their dormitory, darkness descended on Shanghai. Darkness descended, too, on Bright Loyalty's troubled mind, for he was disturbed and mystified by what he had seen and heard. The two young men were the same age, 28, but Mighty Tower seemed to know more about things than Loyalty. If only he were a Christian too! Now Loyalty plied his friend with questions:

"'To rebel is right'. How do you figure that out? I thought we were supposed to obey, not to rebel."

Mighty Tower answered: "Well, Chairman Mao doesn't want people to rebel against him, of course. But to rebel against someone else — that's great."

"And what's this business about 'the four olds'?"

"Oh, that's easy. They mean old thought, old culture, old customs, old habits. Anything from before is bad, so they say."

Bright Loyalty went on: "'Bombard the headquarters'. What does that mean?"

"Maybe it means the Communist Party members who are against Chairman Mao — the revisionists, he calls them."

"But how can anybody 'bombard' anybody else? It takes an army and big guns to bombard something."

"Maybe that's what Chairman Mao has in mind ... Maybe we're headed for civil war."

Bright Loyalty pursued, in such low tones that Mighty Tower could hardly hear him: "How did all this get started, anyway? Do you know?"

"It really started with the play that Deputy Mayor Wu Han wrote, *Hai Jui Dismissed from Office*. In the play he called the official Hai Jui, but it was really Marshal Peng Dehuai. You remember, Chairman Mao sacked Peng after he criticized the Chairman about the Great Leap Forward. That play was too much for Mao to stomach, and he stirred the students to demonstrate in the street. Like we saw today. Mao thinks the country is full of revisionists ..."

"What do you mean, 'revisionists'?"

"Basically," Mighty Tower replied, "they are the officials who don't agree with Chairman Mao over the Commune System, the Hundred Flowers and the Great Leap Forward. They say all those campaigns were impractical and doctrinaire."

Loyalty interjected: "Well, they were impractical and doctrinaire, weren't they?"

"Shush! Don't say that out loud!"

"But," pursued Loyalty, "Liu Shaoqi and others are saying those things. Is it wrong for me to say them?"

The two young men had arrived at a stretch of sidewalk with few other pedestrians. Taking Loyalty's arm so that he could walk in step with him, Mighty Tower put his mouth close to his friend's ear and whispered: "Can't you see? It's a power struggle between Mao on one side and many of the other top brass on the other."

"Where does Zhou Enlai fit into the picture?"

"He's the smartest of all," Mighty Tower replied. "He plays on both teams at once. No matter which side comes out on top, he's a winner."

Excited at the inside information, Loyalty unconsciously gave his friend a shove and interrupted: "Say! How do you know all this stuff?"

Mighty Tower grabbed Bright Loyalty's arm again and renewed his whispering: "That's simple: My uncle is a clerk in the office of Deputy Mayor Wu. All the official communications come across his desk. Not long back there was a letter written by Mao Zedong himself, telling Wu to take that play about Hai Jui out of the theater or else suffer the consequences. My uncle never could keep a secret, especially a juicy one. But you and I had better keep our mouths shut. Understand?"

Bright Loyalty Lee stared in disbelief at the public notice, written in the largest characters he had ever seen on the bulletin board of his commune, the Golden Streams Weaving Factory:

"The entire factory will close tomorrow afternoon, August 21, 1966. All comrades will assemble on the drill ground at 1 p.m. to receive instructions from students.

(signed) Ye Ming, Manager
Golden Streams Weaving Factory."

As he turned away from the notice Loyalty shook his head in confusion. *Students? ....instruction? ....factory closed? ...* Abruptly, he controlled himself, and walked resolutely toward the dormitory. After all, would someone see him shaking his head? And would that motion be interpreted as dissent to a public announcement? And how long before supposed dissent could sink a man into deep trouble?

Arriving at the dormitory, Loyalty saw that Mighty Tower was the only person there.

He blurted out: "Tower, you can't guess what's just been

written up in big characters on the bulletin board. It says...

Mighty Tower interrupted him: "Yes, I know what it says. And you and I are going to be involved whether we like it or not. This note just came from the office. Look!"

Loyalty took the sheet of paper that Tower shoved at him. It had been printed on a gelatin duplicator, in a hurry. But it also bore the chop of Ye Ming, the manager, in glaring red ink; it was official.

"The following will appear at my office at 7.30 p.m. tonight. They will be excused from political studies at that time.

(signed)Ye Ming, Manager
Golden Streams Weaving Factory."

After the signature and chop appeared twelve names, including office workers, a cook, Teacher Ran from the primary school connected with the factory, and both Bright Loyalty Lee and Mighty Tower Gou from the men's dormitory.

Never before had Bright Loyalty seen such seriousness on the Manager's face, nor heard that slight tremor in his voice as he spoke to the twelve people assembled.

"Comrades," he addressed them, "we are seeing a change here in Shanghai. There is no point in hiding from you that we have been thrown right into the middle of that change. Rather — tomorrow afternoon we will be thrown into the middle of it."

The Manager paused for a moment as if to digest what he himself had said. He cleared his throat noisily and went on: "Tomorrow the students are coming. To lecture us. The actual word on the communique is 'to teach you'."

The Manager shuddered ever so slightly. The word "teach" was the word used of instructing criminal elements with a view to reforming them.

He continued: "How many students are coming I do not

know. It could be three or three hundred. What they are going to say I can only guess. Probably an enlargement on their slogans we heard the other day on Nanjing Road."

By this time the Manager was stammering, which was very out of character for him, confirmed Communist Party member that he was. With an effort he controlled himself and got down to the business in hand: "You twelve are the Reception Committee. Make yourselves red arm bands like theirs but instead of the words 'Red Guard' write 'Host' on yours. Buy tea and candy. Be ready to meet them at the main gate at noon. Much may depend on how you receive them on behalf of the factory."

The Manager paused irresolutely. With that uncharacteristic tremor in his voice he went on: "The more you fellow-workers know about the situation the better you will be able to meet it. This factory is directly under the municipal government of the City of Shanghai. Unfortunately, the city officials have recently taken a road displeasing to the authorities in Beijing. Rumor has it that the Red Guards are functioning directly on the orders of Chairman Mao and that they will close down every unit operated by the City of Shanghai — including this factory."

By this time the tremor was so pronounced that the Manager could hardly get the words out. His face was wet with perspiration. He swallowed twice and began again: "So, we are caught between the devil and the deep blue sea. Chairman Mao says: 'The students are my arm and hand, and when you follow them you follow me'. He also says: 'Political power grows out of the barrel of a gun'. He heads the armed forces. We have no alternative but to follow him. And that means to follow the students with the 'Red Guard' arm bands."

Twelve noon saw the Reception Committee lined up at the

main gate of Golden Streams Weaving Factory. Each man and woman wore a red arm band, which from a distance appeared to be Red Guard bands. Only a closer view revealed that instead of the characters "Red Guard" there were the totally innocuous characters, "Host".

At 12:15 the first Red Guards appeared, four of them, arms locked and walking in step. They halted in front of the main gate some twenty feet from the Reception Committee, red arm bands shining all the redder in the noonday sun.

Bright Loyalty Lee stepped over to the group and said: "Good afternoon. Won't you please come in?"

The reply was curt: "No! Not until our leader arrives!"

With that the spokesman turned his back on Bright Loyalty, and the other three followed suit. At 12:45 eight more Red Guards arrived, in step four abreast.

Bright Loyalty stepped out and greeted them as he had done before: "Welcome to Golden Streams Weaving Factory. Won't you come in?"

"Cut out that bourgeois 'welcome' business!" came the blunt response. "Of course we are welcome. We invited ourselves to come."

Holding down the resentment that welled up in him at their rudeness, Loyalty continued: "Come into our reception hall. It is still a little time before the meeting."

The twelve Red Guards strode through the main gate and straight into the reception hall, not waiting to be ushered in. Loyalty and the others on the committee followed, cowed by their overbearing attitude.

Inside the reception hall, Loyalty said: "Please be seated."

"No, we'll stand."

Outwardly unabashed, he pursued, waving to the big table in the center of the room: "Please sit down and have some tea."

The Red Guard leader approached to within six inches of Loyalty's face and spat out the words: "Now listen to me! No more of this feudalistic, decadent, bourgeois stuff! We will not sit down. We will not drink tea. Not even hot water. Now! Show me where the meeting will be held!"

Keeping as pleasant a face as he could manage, Loyalty led the way to the drill ground. Like dogs with their tails between their legs the others on the committee followed. Some were wondering if the stammering factory manager could endure the insolence of the Red Guards. Those of more practical turn of mind were thinking of the pots of nice fragrant tea going to waste in the reception hall.

Arriving at the drill ground, Loyalty pointed out: "Here is a wooden table you can use for a platform. There is a microphone and a stand..."

"Where's your manager?" the Red Guard leader broke in.

"He'll be here shortly and chair the meeting."

"Who asked him to chair the meeting?" was the sharp rejoinder. "That's a bourgeois practice. It's condemned with the Four Olds!"

At five minutes of one the gateman struck a length of suspended railway rail with a hammer. Workers, office employees and cadres poured out of dormitories, offices and mess hall, and within three minutes the drill ground was a sea of people. By this time dozens more Red Guards had arrived. Loyalty noted how they scattered themselves out among the factory people.

Without introduction and without formalities the Red Guard leader leaped onto the table and shouted into the microphone: "Down with the Four Olds!"

The slogan was a cue for a concerted audience response. The Red Guards all shouted in unison: "Down with the Four Olds!"

Again from the leader: "Long live the Great Cultural Revolution!"

Again from the crowd: "Long live the Great Cultural Revolution!"

By now the factory people were catching on. A few had

joined in on the second slogan. Now came the third: "Long live Chairman Mao!"

This time the response was a great crescendo from almost every mouth on the drill ground: "Long live Chairman Mao!"

As suddenly as he had exploded with the slogans the leader backed away from them, and spoke in a conciliatory and sincere tone: "We are not here today to shout slogans. We are here to explain to you what the Great Proletarian Cultural Revolution is all about, just as Chairman Mao explained to us in person in Tiananmen Square in Beijing. I come to you therefore in his name and in the name of our Great Chinese People's Revolution."

Applause burst out across the drill ground.

The speaker then listed the "olds" to be done away with — old thoughts, culture, customs, habits. He concluded: "The first target we will hit is the teachers — from day care up to university — for these people poison the minds of the young."

Again came deafening applause. *Is this all spontaneous?* mused Bright Loyalty, who had gradually worked his way from the platform toward the back of the crowd. *Is that applause real? Or is it a new bandwagon people are scrambling onto?*

As soon as the third speaker was finished, Loyalty retreated to the dormitory. The Red Guards had made a farce of the Reception Committee; he was obviously not needed. Exhausted both physically and emotionally, he flopped onto his bunk and dropped off to sleep. He awoke to find Mighty Tower shaking him and hissing into his ear: "Loyalty! Loyalty! Get up! Come quick!"

Mighty Tower led Bright Loyalty across the drill ground toward the factory's primary school. From a distance they could see a crowd around the teachers' living quarters adjacent to the school, especially thick at the door of one room. As Tower and Loyalty drew nearer they saw the reason for the crowd. All eyes were fixed on a dead cat, impaled with a long nail high in the center of the door of Teacher Ran's bedroom.

Coming up to the group, Bright Loyalty stared in disbelief at the dead cat. It stared back at him with horror written in its gray eyes. Its tongue had been cut out and was hanging from its jaw by a sliver of flesh.

The two men rushed past the dead cat into Teacher Ran's room. Disorder met their gaze. Books were scattered all over the floor, mixed with papers, pens, pencils, ink bottles, shattered cups and dishes, torn clothing, lamps and students' exercise books. Furniture was overturned, a clock had been smashed, bedding was dumped in a corner, and house slippers and shoes were thrown onto the kitchen stove.

Teacher Ran was not there. But it seemed that everybody else was, "three Teos and four Lees", as the saying is, going in and out at will and helping themselves to this and that from the wreckage. Loyalty was shocked to see such casual theft of Teacher Ran's belongings. He stopped a teenager who had just pocketed a pair of white socks, after first carefully matching them to see that they were a pair, and demanded: "What do you mean, helping yourself to Teacher Ran's things?"

The teenager replied casually: "Oh, I'm just picking up some souvenirs. The Red Guards have already gone with everything worth taking."

The Red Guards had left something behind, however. A new slogan was freshly printed in huge characters on the whitewashed wall with one of Teacher Ran's own colored chalks:

"Down with the Four Olds! Old Thoughts, Old Culture, Old Customs, Old Habits!"

As he looked at the disaster and disorder around him, little did Loyalty realize that nine days later he would see his own home in equal disarray.

But he did suddenly awake to the fact that somebody should do something about this catastrophe. He ran to the factory office to find someone high enough on the totem pole of authority to stop the stealing. As luck would have it, the factory secretary was just locking up for the night. Loyalty blurted out without the usual formalities: "Quick! Bring the Manager's seal and strips of paper to seal up Teacher Ran's apartment! Her stuff is all being walked off with!"

"Don't be in such a hurry, young man!" replied the secretary. "What's the trouble?"

In a few short sentences Loyalty explained, and the more he told the lower the secretary's face dropped. Grasping the situation quickly, he dashed back into the office, opened the safe and took out the little black box with the Manager's chop and red ink in it. On the way back to the door he grabbed a sheet of paper and a pot of paste. Then he and Loyalty ran across the compound to the teacher's residence.

When the pilferers saw that a company official was sealing up doors and windows with the Manager's seal, they lost interest in "souvenirs", for no one would normally risk an official's anger by breaking his seal. So the apartment soon cleared of people. But the crowd around the teachers' quarters was increasing.

Seeing Tower, Loyalty plucked his sleeve and started walking away, whispering: "Better get away before they find out who called the secretary!"

Mighty Tower had a sudden thought: "What happened to Teacher Ran? We forgot her!"

The two friends dashed over to the gatekeeper's lodge, and Loyalty shouted at the old gatekeeper: "Hey! Can you tell us where Teacher Ran is?"

The old man shouted back: "Well, those visitors took her away with them an hour ago."

"Did she come back?"

"If she did I didn't see her."

Loyalty turned to Tower: "Come on! Maybe we can find her!"

The two ran out of the compound, then slowed to a fast walk realizing what a spectacle they would make running along the public street. Once outside factory grounds they automatically turned toward a large intersection three blocks away.

As they walked along they glanced up the narrow alleys leading off the street. But life in the alleys was dragging on as usual. No sign of a kidnapped Teacher Ran — if, indeed, she had been kidnapped.

As they approached the main intersection they heard the beating of gongs and drums to the right, up the main thoroughfare. The two friends were breathing hard from excitement and exertion. Mighty Tower suggested: "Let's stop a minute to catch our breath, and see what the gongs and drums are all about."

Back of them along the sidewalk was an awning that an outdoor shoe repairman had rigged up over his sewing machine. They stepped back under its shadow. They did not have long to wait. The gongs and drums got closer, and a crowd began to gather.

The parading group stopped squarely in the middle of the intersection, and a young man jumped up on a hand cart. It did not take long to identify him. He was the Red Guard leader who had been first speaker at the drill ground a few hours before.

He shouted at the top of his lungs: "Bombard the headquarters!"

The crowd echoed back: "Bombard the headquarters!"

The shouters held clenched fist high to heaven. Around each arm was a red arm band.

Only then did Loyalty and Tower notice someone else on

the cart with the Red Guard leader. This person was kneeling on the cart floor, head bowed, hands tied behind back, dunce hat on head, and from the neck was hanging a board with characters written on it.

Tower whispered to Loyalty: "Who in the world is that, kneeling on the cart?"

The Red Guard was shouting again, this time through a megaphone: "Let me introduce the latest dunce in Shanghai. But first I'll read the criminal charges against her. Here they are, written out on the board around her neck:

"'First. Misleading and deceiving the youth of Shanghai with bourgeois ideas.

"'Second. Holding to old customs, thoughts, culture and habits.

"'Third. Running dog of the Revisionists of Shanghai City Government'."

With extra venom in his voice, the Red Guard concluded: "Here she is — Teacher Ran, of the Golden Stream Weaving Factory Elementary School. Come on, Comrades! Spit on her!"

22. The Demon At Work
Summer 1966

THE NEXT DAY was Sunday, and for Bright Loyalty it was a free day. There was no church service to attend, for Shanghai churches had been closed one by one, confiscated, and converted into warehouse, factory, school or theater. But small groups of believers were still meeting in private homes, and Loyalty expected some would gather in his mother's house after nightfall.

Strong Hero Liang was at Jade Moon's place too, as usual, and solicitous of Lotus Flower as usual. In the afternoon the four of them strolled through Fuxing Park, then went home and admired Hero's stamp collection. Loyalty and his mother and sister were to look back on that quiet Sunday afternoon as the lull before the storm.

Old Pastor Bao led the evening service. No hymns were sung; it was too risky. After the meeting the six others left at intervals by ones or twos. Then Loyalty turned to Pastor Bao and said: "Something terrible happened at the factory yesterday. Maybe you can fill me in on the background of this thing. I don't understand...."

Jade Moon interrupted in a whisper: "Excuse me, Loyalty, but maybe someplace else would be better to talk than here ..."

Unconsciously she glanced back over her shoulder as if a spy were lurking in the shadows of the room, then continued in a lower voice: "You and the pastor go up the spiral stairway to the attic, and out to the flat roof. You know, where I hang my laundry. It's the only place you can be sure of being alone."

Loyalty and the pastor exchanged glances, then excused themselves from the others and climbed the spiral stairway. With a light breeze blowing, it was refreshingly cool on the roof. Loyalty knew the place well, but it was Pastor Bao's first time there. Instinctively the old man looked behind the chimney pots, relics of the coal fires that had once burned in the grates down below, and behind the little wooden structure that housed the door they had just come through. Relieved, he took a deep breath and said, "*Wa!* This is a nice place! We can talk freely here."

"You're right, Pastor. Now, here's what happened yesterday..."

Bright Loyalty told of the Red Guards' visit to the factory, of the ransacking of Teacher Ran's room and how she was disgraced on the street.

"Hmm...." said the pastor thoughtfully. "I'm afraid we are going to see more of this."

"Who are they really aiming at?" asked Loyalty. "An elementary school teacher like Miss Ran is awfully low in the pecking order, isn't she?"

"Loyalty, that was just a practice run. Their real game are the high-ups in your factory. Didn't you say that the Manager was agitated when he talked about the Red Guards? Well, maybe he knew what to expect."

Loyalty took another tack: "In the speeches yesterday they continually attacked 'the capitalist class', as they called them. But what's the point? There are no functioning capitalists in China today. Haven't been since Liberation ...."

Pastor Bao bowed his head in thought for a moment.

"Right, Loyalty," he said. "But the people who were capitalists before 1949 are still here. At least some have survived. And these people are prime targets of the Red Guards — and their children and grandchildren. Just like in the Old Testament, the sins of the parents are visited on the children. Mao Zedong is a hundred percent revolutionary, and he wants a continuing revolution."

After a moment's silence, the old pastor went on: "It's a

serious mistake to forget what Mao himself said, that revolution is not a dinner party, nor doing embroidery. It is an act of violence by which one class overthrows another. Apparently he reckons that the capitalistic class has not yet been exterminated."

Bright Loyalty pondered this. "So, what we have today is a revolution within a revolution, a tornado within a tornado?"

"Yes, that's it. Except that before long the tornado may develop into a typhoon, and that typhoon may hit Shanghai hard. We've only seen the beginning of the havoc the Red Guards can deluge us with."

Suddenly a scream tore through the night air, exploding like a volcano from the far side of a chimney pot.

"Ah ha! You fascists! You capitalists! I've caught you at it! You're plotting counter-revolution!"

Loyalty and Pastor Bao jerked around, startled that someone else was on the roof top with them. It was a middle-aged woman, who continued to explode: "Thought you would come up here and hatch your counter-revolutionary plots, did you? Well, I'll report you ... scum to the Red Guards. I see you don't think much of them. Well, they think less of you and you'll soon know it!"

Loyalty whispered to Pastor Bao: "It's The Demon from the ground floor. I'll talk with her ..." Then, turning to The Demon: "It's true we did not know you were here on the roof. By the way, how did you get up here?"

"That's none of your business! But I've known for a long time that Jade Moon comes up here and sends signals by the way she hangs clothes on the line ...."

Before they could restrain themselves both Loyalty and Pastor Bao burst out laughing. The idea of making laundry into a secret code was too much for them. Unfortunately this infuriated The Demon.

"What? Laughing at me, are you? I'll give you something to laugh about!"

Pastor Bao tried to patch up the *faux pas*: "Oh, no! How could we be laughing at you? Just something that struck us funny at the moment. Please forgive us."

The Demon's rejoinder was pure acid: "Forgive you? How can I ever forgive the scum of the earth for the harm you have done me?"

"Harm? Harm?" the pastor asked mildly. "When did I ever harm you?"

"You capitalist swine have crushed us working people. And now it's our turn to crush you! I'm going right now to report you to the Red Guards!"

With that parting blast she twisted herself around, grabbed hold of the parapet, threw one leg over and then the other and disappeared from sight.

Loyalty and Pastor Bao ran over to the place where she disappeared; looking over the edge they saw an iron ladder attached to the side of the building. As they watched, The Demon left the ladder and wormed her way into a window.

"She had a ladder put up from the back window of the upstairs hallway!" exclaimed Bright Loyalty, "and mother didn't know about it! Imagine going to all that trouble just to spy on mother's laundry!"

While Loyalty and the old Pastor were on the roof holding what they thought was a private conversation, another conversation was going on in the room below. For the first time in a month, Strong Hero and Lotus Flower were together alone.

Jade Moon had said: "You two stay here. I'll go down to the kitchen and make a pot of tea." She left the room with teapot in one hand, tea canister in the other and tea cozy tucked under her arm.

"Dear, dear Mama!" said Lotus Flower. "She always knows the right thing to do and say. She's been saving a few spoonfuls of chrysanthemum tea." She looked at the clock on the wall. "It will take her eight minutes to boil the water and make tea. With two minutes for going and coming, that means she is giving us ten minutes alone!"

Hero lost no time in opening the subject nearest the heart of both of them: "I applied again to the political cadre at the starter company for official permission to get married. I've just had his reply. I hope you don't mind my being frank. There's nothing to gain from trying to hide anything from you. Even if I tried, you'd weasel it out of me. You're too smart, like your mother I guess ..."

"Just cut out beating around the bush!" Lotus interrupted. "Smart, am I? At least smart enough to know that you are not getting to the point!"

"The point is," continued Hero, "that I don't like his point. I can't see any sense in the world in what he says ..."

"Come on! What did he say?" The girl's voice was edged with irritation.

"Well, honestly, Lotus, I'd give a mint of money if he hadn't said what he did say ..."

At that, Lotus Flower jumped up, grabbed Hero by the shoulders and gave him a shake. He grinned. He liked the feel of her hands on his shoulders, even though he knew she was losing patience with him.

"Out with it! Cough it up!" she commanded, pommeling him on the back and shoulders with her fists as if to dislodge an object from his throat.

"Hold off! Hold off! I can't talk while you're beating me!"

Lotus Flower let up, though she had discovered that pounding him physically was rather nice.

He began again: "His reply was — I'm sorry to have to say this, because it's just not true — that you are a political risk. Both your father and your brother were sentenced to Reform through Labor. That means they are non-persons and may never regain their rights as citizens. He says our Unit cannot risk criticism by allowing such a marriage."

"That's certainly strange," Lotus Flower countered. "When I applied to my Unit at the clothing factory they raised no objection to your father, even though he was a teller at the Prosperous Clouds Bank in the old days, and is still part of the skeleton staff that keeps its Shanghai office. Nothing could be more capitalistic than a British bank..." Her voice trailed off in puzzled tones.

Hero reminded her: "But they haven't arrested him yet." Then he added as an afterthought: "The truth is we never know from one day to the next if they will arrest him."

Lotus Flower asked, changing the subject: "Where would we live if we were married?"

"That's a question I can't answer. Where is there a vacant place? One room, even. I'm in a dormitory room now with thirty-nine other men. Maybe I make less of a demand on housing if I'm single!"

"At least we are old enough to get married according to law. I'm 24, and you're 30. Even the Party can't hold our age ..."

Just then there was a clatter on the circular stairs coming down from the attic. Feet appeared first, then legs, then torso of Pastor Bao. Bright Loyalty followed.

"Oh!" said Loyalty. "Sorry to disturb you. But we've been disturbed ourselves."

He told of their being surprised by The Demon. Hero jumped up, snapped his fingers and said: "It doesn't sound good for the two of you. Nor for your mother either."

Pastor Bao said hurriedly: "I think if you'll excuse me. I'd better..."

He was interrupted by Jade Moon arriving, tea canister in one hand and teapot in the other, covered now with the cozy. She was flushed with her exertion, and the warmth spilled in her words: "Oh! I'm glad you're back downstairs, Pastor Bao! You'll have a cup of tea, won't you?" She reached up to take cups from the shelf that ran along one side of the room.

"I'm sorry, Jade Moon. But I mustn't delay, as much as I would like a cup of tea. I don't know what might happen to my wife if I'm not home. So — may I say — thank you and good night." With that the old pastor turned and walked out the door.

Jade Moon was crestfallen. Pastor Bao had never acted so abruptly before. Nor had he ever refused a cup of tea.

"Mama, it's like this ...." Bright Loyalty said, and explained again what had happened on the roof.

Jade Moon was aghast: "What? Me? Me sending secret signals by the way I hang up clothes? How ridiculous!"

Unlike Loyalty and Pastor Bao, however, she did not laugh. The dead seriousness of such an accusation gripped her hard. By the latter half of 1966, humor was becoming a lost art.

Loyalty concluded his account with The Demon's threats and her disappearance over the parapet. Jade Moon the mother was thinking a thousand thoughts. At the same time Jade Moon the hostess was pouring out three cups of tea — a cup for each one except herself.

"Please have some tea," she said automatically, making the customary gesture towards the cups on the table.

"I think you'll have to excuse me, too," said Hero regretfully. "I've got to check in at the dormitory by 10 p.m." He did gulp half a cup of tea. Then he grabbed his cap, said good night and left. Once on the street, however, he did not turn in the direction of his dormitory but in the opposite direction. He overtook Pastor Bao and walked home with him.

For Pastor Bao, The Demon's threats turned into reality sooner than he expected. That same night at 1 a.m. there was thunderous knocking at the door.

Suddenly awakened but still half asleep, the pastor and his wife Danrong jumped out of bed. Danrong threw a dressing gown around herself. The pastor climbed into a pair of trousers, and just managed to get to the door and open it before it was broken down. Three young men with red arm bands burst into the room.

"Are there only three of you?" the pastor asked in disbelief.

"Yeah. How many did you expect? Three are enough to take care of old fogies like you."

What they lacked in numbers, however, they made up in fierceness. There was no mistaking that they had come to ransack, steal and destroy.

Since the Bao's living quarters were now reduced to one room, it took little time to turn out everything. With one swift motion a Red Guard turned the rope-strung bed, covers and all, up against the wall. This revealed a leather-covered chest, and without waiting for it to be opened the Red Guard kicked it open, then turned it upside down and dumped the contents on the floor. He sniffed in disdain at the pile of books, pamphlets, old magazines and old letters.

"Stretch out your hands!" demanded the leader. The pastor and his wife did so, obediently. "Where are your wedding rings?"

"They have been sold."

"You rascal! You lie! No one would sell his wedding ring!"

"Please do believe me. I cannot lie. I have never told a lie in my life."

"All right, if you sold them, where is the receipt? When, where, and how did you sell them? Who bought them? For how much?"

Pastor Bao calmly answered as many questions as he could. "But, I do not know where the receipt is," he said. "It has been so long."

"If you can't show me the receipt, that means you have hidden the rings! Come on, quick! Find them! Our policy is: 'Compliance, light punishment; defiance, heavy punishment'. Find them quick!"

"I'm sorry. It's as I told you, they were sold years ago."

"You liar! You call yourself a Christian minister and yet you are telling me a lie!"

In the midst of the tirade Pastor Bao suddenly thought of the words of Christ, "Lo, I am with you always, even to the end of the world." Remembering that promise and sensing that presence made the old pastor smile.

The Red Guard leader saw the smile, and his reaction was sardonic: "What're you smiling about? I'll wipe that smile off your face!"

But it had distracted his attention and he dropped his eyes from the pastor's face. His eyes lit on a chair, and he picked it up and placed it on top of the table. Then he did the same with the other three chairs in the room. The object, apparently, was to make room for the contents of drawers and cupboards being dumped out on the floor.

The Red Guards grabbed the pastor's Bibles, commentaries, dictionaries, Bible study books, hymnbooks and whatever else they could lay hands on and threw them into the leather-covered chest. Still there were more books, which they heaped onto the bedspread, tying the four corners together so they could carry them away.

"We'll see that these books on religious superstition are put through the pulp mill," said the Red Guard leader, licking his lips with satisfaction, "and made into paper for printing the sayings of Chairman Mao."

The largest of the Red Guards remarked: "Why should you have four chairs when there are only two of you?"

He picked up a chair off the table, raised it high over his head and brought it down with a crash on the corner of the table. It flew into a dozen pieces. He picked up a second chair and did the same.

"Now," he said, "you are like the people, with only one chair each!"

The leader spoke up again: "We'll seal up that piano. No more decadent bourgeois music from this place!"

He picked up an old letter from the pile on the floor and ripped it into strips with a kitchen knife. Knocking the lid off the rice pot, he scooped up a handful of rice and used that to paste the strips of paper across the cover of the piano keyboard.

"Now!" he said, "Just seal it with my seal and there'll be no more playing on this thing!" That he proceeded to do.

As Danrong watched her beloved piano being sealed up, she knew it would be a long time before she touched the keys again — if ever.

"One more thing," said the leader. "I'm going to fix up a sign for you to wear tomorrow."

He picked up a cardboard box that had spoons, chopsticks, forks and so on in it. These he dumped on the floor. With a butcher knife he cut out the two larger sides of the box, and using a brush pen of the pastor's he wrote in large characters on one piece of cardboard: "I am a Christian pastor and a liar."

And on the other piece: "I am a running dog of the foreigners."

With the same knife he cut down Danrong's makeshift clothes line that stretched across the back of the room, and with the cord strung the two pieces of cardboard together into a sandwich board.

"Here! You wear it like this!" He draped it over the pastor's shoulders, and told him: "Tomorrow morning at sunup you will stand out on the street corner. You will stand there all day, rain or shine. People will have a good look at you and see what your sins are!"

Two Red Guards picked up the leather-covered chest, the third hoisted to his shoulder the bedspread filled with books.

The leader's parting shot was: "You don't know how lucky you are to get off so lightly! We should beat you up, you bourgeois scum! If you were ten years younger we would really do you in!"

Then he shouted: "Down with the capitalists!"

All three shouted together: "Down with the capitalists!"

Again, the leader: "Down with the Four Olds!"

All together: "Down with the Four Olds!"

With that they left. Pastor Bao closed the door after them. Then he slowly took the two remaining chairs off the table and set them on the floor. The old man and his wife sat down on the chairs. He took her hand in his and they sat silently and looked at the destruction.

23. Ransacked!
Autumn 1966

THE DEMON'S dealings with Jade Moon were indirect, more subtle and slower. She took her time because she wanted to square accounts with her once for all. And what better chance than while the Red Guards were on rampage? Let them do the dirty work and she would reap the benefits!

The Demon heard that a letter of accusation, even an anonymous one, sent through the mail could lead to a house being ransacked. So she sat down and wrote to the Vegetable Distribution Center where Jade Moon worked:

"You are not aware of the fact, but you harbor in your Unit a diehard capitalist and counter-revolutionary. She puts on a face of being poor, but she comes from a capitalist family. Her father was a banker under Chiang Kai-shek and she has many treasures stored up. Her name is Jade Moon Lee."

The Demon did not sign the letter. She sealed the envelope, affixed a stamp and dropped it into the post box, feeling great satisfaction with what she had done.

After the confrontation on the roof, Jade Moon was increasingly uneasy. At night, if she heard the beating of gongs and drums, she would suddenly sit up in bed, and could not lie down again in peace until the sound had faded into the distance.

One day when she came home from work her face was gray and her voice tense. She told Lotus Flower: "Today our work brigade leader called us all together. He said he had been informed that there was a capitalist and counter-revolutionary in our brigade, and threatened: 'That person had better confess voluntarily before it's too late'. He mentioned no names, but everybody in our brigade comes from a worker or peasant family except me. Was he pointing at me?"

The next morning after an uneasy night, Jade Moon told her daughter: "When you get home from work this afternoon, take this bundle to your Grandfather Lee's house. These are the most valuable things we have."

The bundle was not large, about the size of a hat, and was packed in a square of blue cloth with the corners of the cloth tied across the top. Jade Moon placed it on a shelf and threw some old clothes over it.

That afternoon Lotus took the bundle down from its hiding place and started out. The more casual she tried to appear the closer she gripped the bundle and the more she felt enquiring eyes fixed on her and on what she was carrying. It was a twenty-minute walk to Grandfather Lee's house, but today it stretched out to a century. Finally, perspiring profusely and breathing heavily, she arrived at Grandfather Lee's doorstep.

"Made it!" Lotus Flower breathed to herself. Then she shouted the usual loud "*Kai men!* Open the door!"

Grandfather Lee took in the situation at a glance. He silently accepted the bundle, silently took it over to a drawer, silently unlocked it and placed the bundle inside, and silently locked the drawer again. When it was safely put away he told Lotus: "These are a few things that your parents have saved from the past, and also some things that your late grandmother and I gave them at their wedding. I don't believe you have ever seen them..."

He was interrupted by a burst of urgent knocking. Lotus Flower opened the door. She could not believe her eyes! Standing before the door were two women she recognized, from her mother's work brigade. One she had dubbed

"Poker Face" and the other, "Miles of Smiles". And now, for some unknown reason, in front of her grandfather's door stood Poker Face and Miles of Smiles!

Miles of Smiles said, most cheerfully and sweetly: "Your mother said you were here and that you brought a bundle of things here with you."

Lotus Flower's heart sank. Her first thought was to accuse her mother: *Mama! Why did you tell them? Why did you say I was here?*

Miles of Smiles was going on, still cheerfully and sweetly: "The Vegetable Distribution Center told us to come and fetch the things. And you are to go back with us."

Lotus Flower looked at Grandfather Lee. He was silent, yet she knew he was boiling inside. He arose with difficulty, went over and opened the drawer, silently took out the parcel and silently placed it on the table.

For the first time Poker Face spoke: "We will make proper disposition of these things." She it was who took the bundle in her hands.

The three of them had already walked several steps when Lotus turned and looked back. Grandfather Lee was standing by the door, holding onto it with both hands and looking at her silently.

With Poker Face on her left and Miles of Smiles on her right, Lotus was marched through the streets of Shanghai to the Vegetable Distribution Center. It was already closed for the day, and as they walked across the stone floor of the big vacant room just inside the gate their footsteps echoed and re-echoed with a hollow sound. After the pulsing life of the city outside, the quietness and solitude of the place was disturbing.

Poker Face and Miles of Smiles took the girl to a small reception room at one side of the big room. Poker Face commanded sternly: "You stay here until we come back!"

They turned and shut the door. Then Lotus heard the

sound of a key turning in the lock. She was a prisoner! She listened as they mounted the wooden staircase and headed for the office upstairs, and wondered what mischief was brewing up there. No doubt her mother was there — otherwise why should they bring her to the Center? And what were they doing to her mother?

Lotus looked around at her prison. A few straight-backed chairs flat against bare walls. In the center of the room a square wooden table. On the table a newspaper. That was all. She picked up the newspaper and looked at the date: 2 September 1966 — today's paper. The entire front page quoted a speech by Zhou Enlai, the most important man in China after Mao Zedong himself. Lotus Flower began to read:

"The Great Cultural Revolution has completely eradicated old capitalistic thinking .... The capitalistic class has been demolished, but the capitalists themselves, the people, are still here. Their heart has not died ...."

The more Lotus Flower read the more her mind was flooded with questions: *Zhou Enlai says the Cultural Revolution is aimed at the capitalists. But my parents are not capitalists. Why are they harassing my mother? And why pull me into it? Should I face them and demand to know why they are keeping me here? If I say that, will it make things worse for Mama?*

There were footsteps on the stones outside the room, and the sound of key turning in lock. The door opened. Poker Face came in, pulled a chair up to the table, plopped down on it, propped her elbows on the table and looked at Lotus Flower.

"Your mother has told everything," she said. "She's upstairs now writing out her confession. Has your mother transferred anything else out of the house?"

Her face began to loosen up in something approaching a smile.

Lotus Flower answered: "I don't know." But to herself

she wondered: *If Mama has told everything, why are you asking me about taking things out of the house?*

Poker Face asked more questions. She was not pleased with the answers. Finally, with her stern face in control again, she stood up haughtily and commanded: "Stay here! Don't leave!"

There was not really much point in saying that, as after she went out of the door she turned the key in the lock again.

So Lotus Flower was locked in the room with her thoughts. Two questions were fighting with each other for her attention: *What are they doing to Mama? And why are they against us?*

Lotus felt that the four walls were closing in on her, that the world was closing in on her and her family, and that things were getting darker and darker. Then she realized that it was dusk outside and that the room *was* getting darker. She reached up and turned on the one electric bulb which hung by a cord from the ceiling, and the light made her feel better.

Hurried footsteps sounded outside the door, and it was unlocked and pushed open. Poker Face walked in and placed a tiny loaf of bread on the newspaper in front of Lotus Flower, on what Zhou Enlai said about eradicating the capitalists. Then, still without a word, she turned around and left. Lotus grabbed the bread and finished it off in a few bites. It was past suppertime and she was hungry.

Before long there was the sound of many people in the big room outside and the noise of gongs and drums being moved around. Someone opened the door and said: "Go up to the office."

Going out into the big room, Lotus was surprised at the hive of activity — here some young people doing a pantomime, there others waving red flags, still others practising on gongs and drums. Making her way through the crowd, she ran up the stairs. Up there it was dark and quiet, in contrast to the noise below. The office door was open. Lotus tiptoed up to it and looked in. Her mother was sitting there by herself, her back to the door, writing something.

"Mama!" Lotus shouted and rushed to her.

Jade Moon jumped with fright. "You're here, are you?" she asked, surprised.

"I've been locked up in a room downstairs ever since they brought me from grandfather's house!" Lotus Flower stopped to catch her breath. She was still panting from running up the stairs. "Mama, I didn't tell them a thing!"

There was a faraway look in Jade Moon's eyes. Lotus thought she had not heard her, so she repeated with emphasis: "I didn't tell them a thing."

Jade Moon suddenly went limp, as if all the fight had gone out of her. She said, almost in a whisper: "I told them. I told them everything." With a bitter smile she continued: "They had a meeting. They pressed me hard to hand over everything." She shut her eyes tight and shook her head as if trying to get rid of the memory, "I...I...didn't think it was worth it holding out against them. They kept talking about 'treasures'. If it's only *things* they want, they can have them."

Lotus blurted out: "But they kept me locked up for hours, and they insulted and abused you. That's worse than stealing." She began to cry. The two of them held onto each other and cried together.

"They've come back. They'll take us now and ransack our house," Jade Moon whispered tensely.

For a moment, mother and daughter lay still on the three benches they had pulled together for a makeshift bed. As they listened, the gongs and drums drew closer, beating in unison: *Dah...dah... dah, dah, dah,* two slow and three fast.

Jade Moon gave Lotus a quick hug as they lay together on the benches. Then they sat up and slipped into their shoes.

Poker Face burst into the room, shouting: "We've finished those other houses! Now we'll do yours!" The two women followed her out of the office and down the stairs.

Down below, she began prancing back and forth in front of the Red Guards like a victorious general, giving orders to the flag bearers and beaters of gongs and drums. Jade Moon had never seen her so animated before. After she had her troops in order, she placed Jade Moon and Lotus Flower at the tail end of the procession. Then she gave a command. Gongs clanged, drums rattled and off they marched.

In those extraordinary days, gongs and drums were sounding from morning to night and from night to morning. Since it was eleven p.m. already, few people turned out to see what this particular processsion was about. Only The Demon was still awake, and she was there to welcome them. She opened the big double doors downstairs and let the marchers in. Jade Moon fumbled with the keys to the room. Poker Face barked at her: "Quit your stalling! Get on with it!"

Once inside, the Red Guards jerked drawers out and dumped the contents onto the floor. The first drawer or two turned up little to please them: some rubber bands, worn-out shuttlecocks, a couple of wooden combs, children's picture books, a beret Lotus Flower had worn as a child, old clothes and house slippers.

A swipe here and everything was knocked off a shelf. A sweep there and everything came tumbling out of a cupboard. The pile on the floor grew by the minute.

Suddenly an older Red Guard spied the circular stairway. No doubt reckoning that the Lee family treasures were hidden in the attic, he climbed up, lifted up the old castoffs and examined them one by one. Finally, with a look of victory on his face, he came back down the stairs holding the treasures in his hands: a cracked aluminum saucepan, a pair of old wine pitchers with the handles off that Jade Moon had used for flower vases, and an old surgical corset that Grandmother Song had worn years before to keep her back straight.

By this time all the old suitcases had been pulled out from underneath the bed. One was filled with foreign-style spices that a westerner had given Grandfather Song when he left Shanghai in 1948. The small boxes intrigued a young Red Guard. Sure they contained the Lee family treasure, he methodically pried the top off each box with a screwdriver and dumped the dusty lot in a pile on the floor. There it was, all piled together — cinnamon, paprika, nutmeg, sage, rosemary, chili, mustard, peppercorns, garlic salt, allspice, curry powder ... Finally, for fear he had missed something, he took the screwdriver and stirred the mound, scattering it wider and wider on the floor.

In the meantime Poker Face herself was going through the family's books, inspecting them and throwing them one by one onto a pile. She picked up the precious New Testament, looked inside for a moment, closed it and examined the covers, and threw it on the pile of books to go. Jade Moon bit her lip. It would only make matters worse to remonstrate.

Poker Face then picked up a copy of Sung Dynasty Poems and inspected it closely. "Hmmm.." she ruminated. "This must be one of the Confucian Classics...." She opened it and began to read:

"At the willow tree precipice
Taste the wind and
Sample the moon."

She asked no one in particular, "What's the meaning of this? Is it revolutionary or counter-revolutionary?"

Not getting any answer, she balanced the book on her right hand and hefted it for weight. No doubt about it, whether or not a book was revolutionary depended on its weight. In the end she put it back in its original place. Apparently it was not heavy enough to be counter-revolutionary!

The Red Guards went on until they had examined every

nook and cranny of the two rooms and the attic above.

Afterwards they made a list of everything they were taking away: the contents of the bundle Lotus Flower had taken to Grandfather Lee's house — Jade Moon's wedding ring, the gold chain Grandmother Lee had given Jade Moon after Victory was born, and other ornaments — together with the things they turned out that night — brass, pewter, jade, photographs, books — yes, and the cracked aluminum saucepan, the handleless wine pitchers and Grandmother Song's corset — all these things, some of which Lotus saw that night for the first time in her life, became just items on a list.

Then they left. The place looked as if a tornado had struck it. Everything was in the wrong place. The beds were all turned up. After surveying the wreckage for a few minutes Jade Moon looked at the clock. It was 1.30 a.m. Two hours had been long enough to snatch from them everything of material value they possessed.

For some people, a midnight tragedy spells no more sleep that night. But for Jade Moon and Lotus Flower it had the opposite effect. They made their beds, fell into them and dropped off to sleep at once. For one thing, they had anticipated the ransacking for over a week and when it finally came it was something of an anticlimax. Then again, the day had been long and taxing for both of them and by 1.30 a.m. they were physically exhausted.

They slept right through until a shout of "*Kai men*! Open the door!" awakened them at 9 a.m. Startled at first, they were immediately relieved to recognize a familiar voice. It was Bright Loyalty!

When he stepped into the room, his face fell and his mouth flew open. He burst out: "*Aiya*! It's happened to us! Were you here when they came? Did they hurt you? Did you know them?...

"Just sit down," Jade Moon said, "and I'll tell you all about it."

After Jade Moon's account, Lotus added her postscripts. Then, talked out for the moment, the three sat and looked at the wreckage.

Jade Moon broke the silence: "Here's the list they gave us of the things they took. According to their point of view, I guess they think they're being honest. This is a receipt, as it were. But it's a strange kind of honesty!"

She made rice gruel and this, with some boiled peanuts Loyalty had brought, was their breakfast. After eating, the three of them started in on the sizeable job of bringing order out of chaos.

Loyalty swept up the pile of assorted spices and their erstwhile tins. It proved not an unpleasant task, as some of the spices were still aromatic even after their eighteen years in hiding.

"It's an ill wind that blows no good," remarked Jade Moon. "They got rid of the spices for me. I could never use them, yet I didn't have the heart to throw them away."

"Oh! Look what I've found! shouted Lotus. "What's this?" She held up an old-fashioned black silk dress.

Jade Moon replied: "That's Grandmother Song's burial gown. I've kept it here for years while she ... while she's living someplace else." She steadfastly refused to let cross her lips the fact that her mother lived in a public toilet.

"But," Lotus Flower wanted to know, "if the Red Guards get worked up about destroying *old* things, why didn't they take *this*? Nothing could be more old-fashioned than a silk burial gown!"

"Well," Jade Moon replied, "I'm glad they didn't take it. Grandmother Song may be suffering indignity now, but she deserves to be dignified in death."

"But nobody is *buried* these days," Loyalty interrupted. "They cremate people. Does Grandmother know that?"

Jade Moon replied: "Even if she does, she will insist on wearing her gown to the crematorium!"

After two hours of straightening up, the house showed a semblance of order, and the Lees sat down to rest.

"Mama, it's good you have only two rooms!" said Loyalty. "For the families still in single houses, it can be bad. Take the Xiong family. Their house is right over the wall from our dormitory, and the Red Guards ransacked it for two days and three nights ..."

"Impossible!" interrupted Lotus. "Why, they could take a house apart piece by piece in that time!"

A solemn look came over Loyalty's face, and he told his sister: "It's hard to believe, but that's exactly what they did — took the house apart piece by piece. They climbed up on the roof and tore up the tiles. They were looking for gold that was supposed to be hidden somewhere. For two days and three nights all we could hear was the sound of tearing up the tiles and then smashing them onto the ground below. They reckoned they had finished ransacking that house only after every single tile had been torn away."

Jade Moon changed the subject: "Loyalty, you'll stay for dinner, won't you?"

"I'm sorry, Mama, but I have only a half day off. I've got to report back for guard duty at 12:30 ..."

"Guard duty! You have security guards at your factory, don't you?"

"Yes, but the office cadres are very jittery since the Red Guards held that rally on our drill ground nine days ago. And now the Red Guards are organizing a unit inside the factory..."

"Aiya, Loyalty," Jade Moon interrupted. "Only the Lord can protect you. Why, you may have civil war right inside your factory compound!" She had the sudden feeling that the Red Guards were everywhere, all around them, squeezing

her in a vice. Nervously she glanced back over her shoulder
— could a Red Guard be standing in the corner? She quickly
shook her head, to disavow such a thought.

"There's something else that worries me," Jade Moon
lowered her voice. "What's going to happen to Big Sister?
The Demon has worked out her spite on us and on Pastor
Bao — will she let Big Sister alone? She hates Big Sister,
because Big Sister stands for all that she hates. And for a
blind person to be ransacked might be more of a shock than
she could stand. Before you leave, Loyalty, we had better
have special prayer for Big Sister. I believe that only the Lord
and a miracle can keep the Red Guards away from her."

24. Murder At The Foot Of The Ladder
Autumn 1966

AFTER THEIR PRAYER TOGETHER, Bright Loyalty said a hurried goodbye, grabbed his cap and left. As he stepped out onto the street he had the sensation that he had left tumult and turmoil behind. The atmosphere of Sunday noon engulfed him in serenity. Families were taking their day-off stroll along the streets, the children dressed happily in bright colors. It was the first Sunday in September and there was a hint of autumn in the air. *Where does that idea of autumn come from?* Loyalty asked himself. Then he identified the aroma of roasting chestnuts wafting up from a roadside *wok* full of hot black pebbles nudging the chestnuts to just the right degree of roastedness. He breathed deeply. It was a consoling smell.

Almost mesmerized by the pleasant Sunday atmosphere, Loyalty walked along, more carefree than he had been for a long time.

Shortly, however, he found himself approaching the intersection where nine days before he and Mighty Tower had watched Teacher Ran in the pushcart. It seemed to him that the drumbeat from that day was still throbbing in the street. But softly, as if from a distance: *Dah...dah...dah, dah, dah.* Two longs and three shorts.

Loyalty snapped his fingers several times to break the sound of the drums. Then, as he turned into the street where the weaving mill was located, the sound grew louder. For the first time he realized that he was not imagining it.

He quickened his pace. And the drumbeats grew louder and louder: *DAH...DAH!...DAH, DAH, DAH!*"

In front of him loomed a crowd of people around the main gate of the factory. All at once he felt uneasy. Were the Red

Guards having another rally inside the compound? If so, what would it mean this time? Who would be singled out for insult and disgrace? With difficulty he made his way through the crowd at the gate, who apparently wanted to see what was happening inside — but from a safe distance.

Once inside Loyalty could see the action centered on the same platform that had been put up for the first rally. *Hmm! Why didn't we take that platform down?* he mumbled to himself. *It was a standing invitation to them to return!*

The drums were throbbing, throbbing. Flags on the platform were waving in rhythm with their throb, and dancers were dancing to the same rhythm.

As Bright Loyalty approached, a Red Guard with megaphone in hand leaped to the platform. It was the cue for drums to die and flags to furl.

Slogan shouting came next: "To rebel is right! Down with the counter-revolutionaries!" And a new slogan which Bright Loyalty had not heard before and did not understand: "Down with cow ghosts and snake demons!"

Now more Red Guards jumped onto the platform. One of them snatched the megaphone and yelled more slogans. Then they began to jump all over the platform, as if the higher they jumped the more revolutionary they were.

It seemed that the onlookers standing nearest the platform somehow epitomized the Red Guards' enemies; now and then a Red Guard would go to the front of the platform, stretch himself on one leg and give a mighty spit onto those standing immediately in front of him. Dodge the spit? They couldn't, they were packed too tight together.

Loyalty looked closer at the spit targets. *Ahh! That's it! Those are the selected enemies of the Red Guards, for today at least.* Hanging from the neck of each was a small piece of board with an accusation written on it. Working his way closer, he read the accusations:

Secret Agent of Kuomintang

Rightist

Revisionist

Rotten Egg

Running Dog of the Imperialists

Landlord's Wife

After each accusation came the person's name, and after each name an "X" as if to show he was condemned already. Looking closer at the individuals with the little boards around their necks, Loyalty recognized cadres from the factory office, including the manager and the woman treasurer. She it was with the label, "Landlord's Wife".

Just then Loyalty spotted Mighty Tower, and worked his way over to him through the crowd.

Tower whispered: "It's happened, just as Manager Ye was afraid. All the top brass are being 'struggled', right here inside our own factory."

There was a lull in proceedings, no sound from the platform. Loyalty whispered to Tower. "Maybe they're calling it off.."

"Don't you believe it," returned Tower. "Just wait."

Red Guards were talking together on the platform, low but fiercely, as if they would be at each other's throats any moment. The leader was jabbing his finger toward the building back of the platform. Finally the others appeared to give in to him.

He shouted into the megaphone: "We want all you people, you citizens of the New China, to have a better look at your enemies. We're going to put them on display for you on that roof."

A small concrete roof jutted out from the building, covering a porch below. The roof was some eight feet off the ground and no larger than four or five table tops put together.

The Red Guard continued: "The first enemy of the people to climb up will be Hong Yulin, the Landlord's wife!"

"Climb up? Climb up what?" Loyalty whispered to Tower.

"Well, there's a fire escape ladder beside the porch," Tower replied uncertainly. "Maybe they'll..." his voice trailed off. They did not have long to wait.

The Red Guard leader took his megaphone and began to prod Hong Yulin toward the iron ladder.

Loyalty gasped: "She'll never make it! She's too fat!"

Fear was written on Hong Yulin's face as the Red Guard prodded her closer and closer to the fire escape.

She carefully took hold of an upper rung of the ladder and placed her right foot on the bottom rung. With an effort she heaved her weight up and placed her left foot beside the right. Then she repeated the process and made it to the second rung. Already she was red in the face and panting loudly. With much effort she finally made it to rung number eight. There she paused; the roof was opposite that rung.

At that point Hong Yulin became aware of a barrier. The fire escape handrail was between the ladder and the roof. There was not enough space between the handrail and the building for her to squeeze through; she was too fat. So then, how was she to get around the outside of that handrail? By this time she was breathing heavily and perspiring profusely. She lifted her right foot gingerly and swung it outside the handrail, hoping to touch the edge of the roof beyond. But the bit of board hanging around her neck got in the way and she could not see where to put her foot.

She pulled the foot back and clung to the ladder for a moment, worn out by the exertion. Then, pushing the board to one side so that she could see, she tried again to swing her right leg around the handrail. Again her foot failed to contact the roof, and she was hanging in space, her heavy body supported only by her left foot.

Hong Yulin looked down. She saw an endless number of

pairs of eyes looking up at her — some making fun, some with hate in them, some sympathetic, some merely curious. She became dizzy and began to shake and shiver. Swaying back and forth, holding on grimly, trying hard to keep her balance, she pulled her right foot back to the rung again.

Seeing her dilemma, the people responded with all the different attitudes their eyes had revealed:

"Climb!"

"Climb up one more rung!"

"Fatty! Grab hold and go on!"

"Look! The fat pig is putting on an act!"

"Ha! Ha! Who got her as fat as that?"

As the calls increased the abuse got worse. Some began to whistle in derision. Still shaking, Hong Yulin tried a third time, but she still couldn't reach the roof. The leg gradually slipped down the handrail. She was virtually hanging over empty space, and had almost lost her balance. The bit of board was again blocking her vision.

By now her toes had touched the roof, but in order to swing farther right she had to shift the weight from her left foot. She hesitated a moment and stopped moving, her body shaking fearfully.

"Push your foot forward a bit!" someone shouted from below.

The advice was well meant but fatal. For as she pushed her foot forward she lost her balance completely, swaying crazily for an instant, teetered over empty space, then came crashing heavily to the ground.

"*Aiya*!" came from the crowd as from one person.

As she struck the ground there was a sharp snap, like a dry stick breaking in two.

"She's broken a leg or something!" groaned Tower.

The Red Guard leader paid no attention to the fallen treasurer. He was too busy urging the other bearers of little boards up the ladder. One by one they climbed up, squeezed behind the handrail and stepped out onto the roof.

It was a motley herd. The clothes of some had been torn when they were dragged bodily to this "struggle" meeting, the clothes of others were filthy from cleaning out toilets. Some had half the hair shaved off their heads, and each had on that board with his name, accusation, and that fearful "X" mark.

By the time the last person was on the roof it was standing room only. Those in front were in a dangerous position, as there was no railing. Amazingly, the roof stood up under the unaccustomed weight and did not collapse.

The Red Guard leader opened the "struggle" meeting by reading Mao Zedong Thought:

"If you don't hit him
he will not fall...
If you don't sweep
out the dirt it will not
run away by itself."

After he finished reading, several Red Guards spoke one after the other on the theme: "Oppose those who are against Socialism by word and deed." From time to time a speaker would be interrupted by another Red Guard who grabbed the megaphone by force, shouted slogans into it, then handed it back meekly to the speaker again.

As the speakers harangued from the platform, Loyalty looked around at the faces in the crowd. He saw a big question mark written across many of them: "When is my time coming?"

Finally the megaphone was handed back to the Red Guard leader, the one who had prodded Hong Yulin to mount the fateful ladder. Loyalty was shocked and abashed to see him now, a university student, a member of one of the most cultured races on earth, and yet he was red in the face and gesticulating wildly like an uncontrolled madman.

What's come over him? Loyalty asked himself. *Could he be demon-possessed?*

The leader began shouting curses and obscenities at the crowd: "You sons of ...! You ... dogs! You running dogs of these ... bureaucrats! How can you let them live their lives in front of you? You should take these bureaucrats off that roof and tear them limb from limb!"

He raved on and on, as if those particular cadres on the roof were the quintessence of the enemies of Socialism. Abruptly, another Red Guard crossed the platform, pulled the megaphone down and whispered something into the leader's ear. Whatever he said, it stopped the torrent of abuse.

"What a relief!" whispered Loyalty to Tower.

But the lull meant only a shift in target. The two Red Guards fixed eyes on the crumpled and moaning figure of the treasurer, still lying in a heap on the ground near the foot of the ladder.

The Red Guard was yelling into the megaphone again: "We have missed something! One member of that devil-lot has failed to appear on the roof as we ordered her to do. We'll see to it now that she gets onto the roof with the other rotten eggs without delay!"

"*Aiya*!" whispered Tower to Loyalty, "She's got a broken leg! She can't climb that thing!"

The Red Guard leader jumped off the platform, megaphone and all, and headed for the figure on the ground. Holding the big end of the megaphone against Hong Yulin's ear, he shouted: "Get up, you lazy ... ! Climb that ladder! Get up there where you belong!"

A murmur ran through the crowd, a murmur of anger and disapproval at such inhumanity to an injured person. Loyalty thought for a moment that the crowd would turn on the Red Guards. But it was not to be. When they heard the rumble of disapproval, two dozen students with red arm bands rushed to the defence of their leader. To Loyalty's horror, he saw them pick up pieces of boards that had been left under the platform when it was built. Others grabbed boards and twisted them out of the platform itself. In short order they were ready to defend themselves.

The leader paid no attention to all this. He was concentrating on the cringing figure of the treasurer. He shouted: "Get up! Get up! Climb that ladder! I'll give you thirty seconds to get moving...."

The only answer from the abject woman on the ground was a moan, then a whimper: "Please! I can't! I can't!"

One of the Red Guards thrust a board into the hands of the leader.

He shouted in a frenzy: "You can't, you say! I'll show you that you can!" With that, he struck Hong Yulin across the buttocks with the board. From the figure on the ground came an agonized "*Aiya!*"

The pain that he had inflicted on her seemed to trigger a tornado of hate for his victim; he struck her again, harder this time, with the edge of the board and lower down on the thigh.

Snap! Again came that sound like the breaking in two of a dry stick.

"Another bone!" groaned Mighty Tower.

Up to this time the other Red Guards had been facing outward, fearing an attack from the crowd. But the woman's moaning and groaning pulled them like a magnet. With the fury of devils let loose from hell, they turned on the prostrate form and struck it with their boards, again and again and again.

Before long there was no sound at all from the ground except the dull thud of wood striking human flesh and bones.

Jade Moon slipped in through the big double doors on the ground floor as quietly as she could. This afternoon especially she did not want The Demon to see her. Once in the lower hallway she slipped off her shoes and went up the stairs in her stocking feet, holding her shoes in her hand. She went straight to Big Sister's room.

Instead of the usual call outside the door, Jade Moon turned the knob and tried the door, softly, to see if it were locked. It was not. She pushed the door gently and it gently swung open.

"Big Sister!" Jade Moon whispered. "Big Sister!"

A voice answered from inside the darkened room: "Oh! It's you, Jade Moon. Please come in."

Jade Moon lost no time with formalities but started at once: "Big Sister, a terrible thing happened yesterday at Loyalty's factory, just after he left here. They ....*they* beat a woman to death in public. She was a high-up in the factory and a member of the Party, and afterwards all the other office cadres had to wear dunce caps and were paraded through the streets in a truck with their heads down and their accusations hung around their necks. And the truck was one of their own trucks from the factory and ...." Jade Moon stopped, out of breath.

"You're all excited, Jade Moon," said Big Sister quietly. "Just take it a little slower. You'll get a heart attack!"

"Thank you, Big Sister. But I didn't come to tell you all this, really. I want to ask you something more personal: Do you have a place where you could take refuge until these troubles blow over?"

"Thank you, Jade Moon, for your concern for me. I know there's trouble all around, like what happened to Pastor Bao and his wife, and what happened to you night before last. And just think — it all started from you hanging your laundry on the roof. How ridiculous! By the way, are you going to keep on hanging your laundry up there?"

"Why, of course. If I stopped now, The Demon would grab hold of that as sure evidence that she was right." Jade Moon leaned forward and lowered her voice. "But now, about you. I don't want anything to ... to... to happen to you..."

"Jade Moon," Big Sister interrupted, "For me personally, I'm not concerned in the least. During the Japanese War I stayed in Shanghai. I see no reason to leave now."

"But, Big Sister, this is different. Only God and a miracle can keep you from having serious trouble ...."

"You're exactly right, Jade Moon. I believe in God and I believe in miracles. And I believe that God has already planned a miracle for me."

By Wednesday of that week the usual flow of Shanghai life was logjammed by the ubiquitous Red Guards. Lorries that normally brought vegetables to the Distribution Center were commandeered to parade through the streets a hapless jumble of people disgraced with dunce caps on their heads and denunciations around their necks. So there was little to do at the Distribution Center, and the workers were given a half-day off. Jade Moon arrived home at 1 p.m.

Strange, she said to herself. *I get a half-day off, thanks to the Red Guards, and I spend the time straightening up the house after they wrecked it!*

In repacking clothes the Red Guards had scattered on the floor, she found that some had collected mildew over the summer, so she decided to wash them at once.

Jade Moon tied the clothes in a sheet and took them to the communal bathroom downstairs. She washed them in a wooden tub with a bar of brownish-yellow soap, then dumped them back into the sheet for the trip to the roof. The September sun was hot, but there was a fresh easterly breeze blowing off the ocean. Jade Moon breathed deeply of the fresh air and thanked God she was alive.

She was hanging up the last piece — the sheet — when she heard a scream, then a thud in the courtyard back of the house. She ran to the parapet, leaned over and looked down.

To her horror, there in a heap in the courtyard lay The Demon, still holding in her hand a rung of the ladder — her ladder which she had installed to spy on Jade Moon on the roof.

The rung gave way and she fell! Jade Moon realized instantly. She ran into the attic, down the spiral stairway, down the main stairway and out the back door to the courtyard. It was empty, apart from The Demon lying there senseless but alive, moaning piteously.

Jade Moon breathed a prayer: "Oh, Lord, have mercy! Show me what to do!"

The answer came at once, almost audibly: "Don't touch her. Call the police."

She dashed out of the house, knowing that a policeman was on duty at the corner. She was surprised to find not one but two policemen there. The three of them ran back to the house. The Demon was just as Jade Moon had left her, still in a heap on the ground, still clutching a faulty rung of the ladder.

"I'll have to get a stretcher," said the older of the two men. "Be back in a minute." And off he went.

The younger policeman stooped down and took the metal rung out of The Demon's hands. He held it up and examined it.

"Hmmmp!" he grunted. "See this fissure here?" He pointed at one end of the rung, where it had literally come apart. "This," he stated emphatically, "is a product of a backyard furnace from the Great Leap Forward time. Very poor stuff."

He looked up at the ladder and went on: "It's a wonder anybody would ever use this stuff to make a ladder."

Jade Moon could only nod in agreement before superior male knowledge. After all, what did *she* know about iron and making ladders?

The policeman took out his notebook and jotted down

details of the accident: who reported it, to whom and the exact minute of the report — as well as he could remember the minute. By the time he had done this the older policeman was back with a stretcher.

Jade Moon asked: "Where are you taking her?"

"To the Sixth Municipal," replied the older policeman.

Jade Moon let the men and their still-unconscious burden out the big front door. For some reason which she herself did not understand, she did not return to the roof to finish hanging up her laundry. Instead, she went back to the rear courtyard. She looked carefully around, grateful that there were no prying eyes.

Ah! What's that in the corner? Something brown, and plastic. Jade Moon bent down and picked up the object. The Demon's billfold. It was open.

Hmm, she conjectured, *it must have been thrown out of her pocket when she fell, and flew open when it hit the ground.* She searched the ground nearby, and found a few small bills, a few coins. Then she spotted a piece of white paper. It was lying to one side, folded two or three times.

She stooped, picked it up, and unfolded it. It was a note, addressed "To Whom It May Concern."

"Hmm," Jade Moon said, almost aloud. "Who *does* this concern?"

She read: "To Whom It May Concern,
This is to certify
that one of the outstanding
counter-revolutionaries of Shanghai is
Lan Aimi, alias Big Sister,
331–5 Long March Road, Shanghai.
She poses to be blind and poor, but
this is a front for her counter-revolutionary
activity and her espionage. She is a spy for
the Chiang Kai-shek clique on Taiwan.

(signed) A Patriot"

Jade Moon read the note through twice, then crushed it violently and thrust it into her bosom. Leaving billfold and money on the ground, she ran up the stairs to her room, locked the door and fell down on her knees beside the bed.

She prayed, "Oh, Lord! Thank you that this note was delivered into my hands and not into the hands of the Red Guards. Dear Lord, it was addressed 'To Whom It May Concern', and you sent it to a person who is very concerned. Thank you."

Later that afternoon Jade Moon was beginning to prepare supper in the communal kitchen on the ground floor. She lit the fire under the *wok* with a spill of white paper of considerably better quality than one normally uses for the purpose.

After supper, Jade Moon sent Lotus to fetch Big Sister. The Lees' two rooms provided a little more privacy than Big Sister's one.

Once the door was closed and locked, Big Sister said: "I know what you're going to tell me. I heard the policeman from up at the corner. He and another man were carrying out something heavy. Was it The Demon? Earlier, I heard a heavy thud, like someone dropping a sack of cement from the roof. Did The Demon fall down from some place?"

"Well, Big Sister, you're amazing! The strength from your eyes has gone to your ears. You know half the story already." Jade Moon told her the rest, beginning with the laundry in the wooden tub and ending with the accusing letter burning under the iron *wok*.

Afterwards Big Sister sat silent for a long minute, hands folded in lap. "Let's thank the Lord," she said finally. "This is the miracle He planned for me."

"Lotus, it's your day off. How would you like to make a trip to town for me?" Jade Moon asked. "I hear the Christian bookstore has been closed down, but I know Miss Ni the manager, and I'll give you a note for her. Maybe she can go in the back door and bring out at least a New Testament. I miss my Bible so much since ...since...I lost it the other night."

"Yes, Mama, you write the note and I'll take it into town," Lotus agreed.

"Give Miss Ni my loving regards," Jade Moon said before leaving for work.

Lotus Flower waited until the morning rush hour was over. Even so, it was all she could do to fight her way aboard a trolley. She found Miss Ni's address all right. She was still living above the bookstore, which was locked and sealed with strips of paper stamped with red ink.

After she read the note, Miss Ni invited Lotus upstairs. "Have a cup of tea while I go down and get a New Testament for you," she offered. "You're fortunate to come this morning. The city government sealed my stock and records a long time ago. But now they have unsealed everything inside the shop and required me to inventory it all. Later today, they are coming to seal everything back up again."

When Miss Ni returned, Lotus slipped the New Testament into her black bag and zipped it closed.

"Excuse me," Miss Ni said, "I have four friends helping with the inventory, so I must run." She escorted Lotus to the door that led out onto the street. As they were saying goodbye, an ominous sound struck their ears: *Dah...dah... DAH, DAH, DAH*, Two slow beats, three fast.

The two women looked at one another, and Lotus said it for both of them: "I wonder who they're after today.."

The sound of drums came closer: *Dah!...dah!...DAH! DAH! DAH!* A serious note came into Miss Ni's voice: "I think I'd better be inside."

Lotus recognized this as her polite way of saying: "You had better leave!" So she said goodbye and turned to walk away just as a troupe of Red Guards with drummer leading turned into the lane. As she passed them, Lotus Flower tried not to look at the troupe. She squeezed the black plastic bag and its precious contents a little tighter to her side, as if the Red Guards might have x-ray eyes and see what was inside.

She turned the corner into the main street, then stopped. Were the Red Guards really headed for Miss Ni's place, or for somewhere farther down the lane? Ominously, at that very moment the drum beat stopped. Lotus looked back around the corner, and her heart sank heavy as lead within her. The Red Guards were going in Miss Ni's door!

What shall I do? Lotus asked herself. *I can't just go away and leave her! But I can't do a thing to help her! And what if they catch me with my New Testament?*

Perturbed and undecided, she lowered her head and began looking into the window of a shop across the street. After all, there can be more than one reason for window shopping.

Suddenly Lotus Flower heard a *THUD*! as a heavy object struck the ground up the lane she had just left. She turned around to see a box in the middle of the lane. As she watched, a Red Guard stepped out of Miss Ni's door with a second box and *THUD*! down it came beside the first. Another Red Guard emerged with a loose stack of books in his arms; he threw them on top of the boxes and they scattered in all directions.

What are they doing to Miss Ni's books? Why, she was inventorying them for the city government!

Lotus did not have to wait long for her answer. Another Red Guard shot out of the door with an armful of file folders. These, too, he threw on top of the pile. Then he took several sheets of paper from the file folders and wadded them up. As Lotus looked on in disbelief, he pulled a box of matches out of his pocket and lit a piece of wadded paper. Methodically wadding up more loose sheets of paper, he added these to the blaze. Other Red Guards tore the covers off books and ripped the books into pieces. Before long the small blaze had burst into a bonfire.

That's terrible! Lotus Flower reacted angrily. *Those are Bibles and hymnbooks and Bible-study books! Why are they burning them?*

But the worst was yet to come. When book after book had been thrown into the flames, suddenly there was a commotion in the doorway. A Red Guard was pushing the elderly Miss Ni through the door and onto the street. She was screaming in pain. The Red Guard had twisted her arm up behind her back and was pushing her forward by pushing on the arm. As Lotus Flower looked on, she almost screamed in horror herself.

Still holding Miss Ni's arm, the Red Guard thrust her down on the ground perilously close to the fire of burning books. "There!" he shouted at her. "You worship your Bible, don't you? Well, worship those Bibles in front of you now!"

There was another scream of pain from the doorway and a second Red Guard threw a second woman into the street. Then he picked her up bodily and thrust her down next to Miss Ni, again dangerously close to the roaring bonfire. Then an older man was thrust out the same way. And another. And another.

Lotus Flower looked in desperation at the five people, all elderly, around the fire. Still on their knees, they began to back away; the Red Guard leader kicked first one then another, forcing them closer to the fire.

He was shouting now at the top of his voice: "You're all religious people, aren't you? Worship those Bibles now while they're burning! Get closer, you! And you! And you!" And he kicked and kicked.

Sickened and faint, Lotus Flower turned away. Instead of taking the trolley, she walked all the way home, hoping the fresh air and exercise would keep her from going out of her mind.

Some time later she heard that two of the elderly people

died of burns and a third committed suicide because he couldn't endure the pain.

25. More Red Guards
Autumn 1966

AT THE END OF SEPTEMBER conflict between the Red Guards and the weaving mill cadres reached a climax. It would have come sooner but for a number of Red Guards leaving Shanghai on "link-up" junkets for "experience-exchanges" with Red Guards in other cities, notably Wuhan and Beijing. For the purpose they rode the trains free of charge on "link-up tickets." While they were away the factory cadres breathed more easily, but on their return the Red Guards, armed with fresh slogans and new techniques, attacked with renewed vigor.

The man under greatest pressure was Manager Ye Ming. The pressure came not only from the Red Guards on the outside but also from within his own soul, where a guilt complex had built up concerning the death of the treasurer. Going about the factory compound he would grab anyone he met and explain, "She didn't want to be treasurer. I insisted and I am the cause of her death."

Loyalty ran into him one afternoon in front of the office. The Manager caught him by the shoulders and held him in a vice-like grip while he went through his obsession, concluding, "I am to blame for her death."

As Loyalty looked into the Manager's bloodshot eyes he felt he was seeing a man losing his reason. It was only with some difficulty and many apologies that he could break free.

On the last day of September the Red Guards moved in and announced they were taking over the factory. It was obvious, of course, that these rampaging students knew nothing about running any department of a weaving mill, from the typist's desk in the office to the foul, steamy dyeing vat at the far end of the compound. But they dominated the entire factory and settled like a miasma on every single individual.

A dozen of them moved in bodily. They claimed the best beds in the dormitories and preempted first place in the food line. For Loyalty this alien influence in the factory was like a cancer. He knew that though hidden for a while it would eventually break out in its innate malignancy. And he realized that as a Christian he was singularly vulnerable.

In the last few weeks Mighty Tower Gou had been joining him in reading the Bible.

"I want to be frank with you," Loyalty said to Tower. "If *they* catch us reading the Bible together it might go hard with you. You might even be 'struggled'."

"Well, Loyalty, who knows who is going to be 'struggled' next? I'd rather we went on doing as we have been doing."

As the two friends were reading the Bible together one evening, they did not notice that a Red Guard had quietly stolen up behind them. He reached over Loyalty's shoulder and grabbed the book out of his hands.

"What do you mean by reading something that is not Mao Zedong's Thought!" he shouted.

"It's my own book that I brought here. It's a Bible."

"So, you're a Christian, are you? I thought those people all died out long ago!"

"No, they did not die out. You're looking at one now."

"Why do you want to read a book full of myths like Jonah swallowing a whale and the camel that went through the eye of a needle? Ha! Don't you know that under the guidance of Chairman Mao religion will wither on the vine?"

"That's hard to believe, as long as God's love is in the world," said Bright Loyalty quietly.

"Love! That's the big mistake you Christians make. It's hate, not love, that's going to conquer the world. Hate will cut down the capitalists and imperialists once for all. You can't wage class warfare without hate!"

"Well, I guess we'll see in the end which wins out, love or hate."

"In the end! You Christians always "hide from this life, dream about the next world," as the proverb says. We Communists believe in facing the real world here and now. *That's* what I think of your Bible!" The Red Guard slammed the Bible down on the floor and stomped on it.

On a dull and threatening October afternoon Strong Hero and Lotus Flower walked up to the ticket window at the entrance to Fuxing Park. Hero put down a two-cent piece for his own ticket and another for Lotus Flower's.

After they surrendered the tickets at the gate, Lotus teased: "So, you paid two cents for me; do you think I'm worth it?"

"Worth it?" responded Hero, "Why, I'd pay even twice that amount for you!"

Lotus Flower burst out with a loud and happy laugh. Just then a bent old park sweeper with her broom and her dustpan on its long stick passed by.

"What are you laughing about, young woman?" demanded the old sweeper. "There's nothing to laugh about these days."

As if heaven itself concurred with this view, at that instant it began to rain. Lotus ignored the old woman's remark and put up her umbrella. Hero had brought his umbrella, too, but he left it folded and tucked under his arm.

Lotus asked: "Why don't you use your umbrella?"

"Because," he answered, "I'd rather help you use yours."

Hero slipped his hand under Lotus's arm and took hold of her umbrella. In response, Lotus Flower pressed his hand a little closer to her body.

"Don't you know," Hero went on, "that with candy two pieces are better than one but with umbrellas one is better than two?"

Again Lotus laughed happily, though not as loud as

before. No matter, the old woman with her broom and dustpan was already out of earshot.

The two were walking in step now, and close together to stay dry under the one umbrella. With the umbrella they could talk in lower tones and in more privacy than without it. And walking close together gave a nearness which felt very comfortable. They preferred rainy days for walking in the park.

After a while they found a stretch of walkway with few other people. Hero confided: "Something happened at our house — between my sister Rosebud and Mama. You know Rosebud is only ten but she's terribly enthusiastic about the Red Guards, especially since they organized in her school. Imagine, Red Guards in an elementary school!

"Well, the first thing Rosebud did was to insist that Mama buy a little bust of Mao Zedong, about six inches high, white and made of plaster of paris. Well, Mama gave in and bought it. *Then* Rosebud didn't like it when Mama put it on the little table by the door. She wanted it in the place of honor at the opposite side of the room, on the table where we always keep the Bible.

"That was too much for Mama. The symbolism was too obvious. So, we have the Great Helmsman's bust, but it sits on the table beside the door."

Then the subject shifted to The Demon's fall from the ladder and how that had saved Big Sister from plenty of trouble.

Hero reacted: "I'm glad she's out of danger, at least for now. It shows what God can do for His children. Say, couldn't God do something special for us and help us get married soon?"

Lotus giggled. There was still a lot of the little girl in her. "Umm.... We could ask Big Sister to help. Her prayers are pretty potent."

"Oh!" Hero interrupted. "The clock up there says 3:20. I

promised Mama I'd go by the school and pick up Rosebud at
four o'clock and walk home with her. Mama's worried about
her, the way things are going."

Walking through the streets in the rain, still very close to
each other, Hero and Lotus arrived at Progressive Elementary
School just before four o'clock. Instead of going into the
school grounds, they decided to wait across the street from
the main gate.

As they stood there a commotion broke out in the school
yard, at first far inside then coming closer and closer. Red
arm bands appeared inside the school gate. They were worn
by a dozen or more pre-teenage girls, little look-alikes each
with a pigtail down her back.

"Hmm! Those kids are Red Guards!" muttered Hero. "I
wonder what they're up to..."

As they watched they saw that a woman teacher was
the center of attention. She was walking as fast as she
could, but the girls with red arm bands were jumping and
running around her in circles and shouting insults at her.
Lotus was shocked to hear the words they were using. She
clapped her hand over her mouth in shame; she had never
before heard children abuse a teacher with such foul and
obscene language.

As the group spilled out of the school yard and passed the
flower beds which flanked the gate, one of the girls picked up
a piece of the broken brick which bordered the flower beds.
She drew her arm back awkwardly and threw the brickbat at
the teacher who, distracted by the children's insults, did not
see it coming. A sharp corner of the brickbat struck her on
the forehead above the right eye. It penetrated the skin and
drew blood.

The sight of blood had an electric effect on the children,
turning them into maniacs. They had drawn blood; they
wanted more blood.

As the teacher stood half dazed, trying to wipe the blood

out of her eye, another girl picked up a brickbat and hurled it at her. It missed her and glanced off the shoulder of a schoolmate. A third girl picked up a whole brick from the flower bed border. It was too heavy to throw, so she took it in both hands, ran up back of the teacher and with all her strength crashed it into her head.

The teacher groaned with pain and tried to run from her tormentors, but she could not see clearly. She stumbled and fell, hitting her head on the curbstone. The third blow to her head was too much and she passed out.

Across the street, Hero and Lotus were horrified. Hero yelled: "Come on! Let's see if we can help!" At the same time he dropped the umbrella and yanked Lotus from the sidewalk onto the street.

Hero grabbed the girl who had hit the teacher in the back of the head; she was still holding the brick in her two hands.

"Here!" he yelled at her. "Cut that out! You'll kill her!"

Lotus grabbed the right arm of the girl who had thrown the first brickbat and was now holding a second one, ready to throw it.

As if by prearranged signal, the two girls began to kick, scream and bite. Twisting and turning, they both freed themselves. In the meantime another girl, seeing the teacher flat on the ground, jumped onto her, shoes and all, and began to jump up and down on her. In short order other girls followed suit, so that in seconds a half dozen girls were jumping up and down viciously on the prostrate body, screaming expletives and obscene words at the top of their voices.

Hero grabbed one of them by the arm and jerked her off so violently that he flung her to the ground. Lotus yanked another girl off; this one was small and looked like a ten-year old. However, when they pulled one off, two more jumped on. The girls were yelling and screaming and driving them-selves into a frenzy, like so many dervishes gone mad.

A half dozen of them now turned on Hero, kicking, clawing, screaming, biting. Others attacked Lotus.

"Help! Help! Help!" Hero yelled at the top of his lungs. But no one came. The tragic figure on the ground was bleeding from the mouth and the only motion she made was when a girl jumped on her body.

Eventually Hero realized that no one was coming to their aid and that it was time to beat a retreat — if they could. Grabbing Lotus Flower by the hand he yelled: "Let's go!"

They headed back across the street. To their surprise, none of the girls pursued them. Hero picked up their umbrella from the ground where he had flung it and raised it over their heads again, for it was still raining. Then the two of them turned and looked back across the street.

They saw a strange sight. The death dance on the body of the teacher had abruptly stopped. The arms and legs that had dealt out destruction suddenly went limp. The bedlam had fizzled into silence.

A shrill voice piped up: "Look at the blood!"

And another: "She's not *dead*, is she?"

Then one of the little girls leaned up against the gate post and vomited. Another bent over, vomited onto the sidewalk and then collapsed in a faint. The rest simply stood and looked, first at each other and then at the motionless figure on the ground. Suddenly they were all little girls again, vulnerable, sad, self-accusing, horrified.

One by one they picked up their book satchels and silently slunk away.

Hero and Lotus again crossed the street to the scene of carnage. By this time a crowd was beginning to gather. Two figures were still prostrate on the ground, the teacher and the girl who had fainted.

Strong Hero felt the wrist of the teacher, and could find no pulse. He put his ear on her chest and could hear no heartbeat.

He said, to no one in particular: "I'm afraid she's done for."

Then he went over to the girl who had fainted. She was lying half on the sidewalk, half on the street. He turned her over onto her back, and then almost fainted himself.

The girl was his little sister Rosebud.

Lotus walked home with Hero and Rosebud, afraid the child might faint again. As if by agreement, they refrained from questioning her. The three of them walked silently through the wet streets of Shanghai.

As soon as she saw her mother, Rosebud burst into tears. When the sobbing finally subsided, Mother Liang asked: "Now Rosebud, what's the cause for this?"

"Mama, I didn't do it! I didn't throw a thing! I didn't stomp on her at all!" And she broke out crying again.

Hero spoke up: "Rosebud, is it okay if I tell Mama what happened?"

Rosebud nodded her head. The tears welled up again. Hero quickly told of the tragedy he and Lotus had witnessed.

When he finished, her mother looked at Rosebud and said: "And what part did you have in all this?"

"Mama, I didn't do *anything*. It was the Red Guards. They won't allow any of the rest of us to 'struggle' the teachers. Because we aren't Red Guards. And I can't be a Red Guard because our family's on the Black List."

"Well, then," her mother pursued, "why were you there when they stomped her?"

"Mama, I wanted so much to be a Red Guard. All the girls who are popular are Red Guards. I prayed to Chairman Mao that I could be a Red Guard, but ...."

"*Prayed* to Chairman Mao?" her mother interrupted. "How on earth can you pray to a man in Beijing if you are in Shanghai?"

"Oh, no, not to the Chairman Mao in Beijing but to the Chairman Mao over there on the table." Rosebud pointed to the white plaster bust of Mao on the table beside the door.

"To *that* Chairman Mao?" her mother blurted out in astonishment.

"Yes, Mama."

"When do you pray to him?"

"Twice a day."

"Well, I never ...." her mother began and stopped.

"Yes, twice a day. In the morning on my way to school I ask his direction. And in the afternoon I report to him."

Rosebud must have seen her mother's face fall, for she said quickly: "Isn't that all right? A lot of the kids in our class do it."

Mother Liang turned to Hero and Lotus: "You two stay here. Rosebud and I are going into the back room to talk some more."

Lotus felt that this was her cue. She said to Hero: "I'm so sorry all this happened. I'd better be going now. Anyway, you'll have to report back to the factory by 6 p.m."

Saying goodbye, however, was not a quick and easy business. First there was goodbye inside the room. Then Hero let her out the door, closed it all but a crack, and they said goodbye again in the hall. Finally, Hero held her hand a moment in silence. That was all he dared to do in a place as public as the hall.

A little girl's voice coming from inside the room broke the silence. "Dear Mr. Chairman Mao, please forgive me for not getting to stomp on that old teacher. I wanted to show them that I could be just as good a Red Guard as they are!"

Bright Loyalty had lost his good ball-point pen. It was Liberation Brand, and they were scarce and hard to buy. And to lose it was to have no respect for the workmen who made the pen in the first place with their ingenuity, sweat and toil.

Loyalty went back to the looms where he and Tower had been doing repair work all day, but the pen was not there. Could he have dropped it going to the toilet? He took the familiar path to the back of the compound, searching along both sides as he went.

It's quiet back here this time of day, he said to himself. As he approached the toilet, however, he heard a familiar *slosh-slosh* and smelled heavy ammonia odor. Old Hunchie the Hunchback was emptying the cesspit — ladling out the liquid manure with a small wood bucket wired to the end of a bamboo pole, and pouring it into the "honey cart", as the factory workers euphemistically called it.

Normally Loyalty did not care to be around for that operation, but today he was intent on finding his pen. So he went into the toilet. Added to the shock to his nose was now a shock to his eyes; it was not Old Hunchie emptying the cesspit, but the Assistant Manager of the company!

"Oh! Oh! Excuse me!" said Loyalty, embarrassed and starting to retreat.

"Don't run off, son," the Assistant Manager said, leaning for a moment on the long pole with the dripping bucket at the end. "You're just in time to give me a hand." He waved to a second ladle leaning against the wall.

Swallowing twice and trying not to breathe too hard — the stench was always worse when the pit was being emptied — Loyalty dutifully grabbed the ladle and dipped the action end into the mess below. He murmured to himself: *First time in my life to do this.*

The Assistant Manager was happy to have someone to talk to: "I'm glad to see you willing to do this, son. The Red Guards assigned me to this job. I'm grateful to them for pointing out to me the path of patriotism and duty. They have stressed this in their nightly classes ever since they took over the factory. Why shouldn't I do a job that the common people do every day of their lives, especially the peasants in the countryside?"

Bright Loyalty didn't answer. As he heaved bucket after stinking bucket of liquid manure into the cart, he was thinking of something else. Finally he asked: "Who showed you how to do this? Did one of the Red Guards come back here to show you?"

Loyalty was ashamed to look the Assistant Manager in the face. He kept on dipping, heaving and emptying as if his question was a very casual one, hardly needing an answer.

But the Assistant Manager did answer: "Oh, no! What would the Red Guards know about this job? I learned it from Old Hunchie, of course."

Bright Loyalty dipped, heaved and emptied several more times, then asked again: "Do they come back here to supervise your work?"

"The first couple of days they did, but not any more. You can't imagine how grateful I am for this opportunity to identify with The People."

Loyalty dipped, heaved and emptied again. Since the Assistant Manager apparently wanted to talk, he asked again: "When did you start on this today?"

"At three o'clock this afternoon."

"Has there been anyone at your desk since then?"

"Oh, one of the Red Guards is there."

Bright Loyalty thought about that desk in the office, empty except for some teenage student with a red armband. As he conjured up that picture in his mind, he inadvertently missed the hole in the tank and hit the rim around the hole instead. Dried out by standing unused against the wall too long, the bucket shattered on the impact and flew into a dozen pieces, dumping the odoriferous liquid down the side of the cart and splashing Bright Loyalty generously.

The profound stench hit him square in the face. It was more than he could take, and he began to retch from the bottom of his stomach. He ran out of the toilet, gasping for fresh air. He made for a tree beside the path, put his arm up against it and laid his head against his arm, still retching miserably and uncontrollably.

In a moment the Assistant Manager came out, put his hand in a fatherly way on Loyalty's shoulder and said: "That's all right, young man. Maybe you'd better go and have a rest now."

Controlling himself as well as he could, Loyalty slowly walked to the dormitory. After taking a shower and washing his clothes, he asked Mighty Tower to go for a stroll. As they walked, he told his friend about the Assistant Manager. Then he asked thoughtfully: "I've heard about 'brainwashing'; is *that* what it means to be 'brainwashed'?"

The Red Guards held forth nightly on the platform near the spot where the treasurer met her demise. Unfortunately, the intellectual content of the lectures was limited to the Red Guards' standard slogans. The lectures were peppered with, "Chairman Mao says...", followed by what he had told the Red Guards in six glorious rallies in Beijing in August. It was difficult to challenge them on such points, for after all *they* were there and no one else was.

The Red Guards were as securely in charge as if everyone in the factory were handcuffed. No absenteeism was allowed at the night sessions. A Red Guard girl whom the factory hands dubbed "The Counter" saw to that.

One night The Counter climbed the platform and interrupted The Leader in the middle of a sentence. After listening for a moment, he barked into his megaphone: "A strange and unforgivable thing has happened. The former manager Ye Ming is absent. Six of you will go look for him at once, three teams of two men each. You .. and you...and you..." He pointed to six young men. "Search the compound thoroughly, then report back to me."

Mighty Tower and Bright Loyalty looked at each other. They were standing close to the platform; both had been pointed at.

"Let's go!" said Tower.

After they were a little distance from the crowd, Loyalty remarked, "It's great to move around a bit and not just stand there!"

"You're right, Loyalty," Tower answered. "But I don't like the Manager being absent. He looked okay when I saw him this afternoon, except for that faraway look on his face that he's had since The Incident, only today more faraway than usual...I wonder..." Tower's voice trailed off.

"Wonder what?" Loyalty asked.

"Well, you never can tell what a man will do if he has one thing on his mind for weeks. Especially if that one thing is somebody being murdered." Mighty Tower did not elaborate but he quickened his pace across the drillground.

"Where'll we go first?" Loyalty asked.

"Let's go over to the looms," Tower suggested. "Plenty of places there for a man to hide."

The area was only semi-lit. Little electricity was wasted while everyone was at a meeting.

As they neared the loom room Loyalty sniffed: "What's that strange smell? I don't think I ever smelled anything like that around here."

Entering the huge loom room they looked for a light switch. The small flashlight Tower had with him helped.

Loyalty couldn't get that smell off his mind: "Tower, it's worse in here. What do you think it is?"

"No idea. We'd better take a good look."

They finally got enough lights on to pick their way back through the looms. Loyalty said thoughtfully: "That smell is like burnt meat. But not exactly, either. It's worse."

The objectionable odor grew stronger as they worked their way farther down the aisle between the looms. At the far end of the room it was overpowering.

"Now, *where* does it come from?" Bright Loyalty asked. Then he answered his own question: "Tower! Look here! Isn't that something on top of that motor?"

The two friends looked up, and with the help of Tower's little light they saw a human body slumped over one of the electric motors that powered a line of looms.

"Don't touch him!" yelled Tower. "The electricity might still be on!"

Jabbing the beam from the flashlight here and there, they searched feverishly for the switch that controlled the motor. Finally they found it. Sure enough, it was on the "ON" position. Tower quickly pulled it down to "OFF".

With effort they pulled the body off the motor. One hand was tightly gripping the positive pole, the other the negative. They knew even before looking into the face that it was Ye Ming.

They stretched him on the floor and searched for signs of life. There were none. No pulse, no heartbeat, no breathing. The body was already cold; he had been dead for some time. Tower flashed his light back onto the motor and read the telltale figure: "440 VOLTS".

"He died quickly," he said. "No one could live long with that voltage going through his body."

"Could he have left a note?" wondered Loyalty. He unbuttoned the pockets of the Manager's jacket.

In the left breast pocket they found a neatly-folded piece of paper. Loyalty opened it out, and by Tower's light they read:

"To the friends I leave behind:

I Ye Ming, take full responsibility for the untimely death of Hong Yuling. I hope that in some way my death may atone for hers.

(signed) Ye Ming"

26. The Episode Of The Split Pants
Winter 1966 — 67

LATE ONE AFTERNOON in December a new face appeared in the men's dormitory of the Golden Streams Weaving Factory. The red armband with the black characters "Red Guard" was the same as usual. The air of insolence and superiority was the same. But the man himself was new and his questions were those of an outsider:

"How many Red Guards are sleeping in this dormitory?" The visitor jotted down the answer in a notebook. "How many are eating in the mess hall?" More jottings. "What is the name of your leader?"

A few of the workers gathered around and answered his questions. Others, including Mighty Tower and Bright Loyalty, found it convenient to putter about doing little chores in the middle distance — but not out of earshot.

After the visitor left and they were on their way to the mess hall, Loyalty asked Tower: "What do you make of him?"

He replied: "I'm not a prophet, but something tells me that his coming here is for no good."

That night at the regular harangue The Leader was nervous and more unsure of himself than Bright Loyalty had ever seen him.

Without preliminaries he pitched in: "There was a spy on this property this afternoon. You men in the dormitory should have had enough sense to report him to me at once. He is from Du Huan University and represents an upstart and unorthodox group that call themselves Red Guards and are not. If he or anyone else from Du Huan University comes through our big gate again we will throw them out bodily!"

Over the next few days Tower and Loyalty realized that the situation was worse than they had first thought. Sandbags were piled up at either side of the main gate, and a wall of sandbags built across the entire entrance a few feet back from the gate. This allowed the big double gate to open and close, but compelled anyone entering the compound to zigzag around the obstructions before he could come in.

The Leader also had the factory's carpenter turn out plywood shields complete with handhold on the back, and clubs the size and shape of baseball bats. The free time between five and six p.m. now became drill time. Every worker in the factory, male and female, marched, counter marched, drilled and fought mock battles every day for an hour. What had formerly been called "the drill ground" now became a drill ground in reality.

Seeing the warlike preparations, Tower shook his head and said to Loyalty: "It doesn't look good."

"I don't know whether anyone else in this factory knows it but I want to share with you, Tower, that this is Christmas Day, the day when Jesus was born. I wish we had peace and goodwill on earth like He came to bring."

"Well," returned Tower, "let's hope that today at least will be peaceful."

But it was not to be. At three o'clock the factory alarm sounded — three shorts and three longs, the Red Alert. Looms were instantly shut down, lights in the office went off, supper fires in the kitchen were covered. Every worker, young and old, grabbed his shield and club and headed outside. There they found Red Guards shouting: "To the big gate! To the big gate!"

Tower and Loyalty had put down their repairmen's tools

and tumbled outside with the rest of the workers.

Tower whispered: "Don't be in too big a hurry. Let somebody else get there first. This isn't our fight."

As they ran across the drill ground toward the entrance, they saw that the double gate itself, a steel frame strung with link fencing, was already closed. Outside were three lorries disgorging Red Guards, who carried lengths of iron pipe and construction steel.

Suddenly a Red Guard outside gave an order and those who had already made a rush on the gate fell back from it. The same man gave a signal to one of the lorry drivers, who backed his vehicle away from the gate.

"He's going to ram the gate!" Loyalty shouted.

With the motor revved up as fast as it would go, the lorry lunged forward and crashed into the gate. Not being made to withstand such an impact, the gate collapsed and the lorry rolled over it. The wall of sandbags inside the gate fared little better. The heavily armed crowd of Red Guards poured in after the lorry. They flailed right and left with their lengths of iron and steel, as if cutting down grain with scythes.

Almost to a man, the factory workers turned tail and ran, leaving the handful of resident Red Guards to face the onslaught alone. Attackers outnumbered defenders three to one, so the battle was soon over.

It was not until lights were out that night in the dormitory that Tower and Loyalty discovered almost every man there had decided as they had: "It's their fight, not ours."

Strangely, no one was killed in "The Battle at the Gate", as the workers called it. But The Leader went down with two broken legs and The Counter with one, and most of the defenders were injured.

Far from restoring the original administration at Golden Streams Weaving Factory, the victors merely moved into the slots vacated by the vanquished. A new set of Red Guards appropriated free housing in the dormitories and free meals in the mess hall.

There was, however, one big difference. The newcomers stopped the daily drills and nightly meetings; instead, they sought to win over the workers gradually. So an alliance developed between workers and Red Guards in the weaving factory. This was more effective, but the workers were to rue the day when collaboration began.

Like millions of other thinking people, Tower and Loyalty were astonished one day, horrified the next and mystified the third day by what they saw and heard. Their safety valve that new year of 1967 was an occasional walk together in the park, when they could air their feelings to each other.

As they strolled together on a free day, Tower remarked: "What a time to be alive! It seems it's all right if people don't have food to eat, clothes to wear or a place to live, but the one thing that is not all right is not to be a revolutionary!"

"At what point of the revolution are we now? Can you figure that out?"

"Well, in many places Red Guards and workers are uniting, like in our factory, and that's quite a power base. What I would like to know is, in all these surges of power, where is the Communist Party itself? It hasn't stuck its head above the surface anywhere."

"And where," asked Loyalty, 'is the People's Liberation Army?"

"Now there you've put your finger on something!" Tower replied. "We may just hear from the army one of these days."

"One thing certain is that we're dealing with a lot of uncertainties. Which way the wind blows next is up for grabs."

"Right, Loyalty. And I've been thinking that in all this uncertainty you're a lot better off than I am. You have your Christian faith and I have no religion at all."

"I have to admit," said Loyalty thoughtfully, "that I've got very few things to show you as tangible evidence of my Christian faith. We are a church without buildings and without Bibles. Even my New Testament they took away on New Year's Day..."

"But material things such as buildings and books are not the final thing. You've got a faith in your heart that doesn't depend on external things."

"Well, Tower, there's no reason why you couldn't have that faith in your heart, too.... Why don't you go home with me sometime and talk with old Pastor Bao about it?"

As January dragged on, production slumped at the weaving factory. The supply of yarn from spinning mills was disrupted by Red Guard intrusion into them, and even on days when they could operate, the looms would suddenly stutter to a stop when the electricity went off unannounced. Spare parts were harder and harder to get, and Mighty Tower and Bright Loyalty were reduced to patching up hopelessly worn out parts or making do with substitutes of their own concoction. This meant more breakdowns of the looms and longer hours of work for the two friends.

One morning four cadres arrived from the municipal government, obviously a Committee of Investigation. Walking down an aisle of silent looms, the four men ran across Mighty Tower and Bright Loyalty in the middle of a pool of pieces of a dismantled loom.

"What's the trouble here, comrade?" one of the men asked Loyalty.

"We are replacing some of the comb for the warp. The loom is very old, comrade."

One of the men turned to Tower: "How is it that you two are the only people at work in this entire room?"

"I guess no yarn came in yesterday so we can't operate today."

"How often are you shut down?"

Tower calculated a minute, counting up on his fingers: "About half the time."

The two older men exchanged knowing glances. The cadre asked again: "Do you know why you haven't been supplied with yarn?"

Mighty Tower answered innocently: "Well, we haven't been told that."

Again the two men exchanged glances.

Just then Bright Loyalty noticed a noise behind him. Turning, he saw a half-dozen Red Guards, leaders of the new faction that had taken over the factory, descending upon them.

The New Leader barged up. With no introduction or preliminaries he burst out: "See here! Where do you guys come from?"

The senior of the four men drew himself up erect and replied: "From the Municipal Government of the City of Shanghai."

"And what do you mean, coming into this factory without my consent?"

"Excuse me, but this factory is owned and operated by the City of Shanghai. It is our responsibility to..."

He got no farther. The Red Guard slapped his thigh angrily, looking as if he would rather have slapped the man's face. "Get yourselves off this compound in two minutes or I'll throw you off myself!"

Again the two older men exchanged glances. Without a word they turned and walked quietly out of the building. The Red Guards followed, muttering invectives under their breath.

After both groups had gone out of the door, Loyalty scrambled to his feet and said: "Let's watch them leave the compound."

The two friends stood in the shadow by the door, where they could see the main gate fifty yards across the drill ground.

The four visitors managed to maintain their dignity as they walked toward the gate, even though the Red Guards were breathing down their necks like a pack of hungry wolves. As they reached the gate, however, four of the Red Guards in a perfectly synchronized action lifted a right foot, placed it against the small of a visitor's back and gave a mighty push.

Three of the men fell flat on their faces on the street, but the fourth twisted to one side and managed to keep his feet. Infuriated at being stymied, the Red Guard who had tried to push him took a step nearer and kicked the man's buttocks with all his force. Again his victim saw the foot coming and twisted away. He almost got clear, but a loose nail in the toe of the Red Guard's shoe caught his pant leg at the thigh and neatly slit it up through the seat. White underpants suddenly ballooned out through the slit and flapped in the breeze, in sharp contrast to the dark gray of the trousers.

Their dignity scuttled, the four men beat an inglorious retreat up the street. The Red Guards stood in the gate and laughed at their discomfiture, particularly at the efforts of the one man to hold together the split in his trousers.

Unsmiling, Tower and Loyalty looked at each other.

Loyalty said: "It's the first time I've heard a Red Guard laugh."

"Yes," Tower agreed. He thought for a moment. "The Red Guards are out to destroy the old bureaucracy. But they don't realize they are setting up a new bureaucracy of their own — only one less efficient and with less humanity to it."

"Have you heard any more from the four cadres since they left your factory so unceremoniously?" asked Pastor Bao. It was a Sunday afternoon in January, with the sun bright in a windless sky. Bright Loyalty had arranged for Mighty Tower to see Pastor Bao, and now the three men were on the Lees' rooftop.

Tower answered the pastor's question: "No, we haven't

heard a thing from them. Why do you ask?"

"Because," replied the pastor, "these old stagers in The Party and in the government will not take defeat and disgrace lying down. Perhaps the Red Guards are too young to understand that — there's so much they don't understand. They know only to destroy; not to produce. Theirs is a mutation of Marxism that can have only a short life."

"But," argued Tower. "Chairman Mao himself originated the Red Guards."

"Right you are, Mighty Tower, for the purpose of weeding out some of his personal enemies from the political cabbage patch. Such as Liu Shaoqi. After they are dug out, the Red Guards will be dug out, too. When Mao Zedong is finished using the Red Guards he will turn on them and destroy them."

"Why do you say that, Pastor?" Loyalty asked. "Right now the Red Guards seem pretty well in control."

"Because the Bible says that whatever a man sows that shall he also reap. That goes for a nation, a movement or a man. The reaping may be delayed but it will come, as sure as sun up."

"You know, Pastor," said Tower, "it's things like this that the Bible says which really make me think. I've come to the conclusion that faith in a person's heart is very helpful at a time like this. It's obvious that anything material can be taken away from you, but what's in your heart, nobody can snatch that away from you."

The conversation went on, happily uninterrupted because no one had bothered to repair the iron ladder since it parted company with itself that day and dumped The Demon in a heap on the courtyard below. That afternoon Mighty Tower prayed the penitent's prayer, "God, be merciful to me a sinner," and joined the household of God.

The Episode of the Split Pants kicked off a series of events that proved the nemesis of the Shanghai Red Guards, for it eventually brought the People's Liberation Army into the equation. For months the army had been "X" — the unknown quantity — and the troops had kept their hands off the monstrous events that were rocking Shanghai.

The army's dilemma was that it could move only on orders from Chairman Mao. And it was the same Chairman Mao who had unleashed on the Chinese people the pack of wild dogs called Red Guards; he would have to corral and muzzle that pack. In his estimate the time was not yet. But, beginning with the Episode of the Split Pants, pressure began to build up on the Chairman. The bureaucracy was at stake, and with the bureaucracy the whole warp and woof of government.

In the meantime the Red Guards at the weaving mill posted sentries on 24-hour duty. Instead of the link-fence gate they installed steel plate, and they doubled the sandbag barrier back of the gate. All leaves and days-off were cancelled and no one was allowed to go outside the compound. A 24-hour yellow alert was declared. Where the guns and ammunition came from, Mighty Tower and Bright Loyalty never knew, but by the end of January the sentries were carrying loaded rifles and the Red Guards had pistols.

Late one afternoon Tower and Loyalty were repairing a loom in the far corner of the loom room, where they felt free to talk.

Tower asked: "Did you ever imagine this factory being turned into an army camp?"

"Worse than that. A fort really. All we need is a moat and a drawbridge."

"Loyalty, you know the Bible better than I do. Does it say anything about all this?"

Loyalty put down his screwdriver and thought for a minute. "Yes," he said. "Jesus said, 'They that take the sword shall perish with the sword'."

"Well, what are you and I going to do if they hand us a gun and order us to shoot somebody?"

"Tower, that's a question I sure would like to have an answer to."

27. Enter The Army
Summer 1967

EARLY ONE MORNING IN JUNE, Mighty Tower woke with nausea, a fever and a terrible pain in the middle of his stomach.

"What in the world is it?" Bright Loyalty asked.

"I guess it's my chronic appendicitis."

"I'll run over and get the nurse," Loyalty said.

He slipped into his clothes and ran across the drill ground in the half light. The nurse lived in a room adjacent to the clinic. In short order she was up, grabbed her black bag and was on the way back across the drill ground with Loyalty. She found that Tower's temperature was 102 degrees and his pulse rate 90. With the other symptoms, she agreed that appendicitis was likely.

"We'd better get you to the hospital quickly so they can make a white blood count," she said.

"But how are we going to get him there?" Loyalty asked.

"Hmm..." the nurse thought a minute. "The last emergency I had, I borrowed a pedicab. The kind built for cargo, you know. That worked okay. But who would pedal it?"

"I'd be glad to — if you could get permission for me to leave the factory," said Loyalty.

"No trouble there. This might be a life-or-death matter. You get some clothes on him and I'll see about pedicab and permit."

In ten minutes the nurse was back, astride the action end of the pedicab. "Here are the permits," she said.

Loyalty spread Tower's bedding on the floor of the pedicab, and he and the nurse helped him climb aboard.

"I'm sorry, Tower," Loyalty apologized. "This isn't going to be the most comfortable ambulance."

"No matter," Tower muttered. "I just hope they can get rid of this awful pain for me."

The gateman and the nurse helped Loyalty maneuver the three-wheeler around the sandbags and out through the gate. The two of them stood in the gate and waved cheerfully as Loyalty mounted the makeshift ambulance and slowly pedaled up the street.

It was a mile to the hospital. Loyalty took off one layer of clothes after another as he got hotter and hotter at the unaccustomed exertion. Finally arriving at the big gate of the hospital, he was relieved to dismount and push the cart into the emergency ward.

The on-duty personnel acted as if it were routine for a patient to be trundled in in a pedicab. Very efficiently, one nurse took his temperature, another his blood pressure and pulse, another drew a blood sample, a fifth checked his ID card and permit, a sixth supervised the whole operation, while a seventh was standing by consulting the Little Red Book of Chairman Mao. After all, there is nothing quite like socialist efficiency.

A doctor arrived in white smock and nose mask. He looked over Mighty Tower's chart, asked him about his pain and punched his stomach sharply, for which he was rewarded with a resounding "*Aiya!*" from the patient.

A nurse brought a report on the blood sample and handed it to the doctor. He said to Mighty Tower: "You have acute appendicitis. We will operate as soon as the acupuncture man can stick you with his needles."

"Acupuncture?" mumbled Tower.

"Oh, yes. Cheaper. And more efficient than cocaine, ether or chloroform."

Loyalty pulled up a stool and sat beside Tower's stretcher. He had never before touched him physically, although they had known each other so long. But with a high fever raging and an operation just around the corner, his reticence evaporated and he placed his hand on his friend's forehead. "Mighty Tower," he said softly, "A word from the Bible just came to me: 'All things work together for good to them that love God'. I don't know exactly how God manages the 'all things' part, but I do believe it."

An hour later the nurse told Bright Loyalty he could go in and see the patient. Tower was smiling as the acupuncturist removed the last of the needles, giving them a final twirl in a rather affectionate way.

"How'd it go?" Loyalty asked.

"Fine. Didn't feel a thing."

"Are you going to be all right here by yourself?"

"Don't see why I shouldn't. They seem very efficient in this hospital."

"Here's your bedding," Loyalty said, depositing it on the foot of the bed. "Maybe the nurse will put it under you by and by."

Then he went on: "Guess I'd better get that three-wheeler back to the factory. They might need it. In a day or two I'll come back and check on getting you out. By the way, you won't forget what I told you a while ago, will you?"

"No, I won't forget. I'm sure glad you did some memorizing before you lost your Bible on New Year's Day."

Loyalty enjoyed the trip back; without the load, it was almost as good as a bicycle. Everything went smoothly until he reached the intersection at the top of the street leading down to the factory. To his surprise, a soldier in battle dress with rifle and fixed bayonet stopped him and ordered: "Pull out your ID card!"

Then, after examining it: "So! You're from Golden Streams Weaving Factory! No admittance today. And stay away from there! Did you hear me? Stay away from there!"

Nonplussed, Loyalty pulled the three-wheeler over to the curb. He thought: *They won't like it if I don't get this thing back on time!*

He found himself standing under that same awning where he and Mighty Tower had stood the previous August, watching Teacher Ran being disgraced in the middle of the street. Suddenly he heard a shot from the direction of the factory. Edging around the corner, Loyalty was horrified by what he saw: soldiers with rifles, several army lorries and a half-track with its gun pointed toward the factory gate!

Aiya! Soldiers! Guns! he mumbled to himself. Glancing back around the corner at the soldier who had ordered him to stay away from the factory, Loyalty saw he was busy checking the identity of pedestrians, so he sidled down the street toward the factory in the shadow of the buildings.

As he rested for a moment in a doorway, a thousand questions stormed his mind: *Where are my friends inside the factory? Do they have guns? Will the Red Guards fight? Will the half-track open fire? Who will get killed? Couldn't they find a solution to this problem without shooting it out?*

As if in answer to the last question, several rifle bursts came from inside the gate, the bullets ricocheting off the half-track and the brick wall opposite the factory. The soldiers in the street ducked for cover behind the lorries.

A sound squawked out from one of the lorries. Though Loyalty did not recognize it at the time, it was an electronic bull horn, the first he had ever heard.

"This is the People's Liberation Army," it squawked. "Open the gate at once! If you don't open it, we'll blow it open!"

Loyalty edged on down the sidewalk, hugging the houses. He was now opposite the first building in the weaving mill compound. By this time there were no people in the street itself, but a number of brave souls were crouching in doorways, intent on what was happening at the factory gate. Loyalty himself was so intent on what was going on that he tripped over a figure huddled in a doorway.

"*Ai!* Watch it!" said the man, too interested in events to resent being kicked accidentally.

"Oh! I'm sorry," apologized Loyalty. "Did I hurt you?"

"No, but *you're* going to get hurt if you don't take cover! Didn't you hear those bullets whistling past?"

"Yes, but the trouble is I'm from the weaving factory. I happened to be outside this morning. And I sure would like to know what's going on inside!"

"I hope those Red Guards get what's coming to them," said the man fiercely. "They embarrassed my sister terribly...."

"Your sister? Who's that?" Bright Loyalty interrupted.

"Ran Xin. She teaches the elementary children inside."

"You don't say! I know her very well."

"And what's your name?"

"I'm Bright Loyalty Lee. And yours?"

"Just call me Ning. My sister told us about you and how you kept her things from all being stolen!"

At that point another shot rang out, fired from behind the gate.

"We'd better go inside!" Loyalty's new acquaintance said.

Loyalty hesitated.

"Oh, it's all right," the other man said. "I live here. On the fourth floor. Come on, we'll go upstairs. Maybe we can see something from up there."

The two men ran up the stairs to the fourth floor, where the windows opening out onto the street gave them a ringside seat. As they looked down the street, however, Loyalty caught another movement out of the corner of his eye.

He grabbed Ning and pulled him back into the shadows of the room, hissing: "Don't move! Look straight across the street, beyond the first row of buildings. What do you see on that flat roof of the second building?"

"*Aiya!* There are men on the roof! Soldiers! And look — more of them are dropping down from the roof next door! Now, what are they up to?"

"They're on the roof of the loom room," answered Loyalty. "My guess is that in a minute they'll collect on the corner of the roof that overlooks the main gate. The Red Guards down at the gate don't know they're up there."

"They're stealing up behind them!" There was a ring of admiration in Ning's voice. "They haven't been in the People's Liberation Army for nothing!"

"They've got automatic rifles," continued Loyalty. "If the Red Guards know what's good for them they'll surrender chop-chop!"

That's just it," returned Ning. "How can they? They don't know those guys are on the roof."

Just then the electronic bull horn squawked again: "One more time! In the name of the People's Liberation Army, open the gate! We'll give you one minute!"

The ultimatum was answered by a dozen rifle shots from inside the gate. Not a shot came in answer; only a strange silence.

Loyalty and Ning looked across again at the roof of the loom room. A half dozen soldiers were down on all fours, creeping slowly up to the edge of the roof, their rifles ahead of them.

Ping! A single shot rang out from below, aimed at the roof. The defenders had spotted the men. But it was too late.

Rat-ta-ta-ta-tat! Rat-ta-ta-ta-tat! Automatic weapons rained leaden death on the men and women at the gate.

A pause. The men on the roof were reloading. Then again: *Rat-ta-ta-ta-tat! Rat-ta-ta-ta-tat!*

On it went, the hail of death. As best he could, Bright

Loyalty counted the shots — over a hundred in less than thirty seconds.

Loyalty and Ning could not see what had happened to the defenders at the gate. They could only stand and look at each other. Ning said: "I guess that's the end of the Red Guards in the weaving mill."

Loyalty's thoughts were more personal: *I wonder how many of my friends are dead.*

As Loyalty learned later, the soldiers on the roof dashed down to the drill ground, shooting at anything that moved. They had no sympathy for the Red Guards who had been shooting at their fellow-soldiers outside the gate, and they only realized too late that many of the factory workers themselves hated the Red Guards cordially. As happens in war, the innocent suffered with the guilty in The Second Battle at the Gate.

Loyalty said goodbye to his new friend Ning, descended the stairs and was surprised to find that the soldiers had already sealed off the street. They were not allowing in any of the hundreds of curious who wanted to see the shambles of battle. The crowd behind the barrier only grudgingly gave way before the lorries which, with sirens screaming, were carting the wounded off to hospitals and the captured to jails.

The soldiers did allow people to leave the street, however, and Loyalty quickly made his way back to where he had left the pedicab. To his relief it was still there; in the excitement no one had bothered to run off with it. For a full two minutes he sat on the saddle, undecided what to do. After all, what does one do when one's factory has just been shot up in a minor civil war?

Loyalty's mind was made up for him as a soldier jabbed his bayonet at him and ordered: "Move along! Move along!"

He started pedaling the three-wheeler with due alacrity.

Only after a minute or so did he realize he was retracing his route to the hospital.

Mighty Tower saw him coming in, and said banteringly, "No, I'm not ready to go home!" Then his face fell as he saw how serious Loyalty looked.

It took Loyalty five minutes to tell of The Second Battle at the Gate. A neighboring patient raised up on elbow to hear more clearly. Then another and another, until all the patients in the ward were propped up on expectant elbows. It was the most excitement they had had for many a day.

When the first telling was told out, Loyalty paused.

Tower said seriously: "Loyalty, it looks as if I have lost my appendix but saved my life — and maybe yours to boot."

As if it were a cue, they said in unison: "All things work together for good to them that love God."

Tower added: "I'll never forget that verse as long as I live."

Pastor and Mrs. Bao, Mighty Tower and Strong Hero were all at the Lees' for Sunday supper and a Bible study afterwards. Once the study was over, the women stayed downstairs and the four men climbed to the roof "for a breath of air," as Loyalty put it.

The old pastor spoke first: "Let me congratulate you three men that you have survived the first year of the Great Proletarian Cultural Revolution. As you think of the men your age and younger that you knew a year ago, how many are still alive? And of those, how many still have their freedom?"

Silence fell over the group as they remembered all that had happened during that year since the Cultural Revolution first swung its scythe of death and destruction through society.

Pastor Bao went on: "The Red Guards were so naive! They didn't realize Chairman Mao was manipulating them for his own ends. And they overstepped their charter, too.

Now Chairman Mao has disowned them as 'politically immature' and says 'they can't cope'."

Hero asked: "What's going to happen to the Red Guards now?"

"Chairman Mao has turned his back on them," replied the pastor. "It was very significant when six months ago he knocked their 'Shanghai People's Commune' off the map and replaced it with 'The Revolutionary Committee', or 'Three Links', as he called them — the army, the Party cadres and Red Guards. He conveniently placed the Red Guards last and least! Their days are numbered. The old man outwitted them."

"What about you, Pastor?" Tower asked. "Will you ever get back the books and things the Red Guards took from you?"

"That's the least of my worries, Tower. The Bible speaks of 'taking joyfully the spoiling of your goods', and I guess that goes for the Red Guards and what they did to us."

Then Pastor Bao summarized his view of the Cultural Revolution: "This is a drama in which there are no heroes, only victims. The people are victims of the Red Guards, the Red Guards are victims of Mao Zedong, and Mao Zedong is a victim of his own illusion of perpetual revolution."

28. A Would-Be Rapist
North China. Autumn 1967

BRIGHT VICTORY LEE slowly pulled off his white smock. He threw it onto the foot of the cot and then threw himself down after it. He was bone weary.

"Tired?"

The question came from a nearby cot in the dormitory.

"Right. I *am* tired. If we just didn't have all these emergency cases! When are we Chinese going to quit beating each other up?"

"Are you asking me?" It was the question to answer a question.

Victory had just dropped off into a doze when an office boy shuffled in, clasping newly-arrived mail. He shouted: "Bright Victory Lee!"

"Here!" Victory shouted back, sitting up in bed. He took the letter and read the address:

"Deliver to: Mr Bright Victory Lee
Physicians' Assistants' Dormitory
Sixth Municipal Hospital, Beijing City"

More closely, he looked at the return address in the upper left-hand corner of the envelope:

"Sent by: Huang
Datong Municipal Health Center
Datong, Shanxi"

Suddenly, Victory didn't feel so tired anymore. He ripped the envelope open enthusiastically. But he did not begin reading at once. For a full minute he luxuriated in the beauty of True Virtue's handwriting and basked in the warmth of her presence reflected from the sheet before him.

The contents, like Virtue herself, were businesslike and to the point:

"I have spoken to Director about your request. He is willing to enquire at Mine Number Three to see if they still need a barefoot doctor. (Of course, you are much more than that now.) But he was so shocked at the idea of anyone leaving Beijing and returning here voluntarily that he insisted on me enquiring if this is *really* what you want to do..."

The signature at the bottom of the letter was simply, "True Virtue".

It did not take long for Victory to answer her question:

"Yes, that is really what I want to do. However, I would apply for a transfer from Beijing only on the written agreement that my status in the mines would not be 'free-worker' but 'Assistant to the Director of Datong Municipal Health Center.'"

Director Zhuo of Beijing's Sixth Municipal Hospital sat back in his swivel chair, put the five fingers of his right hand against the five fingers of his left hand and gazed at Bright Victory through the maze of the fingers. Victory knew this was the sign of the Director giving serious consideration to a matter.

"Yes, sir, that is what I want to do," Victory said.

The Director continued: "Actually, all this emergency work should level off, now that the army is more in control of units where," he paused, grasping for the right word, "I might say... there have been problems before. But, one thing, Lee: I will release you from this hospital only to the Director of the Municipal Health Center at Datong, Shanxi, not to the mine's commandant. And another thing, for your private ear only: Normally I would refuse to transfer out of this unit anyone as efficient and helpful as you are. But I have a soft spot in my heart for Datong, Shanxi. You see, I come from that place."

"Brothers and sisters, Bright Victory Lee has been reassigned to the Datong Municipal Health Center. He will leave

Beijing if he can get his papers in order."

A chorus of approval rose from the dozen or so Christians meeting in Elder Feng's house as True Virtue Huang shared this good news. They all remembered Bright Victory warmly. Shortly afterwards the meeting closed and the believers left by ones or twos in order not to attract attention.

As True Virtue started to leave, Elder Feng said: "It's dark tonight, Virtue, only a new moon. Maybe someone should walk home with you."

"Oh, I'm not afraid, thank you."

"But you know things have not yet quietened down after all the disturbances, and it's already past nine o'clock."

"It's all right. After all, this is our own neighborhood, and it's only a ten-minute walk home."

Saying that, True Virtue buttoned up her jacket and stepped out into the darkness. Once outside, however, she felt a little shiver run up her backbone.

"There's nothing to be afraid of," she assured herself. "But maybe I'd better pray first."

So at the main gate of the compound she stopped and prayed: "Dear Heavenly Father, it's a dark night and I'm alone except for You. Please protect me. Amen."

Then with renewed confidence she straightened up, threw her shoulders back, breathed deeply and stepped out into the street. The new moon in the west was only a sliver of itself, but there was still enough light for her to pick her way along the path.

The only place I really don't like going is across the dry stream bed with the bushes and trees around, she said almost out loud.

True Virtue enjoyed the walk in the crisp autumn air, but as she approached the dry stream bed she had a premonition. Was someone following her? She was afraid to look back. She quickened her step, thinking: *I wish those bushes were not so close to the path.*

Just then she heard a man's voice behind her. "Excuse me, but could you tell me if the Yang family lives near here?" It was a cultured voice with a city accent.

Being of a practical turn of mind, True Virtue asked, "Which Yang family?" She had unconsciously stopped and turned to face the man.

He did not answer her question, but with his left hand grabbed her right wrist. Then, to her horror, she saw a glint of metal in the man's right hand. It was a knife.

"Don't raise your voice and I won't hurt you," he told her. "But if you scream, I've something here that will silence you — forever!"

True Virtue breathed a quick prayer: *Oh, Lord! Help me!* Then it seemed to her the Lord said: "Virtue, why pray silently? Pray out loud!"

To the attacker she said: "No, I'm not going to scream. But before you...."

He interrupted: "Come! Right now! Into the bushes!" And he gave her a yank.

"Please let me finish what I was saying!" Virtue dug her heels into the path with the stubbornness of a North China mule.

"Oh, all right. What were you saying?"

"Before anything else, I have one request first."

The attacker pulled again on her wrist. But True Virtue was not to be pulled that easily.

"Well, what is it?

"Just let me pray to my Heavenly Father first."

"Your 'Heavenly Father'? Who under the sun is that?".

"Never mind now. Only let me pray to Him before ..." Virtue was finding it difficult to speak, "...before anything else."

"Well, okay, if you insist. But no funny business! Remember, I've got this!"

He loosed her wrist, and at the same time lowered the knife in his right hand and drew it across her throat, while making a suggestive rasping sound deep back in his own mouth.

Without commenting on his gruesome threat, True Virtue dropped to her knees and began to pray: "Oh, Heavenly Father, I told You before I left the house that it is dark and I was alone except for You and I asked You to protect me. And a few minutes ago I prayed silently for You to protect me and You said I should pray out loud, so now, for the third time, please protect me."

True Virtue looked up. Her attacker was standing over her, the knife high in his right hand. She stood up.

"Did you hear me pray to my Heavenly Father?"

The man did not answer. He simply stood motionless with knife held high.

"Aren't you going to answer me?"

Still no response.

"Well, goodbye," Virtue said, and started walking away. After a few steps she looked back. He was still standing there, knife held high, in the same position. Quickly she half ran, half walked back to Elder Feng's house.

"... And that's the way it happened," True Virtue concluded her story to the three or four believers at the house. "The last I saw of him, he was still standing there."

"All of us will go home with you this time, Virtue," Elder Feng said. They quickly lit torches and set out.

As they approached the dry stream bed, True Virtue caught her breath: "Oh! He's still there!"

Sure enough, he was still standing in the same spot she had left him in, knife still upraised.

Elder Feng blurted out: "He's frozen! He can't move!"

Another brother questioned: "Can he talk?" Not getting an answer, he answered his own question: "Guess he can't!"

Silence fell on the handful of people lit up by the flickering torches. Finally, Elder Feng said: "Virtue, you got him into this fix, you'll have to get him out."

For the second time that night Virtue dropped to her knees on the path and prayed: "Dear Lord, if it shall please You, heal this man from being frozen in one position."

As she finished praying, she heard a clatter as the knife dropped. Gradually the hand lowered.

Virtue addressed her ex-attacker: "All right, now I'll tell you who my Heavenly Father is. He is the maker of heaven and earth and people and He has all power. He is my Father and He looks after me."

The erstwhile attacker was now attacked. Not by people but by an Invisible Force he did not understand. He began to shake and tremble with fear. Almost collapsing, he had to be helped along the road to Elder Feng's house. Once inside, the Christians more fully explained to the young man the mighty power of God.

It did not take much exhortation; what he had experienced was convincing enough. He confessed his sins and prayed for forgiveness from an all-powerful Heavenly Father.

Word of True Virtue Huang's miraculous escape from a would-be-rapist spread as only such news can. The next Sunday night Elder Feng's house was filled to overflowing, and the courtyard was packed with non-Christians.

All necks were craned to get a glimpse of the young man himself, well inside the house. There was much whispering and exchanging of opinions: "You mean to tell me they didn't turn him over to the police?"

"He needs a bullet through the back of his head for trying *that!*"

"You say he was frozen with his hand held up all that time?"

"Why has the Feng family taken him in? — are they related?"

And on and on and on.

Elder Feng was very conscious of public reaction, especially on such a sensitive issue as attempted rape, and he had decided that the best way to quieten the clacking tongues would be to let the young man tell his own story for all to hear. Over the past few days he had discussed this with the other believers, including True Virtue and her parents, and in the end all agreed that to bring the matter out into the open was both sensible and scriptural.

Because there were more people in the courtyard than inside the house, Elder Feng held the meeting outside that night. The day had been warm and there was no wind; an outside meeting was possible.

Elder Feng opened the meeting by saying: "You have heard of the remarkable events a week ago tonight. It is only right for you to know what happened, and to recognize the power of God in protecting His child and later in bringing another person to repent of his sins and ask forgiveness. That young man will tell his own story. His name is Han Changping."

The young man stepped out to the courtyard and began: "My name is Han Changping and I was sent here from Beijing, 'up to the hills, down to the country', as they say, to learn from the peasants. This was my punishment for being an enthusiastic Red Guard for a year and doing everything a Red Guard was told to do.

"When I arrived in this place, I had no friend to help me, no relative. I was supposed to learn from the peasants, but they refused to teach a city boy anything. Finally I found myself living in a cowshed and trying to survive by sorting some grain out of the cow's food and cooking that. I was so lonely I didn't know what to do. No one would befriend me. Nobody loves an ex-Red Guard.

"In desperation I decided last Sunday to look for a girl to give me some comfort. I tried to be friendly with three different girls that day, but none would even talk with me. I was so lonely and homesick I thought I would die. Then a demon must have got into my heart, because I decided if no girl wanted to be friendly with me I would force myself on one. That is the reason I tried to do the wicked thing last Sunday night.

"But when the girl began to pray on her knees I was suddenly overwhelmed by another Power, greater than the power of the demon within me. The young woman spoke of her 'Heavenly Father', and it was He who froze my arm up in the air so that I could not stab her. And it was He who later answered the prayers of this same young woman and cured my paralysis, for I was frozen and could not move for half an hour.

"Then, instead of killing me on the spot, these people brought me to this house. In fact, they half carried me, I was so weak. Here they explained to me who the Heavenly Father is. More than that, they took me in, gave me the first decent meal I have had in a month, and even gave me a bed to sleep on.

"I cannot but humbly put my trust in the Heavenly Father and in Jesus Christ whom He sent to earth. That's all I have to say. Thank you."

Elder Feng arose: "You have heard tonight about a miracle, how God delivered a young woman from dishonor and death. Why does God do such things? It is because today we have no church buildings for you to see and no Bibles for you to read. But God is still very much alive in China, and He reveals Himself by His mighty acts."

As Elder Feng spoke, a stillness descended on the hundreds of people in the house and courtyard, broken only now and then by an earnest "Amen!" from the believers.

"This miracle was not for the young woman's benefit alone," he continued, "but for all you here tonight, to inform you that God cares for His own and that He invites you to come to Him and be saved."

As he finished speaking, a murmur of reaction rippled across the crowd. Some twisted and squirmed uneasily, then turned and made their way out of the courtyard. Others remained inside and began to ask the Christians, "Can I, too, know the Heavenly Father you are talking about?"

The following Sunday True Virtue came early to the house meeting.

"You see what has happened after God so miraculously delivered you!" Elder Feng said to her. "Many more are here tonight than ordinarily. As long as some can stand in the courtyard it's all right. But later, in winter, what are we going to do?"

True Virtue thought for a minute, then suggested: "Is God saying to us that we should start another house meeting? If so, where? And who would lead it?"

"Well," answered Elder Feng, "your last question first: I believe there is never a church without a pastor."

Virtue pricked up her ears: "How can you say that?" she asked. "All the seminaries and Bible schools are closed. No leaders are being trained nowadays."

"I know what you are saying, Virtue, but this is what I mean: In every group of God's people, He has His own leaders with gifts to shepherd the flock."

He lowered his voice: "After the meeting a week ago, the police came on Monday morning, wanting to know why the big crowd was here. I told them the whole story. No point in hiding anything from them — they already knew the external facts. Only, of course, they did not accept that God was involved — they don't believe there is a God. Virtue, I'm telling you all this because the police may pay special attention to you in the future."

It was not True Virtue, however, to whom the police paid attention. One night four policemen carrying rifles appeared at Elder Feng's door. The tallest one said: "We want to talk with Han Changping."

Changping came to the door and asked: "Yes?"

"You will go with us. You will be asked a few questions."

Standing to one side, Elder Feng spoke up: "Will you please come inside the house to ask your questions?"

"No. We police will not ask the questions. He will be questioned by members of the Datong Revolutionary Committee."

Elder Feng's heart sank. *The Revolutionary Committee!* he thought to himself. *That's dominated by the army!*

Aloud he said: "Please let him pick up his jacket."

Following Changping inside, Elder Feng said to him: "And take your bedding bundle, too. They may not let you come home tonight."

"Han Changping, aged 18, single, a native of Beijing City, is hereby charged with bodily assault, attempted rape, and assault with a dangerous weapon with intent to kill."

The accusation was read in on-stage falsetto by a young woman in the uniform of the People's Liberation Army.

Han Changping stood alone, motionless, before a plain wood table at which sat two secretaries and three judges, all in army uniform. The center judge was a woman.

The woman judge spoke: "Han Changping, do you or do you not acknowledge that the accusation as read is true, correct, and accurately set forth?"

"I acknowledge."

"Do you or do you not confess to these crimes as committed by you on Sunday night, September 10, 1967?"

"I confess."

"Do you or do you not understand that each of the aforesaid crimes is punishable by as much as twenty years in prison?"

"I understand."

"Do you or do you not realize that the total punishment for the aforesaid three crimes could mean a total of sixty years in prison for you?"

"I realize that."

At each answer from the accused, a half-audible sigh went up from the crowd standing in the courtroom, among them Elder Feng, True Virtue Huang, her father and mother and other Christians.

The woman judge continued: "Can you, Han Changping, give any reason why you should not be subject to the punishment as prescribed by the government?"

"Your Honor, I am guilty and I deserve to be punished. I am truly sorry for what I did and I throw myself on the mercy of the government."

The woman judge stood up and addressed the crowd: "This is a People's Court. You the people have heard indictment and confession. Do you have further charges against Han Changping?"

Utter silence descended on the courtroom. It was broken by a female voice: "Your Honor, may I speak?"

"Identify yourself!"

"I am True Virtue Huang. I was the victim of the assault in question. If there were a complainant in this case I would be the complainant. But I have not in the past lodged a complaint against Han Changping, nor do I lodge a complaint at this time. Far from that, I request that this court record the fact that I completely forgive him for his actions against me."

Silence again. Again a voice, this time male: "Your Honor, may I speak?"

"Identify yourself!"

"I am Feng Weihua. It was to my house True Virtue Huang came seeking help the night she was attacked. Also, the defendant has lived at my house since that night. I can vouch for his repentance and his desire to live a new life. If this court should give him a suspended sentence I will guarantee his good conduct from this time on."

Again silence. The only activity in the courtroom was that of the two secretaries, feverishly recording proceedings with ball-point pens.

When they had finished and laid pens aside, the judge spoke again; "True Virtue Huang and Feng Weihua will step forward."

They did so, and the judge continued: "The secretaries will read the records of what you both said."

The secretaries read the record.

"Do you acknowledge this as an accurate record of what you said?"

They both responded: "I do."

"In that case, take the pen lying on the table and sign your names in the margin alongside your testimonies."

This they did. The judge sat silent for several minutes, her chin cradled in her hand. Finally she said: "Secretaries, do not record what I am going to say. This is not a part of the trial."

Then she turned to True Virtue and Elder Feng: "What you two have said is far from usual in such cases. Most people demand revenge and punishment, but you have asked the exact opposite. For my personal understanding I ask you: what is your motivation? Are you related to the accused?"

Elder Feng said: "No, your Honor, not in the ordinary sense of the word."

"What do you mean, 'not in the ordinary sense of the word'?"

"I mean we are not blood relatives."

"Then what is your relationship?"

"This, your Honor, that True Virtue Huang and I are both Christians. And since the attack Han Changping has become a Christian also. That is our relationship."

Again, silence. Again, the judge's hand under her chin. Then she told the secretaries: "Record this: Court is recessed while the judges deliberate."

The crowd in the courtroom waited and waited. Finally, some became restless and headed for the door, but they were told this was not allowed. Grudgingly they continued to wait, standing first on one foot and then on the other. They had been compelled to attend many trials during the eighteen years since Liberation.

For her part, True Virtue marked the minutes — ten... twenty.. thirty... Why the delay? Weren't all sentences pre-decided anyway?

Finally, after 35 minutes, the falsetto voice said again: "The court will come to order! Sentence will be pronounced!"

The woman judge stood up and began to speak: "This is a most unusual case. A total of sixty years in prison could be meted out for the crimes committed. But since the accused has repented of his crimes and since the victim refuses to press charges and since a respected citizen is willing to be his guarantor, the court hereby sentences the accused, Han Changping, to a ten-year suspended sentence.

"But since the court must execute judgement on law-breakers, the accused is also hereby sentenced to fifty lashes of the bamboo, to be administered forthwith."

The judge sat down, and the falsetto voice came on again: "The criminal will remove jacket, shirt and undershirt. He will lie prostrate on the floor face down. He will grip the legs of a chair with both left and right hand. If he turns loose of either grip the number of lashes will be doubled."

Changping's first reaction at getting off with a suspended sentence was a surge of elation. But the immediate prospect of fifty lashes with the bamboo was like a bucket of ice water thrown over him.

He slowly removed jacket, shirt and undershirt. He slowly lay down on the floor and slowly gripped two legs of a chair.

Was there designed symbolism in the next scene of the male versus female drama? The woman soldier with the falsetto voice leaped to a corner of the room, grabbed a length of thin bamboo, bounded back to center stage and whacked Han Changping across the shoulders with all her might.

The woman judge counted the lashes: "one... two... three.. four... five..." And on and on until a final: "Fifty."

At about lash number thirty, Han Changping lost consciousness. When it was over, he did not move. He lay in a pool of blood, and spectators with weak stomachs turned faces to the wall rather than look at the sight. Only a callous few jeered and shouted: "Good enough for him!"

The woman judge stepped over and prodded his ribs with the tip of her right shoe. Gazing at the prostrate figure coldly, she straightened up and addressed the crowd: "Is there a doctor here?"

No response.

Again and louder: "Is there a doctor here?"

At that, True Virtue stepped forward.

Surprised at seeing the victim come forward again, the judge asked: "Are you a doctor?"

"No, your Honor, but I am a first-aid medic from the Health Department. If your Honor please, may I take care of him?"

The judge said: "It's nothing to me, what you or anyone else does to him. Alive or dead, take him away."

She went back to her seat, took up the gavel and struck the table. The falsetto voice pronounced: "Court dismissed!"

The Christians borrowed a door for a make-do stretcher and carried Han Changping to the Health Department. On the way he revived in the fresh autumn air. True Virtue heated water and sponged his back and shoulders; though many, the lacerations were mostly superficial. The Health Department had no facilities for in-patients. So late that afternoon Virtue's father came with his mule cart and took Changping to Elder Feng's house. It was not the most comfortable ambulance ride.

"I'm sorry to trouble you, Director Zhou, but is there any news as to my papers?"

The Director put ten fingers together and looked at Bright Victory through the maze. It was his let-me-think-this-through pose.

"Hmm..." he hummed, "hmm... Lee, there's a hold-up at the Datong end. All we need is a letter of acceptance from there, but it hasn't come. Makes me think of when I was in charge of a hospital in South China and the water supply suddenly quit. We finally discovered that a snake had crawled into the pipe, and when it died it swelled up and blocked the pipeline. I think we've got a similar situation now — some snake has blocked the pipeline."

29. The Snake In The Pipe
Winter and Spring 1968

"PAPA, I want to share with you and Mama something from Victory's last letter. He told a story about a snake in a pipe, and how it blocked up the pipe and stopped the water. He didn't make any application, but it was a strange story to tell if he didn't want to make a point."

Papa Huang was sitting near the coal fire, toasting himself after a cold day on the mule cart. "Why should he have to make a point?" he asked. "Maybe he just liked the story."

His wife reacted, half amused and half irritated: "Oh, Papa! You really are Old North China! You never see beneath the surface!" She thought for a minute and then turned to True Virtue: "Pipeline? Pipeline? What kind of a pipeline? Real pipe or something like a pipe? Oh! Could it be his procedure in getting transferred to Datong? That would be like a pipeline, wouldn't it?"

Papa Huang broke in: "Why should a procedure be like a pipe? I don't see the connection."

Mama looked at Papa with a trace of pity on her face. "Well, *you* wouldn't see the connection. That's for sure. But maybe *Victory* meant there was a connection. His procedure *has* been blocked for months now."

She went on, half aloud and half to herself: "Snake? Snake? That means a bad person. You never use 'snake' to mean 'good person.'"

True Virtue burst out in admiration: "Mama, you're as good as a detective!" Then, soberly: "Do you think Victory is telling us a bad person is blocking his procedure?"

"Virtue, it might just be that way. If so, who *is* he?"

Papa interrupted in disdain: "You women and your fancy ideas!"

True Virtue's alarm clock went off at 5 a.m. She turned over, yawned, and lay there for a minute groaning at the thought of going out so early on a winter morning.

"Get out of bed, lazy bones!" she chided herself. "That bandage material has to be laid out for the volunteers by 8 o'clock. No matter that somebody else fell down on the job yesterday."

For the first time since she started work at the Health Department, True Virtue found herself turning the key and letting herself in the back door of the compound at 6 a.m. Once inside, she shivered a bit at the thought of crossing the compound and opening the office in the dark.

But she reassured herself, *people live on the compound — Old Gatey and Orchid Qiu. Maybe her light will be on by now.*

As she approached the office door, key in hand, True Virtue looked up and across toward Orchid's window. Sure enough, her light was on. It was such a cheerful contrast to the pre-dawn blackness that Virtue did not insert the key in the lock at once but stood for a moment looking at the lighted window.

Then, to her utter surprise, the silhouette of a man appeared in the window.

An instant later, the face turned toward the window, and True Virtue backed up against the office door in astonishment. It was her boss, Director Tang!

Why in the world is he in Orchid's bedroom at this time of morning? The question stormed her mind. Her second thought was quieter: *Oh, well, he may be there on some emergency business...*

As Virtue stood in the cold and dark, afraid to go into the office for fear a noise might give her away, she saw the light on the stairs in the building opposite flick on then off, the door quietly open and close, and a figure steal across the compound toward the same door she had just let herself in by.

Business? she thought. *Not at this hour! If not business, what? Could Orchid be having a liaison with the boss? He's a married man with two children! How could such a thing be?*

By this time True Virtue was uncomfortably cold, and finally went inside. It was warmer there; the coal fire in the potbellied stove had been banked the night before. In the darkness she felt her way over to the stove, opened the door and began to punch the coals with a poker. But the fire failed to flare up.

There's nothing for it, she said to herself. *I've got to find some kindling .... and the coal scuttle .. or I'll never get this fire going ... Oh! Why did I ever come to the office at this hour of the morning anyway? Just to fill my mind with questions about Orchid and The Director!*

But the practical was never far from her thoughts, and she reminded herself: *I've got a job to do ... And I'll never do it without some light and heat.*

Reluctantly she flipped a switch. A light came on. In short order she found kindling wood and coal scuttle, and before long the fire was roaring cheerfully.

True Virtue was concentrating on the materials for bandages, when — what was that? A noise.... She stopped dead still and listened ....Yes, there it was again: "Tap, tap, tap."

She looked around, and jumped when she saw a figure outside the door. She turned on a couple more lights, and saw with relief that it was Orchid Qiu standing outside.

Thinking, *what could she want at this hour?* True Virtue stepped over and drew the bolt on the door.

Bundled up against the cold, Orchid stepped inside. Never before had Virtue seen the normally self-possessed woman so distraught.

Without preliminaries she burst out: "Why are you here at this hour? Don't you know you are not on duty until eight o'clock?"

True Virtue drew herself up to her full height, bridling at such rudeness. Then a calming word came to mind: "Return good for evil."

She felt her mounting anger subside, and answered quietly: "I'm sorry if I've broken regulations. But this material had to be set out for the volunteers coming at eight o'clock."

Fear and agitation were written on Orchid's face. Her voice quivered: "Did ... did you... when you came ... did you see a light in my window?"

Now, True Virtue thought, *I see what you're concerned about.* Why, yes," she said aloud, "I did see a light in your window."

Orchid grew more agitated: "Did you ... did you see me in the window?"

"Why, no, I didn't."

"Well, did you see anybody else?"

"Yes, I did. I saw The Director. I wondered if he had some urgent business ...."

Suddenly Orchid went into hysteria: "No! No! No! You didn't wonder *that*! You *knew* why he was there!"

She broke out sobbing. Great long hysterical sobs such as True Virtue had seldom heard before. Intuitively, Virtue gathered her into her arms and let her weep on her shoulder.

When Orchid had sobbed all her strength out, Virtue eased her onto a chair. Then she stepped over to the stove, took the tea kettle which was always there and poured a cup of tea. "Drink this and you'll feel better."

Having to do something physical, even if it were only holding a teacup and sipping the hot liquid, steadied the older woman.

After a few minutes she spoke in a controlled voice: "For a long time I've needed someone to confide in. And I think you are the one. In fact, I *know* you are the one. In a minute you will see what I mean.

"For years I have had a relationship with The Director. It began under pressure from him when I learned that he had documents concerning my past in the safe — *that* safe over there in the corner. Oh! If I only knew the combination of that safe!

"After our relationship began, I fell in love with him. But I guess you might say I love him with my right hand and hate him with my left."

"Why do you say it like that?" True Virtue broke in. "You're left-handed."

"Correct, Virtue. My left hand is stronger than my right, and it will win out. I guess that's the reason I'm talking to you now. You know, this kind of relationship cannot last. It's hollow. It's HOLLOW!" Orchid's voice rose again.

"Here," True Virtue said, "let me pour you some more tea."

When she came back with fresh hot water she was surprised at the new tack Orchid took:

"I have sensed for some time that he's getting tired of me. I suppose if a man throws his own wife overboard it's no great thing if he throws Number Two overboard after her.

"The problem is that he now has his eye on Number Three. I can tell it by the way he looks at her when she walks past him. Just like he used to look at me. How foolish I was not to turn him down flat in the first place, no matter what's in that safe!"

As she listened Virtue felt a flush creep up her neck, suffuse her face and go on to the roots of her hair. She felt her hair stand up on end. She looked at Orchid and Orchid looked at her.

"Yes," Orchid sighed. "That's it. He now has his eye on you. To make you Number Three."

True Virtue burst out: "How can he think such a thing! He knows I have an understanding with Bright Victory Lee!"

"But don't you see, True Virtue? He's the one man who can keep Victory from returning to Datong. And from his own standpoint he has every reason to keep him away!"

"... And that's the allegory of the snake in the pipe as Victory wrote it to me. And that's the story of the real snake in the real pipe as Orchid Qiu told it to me the other morning before daylight."

It was Sunday afternoon. Han Changping had gone off with a preaching band to a village, leaving True Virtue to talk quietly with Elder Feng and his wife.

"So," remarked Elder Feng, "that's the snake! And he doesn't seem to mind how many people he gets his fangs into as long as he can have his own will on women, even if the poison is blackmail."

"But what am I going to *do*, Elder? How do I meet this problem?"

"Well, the Good Book has some good words on this subject; try this on for size: 'Watch and pray!' *Watch* — don't allow yourself to be alone with him; always be sure at least one other person is present. Then *pray* — God will surely answer your prayer and provide you a way out.

"You saw God work for you in answer to prayer once already. He can do the same again."

Late one afternoon True Virtue came back to the office to find Orchid Qiu alone. "Where's The Director?"

"He's out. Taking care of some debts before Chinese New Year."

True Virtue said to herself: *Now is the time to be frank.* Aloud she said: "Could we go over to your room and talk?"

"Why... why certainly."

Not since that revealing pre-dawn session had either woman brought up the subject heaviest on both their hearts.

True Virtue opened the conversation: "I have one thing to ask you and another thing to tell you."

"Good. The question first."

"When you told me about the documents in the safe you said you 'learned' they were there. How did you 'learn' that?"

"Why ... why... he told me, of course."

"Did you learn about those documents from someone else?"

"No ... I didn't..." A look of incredulity spread over Orchid's face. "Virtue! I never thought about that! Do you mean to infer that there may not be any documents after all?"

"I don't know. But it's worth thinking about." True Virtue paused a moment to let what she had said sink in. "Now the second matter: a simple fact. You and I are not in this thing alone. We have God on our side."

"God? But I ... I don't believe in God. I know you do, but I've always been taught there is no God."

"Well, we won't discuss that right now. But the God I believe in is on the side of the oppressed and the needy. And if there's anybody I know who fits into those categories, it's you. So whether you believe in God or not, He is on your side."

"Lee, I've called you in to give you some news." Director Zhuo of Beijing's Sixth Municipal Hospital put his ten fingers together and looked through them at Bright Victory.

He went on: "I have an idea now who the snake-in-the-pipe at Datong might be. Look at this." He tossed over an official envelope.

Victory looked at the return address in the upper left-hand corner:

Central Office, Department of Health
People's Republic of China
Beijing City

"Shall I read it?" Victory asked.

"Right."

He opened the letter and read:

"Director Zhuo, Sixth Municipal Hospital
Beijing City

Comrade Director,
It has come to my attention that there is malfeasance at the
Datong Municipal Health Center, Datong, Shanxi. You will
proceed there without undue delay to make an audit and
otherwise investigate with particular reference to Director
Tang of said office. You have been appointed to make this
investigation because you are from that place and therefore
may enjoy certain advantages that an outsider would not.
            Sincerely,
            (NAME WITHHELD)
            Director, Department of Health."

"Do you see what I mean, Lee, about a snake-in-the-pipe?"
But Bright Victory did not see. His mind went blank as he
tried to relate the letter before him to the delay in processing
his transfer to Datong. The blankness must have shown on
his face.

Director Zhuo was observing him closely: "Ha! I see that
you don't see! It's the simple human equation that when a
man goes wrong in one area — money, for instance, as the
letter intimates — he is also apt to go wrong in others — such
as relationship to his staff. My guess is that when we begin to
take the roof off Director Tang's little playhouse, we shall
find a number of skeletons in the closets."

Chinese New Year, that ancient and glorious festival, was
only one week away; what would be more natural than to
return to one's home turf to celebrate the holidays with
relatives and friends? And incidentally one could, of course,
investigate goings-on at the Datong Health Center.

It was with great satisfaction, therefore, that Director
Zhuo stepped off the "soft berth" coach and onto the station
platform at Datong. Home for the holidays! He balanced his

load carefully — suitcase plus several jars of pickles and preserved ginger in his right hand, and briefcase plus assorted dried plums, peaches and apricots, peanut candy and a tin of MacIntosh biscuits from Hong Kong in his left hand, each slung neatly in its own mesh bag.

Who would have dreamed of the contents of the briefcase? There the papers were: evidence against Director Tang of Datong Medical Center, the notarized order to investigate, and — in code — the combination to the safe in Director Tang's office.

Ten days later, on the third day of the lunar new year, three more men arrived by train from Beijing. Obviously they had never been in Datong before. They looked around uncomfortably and finally enquired of a policeman the way to the New China Hotel.

That night Director Zhuo called on the three men at the hotel. They invited him to their room and locked the door behind them. After exchanging identification the four began to talk.

"So, you are the auditor," Director Zhuo said, "and you two are the bookkeepers. Do you have detailed orders as to what to do?"

After discussing with them some of the medical terms they would run into in the accounts of the Health Center, he concluded: "I'll come by tomorrow morning at eight. We'll walk over from here."

On the fourth day of the lunar new year the Datong Health Center was struggling to function again after the longest shutdown of the year. But the holiday camaraderie spilled over into this first workday. It was with evident good pleasure, therefore, that Director Tang received the calling card brought in by Orchid Qiu. He read the name and post of his distinguished visitor:

Dr Zhuo Huiying
Director, Sixth Municipal Hospital
Beijing City

"How nice of him!" Director Tang exclaimed to Orchid. "He must be here for New Year and he's calling on me before returning to Beijing! Get out the best tea and the sticky rice balls and the sesame candy!"

Director Tang dashed out to the main office and welcomed the visitors with cordiality and warmth. After all, visitors from Beijing are hard to come by in the provinces. He bowed the four men into his inner office and scurried to pull up chairs.

As he observed the welcome, complete with sticky rice balls and candy which Orchid was now serving, Director Zhuo said to himself: *He doesn't suspect the ax that is about to fall!*

"You're entirely too kind, Comrade Director," he said aloud. "The new year's holiday ended yesterday and you are carrying it over to today." Then he introduced "my three friends from Beijing." They exchanged calling cards in proper style and Director Tang made appropriate remarks.

After conventionalities had ground on for a few minutes, Director Zhuo decided it was time to end playacting. With an "excuse me", he laid his briefcase on Director Tang's desk, unlocked it and took out a sheaf of official papers. Separating out a document, he handed it to Director Tang and said: "Please read this."

As he read, Director Tang's face fell. The further he read the lower it dropped. Finally the paper dropped to the floor from lifeless and unfeeling hands. Tang looked at the visitors, wonder and disbelief written across his face.

Director Zhuo asked: "Do you understand what you have read?"

"No .... yes ... but ...."

"Right!" returned Director Zhuo. "Consider yourself

under house arrest. Do not leave this property until we have finished the investigation."

Orchid Qiu, standing to one side after serving the refreshments, saw and heard the whole drama. Her bosom rose and fell with conflicting emotions: Was the Director really being investigated? And under house arrest? What did all this mean to her?

Suddenly she realized that Director Zhuo was speaking to her: "Call all the comrades in for a meeting. Everybody, from Dr. Hua down to the gateman and the cleaning woman. They are to come right now."

Without even remembering to say "Yes, sir", Orchid turned, grabbed her wadded jacket, slipped into rubber shoes and struck out across the compound.

Director Zhuo turned to the auditor and bookkeepers: "We don't want Tang to feel bad that we are not doing justice to what he has served." Then, "Thank you, Dr. Tang, for the tea and edibles."

"Yes, yes," the other three men chimed in. "Thank you, Dr. Tang."

The four men dug into the sticky rice balls and sesame candy, all the while enjoying the discomfiture they knew lay behind the scowl on Tang's face.

They had just finished off the last bits when the workers began to trickle in, all ill at ease and all wondering why this special meeting with the men from Beijing. But Director Zhuo put them at ease immediately by addressing them in the local dialect and by joking about the amount of food they must have eaten over the holidays.

"You talk like a native of this place!" interjected Old Gatey.

"That is due to the fact, my friend, that I am a native of this place!" Director Zhuo continued: "You are all wondering why we four men are here. For your interest I shall read our orders from the Chief of the Department of Health in Beijing."

He proceeded to do so, then concluded: "Your work will go on as usual. The only restriction is that no one will leave Datong for reasons either public or private during the investigation. Thank you. You are dismissed."

Director Zhuo turned to True Virtue and Orchid: "While the auditor and bookkeepers begin on the books, you two will help me inventory the contents of the safe."

The scowl on Tang's face turned to amazement as he watched Director Zhuo pick up a manila envelope from his briefcase, take out a sheet of paper, then twist the dial a few times and open the safe — *his* safe, for which he thought he alone had the combination.

"You, Comrade Qiu, will remove the contents of the safe and call them out while Comrade Huang writes them down. I will make a final check on each item ...."

At noon True Virtue went across with Orchid to her room, ostensibly to eat her lunch there. But once inside the room Orchid grabbed Virtue, put her head down on her shoulder and wept.

"Just to think that all the time I believed he had incriminating documents against me in that safe," she sobbed. "And there wasn't a *thing* about me!"

"Yes, Orchid, it was blackmail by bluff."

"The scoundrel! The liar! How could he do such a thing to me? And time after time he told me he loved me! I'll never believe a man again!"

Once more there was a burst of weeping. But it didn't last long, because it came from relief and not sorrow.

As Orchid Qiu wiped away her tears she suddenly looked at her left hand.

"Do you remember, Virtue, that I said my left hand is stronger than my right? And that my left hand never loved him? Today my left hand has won out. I'll never let him touch me again!"

"And do *you* remember, Orchid, that I said God is on your side?"

Orchid gave a slow and thoughtful nod.

"Well, just a postscript to that," went on True Virtue, "I asked God, since He was on your side, to please *do* something for you. And now He has done it."

"Huang. So your name is True Virtue Huang," said Director Zhuo thoughtfully. "When I was a boy here in Datong I knew a man named Huang. He used to give me a ride home from school on his mule cart. He had an old gray mule named Mandy ...."

"That was my father. He still drives a mule cart."

"Hmm," said Director Zhuo, and put his ten fingers together. "Not to change the subject, but there's a good chance that Bright Victory Lee will come back to Datong. Do you remember Bright Victory Lee?"

A blush crept up Virtue's neck and colored her face.

"Yes, I remember him."

"Hmm," said Director Zhuo. "I thought you'd remember him."

30. The Clinic At Mine Number Three
Spring 1968

"DR. HUA, now that you are Acting Director of Datong Medical Center, the first thing you need to do is to beef up your staff."

"Right you are, Comrade Director. There's one man I'd like to have back here, but ..."

"Who's that?"

"Well, I understand he currently works on your staff in Beijing, and ...."

"You mean Bright Victory Lee?"

"Now that you mention his name, that's the man."

"Dr. Hua, I have discussed this with Bright Victory Lee. If you want him, just write a letter asking for his transfer. I'll take care of the rest."

It was a crisp, windy March day when Bright Victory stepped off the "soft seat" coach onto the Datong station platform. In contrast to the loneliness of his first arrival in Datong almost eight years before, this time here were friends to meet him — Dr. Hua, Orchid Qiu, Elder Feng, Mama and Papa Huang and True Virtue.

After greetings all around, Virtue's father said: "I've brought the mule cart, if you care to ride. I see you've got more baggage than when you left here."

"Right you are," Victory laughed, thinking of all the gifts he had brought along for the very people who had met him. "But I don't see all of us getting onto the mule cart. Could you be so good as to take my baggage along to the Health Center? And the rest of us will walk."

Mama Huang broke in: "When you've got your things set in, don't forget to come over for supper."

Victory answered heartily: "That I won't forget!"

Elder Feng and Dr. Hua excused themselves at the turnoff to their respective houses, and after arriving at the Health Center Orchid Qiu disappeared discreetly to her room.

When the mule cart arrived, Virtue said to her father: "You take Mama home and I'll help Victory take his things to the dorm." Without a glance at Victory, she picked up his old rattan suitcase and walked away with it.

Hmm, said Victory to himself, looking after her, *History repeats itself. She did that once before!* With his left hand he picked up his old bedding bundle and with his right gathered together a box, a basket and several crocks, jars and tins suspended in sundry mesh bags.

True Virtue had the door of the drab yellow building open and the rattan suitcase inside by the time Bright Victory with his heavier load had struggled up. The men's dorm was empty; not a soul was in sight.

She turned to him and said: "It's nice seeing you again."

"Well, it's nice seeing you!" he responded. And seeing was not enough. He caught her to him, then found her lips and kissed her.

True Virtue twisted herself free from his embrace, stood as tall as she could and demanded: "Bright Victory Lee! How *could* you! We are not even engaged!"

"Well, we'll take care of that right away. Will you marry me?"

"That's not for me to say. When it comes to marriage, you will have to talk to my parents."

And she turned her back on him and strode off.

In the first interview with his new boss on Monday morning, Bright Victory's ruffled feathers were rubbed the wrong way again. After they had gone over Victory's responsibilities, both in and out of the Health Center, he brought up the proposed clinic in Mine Number Three.

Dr. Hua exploded: "Young man, it is highly questionable whether you should do anything at all in those mines."

Victory was taken aback. With effort he controlled his voice. "May I ask why you say that?"

"In the first place, we've got enough on our plate already, with Dr. Tang dismissed. Secondly, they're only a bunch of jailbirds over there. They don't deserve much consideration."

At the slam against the prisoners, Victory felt his hackles rise. "Sir," he burst out, "I can't forget that I was a prisoner myself there for years. And some very good friends of mine are still there."

The hardness in the doctor's voice eased a bit: "Well, you can go there out of working hours if you like. But don't give out any of our medicines in those mines! I don't want even one bottle of medicine going to the mines through that front door!"

The following Sunday True Virtue was on emergency duty at the Center, and Victory realized this was his chance. But by the time he arrived at the Huang cottage the wind had gone from his sails. For the whole afternoon he talked about this, that and the other, with no courage to bring up the matter that filled his heart and mind.

Finally he picked up his cap and started for the door. Then with great determination he turned around and blurted out: "There's something I've been meaning to say to you...."

"Well, what is it?" replied Mama Huang. "You've had all afternoon to say it."

"Yes, but it's ... well ..." Victory swallowed twice, then coughed, but the lump in his throat wouldn't go away. "It's special."

"Well?" again from Mama Huang.

"It's about True Virtue."

"Too bad she's not here. I don't like talking about a person behind her back."

"Well, the truth is, she said I should talk to you."

"Okay, go ahead then."

Victory stood up straight and took a deep breath. He backed toward the wall, hoping the shadow would hide the red that was rising in his face. With supreme courage he finally produced the question: "Could I ask for the hand of True Virtue in marriage?"

"Hmmp! So that's the reason you came back to Datong!" put in Papa Huang. "I always thought you looked at her sort of dreamy-like."

"Now, Papa, don't be so hard on Victory."

But Papa was properly aroused: "It's marriage you're thinking about, is it? To do it properly, the boy's parents should approach the girl's parents ..."

"Papa, you know that's impossible. His parents are a thousand miles away."

A touch of mellowness stole into Papa Huang's voice: "If it's marriage you'll have to go about it the proper way."

"What's that, Mr. Huang?"

"You can't sew without a needle. You've got to have an old-man-under-the-moon."

"What's 'an old-man-under-the-moon'?"

"He means a middleman," Mama explained.

"A middleman?" Bright Victory wondered. "But it's nineteen years after Liberation, and all those feudalistic ways ..."

"Son, you're talking about the government now and what they say. But the government is outside and the family is inside. There are some things that even the government of China can't change."

"Bright Victory Lee! You're a sight for sore eyes! Praise God you're back!" In a very un-Chinese gesture, Pastor Ling grabbed Bright Victory and hugged him. The two men wept tears of joy on each other's shoulders.

Bright Victory had foreseen the emotional reunion with

his old prisonmates and had told the lineup outside he would see them only one at a time. As the evening wore on, he saw more friends than patients. And Pastor Ling was the one he most wanted to see.

"It's great that you're back! It's great you've opened this clinic! And it's great you've set the time for evening, after working hours!" He went on and on, as one friend does who hasn't seen the other for a long time.

Victory laughed. "My new boss thought he was putting limitations on me, saying I could come here only after my working hours. But that's the only time it would be worth-while coming — because that's when you're free."

The old pastor started up again: "Victory, since you left, God has raised up others to pray with me. Not just one but over twenty men! We've got a *church* down in the mine. It's a real 'underground church' if there ever was one! I'm pastoring a church again! Maybe the greatest thing is that Straw Boss Liu has turned to the Lord. He helps me arrange meetings now, and..."

Bright Victory laughed again. "Excuse me, Pastor, but this is officially a clinic. Others are waiting outside. Can I doctor anything for you?"

The pastor held up his fingers, some missing, some bent, some lacerated, some bruised. "Well, I guess you could fix up my fingers for me."

The following Sunday afternoon Victory called on Elder Feng. *If anyone has to be a middleman, I guess he's it,* he thought as he approached the Feng family courtyard. But, as on the previous Sunday, he found it hard to broach the subject he had come to discuss.

First he told of the new clinic every Monday, Wednesday and Friday night at the mine. "But a real problem is that Dr. Hua has ruled against me. He was pretty rough. He said, 'Don't take one bottle of medicine to the mines through that front door!'"

"Why is that?"

"Well, he says it's a different unit from the Health Center and they have their own financing."

"In that case, son, we'll look for a 'back door', as they say. Better still, we'll ask the Lord Jesus to open a back door for you. He is the Door and He can open doors."

Victory asked: "How are things going with the church?"

"Well, the believers have their external problems and their internal shortcomings. But do you know what I feel, Victory?"

"Why, no ....What is it?" Bright Victory sensed that this was a leading question.

"I feel that the Christian church in China is on the verge of the greatest expansion in its history. I can see it over the horizon."

With a start, Victory realized that Elder Feng's eyes were gazing out beyond the horizon. There was the look of a prophet in his eyes for a moment. But then he brought them down to the immediate again, and focused them on Bright Victory: "There's so much to be done! We already have two preaching bands going out on Sundays. How would you like to head up a third?"

They talked on and on about preaching bands. Finally, Victory picked up his cap and started toward the door. Then he paused irresolutely and turned around: "Oh! There's one place where I need your help. Did you ever hear of the-old-man-under-the-moon?"

Elder Feng laughed and laughed. "I was wondering when you would come around to that," he said.

"And that, Dr. Hua, is what is on my mind. You are the head of our unit and I thought it advisable to seek your guidance."

Victory was finding it relatively simple to approach Dr. Hua about an engagement.

"Harrump! It is not only *advisable* but *necessary* to obtain the approval of your unit for an engagement. In your case it is not complicated, as both you and True Virtue are in the same unit."

"Of course, Dr. Hua, I would also ask her parents in the old-fashioned way." He conveniently omitted to mention that he had already asked True Virtue's parents.

"Not these days, Victory! It's nineteen years since Liberation, and all those feudalistic ways have gone by the board."

"But, sir, old-fashioned ways die hard and the family is still important."

"Be careful, son. You're talking about the government and the laws. Today the family is outside and the government is inside. Since Liberation everything has changed, even the way you get engaged."

"Elder Feng, I want to thank you for arranging the engagement. We will look forward to your continued help through the wedding ceremony and beyond."

"Of course, Victory," Elder Feng replied. "We can't drop you in midstream. My wife and I will help as much as we can."

"Well, right now I need some advice. When should we set the wedding date?"

"As to the specific date, you'll have to talk about that with the bride-to-be. But in general it will depend on when you can shoulder the finances of a wedding."

"That's a delicate question," said Bright Victory wryly.

"Why?"

"To be frank, right now almost my entire income is swallowed up by supplies for the clinic in the mine."

"Are there no funds at the mine for medical work?" asked Elder Feng in surprise.

"You know there is a new commandant there," Victory replied. "He told me, 'There's nothing'."

"I don't see how you can support the clinic indefinitely by yourself."

"I agree, Elder, but right now I don't see any door opening for me."

"Well, Victory, if there's no front door, I still believe God will open a back door for you."

"Virtue, you look so fresh and rosy this morning! You look absolutely delectable!"

"Victory! How can you say that? If a thing is 'delectable' it means it's good to eat! And I'll let you know I'm not edible!"

Victory suddenly turned serious. "Virtue, we should talk about our wedding date."

"Yes, Victory, you're right. When do you want to get married?"

"Yesterday."

"'Yesterday'?" she laughed. "That's already gone!"

"Well, if not yesterday then today."

"Victory, you're joking."

"I'm not joking," he replied. "Didn't you ask me when I wanted to get married? The answer is *now*. Having you so close and yet so far away is tantalizing."

"I know what you mean," True Virtue acknowledged.

"But, Virtue, I have a problem. To have a wedding means money — for clothes, for decoration, and especially for the feast. And did you know I'm flat broke? Flat as a plywood board!"

"No, you didn't tell me."

"It's the clinic in the mine," Victory explained. "Almost every cent I earn goes into medicines, bandages, soap, towels and so on. I just can't save anything for our wedding!"

"Maybe I shouldn't say this, Victory, but ..."

"But what?" he asked.

"Well, some of my friends are pushing me to set the wedding date. And unless we set it before long they are going to start talking."

31. Back Doors and Weddings
Spring 1968

"I'M VERY PLEASED, Victory, that you've gone out the last few Sundays with the preaching bands," Elder Feng said. "Now you know how they operate, what they can and cannot do, and what to be careful of."

"Right, I've learned a lot. As I've tried to evaluate the preaching bands, a verse of Scripture comes to mind."

"What's that?"

"'Wise as serpents and harmless as doves'."

Elder Feng laughed. "That doesn't say much about their theology but it does say something about their methods."

"Yes, like meeting the village people at the public market here in Datong and walking home with them. That cuts down on the suspicion of the village police when they see you walking into the village with a local person."

"Right," nodded Elder Feng. "We learned that from experience."

"And I've noticed that the meetings are inside houses," went on Victory, "or in courtyards that are closed on all four sides."

"That's to keep things as low-key as possible," Elder Feng explained. "Technically and legally, the meetings can be stopped by the police and those attending arrested."

"Are the meetings much different from those the missionaries used to hold?" Victory asked.

"In content, no difference. It's still Jesus Christ and Him crucified."

"But what about methods?"

"Well, when Pastor Jim Johnson was here in pre-Liberation days we had absolute freedom to go where we wanted and do what we wanted. He was great for outdoor evangelistic meetings far and wide. Mostly, that meant casting the net in the turbulent seas of busy markets. Today we fish with hook and line in quiet waters. It's a blessing in disguise, for the country Christians bring their own relatives and friends in to hear. This will prove more productive in the end. After all, in China it's your relatives and immediate friends who count, anyway, and our present way of going about it emphasizes the closer circle of people with whom you already have mutual obligations."

"Excuse me, but are you Mr. Dou?"

"Why, yes, my name is Dou. Anything I can do for you?"

"I was told to look in the cabbage section of the market for a man with three white duck feathers stuck in his basket."

Mr. Dou laughed and grabbed Bright Victory by the hand. "You are Brother ....?"

"Lee. Bright Victory Lee. At your service, sir!"

Both laughed and gripped hands again.

"And here are the brethren who are going with us...." Victory turned and motioned two others to step up. "This is Brother Huang ... and Brother Han."

"I'm glad to meet you all....Now just a minute till I have these cabbages weighed out."

As they started walking Bright Victory asked: "So, your place is Sheets Family Village. How far is that?"

"Not far. Just on the other side of the mines. Ours is not a farming village but a coke-burning village. We have a dozen coke ovens and burn coke for the steel industry."

"How many believers do you have?"

"Only four families. But it's going to be great if you can come out and help us."

The four men were walking along the perimeter fence of Mine Number Three. Victory looked up at the barbed wire and the grim sentry boxes with their rifles and fixed bayonets, and beyond them saw the dirty buildings of the camp and the dusty tipples where the coal was loaded onto trucks and mule carts. He grimaced as he looked at the ugly black buildings and thought of the blackness of human suffering hidden away in them.

As they walked down the coal-dust-covered road he thought of the road ahead for most of the inmates inside the barbed wire — a road with no joy and no brightness, only the darkness that was already ground into their souls.

Approaching Sheets Family Village, the road ran between stark brick structures without windows and with only one small door each. Black smoke billowed out of a hole in each roof; some smoke mounted into the sky, writing "pollution" as it ascended, while other smoke curled downward, adding a new coating of soot to the black brick buildings and everything else in sight.

Victory asked Mr. Dou: "Those your coke ovens?"

"Right. That's the livelihood of the village."

Victory looked more closely at the roughly-built structures, and asked: "Does anyone ever go inside?"

"Oh, yes. To arrange the coal and to remove the coke after burning."

Under his breath Bright Victory muttered, *Looks like a dangerous job to me.*

Brother Dou filled Victory in as to the mechanics of the village gathering. Then he sounded a somber note: "Don't be surprised if we have some disturbance this afternoon. The chairman of the local Communist Party is an aggressive man who feels that his calling in life is to make things hard for the Christians. If he turns up, don't be surprised at whatever happens."

"What's his name?"

"His name's Tang. He is the brother of Dr. Tang who used to head the Datong Health Center until he was demoted and kicked out of the Party. Just missed a jail sentence. But perhaps you've never heard of him..."

"And now, brethren, we'll ask each of our visitors for a word of greeting." Brother Dou was addressing the worshipers — eleven villagers plus the three men from town, all sitting on benches in the Dou family courtyard. Above, two bedspreads stretched on bamboo poles gave some protection from the sun. Below, pigs and chickens strolled casually among the worshipers.

Papa Huang spoke first, hesitatingly, with none of the assurance he showed in ordinary conversation. As he himself said, "I'm not for public speaking."

Then Han Changping told of an empty life as a Red Guard, of his utter desolation when he was sent "up to the hills, down to the country," and how finally the warmth, forgiveness and acceptance of the Christians proved the lifeline that pulled him out of the morass of sin, shame and suffering.

Finally Bright Victory told of growing up in Chongqing, and how the family turned to Christ due to the forgiveness shown by Mrs. Deng after her husband was done to death.

Brother Dou motioned to Victory to continue on and bring the message. It was Victory's first attempt at anything remotely related to a sermon. He took off on forgiveness, using the Chongqing incident as a springboard. He was just warming up to his subject when the main door to the courtyard scraped open and three middle-aged men stepped over the threshold.

Bright Victory gave a start. Could that man in front be his old boss, Director Tang? Then he remembered that Dr. Tang's brother lived in the village, was the local Party chairman, *and* could be expected to cause trouble! Here he was at the meeting!

The thought raced through Victory's mind: *I hope he keeps quiet until I'm through!*

But that was not to be.

Victory was quoting: "If you forgive not men their trespasses neither will your Heavenly Father forgive your trespasses," when a voice from near the door broke in: "What book are you quoting from?"

Bright Victory answered: "From the Christian Bible."

"That's a foreign book. We don't need the likes of that in China today!"

Victory surprised himself at his answer: "Because a book comes from another country, does that make it bad?"

"Of course it does! This is China and we are Chinese!"

"Then may I ask: Do the writings of Marx, Engels and Lenin come from China?"

"Hmmp! Think you're smart, don't you?" said the interrupter sarcastically. "I'm here to tell you that this is an illegal meeting. You are more than four people not mutually related. Today I'm giving you a warning. But I ought to arrest all of you!"

With that threat the three men scraped open the courtyard door, stepped over the threshold and left.

After the meeting Sunday night Bright Victory told Elder Feng about the afternoon incident.

When he had finished, the elder was silent a whole minute. Then he said thoughtfully: "Two things, Victory: First, it's no surprise that Satan counter-attacks. In fact we should feel complimented that Satan deigns to recognize us. Secondly, you are going to be thrown into the conflict personally. Just thank God for a challenge worthy of the best that is in you."

"That's what he said, Virtue, just before the three of them stomped out of the meeting yesterday afternoon."

"Well, Victory, if you are going to preach in the future, yesterday was not a very auspicious start. A non-Christian might say it was an unlucky day."

"I guess people may be talking like that," agreed Victory.

"Rumors spread like smoke, especially if a man like Tang fans the flame."

"But, Victory, it may not be ten-tenths bad that Tang is against us in Sheets Family Village," True Virtue told him. "I understand he isn't liked at all by the village people. They say he's puffed up like an oversize frog in a small puddle, just because he's local Communist Party chairman."

"I'd just as soon our paths would not cross again, even so," Bright Victory commented.

"But you must be prepared. Your paths could cross again."

"Victory! Victory! Come quickly! You can't imagine who's come to see you!" Orchid Qiu was almost beside herself with excitement.

Victory quickly finished with the outpatient he was seeing and started across the compound with Orchid.

"And a funny thing, Victory, he asked me for the key to the back door and said he would meet you there, of all places!"

"Say, Orchid, stop, won't you? Just stop a minute."

"But he said to hurry!"

"Yes, yes, Orchid. But stop! Catch your breath a minute."

Finally she did stop. Victory looked her straight in the eye and asked, "Orchid, who *is* it?"

"Oh! I'm sorry! I forgot to tell you. Why, it's Director Zhou, your old boss from Beijing."

"Okay. That's all I want to know. Let's go!"

The two ran to the back door of the compound. To their amazement they found not only Director Zhou there, but a great jumble of boxes inside the door and more being handed in from a truck outside.

Director Zhou greeted Bright Victory warmly: "Hello, Victory, how are you?"

"Very well, thank you, sir. And you?"

"I'm fine, thanks."

Bright Victory curbed his bursting curiosity about the boxes. With great effort he tried to carry on the conversation even while the truck men were jostling him for space to set the boxes down.

"And may I ask what brings you to Datong?" he said politely.

"An uncle of mine passed away, the last remaining male of his generation. So I came not only for the funeral but for other family reasons."

Bright Victory nodded gravely. "I offer you my sympathies in the loss of your uncle." But the question was still beating on his brain: *What are all these boxes about?*

The Director continued: "I'm especially glad to do something for your friend Dr. Hei. Ever since he came back from the earthquake project he has been undecided about his left-over supplies. They were travel-worn and getting out of date, of course. Well, the other day out of the blue he decided to send them to you for your prison clinic. Could you use them?"

Bright Victory suddenly choked up. So much so that he could not get a word out. Mistaking his silence for indecision and lack of enthusiasm, Director Zhou's face fell. Then he noticed the quiver on Victory's lips.

"Director Zhou," finally the words came out, "you... you mean all these things are for me?"

"Yes they are, Bright Victory. For your clinic in the mines ... and here is a letter from Dr Hei as well."

"*How* can I ever thank you? And how can I thank Dr Hei? Your kindness is more than I can stand."

Bright Victory's eyes had filled with tears and he was busy blowing his nose.

Neither of the men had noticed that Orchid had disappeared. Now she was coming back with Virtue in tow.

Breathless, Orchid managed to say: "You remember True Virtue Huang, of course."

"Of course! Miss Huang, how are you? And your mother and father?"

"I'm well, thank you. And so are they. And you, sir, how are you?"

Amazed at the dozens of boxes being piled inside the door, True Virtue's aplomb quickly wore thin and curiosity conquered courtesy: "And what are all these boxes for?"

Dr. Zhou said to them all: "I'm glad just you three are here. I want to share a little joke with you ... All this is off the record. These supplies are a token of personal good wishes from Dr. Hei, because you, Bright Victory, saved his life.

"Since it is a back-door arrangement I thought it would be appropriate to deliver these things to the back door of the Center. Ha! Ha! I hope you don't mind my little joke."

"Mind!" exclaimed Victory. "You'll never know how grateful we are to you for these things. And for the way you have delivered them, too."

"It's marvelous! It's wonderful! The Lord did open the back door, didn't He? And to think it was our own back door here on the compound!"

Bright Victory was ecstatic with joy. He and Old Gatey the gateman had just trundled in and stacked the last of thirty boxes.

True Virtue, the phlegmatic northerner, stood there in the storeroom with keys in hand and enjoyed the sudden development in a quieter way. "Yes, this really puts one over on Dr. Hua," she chuckled. "Just like he says, not one bottle of *his* medicine will go out that front door. It will be God's medicine, not his, and it's 'back door' medicine anyway!"

Virtue laughed deliciously. Then she thought of something, and asked: "Didn't Dr. Zhou give you a letter?"

"Why, he did, for sure. Let's look at it."

Victory took the letter out of his pocket. For a moment he balanced it on his hand.

"Hmm. Feels heavy."

He tore open the envelope. Folded neatly inside the letter were bank notes. Victory held one up — a ten-dollar bill!

After "Oh's" and "Ah's", he counted: "... Eighteen, nineteen, twenty! That makes — let's see — in all two hundred dollars!" Folding the bills, he shoved them into his breast pocket. Then he opened up Dr. Hei's letter:

"Dear Bright Victory,

I hear you are getting married. Enclosed are twenty good wishes for your wedding. Thank you again for saving my life ..."

"Well," said Virtue, "it looks like there's a wedding coming up!"

Bright Victory looked around. The door was closed, and no one had followed them into the storeroom. He grabbed Virtue firmly around the waist and kissed her lips.

True Virtue stiffened, pulled herself away and stood as tall as she could. "Bright Victory Lee! How could you? Don't you know kissing is insanitary?"

"Good afternoon, Brother Dou. I see you still have your three white duck feathers."

Brother Dou laughed. "Yes, I wasn't sure if it would be you or someone else this afternoon, so I stuck them in just in case."

As they passed by the kilns, Bright Victory noticed that one was emitting no smoke. Closer inspection revealed big characters on the door:

OUT OF ORDER

DANGER — NO ADMITTANCE

"The fire went out several days ago," explained Brother

Dou. "Looks like they're in for a big overhaul job on the kiln itself."

As on previous Sundays, halfway through the meeting the courtyard door scraped open and three men straddled the high threshold and stepped inside. Bright Victory avoided eye contact with either Chairman Tang or the other two. He simply continued speaking.

He was in the middle of a sentence when it happened: "Bang!"

He's shooting at me! thought Bright Victory as he dropped flat to the ground.

"Ha! Ha! Ha!" The three men laughed, very amused at Victory's sudden dive for the ground. "Does a firecracker scare you that bad? Next time I'll bring a gun!"

With that parting thought the three men got up noisily, scraped the door open and left.

For True Virtue Huang, like millions of other Chinese brides since 1949, there was no traditional red wedding gown. In fact, True Virtue wore no gown at all, just a new white blouse of mixed cotton and nylon and a new blue skirt.

Going to the local civil affairs office on Friday morning for the legal ceremony, Virtue dared to wear her new blouse, because it could be covered by her blue, button-up Mao jacket, but she did not dare wear the skirt. That was too *avant-garde* to be displayed at the government office. But she did wear a new pair of dark blue pants tailored for the occasion.

Dr. Hua accompanied Victory and Virtue and signed for their unit, a necessary acknowledgement that the unit did not oppose the marriage. In fact he showed his magnanimity by giving the bride and groom Friday and Saturday off.

Elder Feng was not an ordained man. But he was God's chosen leader of that flock, and the members of the flock recognized this. So there was a deep feeling of "rightness" as he performed the Christian ceremony and administered the vows on that Sunday evening. He performed the ceremony attired in an old pair of gray pants and a dark blue, short-sleeved sports shirt with square tails out and only four buttons on the front. Where the fifth should have been, the top of the shirt was open and revealed several square inches of white underwear beneath.

For his wedding outfit, Victory wore a new pair of blue pants and a white, short-sleeved sports shirt made from the same bolt of material that True Virtue's new blouse had been cut from.

The main part of the ceremony came when Elder Feng held up his Bible. Victory placed his right hand on the Bible, palm down, then Virtue placed hers on top of his. Finally, Elder Feng placed his right hand on top of their two hands and prayed, commending them to the Heavenly Father for time and eternity.

After the last "Amen" there was an obvious easing of tension and everyone breathed more freely, stretched, and began to chat with the person sitting in the next seat. A hired photographer took pictures, and the women excused themselves to help in the kitchen.

While the guests sat around waiting for the feast to be served, they nibbled peanuts and sunflower seeds and sipped green tea. It was at this point that the groom poured a cup of tea and held it to the bride's lips for her to sip. Then she reversed the procedure, pouring a cup of tea and holding it for him to sip. The small amount of tea sloshed was the occasion for many jokes and great prognostication as to what dire things would happen to this marriage as a result of spilling the tea.

Apart from the Christians, only True Virtue's relatives and the staff of Datong Health Center were present, with Dr. Hua again much in evidence. It was becoming quite obvious from the lead he took in affairs that he had been a prime mover in this courtship from first to last.

Finally, the bride and groom sat down with the guests around a half dozen tables set out in the courtyard, and ate a solid meal of pork, chicken and duck, stir-fried with spring vegetables and topped off with large quantities of white rice, steamed bread and kettle after kettle of green tea.

They had neither money nor time off for a honeymoon. But they did go to the Huang home and spend the night in True Virtue's bedroom, where a double bed had been brought in for the occasion.

Now that they were married it was in order for Victory and Virtue to work in the same preaching band, so on the Sunday after the wedding Virtue went to Sheets Family Village for the first time. It was the quietest meeting for some weeks because, for reasons unknown, Chairman Tang and Friends did not appear.

Victory and Virtue were just preparing to leave the Dou home when there were sounds of excitement in the road outside. Victory dashed to the door and opened it. An old man was toddling along toward the center of the village as fast as two legs and a cane could take him.

Bright Victory shouted at him: "Hey! What's your rush? Where're you going?"

"Don't you know what happened?"

"No. What?" Victory asked.

"The kiln's collapsed! Chairman Tang's inside!" And the old man toddled on out of earshot.

Victory turned around and shouted to those in the courtyard. "The kiln's collapsed! Chairman Tang's inside! Let's go!" Not waiting for the others, he ran off down the road.

As he approached the kilns, Victory found a crowd gathered around the kiln marked "DANGER — NO ADMITTANCE". What had been a large, imposing kiln was now a huge heap of rubble. It had collapsed in on itself, filling the huge central cavity where the coke was burned.

Bright Victory accosted an older man standing by: "Hey! What happened? Anybody hurt?"

With great aplomb, quite willing to be an authority on the subject, the man replied: "The kiln was old and out of order. It collapsed. Unfortunately there was a man inside."

"Who?"

"Chairman Tang. He had no business being inside but as Party chairman he ..."

"Is he alive?" Bright Victory asked urgently.

"Was a few minutes ago. You could hear him groaning."

"Why aren't they getting him out?"

A bystander joined in: "Oh, he's dead by now. Good enough for him. Fate's caught up with him."

A third person added his wisdom: "Nobody liked him. He was as self-important as a bullfrog. Ha! Ha! Ha!"

Others around joined in laughing and snickering. At that point True Virtue and the other Christians arrived, puffing and panting. Victory shouted at them: "Chairman Tang's in there! Let's get him out!"

Without waiting for their response, he turned and tore into the debris, picking up bricks and throwing them aside. The other Christians followed suit, and before long they had cleared an approach path to the main door of the kiln.

Reminds me of my coal-mining days, Bright Victory muttered to himself.

Now they began to run into debris too large to move by hand: Victory dashed back to the crowd. Some were jeering and sneering — whether at the man underneath or at those working to get him out he wasn't sure. He didn't stop to ask, but found the old man he had been talking with: "Get me three crowbars. Big heavy ones."

The old man balked at being ordered around, but on

second thought he said: "Okay" and started off, mumbling to himself, "You never know who you're talking to."

Victory turned again to clawing at the bricks with his bare hands.

In a few minutes the old man came back with two companions, each shouldering a huge crowbar. With these, Victory and Company rolled the larger chunks back down the path they had already cleared out.

By this time the feverish work had almost exhausted them. Victory gasped: "Let's rest a minute." He was leaning on one of the crowbars when a platoon of soldiers trotted up on the double-quick.

The sergeant in charge, panting, stood for a minute, then recovered his breath enough to ask Bright Victory: "You in charge here?"

"No. Just a volunteer worker.

"Well, you rest a bit. We'll dig. Just let me have that crowbar, won't you?"

Victory, Virtue, Brother Dou and the other Christians sat down on some of the larger chunks they had rolled out.

As soon as Brother Dou had caught his breath, he lifted his voice and prayed loudly: "Oh God! You know that our friend Chairman Tang is under all that pile of brick and rubble. Oh God! Please save him alive. Amen."

The crowd reacted to the prayer with mutterings, criticism and even blasphemy. One loud voice proclaimed: "Not even the Old Man in Heaven could save a person alive from all those bricks! Anyway, that guy doesn't deserve to be saved alive!"

"Ha! Ha! Ha!" General laughter from the crowd followed this blasphemy.

The soldiers worked hard, throwing out bricks and debris. Before long, however, they in turn were tired. Bright Victory offered his group to spell them off. By this time a path had been cleared through the original doorway and a few feet inside the kiln.

After loosening a big chunk of bricks and mortar, Victory heard a sound from the other side. He motioned for those back of him to be quiet, and sure enough, there it was, a moan then: "*Aiya!*"

Victory got down on his knees and pulled some loose debris aside. There in a small cavity no larger than a beehive was Chairman Tang.

Slowly and carefully Victory pulled him out. He and Brother Dou picked him up, carried him out to the street and stretched him out on the ground.

"Bring a pan of water and a towel. And some tea for him to drink." Bright Victory was the para-medic now, giving first aid to the injured.

Before wash pan, towel and tea arrived, Victory went over Chairman Tang's body. Amazingly no bone was broken. Cold water on face, head and hands revived him. He sat up and eagerly gulped two cups of warm tea.

Looking around, Chairman Tang recognized his rescuers. Gone was the sassiness and cynicism of previous Sundays. He felt his body. No bones broken. Only a few cuts and bruises.

Amazingly, he struggled to his feet under his own steam, and said: "I have a confession to make, and an apology. For a long time I have been hard on the Christians. But today you people here made fun of me and left me to die, but the Christians prayed for me and rescued me. From now on, the church will meet in my house!"

PART V

SHANGHAI AND ANHUI
1971

上海和安徽

32. "Up To The Hills, Down To The Country"

Shanghai and Anhui — Spring 1971

"CHILDREN, it looks as if our little family is going to be broken up."

Strong Hero Liang and his sister Rosebud gazed in unbelief at their mother. Hero asked: "Why should anybody want to break up our family? There are only three of us left, with Papa in the Reform-through-Labor camp on the Russian border."

"Hero, it's this program to reduce city population. They're sending more and more people out of the city. 'Up-to-the-hills, down-to-the-country' they call it."

"They've had that program on for years," Hero protested, "as punishment for the Red Guards, for instance."

"Yes, Hero, but now it's been broadened to include ordinary families."

"Like ours?" Rosebud wanted to know.

"Right, Rosey. At the neighborhood meeting last night the district cadres told me that someone had to go from our family, right away, or they'd use force. Now, we have a choice. But later, if it comes to force, it will be the choice of those who have the force."

Strong Hero and Rosebud sat silent. It took a while for that to soak in.

Then Hero reacted: "When are they going to stop thinking up these interminable programs? Ever since Liberation we've had a brand new one every fourteen months, from a trivial Swat the Fly to a tragic Cultural Revolution."

"Now, Strong Hero, it does no good to react like that," said his mother firmly. "We can only face this issue rationally and as Christians."

Hero sat for a minute with his chin cradled in his hand, then agreed: "You're right, Mama. No point in getting heated up."

"This program is aimed at young unmarried people ...."

Rosebud interrupted her mother: "Well, that leaves you out, Mama."

"And it looks as if it puts me in," said Hero.

Mother Liang's eyes brimmed with tears. "Hero, it's hard enough to support three in the family on your income and mine, and send a little to your father up on the frontier. How could I manage to do that on one income? And if you went to the country, I'd have to send you something, too, to keep you alive!" She broke out in tears of frustration and tension.

Then Rosebud spoke up: "Mama, could *I* volunteer to go? Would that satisfy the district cadres?"

"*You*, Rosebud? Why, you're my precious little flower! And you're only fifteen years old! How could I bear to let you go away? For four years!"

"But, Mama, they *are* sending fifteen-year-olds now. Just last week two girls from my class left for Zong Ming Island."

The thought of Rosebud leaving home was too much for Mother Liang. She gathered her up in her arms and wept.

"....So, Lotus, that's the way the family confab went ...." Hero's voice trailed off in thought and he gave a gentle push with the paddle. He had invested ten cents to rent a boat so that they could have some privacy on the lake at Hongkou Park that Sunday afternoon.

"But... her education!" protested Lotus. "What will happen to that if she goes to the country?"

"Rosebud's finished middle school. And we can't pay the fees for high school, even if she could get in, which is doubtful anyway since our family's on the black list ..."

"What does Rosebud herself think of becoming a farmer?"

"Very excited about it. She says anything would be better

than hanging around the house doing nothing.... And there's another thing, too..."

"What's that?"

Hero lowered his voice so that it wouldn't carry to the people in the other boats: "For some reason, Rosebud is wildly enthusiastic for every new program that comes along. Swallows it hook, line and sinker."

At the Dispatch Office the Police Sergeant in Charge of Census took up his ball-point and with one stroke excised Rosebud from the Shanghai Residents List.

Lotus Flower had asked for the day off to be with Rosebud and her mother on this day Rosebud was leaving for four years on Zong Ming Island. The two girls returned to the apartment just as Mrs. Liang was arriving from the opposite direction. She was carrying something heavy and bulky in her black plastic bag.

Rosebud dashed up to her mother, demanding: "Mama, what's in your bag?"

"Wait until we're inside and I'll show you."

Rosebud grabbed the bag from her mother. It was so heavy she could hardly carry it. Once inside, she dutifully handed it back to her mother. Mother Liang put it on the table and carefully folded down its black sides. Of a sudden the secret was revealed — four huge crabs, greenish-black, claws tied together with straw and legs bound to bodies with more straw. They were looking around with their black beady eyes and blowing bubbles out of their mouths.

"Oh! How huge!" Rosebud yelled with delight.

"Yes, they're the largest I could find. They weigh more than a pound apiece. I got them for a special treat because... because you won't be home for a while."

Mrs. Liang boiled up the crabs in a hurry and cooked some fresh rice.

When the crabs were piled high on the table, however,

neither mother nor daughter nor guest had much appetite to enjoy the delicacy. It was too sad a day for even crabs to lighten it up.

The ferry was scheduled to leave for Zong Ming Island at 5 p.m. To their surprise, when they went out at 1.30 to call a pedicab for the baggage, it had begun to rain. Not much of a rain, just one of those fine, steady, insistent drizzles for which Shanghai is famous.

The rain slowed them down, and it was 4.30 before the three women finally reached the barrier blocking the wharf at Wusongkou on the Yangzi River ten miles from the city.

The policeman at the barrier was adamant. "No escorting of passengers beyond this point. Don't you see the sign?"

There was the sign all right: "PASSENGERS ONLY."

"But who will carry her baggage for her?" Mrs. Liang wanted to know.

"She will carry it herself, of course," was the reply.

In the melee and the rush of buying a ferry ticket and loading up Rosebud with suitcase, bedding bundle and odds and ends, they all forgot to say goodbye. After she was a dozen steps away, the two older women did remember and called after her, "Goodbye! Goodbye!" But in the noise and excitement Rosebud did not hear.

The last they saw of her, she was struggling down the passageway, bravely dragging suitcase, bedding bundle and odds and ends.

Mrs. Liang and Lotus Flower looked around them. The rain was getting heavier. The heavens were gray. The ferry was gray. From a distance they watched the slender shadows, each one like the next, struggling up the gangplank. They, too, were gray. The feelings and thoughts of the two women were also gray.

The ferry whistled, and began to pull away from the pier. It nosed slowly into the current of the Yangzi, an inch at a time, too heavily loaded with sad affairs to move. It whistled again and belched out a great cloud of black smoke, as if it were too tired for words.

"It's strange, Loyalty. Why should you be out of work? Are they doing nothing at all at the weaving factory?"

"Almost nothing, Mama. The looms are so old that they have just about broken down for the last time. They should buy new looms, modern ones."

"Well, why don't they?"

"No money. New looms would have to come from abroad, and that means foreign exchange."

"Loyalty, there's one thing I'm worried about. If you are not assigned to new work soon, do you know what's apt to happen?"

"I know what you're thinking about. 'Up-to-the-hills, down-to-the-country', like hit the Liang family."

Just then mother and son fell silent. They listened. What was that sound in the distance?"

"Dah...dah.. Dah, dah, dah!" Two longs, three shorts.

Jade Moon turned pale, and whispered: "I haven't heard that drumbeat for a long time. It was what I dreaded so much before."

"Yes, Mama, and there are gongs along with the drums. Hear them?"

"I just wonder what family they're going to today."

Three nights later, Jade Moon, Loyalty and Lotus were finishing supper.

"*Wa!* Mama, those mustard greens were tasty!" Loyalty exclaimed. "No matter that you had to clip the yellow part of the leaves off. What was left was mature and had a really mustardy flavor!"

All three laughed heartily. After all, it was nice to be able to pull something tasty out of the refuse heap of the Vegetable Distribution Center.

To prove he meant what he said, Loyalty picked up the serving bowl and with a chinaware soup spoon scooped out the last bit of water in which the mustard greens had been cooked.

"There!" he said. "That's my ration of vitamins and minerals for today!"

Again, all three laughed. Loyalty pushed the bowl back on the table in a "now-I'm-satisfied" gesture, and leaned back comfortably in his chair.

Lotus held up a finger: "Listen!"

Sure enough, there it was in the distance: "Dah...dah...dah, dah, dah!" Two longs, three shorts.

Jade Moon gave the slightest shiver, and tried quickly to conceal it. "That's it," she said. "Wonder what family's getting it tonight...."

They said nothing more but listened quietly. Gradually the drumbeat grew louder. And now they could hear the gongs as well.

Finally it was loud — and close: "DAH!...DAH!...*DAH, DAH, DAH!*" They were inside the house! They were coming up the stairs!

"Who let them in?" whispered Lotus.

"Must have been The Demon," answered Loyalty, also in a whisper.

Brother and sister looked at their mother. Her face was white as a sheet.

Outside the door the beat stopped. The door flew open. The Demon strode in. Or rather, limped in, for her left leg was shorter than the right, after her fall.

The beaters of drums and gongs followed.

Without courtesy or conventionality The Demon plunged in: "The Workers' Propaganda Brigade have something to say to you."

She stepped back, and a girl of perhaps eighteen years of age stepped forward. She wore a blue cap with a red star in front, plus a worker's blue pants and jacket.

"Are you Bright Loyalty Lee?"

"Yes, I am," he answered. "What can I do for you?"

"First of all, cut out that bourgeois 'what-can-I-do-for-you' stuff. It's not what you can do for me but what you can do for your country! Don't you love your country? What are you, a full-grown, healthy man doing, sitting here at home on your bottom and not out working for your country?"

By this time the girl was panting for breath.

She's out of breath and out of spiel, Loyalty said to himself. But he was wrong.

Catching her breath, she continued: "Don't you know that every family in Shanghai must provide at least one person for the great program, 'Up-to-the-hills, down-to-the-country'? We know that your mother and your sister both have jobs but you are 'awaiting assignment'. How long do you have to wait before you move off to the farm and do something for your country?"

Her breast heaving with emotion, the spokeswoman stopped for breath again. But she wasn't finished yet. The sting was in the tail: "We'll give you three days to make up your mind. If you're not ready by then to check out of Shanghai, we'll turn you over to the District Cadres!"

With that parting shot, she turned on her cloth-soled heel and made her exit. Dutifully the rest of the Workers' Propaganda Brigade trooped out. Last of all, The Demon limped out.

But that wasn't the end. The grand finale was a blast of gong-and-drum in the upper hall: "DAH!...DAH!... *DAH, DAH, DAH!*" The beat continued down the stairs, out into the yard and along the street until it finally faded away in the distance.

The Lees were not yet to settle down for the night. There was a postscript, in the person of The Demon.

After escorting the drum and gong beaters several blocks, she returned. This time she was polite enough to knock on the Lees' door. But she refused to step inside when invited to do so.

Standing in the hallway outside she shouted, loud enough for all in the house to hear: "This is just to let you know that at the meeting of the Neighborhood Street Committee last night your name was tabulated, Bright Loyalty Lee, as a likely prospect to go to Anhui Province for the rice planting. Remember the deadline! Remember your family is black-listed."

Then, as a matter of private wisdom being shared gratis with people who should appreciate it: "Don't you know it's a mistake you ever got a good job at the weaving factory? You'll never get that good a job again!"

With that, she turned and limped off down the hall.

Loyalty was in need of another man with whom he could share his problem. The next morning, therefore, he walked over to the weaving factory to look for Mighty Tower Gou. He had a hunch he would find his friend in the loom room, where the two of them had experienced both pleasure and frustration.

Sure enough, there was Mighty Tower sitting on the floor, an island in a sea of parts of a dismantled loom.

"So! They've taken you back on, have they?" Tower exclaimed. "I sure could use some help with these old looms!"

"No, Tower, I'm sorry. Nothing like that. I've come to tell you some news and to ask some advice."

Loyalty recounted the visit of the Worker's Propaganda Brigade plus The Demon's personal postscript.

"What do you think, Tower? In the first place, any chance of me being reassigned here?"

"Well, you could enquire at the office. No harm done."

"In the second place, as a friend and a Christian, what would you advise?"

Mighty Tower thought for a long minute. Then he said: "Loyalty, I just don't see that we can buck the system. We're up against *force majeure*. What can you do but look up your District Cadres and ask for reassignment to whatever and wherever they say?"

Bright Loyalty looked around at his fellow fifth-class passengers on *M.S. The East is Red No. 17*. It was his first time on a Yangzi River steamer since the family arrived in Shanghai on the *S.S. Min Jiang* so long before.

He stretched out his bedding and thereby staked a claim to that much deck space. The deck above gave protection from rain without blocking his view of the shoreline. He took a deep breath of the damp salty air and congratulated himself on the long rest he would enjoy between Shanghai City and Wuhu in Anhui Province.

The next morning the steamer was ploughing along past dim mud banks which all looked alike, mile after tedious mile.

"Wish I could see something," Loyalty murmured to himself. But his thoughts were interrupted: "BONG! BONG! BONG!"

"What's that?" He asked his next-door neighbor on the deck.

"Breakfast," came the reply.

Loyalty rolled up his bedding so that he could sit on the roll and lean up against the side of the ship to eat. Retrieving rice bowl and chopsticks out of the cardboard box which did duty as a suitcase, he lined up for the dole-out of rice gruel and fried soy beans.

Having finished breakfast, Loyalty felt like talking. He addressed his neighbor again: "You know what I like about the boat as compared to the train? You can bring more baggage *and* the ticket is cheaper, too."

"I'd never carry as many ducks as that on the train," agreed the other, motioning toward four bamboo crates speared together with a wooden carrying pole at the foot of his bedding.

"The only problem is, you can't *see* anything," went on Loyalty.

"Hmmp," commented his fellow traveller.

Undaunted, Loyalty kept talking: "Could I go up on the bridge for a better view, do you think?"

"Don't know. Never been up there," returned the other.

Loyalty made his way over to the wooden bucket full of water and washed his bowl and chopsticks, replacing them in the cardboard box. Again he addressed his neighbor: "Guess I'll go up topside and see what I can see."

"Hmmp," was the only rejoinder.

Bright Loyalty was one of the few passengers stirring. Apart from a handful making their way either to or from the latrine on the stern of the ship, everybody else had settled back into their bedding as if the best way to spend the hours was to snooze them away.

A few stewards in dirty white smocks gave Loyalty a "Where-do-you-think-you're-going" look. But no one stopped him on his way topside. After all, it was a classless society now, far removed from pre-Liberation days when padlocked iron gates restrained deck passengers from ascending to the sanctum of First Class.

Bright Loyalty bypassed the bridge and climbed on to the top deck, above the bridge. "*Wa!* That's better!" he told himself as he breathed deep of the fresh air. He could see far and wide over the flat countryside of Jiangsu Province and, closer at hand, the occasional steamer, tugboat, barge, ferry, fishing boat or raft floating on the broad bosom of the Yangzi.

Apparently no one else had a yen for fresh air and a view. Loyalty was on the top deck alone. With no one to talk to, his eyes strayed to the deck below where a few second-class passengers were lounging in deck chairs. There was no First Class; Second Class was the top grade of accommodation on the ship. The only activity on the Second-Class deck was a game of mahjong played by four men sitting around a square table.

Suddenly Loyalty was galvanized by what he saw. Two of the mahjong players had their caps off, and one of them had no hair on the top of his head at all. Instead, red lines ran in all directions like a map.

I'd recognize that head anywhere, said Loyalty to himself. *It couldn't belong to anybody on earth but Colonel Chang!*

Quickly his memory replayed the last time he saw that map-like head — at his brother Victory's trial! And this was the very man who had sentenced his father to Reform-through-Labor on Hainan Island!

So! He's still alive! And what's he doing on this ship, with me, out in the middle of the Yangzi River? Does he know I'm on board? Is this a mere coincidence? Or something else?

Questions tumbled through Loyalty's mind, one after the other. Quickly he turned away from the edge of the deck. No point in letting Colonel Chang see him! But how could Colonel Chang recognize him anyway? Surely it was just a strange coincidence — albeit one in a million — that he and Colonel Chang were on the same boat.

Even so, Loyalty's enthusiasm for fresh air and scenery suddenly evaporated. He descended the ladder on the side of the ship away from the mahjong players, and quietly made his way back to his bedding roll on the lower deck.

After lunch Loyalty dropped off into a fitful sleep, and

dreamed that the ship was steaming along on a crazy map on which all the lines were red.

"Wake up! Wake up! They're checking tickets!" It was the voice of the duck dealer.

Bright Loyalty rubbed his eyes and looked around. Two men in uniform were bending over recumbent forms, shaking them awake and demanding something. What was it? Tickets?

As they drew closer, Bright Loyalty heard the words, "Identity papers". He pulled out his ID and handed it to the officer. The man read it twice, then asked the second man: "What's the name? Pull it out, let's compare."

The other man pulled out a slip of paper and held it up beside Loyalty's ID.

"Yep. That's him." He turned to Loyalty and said: "Come with us."

Loyalty turned to the duck dealer, who was looking on with a blank expression on his face, and said: "Just keep an eye on my things, won't you?"

"Can do," the duck dealer answered.

"Follow me," the officer said. Loyalty followed him across the deck, while the second man brought up the rear.

Loyalty wondered, *Am I under arrest?* But he knew it was pointless to ask where they were taking him or why. The three went up the companion way to Second Class and knocked on a door.

From inside came an answering grunt. The officer outside asked uncertainly: "Colonel Chang?"

Bright Loyalty stood before the table in the well-lit cabin. Behind the table sat a heavy florid man in officer's uniform. He had his cap on.

"So, you are Bright Loyalty Lee. I believe we have seen each other before."

"Yes, sir."

"You should know, Lee, that of all the people in the world, the Chinese have the longest memories, and of all the families in China the Changs have the longest. A Chang never forgets."

All Loyalty could say was: "Yes, sir."

"I want you to know that I am now Garrison Commander at Wuhu, Anhui, where you are headed for. Welcome to Wuhu. We shall no doubt see each other again. Next time, I want to send a Lee direct to prison. That is all. You are dismissed."

Loyalty could only say: "Yes, sir."

"Wake up, Comrade Lee! It's time we were out there planting rice!"

"Uuugh," Loyalty groaned, and dropped back to sleep.

"Wake up! Wake up! Get out of bed!"

This time Loyalty got a shake along with the shout. That brought him around.

"Go out and brush your teeth, Comrade. I'll heat up some rice from last night. That'll stick to our ribs better than rice gruel."

The speaker was Yuan Jing, ex-Shanghai like Loyalty, but already in Anhui a year and thus already reckoned a veteran.

Loyalty finally staggered up from his straw sleeping mat. "Phew! What a job to get up! And I've been here only a week. Will I ever get used to country life?"

Before the sun had tipped the horizon, Loyalty and his teammates were ankle-deep in mud in the sprouting bed, slipping the tender young shoots gently out of their ooze and tying them fifty to a bundle with rice straw. These they tossed over beside the path to be picked up later.

When enough bundles had been thrown over to the path to make a load, Loyalty stacked them onto two shallow baskets. He then shouldered the two baskets, one front, the other back, with a carrying pole. After a week of this his shoulder was tender and raw from the pole cutting into the flesh. He gritted his teeth and set off along the paddy bank, making an effort at trotting like the country people when they carry a load. But the pole was cutting into the raw wounds from previous days. Gingerly, he shifted the load to the other shoulder and tried again. That shoulder objected too.

Finally, in highly unorthodox fashion, Loyalty balanced the load on the back of his neck and crept slowly across the paddy fields to where the planting was to start.

"Pheew!" With great relief he lowered the baskets to the ground.

After blowing and panting for a minute, he stooped down, lifted a bundle of sprouts from a basket and threw it out into the paddy field where the rows were to start this morning. Then another stoop and another toss. The trick was to zero the bundle in on the exact area where those particular seedlings would be planted. By this time some of Loyalty's teammates had already sloshed out into the mud halfway up to their knees.

Still warm from yesterday's sun, the mud squeezing up between bare toes felt very pleasant. It was considerably warmer than the air that still had an early-morning chill about it.

Now the real rice planting began. With a bundle of fifty seedlings in his left hand, Loyalty selected a good healthy one to start the day. He bent over and jammed its roots into the mud at just the right space from the last seedling planted the day before.

Then he backed a few inches down the row, selected a second seedling and thrust it into the mud. And on and on until he had planted about half his bundle of seedlings.

Bright Loyalty tried to stand up straight. He tried to stretch. He thought his back would break in two. *If this is the way I feel at the start of the day, how will I feel at the end?* he asked himself.

The sun broke through the early morning mist. The workers now got hot from the sun as well as from the constant bend-and-thrust. Before long, sweat was dripping off faces like rain and running down bodies in rivulets.

For Loyalty the dark cloud of unrelenting physical labor did have a small silver lining — the chatting and laughing and joking while they worked. Sparked by the cheerful Yuan Jing, this camaraderie lightened the load of labor, and was especially pleasant when the men's and women's teams worked together and bantered back and forth.

At noon the team sat on a bank, where their lunch of cold rice had been tied up in a tree to protect it from ants. Pickled cabbage helped "escort the rice", as the saying has it, and the whole was washed down with hot water from thermos bottles. After lunch they all stretched out in the shade for a nap.

Before long, however, it was back to rice planting with more bend-and-thrust, bend-and-thrust, the same motions repeated again and again through the long afternoon.

Only darkness called an end to the endless toil. They had been in the fields fourteen hours since beginning to slip seedlings at dawn.

Arriving at the commune's dormitory after dark, their first duty was to attend a half-hour of political indoctrination. Only after that could Loyalty drag himself back to the dormitory. This was even more difficult than coming in from the field, for the indoctrination class meant sitting in one position for thirty minutes. During that time aching joints and muscles "froze", so that to move afterwards was agony personified.

They still had to cook before they could eat, and Loyalty discovered that the firewood had been used up. There was nothing for it but to take an ax, climb the hill back of the dormitory and search for wood in the dark. After finally locating a few sticks, he limped back to the kitchen and cooked his rice. All this time he was still in wet clothes from the paddy field.

Finally arriving at his sleeping mat, he took off his wet clothes and hung them over a nail, hoping they would be dry when he put them on again the next morning.

After a month of planting rice daily, Loyalty's Work Brigade leader finally gave him a day off. He slept all morning, and in the afternoon he wrote a letter home:

"Dear Mama and Little Sister,

I have just realized that it has been a month since I arrived here and since my first letter.

Because we have been busy planting rice I have had no time to write.

Everything is going well. Please do not worry.

I hope you are both well.

Your son and brother, Bright Loyalty."

33. Caught In The Backlash
Anhui Province — Autumn 1971

ON THEIR DAY OFF, five men from the work team gathered in front of the commune office to listen to radio news over the loudspeaker:

"A hijacked airplane with renegade Lin Biao and his fellow conspirators on board crashed and burned today in Inner Mongolia. They were trying to make a getaway to Russia when the accident happened..."

Loyalty looked at Jing and Jing looked at the three other teammates gathered around the loudspeaker.

"But I thought Lin Biao was Number Two, second only to Chairman Mao himself!" blurted out one of the men.

"And he was editor and pusher of Mao's Little Red Book! How come he's a 'renegade' now?" another wanted to know.

"Sounds like a re-run of how Liu Shaoqi was demoted back in 1968. *He* was Number Two then!" the third added.

Jing commented mildly: "We don't know much about these things. Maybe we'd better wait until we're better informed before we venture an opinion."

Their wings cropped by the teammate from the city, the three made excuses and drifted off, leaving Jing and Loyalty alone.

Loyalty proposed: "Let's go for a walk up the Little River." Little did he dream of the long-term results of that innocent suggestion.

The two friends walked silently along among the many local people heading towards or coming from the ferries that crossed the Little River. In a few minutes they passed the ferries themselves, wooden boats pulled up to the shore, each with a long scull at the stern and one just-as-long oar on the prow. After they had threaded their way among the tea shops and snack stands Loyalty opened up: "Do you think there is any connection between Lin Biao's death — by execution or whatever — and the announcement that President Nixon of America is coming to China?"

"Hmm..." answered Jing, "that deserves some thought. Would a diehard leftist like Lin Biao welcome a visit from an inveterate enemy, president of the most capitalistic nation on earth? And what if Lin Biao was adamant in his objection to Nixon's visit? Chairman Mao would have only two alternatives: either call off the Nixon visit or get rid of Lin Biao. It looks as if he has done the latter."

"Jing, if there's a backlash to this from the extreme leftists, such as some army officers, do you think we might feel it even here in Anhui Province?"

"That's not impossible."

"That brings me to this — something I should tell you." Loyalty recounted the highlights of his family history, how Colonel Chang had exiled his father to Hainan and his brother to Shanxi, and only recently had threatened Loyalty himself.

"So, Jing, that's our family story," he ended, and pulled from his pocket a slip of paper. "Here are the names and addresses of my mother and sister. Please get in touch with them in case anything happens."

Returning two hours later from a satisfying stroll up the bank of the Little River, Loyalty and Jing were hot and thirsty.

"How about a cup of tea before we go back to the dorm?" Loyalty suggested. "Be nice to sit down a bit, too."

"Sounds good. And what about some of those fried dumplings to go with the tea?"

None of the tea shops were particularly elegant. All were made of split bamboo sides on bamboo frames and topped with expendable thatch of rice straw. They looked as if they had already been dismantled and moved more than once, adjusting to the vagaries of floods and crossing points on the river.

The two friends decided on the largest of the tea shops. Loyalty noticed two sheet-iron kettles on a fire outside under the eaves, one freshly filled, the other boiling away merrily and snorting steam out of its long spout like a one-nostril dragon.

Loyalty and Jing stepped over the bamboo sill whose main object in life seemed to be to trip up customers as they entered, and sat down on benches at a square table. The waiter plunked down a mug, tea leaves loose in bottom, before each man automatically. After all, the only reason for going into a tea shop is to drink tea, so why ask what they wanted?

Jing offered: "I'll pick up a dozen dumplings," and off he went.

The waiter came back with his long-nosed kettle and deftly filled the two mugs. Bright Loyalty paid the five cents per cup, and the waiter capped their mugs with aluminum covers, then moved on to the next table. Since his was the only movement in the room, Loyalty watched him and realized with a start that at the second table were four girls. They had not said a word since he and Jing entered, but were quietly drinking tea and eating fried dumplings.

Just then Jing came back with a large bowl of dumplings, each one crispy hot from its time in the *wok* and exuding the most delectable fragrance. "I'll have to take the bowl back. Borrowed it," Jing remarked.

The girls overheard this and giggled. One of them said, in a rather louder-than-necessary tone if she meant only the other girls to hear: "So, they borrowed their bowl, too! Maybe they could take ours back when they take theirs." They giggled again.

By now both Loyalty and Jing were looking straight at the girls quite unabashedly. After all, *they* started it.

"Excuse me, ladies," Jing said, "but do I recognize a voice that I've heard laughing and joking in the rice planting?"

The girls giggled again. One of them asked: "Didn't you recognize us?"

"Recognize you?" Jing exclaimed. "How could anybody recognize you when you hide behind all those hats, scarves, gloves and long sleeves out in the paddy field? Do you ladies come from Iran?"

They all laughed. And at that moment it happened. A great ball of fire and smoke burst through the thin wall of split bamboo on the side where the water was heated.

The waiter, who had just stepped outside, yelled: "*Jiuhuo! Jiuhuo!* Fire! Fire!"

In a split second the ball of fire mounted to the thatched roof and at the same time engulfed the entire side of the bamboo structure.

"Fire! Fire!" the waiter yelled again.

Jing grabbed up the bowl of dumplings and Bright Loyalty the two cups of tea and they headed for the door. After all, they had already paid for both tea and dumplings!

The two men reached the door ahead of the four women. Though the room was filled with smoke by this time, they chivalrously stood aside to let the women out first.

Three of the four made it, but the fourth caught her toe underneath the bamboo sill. She went flat on her face just outside the door, her foot still stuck under the bamboo pole.

With the area near the door ablaze by now, there was no time to lose. Loyalty and Jing jumped outside, dropping tea and dumplings in the process. They grabbed the girl by her hands and feet and carried her away from the burning building.

They were only just in time. By now the thatched roof was a crown of flames and the bamboo uprights and rafters, expanding in the heat, were exploding like mortar fire before bursting into flame.

They carried the girl some fifty feet from the burning

building before they set her down on the ground. Only then did they realize she was moaning with pain.

The other three girls tried to help her to her feet. She gingerly put the damaged foot to the ground, then collapsed again onto the ground, still moaning: *"Aiya! Aiya!"*

"Better take her shoe off. That'll relieve the foot a bit," Jing suggested.

By this time a crowd had collected, attracted by the fire. Before long their attention was transferred from the fire to the injured woman on the ground.

Loyalty said: "We'll have to find some way to get her to the infirmary at the commune."

"Right," responded Jing. "I'll go over to the dumpling seller to see if he has something we can use."

In a few minutes Jing was back with a straight chair, and with some pain the injured girl managed to sit on it. With Loyalty on one side and Jing on the other, and one of her friends holding onto the chair from behind to steady it, they lifted the chair and its occupant and started off.

At first their gait was uncertain and it looked as if they might dump the patient on the ground at any moment. As they progressed, however, they became more adept at handling the ungainly load, and it wasn't long before they were in step and doing better.

The girl steadied herself by placing a hand on the shoulder of each of the men. Loyalty felt the gentle pressure, and it sent an electric shock through him. For the first time in his life a woman other than his own kin had touched him physically. It was not an unpleasant sensation.

As they went along the path, Loyalty noticed that a young boy was following them like a puppy dog. When they finally turned their patient over to the nurse at the infirmary, the boy was still sticking around.

Loyalty asked Jing: "Do you know who this boy is?" Jing laughed. "That's the son of the dumpling man. His father made me pay for the two bowls before he would lend me the chair. And he sent his boy along to retrieve the chair!"

"Jing, did you get the name of the injured girl yesterday?"
"Why, no. Did you?"
"I did not. That was foolish of me..."
Jing laughed teasingly and asked: "Would you like to know her name?"
"Well, no... That is... Why, I guess so. Why do you ask?"
"Sounds as if you are interested in finding it out, that's all."
"Suppose we go over to the infirmary after supper and ask how she's doing..."
"How'll we enquire about a person whose name we don't know?" Jing asked, laughing again.
"Oh! Shut up, you clod!" Loyalty was only half joking. To punctuate his disgust with Jing, he grabbed off a sandal and threw it at him.
Jing caught it and threw it back, warning: "Careful now! He who throws shoes is subject to arrest for assault and battery!"

The girl was sitting on the cot with her leg straight out in a cast.
"We thought we'd come over and see how you're getting on..." said Loyalty, sounding a lot more casual than he felt.
"Oh, I'm fine, thanks," she responded. "It doesn't hurt like yesterday. You know, I want to thank you two gentlemen for saving my life."
"It wasn't as bad as that," Jing assured her. "I don't think you were in any real danger."
"And you carried me all the way back here. How can I thank you enough for all you did?"
"Well," said Loyalty, "there's one thing you can do for us."
"What's that?" she asked. A most engaging smile lit up her face.

"Perhaps you could tell us your name."

"That's not hard to do. My name's Wei Hanah."

Bright Loyalty responded quickly: "Hanah! That's a Bible name!"

"What do you know about the Bible?" she asked.

"I'm a Christian!" Loyalty told her.

"So am I!" Her smile became a beam. "What about your friend, is he a Christian, too?"

"No, I couldn't say I am," Jing spoke up. "But I do have a high regard for Christians. They have suffered a lot."

"By the way," Hanah continued, "do you know there's a Christian meeting in the village?"

"Which one?" asked Bright Loyalty.

"Long Dike Village, the one attached to the commune."

"Why, no, I hadn't heard about it."

"I go over there now and then. Perhaps I could ask one of the men to look you up and take you along."

"Do you mean to say you were working in the Golden Streams Weaving Factory in the fall of 1966?"

The questioner was a young man Loyalty had sat next to on the ferry crossing the Little River. Now they were sitting in one of the tea shops on the bank.

"Right. I was there at that time," agreed Loyalty.

"What was your job?"

"Repairman. Mostly repairing the looms."

"Well, I was there at the same time," said his new acquaintance.

"And what were you doing?" Loyalty asked, surprised.

"Not very much. They called me The Leader."

Loyalty almost fell backwards off the bench. Here was the very man who beat the Treasurer to death with a wooden board! Controlling himself, he stammered: "I'm sorry. I didn't recognize you."

"I'm not surprised. I've grown this mustache. And I wear

dark glasses all the time." The Leader took off his dark glasses.

Loyalty asked: "And what are you doing here in Anhui?"

"Right now I'm harvesting rice, as I suspect you are," he said with a wry smile.

After a pause he continued: "Do you remember some of the slogans we used to shout, such as 'Foment revolution to increase production'?"

"Yes, I remember."

"They were lies. All lies. Now I know that to foment revolution destroys production. Look at the weaving factory. We were a bunch of numbskulls, and we set the experts to one side and made them clean out toilets!"

"Ummh..." grunted Loyalty, as noncommittally as he could manage.

"We worshiped Chairman Mao, but the way he treated us turned worship into hate," went on the Leader.

Loyalty felt uneasy at hearing such a sentiment voiced in a public place. He changed the subject, and asked: "How did you happen to land in Anhui?"

"I was tried before a Revolutionary Committee, and I'm lucky to be alive. But I walk a tightrope every day. The chief judge was a military officer and he sent me to Anhui because he was being transferred here himself and wanted to keep an eye on me..."

At this Loyalty's ears stood straight out from his head. In a quiet voice he managed: "Could I ask what his name is?"

"He's a Colonel in the army, Colonel Chang. I have a constant and abiding hate for that man."

"Excuse me, but I'm looking for Bright Loyalty Lee. Would you happen to know him?"

The middle-aged farmer seemed uncertain of himself, as if out of his depth at the "Up-to-the-hills, down-to-the-country" dormitory for city boys.

Loyalty heard him and stepped over. "I'm Bright Loyalty Lee. Anything I can do for you?"

"A mutual friend asked me to come over and bring you to my house, if you'd like to go," said the farmer.

"I'd be very pleased," responded Loyalty. "Just a moment and I'll get my cap."

It was the second Sunday afternoon after Loyalty and Jing had seen Wei Hanah in the infirmary. Loyalty was half expecting someone that afternoon and had not gone out.

As they walked away from the dormitory Loyalty enquired: "May I ask your name, sir?"

"I'm Sun Kang. I hear you're a Christian."

"Right you are, Mr. Sun. Thank you for coming for me."

Arriving at the Sun home, Loyalty looked around as unobtrusively as he could. Yes! There she was — Hanah, on crutches and with that engaging smile. Was he mistaken, or did the smile grow brighter when she saw him?

Bright Loyalty looked at the summons in disbelief. But it was signed by Colonel Chang himself, with his official chop as Garrison Commander of Wuhu:

"To Bright Loyalty Lee:

You are to appear at once at the office of the Garrison Commander of Wuhu District.

Any delay in your voluntary appearance will be regarded as a misdemeanor punishable by law."

"Am I under arrest?" Loyalty asked Jing.

"The order doesn't say so. But maybe you could take your toothbrush with you."

Loyalty hurriedly threw toothbrush, toothpaste, towel, soap and change of underwear into his plastic zip bag. Arriving at the Garrison Commander's Headquarters, he was relieved when he was not ushered at once into Colonel Chang's presence. What did happen, however, mystified him beyond words.

A woman soldier in the outer office handed him a copy of the Little Red Book, or, as the title has it, *Quotations from Chairman Mao Zedong*. She told him: "Copy out the first three pages on this sheet of paper with this ball-point pen. Not in formal characters like printing, but like you would use writing your mother back home."

Completely perplexed, Bright Loyalty nevertheless did as he was told, and handed the sheet back to the woman soldier.

She said the one word: "Wait."

Bright Loyalty waited. He waited an hour, then two hours. Finally a bespectacled man appeared, middle-aged and balding. In one hand he waved Loyalty's writing, in the other a letter.

He said: "You're okay. No problem." Then he disappeared.

Unnerved and undecided what to do, Loyalty simply sat down. He waited another half hour. What the bespectacled man had said kept revolving in his mind: "You're okay. No problem." If that was so, why was he still there?

Finally he decided to speak to the woman soldier.

Surprised, she asked: "You still here? I told old Ding to let you go."

Loyalty stammered: "I'm sorry. I didn't understand him to mean that."

The woman soldier suddenly brightened up, as if a really valuable thought had struck her: "Now that you're still here," she said, "do you recognize this writing?" She thrust a letter at Bright Loyalty.

He took it politely with both hands, and asked: "May I read it?"

"Sure. That's what I gave it to you for."

As he read, Bright Loyalty was amazed:

"Colonel Chang,

I hate your guts. Some day I'm going to kill you. You won't be the first. It will be a great pleasure to see you dead." There was no signature. The woman soldier repeated her question. "Do you recognize the handwriting?"

Bright Loyalty looked long and hard at the letter, all the time trying to conceal his horror at anyone having the audacity to write like this to an army officer.

Biting his lip to control his voice, he handed the letter back, saying: "Sorry. I've never seen that handwriting before."

Now quite communicative, the woman soldier volunteered: "If Colonel Chang could get his hands on that rascal, he'd tear him limb from limb. I know how he reacts to this kind of thing. You see, I'm his wife."

Then, seeing Loyalty standing awkwardly in front of her, she added: "That's all. You may go."

Never in his life had Bright Loyalty been so relieved to go through a door and leave a place. As he made his way along the streets of Wuhu and back to the ferry crossing, a hundred questions stormed his mind. One was: *How could anyone imagine I would recognize that writing?*

As he sat down on the ferry he realized he was on the very seat where he had sat with The Leader the other day. Then suddenly, up in the sky over the river, Loyalty saw boards with characters written on them:

Secret Agent of Kuomintang

Rightist

Revisionist

Rotten Egg

Running Dog of The Imperialists

Landlord's Wife

In his vision he was transported back to that tragic day at the Golden Streams Weaving Factory, when he had looked long and hard at those epithets. Not only the words but also the exact way they were written was etched indelibly on his memory, every flourish, whorl and tittle. And the handwriting on the boards in the sky was the same as in the letter in the office!

So! Loyalty said to himself, *It was the Leader who wrote the Letter.*

That night after supper Bright Loyalty stole out to the river-side alone. There were several questions in his mind. The first was: should he share this with Jing or not?

After some minutes he decided: *No! Some things can be shared, others not. If Jing knew about this it could get him into trouble. What he doesn't know won't hurt him.*

Loyalty walked slowly along the river bank, his hands clasped behind his back.

The next question is: I told Mrs. Chang that I had never seen that handwriting. That was true. A half hour later I realized I had seen it. As a Christian, what should I do? Go back and tell her? Or let it be? If I tell her, Colonel Chang will kill the Leader. If I don't tell her, maybe the Leader will kill Colonel Chang....

Bright Loyalty stopped walking and reasoning, and began to pray:

"Dear God, please show me right now what I should do. To say or not to say what I know. To come out with it or to keep quiet."

At that moment, he heard a voice behind him, which said: "Let the dead bury their dead."

Bright Loyalty bowed his head and said: "Thank you, Lord." Then he turned and retraced his steps to the dormitory.

34. Tragedy At Ye River

Autumn 1971

AFTER BRIGHT LOYALTY had been attending the house meeting for several weeks, Elder Sun spoke to him at the end of a service: "Loyalty, two or three of us are going to a village up in the hills south of town next Sunday. Could you go along?"

"Thank you! I'd be very pleased," Bright Loyalty replied. "There should be no problem getting the day off, because work is not pressing just now."

"Good. No need to bother about a permit — we won't stay overnight."

The next Sunday morning, therefore, four men started out early to walk the ten miles up to Ye Family Village.

"Too bad it's so overcast and dull," Bright Loyalty commented.

"Never mind," answered Elder Sun. "It won't be so hot walking. Anyway, you've brought your umbrella."

Up in the edge of the hills, Bright Loyalty saw something he had never seen before — a deserted village. The path lay through the center of the village, as it must have for centuries past. But instead of the shouting of coolies and the laughter of children there was dead silence, except for the echo of their own footfalls against the crumbling mud walls on either side of the path.

Roofs had caved in. Windows and doors gazed out at them with sightless eyes. What had once been floors were now patches of weeds waist high.

Loyalty remarked in a voice subdued by awe: "I've never seen anything like this in my life! What happened to the people who used to live here?"

"They're dead and gone, Loyalty. Before the Commune

System was established this village was inhabited. But it was never a prosperous place; the soil is poor, not like down on the plains. When the Communizing Wind blew through, as they say, production was so dislocated that the people starved. Some of them wandered off to other places. But that's not the worst of it..." Elder Sun paused.

"What do you mean, not the worst of it?" Loyalty asked.

"Before these people died, some of them boiled their own children and ate them."

"You don't mean it! I never heard of such a thing!"

"No, son. You didn't live in Anhui while they were setting up communes."

Just then the sky darkened, lightning flashed and thunder rolled. It was eerie, looking through the vacant doors and windows at the lightning flashing beyond. To Loyalty, the roll of thunder seemed like a funeral dirge for the souls of the children sacrificed in the village.

The men put up their umbrellas. The rain was peppering down now and Loyalty jumped, thinking the patter of rain on his paper umbrella sounded like the patter of little feet!

With an effort, he forced himself back to reality and commented: "What a waste of land, just to leave these houses sitting here! Why doesn't the government come in and level them and make rice paddies?"

"You don't understand, son," replied Elder Sun. "Not a man within fifty miles would lift a hand to tear down these walls. They say the village is haunted, and that at night and on dark rainy days like this you can still hear the children who were killed and eaten running up and down the street. No, it will remain a ghost village in more ways than one for a long time to come."

Within sight of Ye Family Village, the men crossed a roaring stream by an ancient stone bridge.

"I've never seen the Ye River dashing at the bridge like that," commented Elder Sun. "Looks fearful, doesn't it?"

Little did he know then just how fearful that river could be.

The rain let up before they entered the village, but the sky overhead remained dark and threatening. An occasional flash of lightning added a chemical smell to the dank air and the thunder rumbled like some cosmic ogre bent on destruction.

As they entered the village proper Loyalty was surprised to see that the main village street was covered over with a permanent roof. He asked Elder Sun, "Why do they have this roof over the street?"

"Never seen this before, son? That's to keep off the sun in the summer and the rain during rainy season. They like it that way, I reckon."

Loyalty didn't say so, but he reckoned he *didn't* like it that way. Especially for today. With it so black and rainy anyway, the darkness under the roof was oppressive and almost intolerable. Loyalty shivered involuntarily, as if the darkness had some foreboding about it.

Rather than light lamps inside the dark houses, the villagers had come out to perform their household duties in the street, where the light was somewhat better. Some were winnowing rice with flat bamboo trays, blowing the chaff away to land a bit farther down the street. Others were washing and chopping vegetables. Here a mother was suspending her little girl by the thighs, her own feet wide apart to avoid the splatter while the child relieved herself. There an old man was rolling a cigarette from an old newspaper, wetting and sealing it with saliva.

Loyalty said to himself: *This looks like a scene from a century ago, even to the deadpan faces. I guess nobody would take a picture of this village street for China Reconstructs!*

"Well, here we are." Elder Sun broke into Loyalty's chain of thought. "Please go in." He waved the three men into a small general store.

They passed bins of rice, salt, sweet potatoes, onions, dried beans, dried shrimp and dried squid on the right, and on the left a decrepit and much-patched glass showcase. Inside the showcase were biscuits, puffed-rice candy, peanut brittle and trays of dried apricots, peaches, plums and persimmons, and piled on top were trays of noodles of various sizes, shapes and degrees of wetness.

At the street end of the showcase, at a convenient height for cigarette smokers, the tiny flame of a weed-pith wick burning in rapeseed oil was always ready to serve either customer or passerby.

Behind the showcase stood a middle-aged man. A smile lit up his face as the men stepped into the shop, and he shook his own two hands vigorously in the old-fashioned way. Of a newer generation, Loyalty stuck out his hand; the proprietor took it and shook it just as vigorously.

"This is Bright Loyalty Lee," Elder Sun introduced. "Bright Loyalty, this is Brother Lou. The meetings are here at his place."

Brother Lou ushered his visitors up to the living quarters above the store. There were no stairs, just a ladder of cross-pieces nailed to uprights that were part of the wall.

Once on the upper floor, Loyalty found the light better, with a window opening out onto the communal roof that covered the street. Several potted chrysanthemums sitting out on the roof and blooming in a variety of colors showed the desire of the Lou family to brighten up an otherwise dull view.

The floor was clean and had been polished, Bright Loyalty suspected, by the daily laying out and taking up of bedding, for this was obviously bedroom by night as well as living room by day.

Four straight chairs were set against the walls, two by two, with a small wooden tea table between each set. Brother Lou motioned his guests toward the chairs and poured hot water from the inevitable thermos, apologizing that it was only *bai kai shui*, "white boiled water", and not tea.

A half hour later Brother Lou came back up the ladder and invited the visitors down to the ground floor for lunch. By this time the rain was again descending in torrents, and Bright Loyalty was glad to get away from its incessant pounding on the tiles.

After lunch they climbed the ladder again, and before long the Christians began to dribble into the store. Those from the village were comparatively dry, but those from a distance were soaked to the skin.

Loyalty noticed that they did not climb the ladder at once but spent a little time down below chatting with Brother Lou or perhaps buying bits of groceries. Then, when there were no other customers in the shop, they mounted the ladder to the meeting place.

Loyalty asked Elder Sun: "Why do the people hang around down below before coming up here?"

"They don't want to attract attention to the meeting," he replied. "When they leave they'll be just as careful."

For a long time Loyalty had anticipated attending a meeting in a village off the beaten track. He was hardly prepared, however, for the kind of meeting it turned out to be. He was surprised, for example, at the absence of hymn singing. Only later did he realize that this was to make the meeting as unobtrusive as possible — singing would immediately attract attention on the narrow village street.

The format of the meeting also surprised him. Apart from a short message by Elder Sun, the time was given over to testimonies by the believers, largely to do with miracles and other remarkable happenings.

One of the men told of his only son, four years old, running a high fever one night and how, after they had circled him on his sleeping mat and prayed earnestly, the fever came down.

A woman told how her young sow was farrowing for the first time and was having difficulty delivering the piglets. The family and Christian neighbors gathered around the sow in the pigsty and prayed for her. Just as they finished, there was a shout at the door. A villager from eight miles away had come to repay ten dollars borrowed six months before — and he was the most famous pig doctor in the county. He prescribed a concoction of herbs that could be bought in the medicine shop, and with that drench and his manipulation of the piglets all were born safely. Since no interest had been charged on the debt of ten dollars, he said he would not charge for his pig doctoring.

"You know that we have neither electricity nor telephone nor running water here in this village," testified another believer. "But we do have a transistor radio. Every night our family gathers around to listen to the Christian programs from Manila. They are in Mandarin so we can understand them. They read the Bible at dictation speed, and we copy it down night after night. Before long we'll have a complete New Testament of our own."

On and on the testimonies went. The note of praise and rejoicing was in sharp contrast to the dark and depressing day outside.

Suddenly, Brother Lou's son, who was tending the store below, called out:

"Papa, we're out of rapeseed oil."

At that, the brother who was speaking fell silent in the middle of a sentence, as if this were the normal thing to do.

In a couple of minutes the boy below shouted again: "It's all right, Papa. I've found the other crock of rapeseed oil."

There was an easing of tension. The brother who had broken off in the middle of a sentence took up again.

Loyalty must have had a quizzical, how-could-that-be expression on his face, for Elder Sun laughed out loud, interrupting the speaker for the second time. This only caused Loyalty to look even more quizzical, which in turn brought more laughter from all. Several slapped their thighs as if it were a great joke.

Finally Elder Sun controlled himself and explained: "Sorry, Loyalty. We should have let you in on it. 'No rapeseed oil' means 'A suspicious person in the store — maybe a spy'. Then later, 'Found the rapeseed oil' means 'The person has gone — coast is clear'."

At that, Bright Loyalty joined in the laughter, even if it were at his own expense.

As the meeting closed, the sky darkened and the rain came down in torrents again.

"You know, Brother Sun, I don't think you'd better try to get home tonight," suggested Brother Lou. "You can all stretch out here on the floor and spend the night, then go home tomorrow."

"Thank you, brother," responded Elder Sun. "I appreciate your thought, but we'll have to get back. We don't have permits to spend the night here, and you know how strict the police are about permits. We could all land up in jail. More than that, it could give the Christians a bad name with the police."

Brother Lou and the other local brethren urged him further, but Elder Sun was adamant. With the rain coming down in buckets, the four visitors left Brother Lou's store at 4 p.m.

When they stepped from the protection of the village street out into the full force of the storm, Loyalty wasn't so sure it was a wise decision to return home, permit or no permit. But it was Elder Sun's decision. After all, he was the leader and he knew local conditions. Bright Loyalty brought his umbrella down to the top of his head and tipped it in the direction of the wind to keep it from being turned inside out.

Just then lightning flashed and with a mighty "CRACK!" struck a pine tree some two hundred yards down the road in front of them. The tree split from top to bottom, and an instant later the thunder rolled over them like a great ocean wave.

Bright Loyalty said to himself: *If I were superstitious, I'd say that was a bad omen.* He looked at Elder Sun. But the older man did not return the look. His eyes were straight ahead. With a firm grip on his umbrella he strode resolutely into the storm.

Before leaving Brother Lou's store, Bright Loyalty had changed his cloth shoes for straw sandals, for the sake of saving his cloth shoes and also for better traction on the stones. He had also rolled up his pant legs to keep them as dry as possible. But the wind blew the rain underneath his umbrella; before long his pants were soaked and his jacket was fast heading in the same direction.

Though their pace was slow, all was going fairly well until they came in sight of the stone bridge over the Ye River.

Loyalty was the first to notice what had happened. "Hey! Look!" he exclaimed. "The bridge's gone!"

Sure enough, the approaches on both sides were still there, but the bridge itself had been swept away by the surging stream! Not a stone of the bridge was left.

As they arrived at the edge of the swirling torrent, they saw another group of stranded travellers, two men standing on the far side. The roar of the water made it impossible to converse across the chasm.

As Elder Sun and Company paused to consider the situation, the two men on the opposite side left the path and made their way along the bank upstream a couple of hundred yards. The watchers saw what they had not noticed before —

that the stream widened at that point, which probably meant shallower water.

The two men went down into the water, took hands and gradually made their way across. At the deepest point the water was not above their waists. In a few minutes they were standing beside the four.

"How was it? Can do?" Elder Sun asked.

"No problem. You've just got to keep to the shallowest part," one of them replied.

Oh hearing that, Elder Sun turned to his three companions and said: "All right, brethren, let's go!"

And he turned and headed upstream along the bank. Somewhat reluctantly, Loyalty and the other two followed.

Arriving at the shallow part, Elder Sun said: "I'll go first. We'll hold each other by the hand like those men did."

With that he lowered his umbrella, held it in his left hand and extended his right hand to Loyalty. Holding hands and facing upstream, the four stepped down into the water.

Loyalty caught his breath; the water was colder than he anticipated. Too, the current was stronger, even here, than he thought it would be.

Step by step, the four felt their way out into the stream. The bottom was gravel, and the grip of their feet on it was good enough. But Bright Loyalty was dreading that deep place in the middle of the river where the two men had gone down waist deep. *If we can just get past that we'll be okay*, he thought. But they had missed the exact crossing point of the other two men. Before they had gone a third of the way across, suddenly Elder Sun slipped down an incline, and slid under the water without making a sound.

Loyalty yelled: "Help!" and held onto the elder's hand with all his might. But the angle at which the older man slid into the water threw his grip out of line. There was a vicious twist on his wrist as the current grabbed the body, and a pain such as he had never experienced before shot up his arm.

Involuntarily his grip on the other hand loosened, and Loyalty saw Elder Sun's hand disappear after the body into the swirling muddy current. In an instant he was gone.

The three men beat a hasty retreat and ran down the river bank, trying to catch a glimpse of the body. Until dark they followed the river, looking, looking, looking, hoping they would find the body snagged on a broken tree trunk or some other obstacle. All was in vain.

As darkness fell they finally retraced their steps to the path at the washed-out bridge. From there they plodded their sodden way back to Ye Family Village to make their sad report to Brother Lou and the other Christians.

Loyalty had a miserable night with the pain in his arm. The next morning the brothers insisted that he get to the infirmary at the commune as quickly as possible. They would go back and search again for the body.

When he arrived at the broken bridge he discovered that an enterprising farmer had already set up a ferry service, charging ten cents per person per crossing. Ironically, Loyalty boarded the boat at exactly the spot where he had entered the water the day before.

By the time he arrived at the infirmary the arm was swollen and painful indeed. There was, however, one alleviating circumstance. Entering the outpatients' department, who should he find there but Wei Hanah. She was still on crutches.

"Hello!" Loyalty exclaimed in surprise. "Are you here to have your cast checked?"

"Oh, no" she replied. "I've been transferred here as orderly. After I'd made several visits here with my broken ankle, I realized how important the infirmary is to the commune and I applied for a transfer. They were in need of an orderly, so I'm it. But what brings you here, may I ask?"

Loyalty recounted the tragedy on the Ye River.

The doctor on duty looked at Loyalty's arm in short order. For some reason, Hanah was able to make herself useful to the doctor while he was treating Loyalty.

The doctor was called away for a minute, leaving them alone. Loyalty surprised himself by saying: "I'm not so glad to break an arm but I am glad to see you again. Sometimes broken bones are useful, aren't they?"

"Loyalty! Loyalty! There's a soldier to see you, a woman soldier! She's waiting outside."

There was urgency in Jing's voice.

Loyalty rolled off his bunk, slid into his house slippers and dashed for the front door.

He was half-relieved, half-perturbed to see standing before the door the wife of Colonel Chang. He said, "How do you do, Mrs. Chang?"

Apparently Loyalty had pressed the wrong button.

Mrs. Chang drew herself up straight and said, haughtily: "When I am in uniform you may address me as Sergeant Ye. The fact that I am married to Colonel Chang is incidental to my service to party and country."

"Oh! I beg your pardon, erh," Loyalty managed to stammer out, "Erh... Sergeant... Ye!"

The sergeant must have noted Loyalty's sincerity; the starch in posture and tone melted a bit: "That's all right, Comrade. But just remember I'm Sergeant Ye."

Then she turned all official again: "Here! I've brought you a letter from the Commandant. I've been instructed you should read it in my presence."

She handed an official-looking envelope to Loyalty.

He took the envelope and after some fumbling tore it open. He read:

"Bright Loyalty Lee:

You spent the night away from your residence without a permit. This time there are extenuating circumstances.

Do not let it happen again. Remember you and your family are on the Black List.

> (Signed) *Colonel Chang*
> Garrison Commander
> Wuhu District"

Bright Loyalty looked at Sergeant Ye with that quizzical expression that so often mirrored his thoughts. The sergeant was quick to pick it up.

"You're wondering how Colonel Chang knew you spent the night away," she said. "Well, he has ways and means. Especially if a person by the name of Ye lives in the same house with him and knows everything that goes on in her native place of Ye Family Village!"

With twenty dollars sent by his mother from Shanghai and fifteen saved from his meager income as a farm laborer, Loyalty bought a Great Wall brand transistor radio, with medium and short-wave bands.

The radio was timely. With Elder Sun gone, it fell to Loyalty to lead the meetings and Bible studies in Long Dike Village. How thankful he was that his left arm was broken and not his right. He could still copy down the outlines of the messages he heard from Manila. His new position gave him more opportunities to help than before. He did not realize that it also made him more of a marked man.

"'Tis an ill wind that blows no one good."

Loyalty repeated the old saying to himself as he whistled his way across to the infirmary to have his arm checked. He just might get in a few words with Wei Hanah! And a few words with Hanah just might turn a broken arm into a lucky break.

When Loyalty arrived, Hanah was sweeping the outpatients' Department. Granted, not very convincingly. Balancing on her left foot and left crutch with her right leg in its cast swinging free, she was sweeping half-heartedly with her right hand. Her broom was several dozen long splinters of bamboo tied together.

She smiled most delightfully at Bright Loyalty when he came in. "Hi!" she greeted him. "Want a job? This place hasn't been swept for days."

It looked it. Candy wrappers, cigarette butts and the shells of sunflower and watermelon littered the ground.

Bright Loyalty grabbed the besom in his one good hand and swept vigorously enough to scatter the dust in all directions. When he had swept up a pile of debris Hanah brought the dustpan, and placed the feet of the two crutches back of the dustpan to brace it steady on the ground while Loyalty corralled the sweepings and urged them up into it.

He was concentrating on completing the operation without letting the dust fly up into Hanah's face. Neither of them noticed that the doctor had arrived and was standing, arms akimbo, just inside the door.

"Well," the doctor finally commented, "I've heard of the blind leading the blind, and now I've seen the lame sweeping for the lame!"

The full moon was beautiful as only an autumn moon can be. Moon Festival Day fell on a Sunday, and after the house meeting Mrs. Sun served moon cakes and tea. The Christians sat around chatting in the moonlight.

But all good things come to an end. The guests dribbled out by ones and twos, until finally only five were left — Hanah, Loyalty, two of Hanah's friends from the dormitory and Jing, who had recently started attending the meetings.

As the five walked the moonlit path together, Hanah on her three legs was not very fast. So the three others gradually drew out in front and for the first time Loyalty and Hanah found themselves walking alone together.

"You know," Loyalty said, "I've been wanting to ask you for a long time — where were you born?"

"In Shanghai."

"I'm not surprised, judging by your accent."

"Now, Bright Loyalty Lee, you know I don't have an accent!"

"Why, everybody has an accent. Except me, of course." The two of them laughed merrily, and Loyalty said to himself, *My! I love her laugh!*

Out loud he said: "Shanghai. That's where I'm from, of course. Were you baptized in Shanghai?"

"Yes, I was."

"And who baptized you?"

"An elderly pastor. Don't suppose you ever heard of him..."

"Who was he?"

"Old Pastor Bao."

"You don't say! He's a very good friend of our family."

On and on they went, comparing notes on Shanghai. The longer they talked the slower they walked. As they finally drew near the girls' dormitory and saw the other three sitting on the steps waiting, Loyalty blurted out to Hanah: "I wish this walk could go on forever!"

His first Sunday out of the cast, Loyalty returned with two of the brothers to Ye Family Village.

The ferry across the Ye River was still operated by the same farmer, but a sign dignified it as "Ye River Nationalized Emergency Ferry Service", and the fare had been reduced to five cents per person per crossing. The bridge was being replaced, but with reinforced concrete instead of stone.

Approaching the village, they noticed a crowd in the elementary school yard at the edge of the village and heard a strident female voice amplified by an electronic megaphone.

"Wait a minute," Loyalty said. "I know that voice. It's Colonel Chang's wife, Sergeant Ye! What's she doing here?"

The three walked on, but at a snail's pace. They wanted to hear what she was saying:

"Something new is happening. The president of that decadent bourgeois country the United States has finally decided to come and see for himself the results of our glorious socialist revolution. He will learn much.

"But from our standpoint as patriotic citizens we must be on guard. We must clear away now the remnants of counter-revolutionaries, rightists and revisionists who are still at large..."

At that point Loyalty and Friends stepped under the roof of the village street, which cut off the sound from outside.

In a low voice Loyalty remonstrated to his companions: "'Counter-revolutionaries, rightists, revisionists'. How could there be any in this village?"

Brother Lou was delighted to see Loyalty again and pumped his arm vigorously. Loyalty was glad his right arm had not been broken, for such vigorous hand shaking could have damaged the break again!

At noon Brother Lou served pig liver sliced with fresh hot peppers, stir-fried in oil at sizzling heat. With white rice and a clear hot soup, that was a meal Bright Loyalty long remembered. For one thing, it was the last meal he would eat in freedom for some time to come.

As before, the meeting was held in the room above the shop. Loyalty grimaced as he remembered the pain he had endured that night in this room.

In the middle of the meeting, Brother Lou's son down below shouted: "Papa, we're out of rapeseed oil!"

Silence fell on the assembly.

A moment later the boy's voice came again: "Papa! We're out of rapeseed oil!"

As the company of believers looked on in disbelief, a green military cap with the single red star of the People's Liberation Army appeared in the hole where the ladder came up from below. In front of the cap, the black barrel of a 45 automatic slid up over the edge of the hole. The gun pointed at the believers.

The soldier barked: "*Budong!* Don't move!"

Shoulders in a military green jacket pushed up through the hole. The man stepped from the ladder onto the floor and moved over against the wall, all the time keeping the barrel of the gun pointed at the people.

A second soldier and a second gun appeared in the hole, and then a third. Finally a woman soldier appeared in the hole. It was Sergeant Ye.

After she had caught her breath from the exertion of climbing the ladder, she drew herself up straight and snapped: "So! So! You ran out of rapeseed oil, did you? Well, you'll get very little oil of any kind where you're going! You are all under arrest as counter-revolutionaries and reactionaries. Specifically, for holding an illegal meeting. It's about time we cleared out the last pockets of resistant elements in this village!"

At the trial in the Garrison Commander's courtyard in Wuhu five days later, both Bright Loyalty Lee and Brother Lou were sentenced to five years in prison. The four women were released. The six other men who had been at the meeting were flogged with bamboo rods and sent home, with a warning of more severe punishment if they were ever caught holding an illegal meeting again.

PART VI

BEIJING
AND MANCHURIA
1976 ~ 1978

35. End Of An Era
Beijing, Summer and Autumn, 1976

BRIGHT VICTORY and True Virtue were sitting under the grape arbor at Datong late one summer evening. Their two children were playing on the ground while Papa and Mama Huang watched them indulgently. The four adults were eating watermelon and spitting the seeds into an open basket, to be dried and enjoyed during the winter. The children had lost interest in watermelon and were chasing each other in a cut-down version of hide-and-seek.

"The lines have fallen to us in pleasant places," Victory said to his wife, leaning back against a post. "It looks as if we can settle down now to the long haul of living simply, serving God and man and raising the children in the way they should go."

Victory did not know of a letter that was even then at the Post Office, waiting to be delivered the following morning.

Victory was busy at the Outpatients' Department when Orchid Qiu made a special trip over from the office to deliver his letter.

"I noticed it was from the hospital in Beijing where you used to work," she explained. "I thought you might like to see it right away."

Victory finished with his patient, then went outside and sat in the shade of a tree to read the letter. It was from his friend Dr. Hei:

"Dear Bright Victory,

I can never forget that I owe my very life to you. You risked yours to save me that day in Southern Hebei.

The government is giving renewed attention to training

doctors. At present there are ten training slots open in this hospital and I have put your name down for one. This is tentative until I receive word from you.

We can make necessary arrangements from here for your change of residence with your family."

"Victory, I've never been so surprised in my life! I can't take it in! To leave Papa and Mama — it just doesn't seem right!"

The usually unflappable True Virtue had reacted more sharply to Dr. Hei's letter than Bright Victory had anticipated. He was not prepared for such a negative reaction.

"But, Virtue," he protested, "things are in good shape here in Datong, with a full-time male nurse holding a clinic every day at Number Three Mine, which is more than I was ever able to do, and old Pastor Ling finally released and living with his son in Kaifeng..."

"But my parents! How can I leave them?"

Victory did not answer at once. He fell into deep thought.

"Parents ..." he began slowly, then paused. Virtue held her breath, wondering what was coming. "Parents are important. But, Virtue, your brother and his family are here; they'll take care of Papa and Mama... And — the thought just struck me — if we are in Beijing, might God open a back door so that *my* parents could be united again?"

True Virtue thought for a long minute. Then she burst into tears. "Forgive me, Victory," she sobbed. "I'm so selfish, thinking about my parents when I should be thinking about your father on Hainan. And your brother still in prison in Anhui. Oh, Victory! Wouldn't it be wonderful if God would open the way for both of them so they could go home?"

It was True Virtue's first time to see Beijing. She was all eyes and ears as the train threaded its way through the suburbs and finally chuffed to a stop in the great central station.

For the two children, Geng, four, and Deng, two, however, the center of attention was not the big city but two panda dolls their grandparents had given them as goodbye presents.

With some effort Victory and Virtue shifted children and baggage out to a motor tricycle taxi stand, and managed to get everyone and everything into two little three-wheelers.

Dr. Hei welcomed them warmly at Sixth Municipal Hospital.

"We have arranged housing near the hospital compound," he told them. "It's on an old-style Beijing alley, and it's an old house. I hope you aren't disappointed at not living in one of the new high-rise buildings out at the edge of the city."

"Far from it," Virtue said. "I don't know how I could adjust to living like a bird on a cliff up in one of those tall buildings."

"There! What a relief to put that basket down!" True Virtue took a hand towel and wiped her face, which was streaming with perspiration. "It seems hotter here in the city than back in Datong," she continued.

"Probably is," agreed Bright Victory, "what with all the buildings and the pavement."

Virtue sat down, fanned herself and looked at Victory, who had just finishing nailing up a shelf for kitchen utensils.

"Anyway, the market is only three alleys away," she told him. "And what a variety of vegetables!"

Victory asked: "Is the house going to be okay for you?"

"Well, it's small," she answered, "only 192 square feet, and there's no yard for the children to play in. But I think I'm going to like it here in Beijing."

The following morning Victory went to Dr. Hei's office for orientation. By no stretch of the imagination could he have been prepared for what he heard.

"You will have classes every morning six days a week,"

Dr. Hei told him. "Three afternoons a week are for private study, and the other three are your practical training. For this you will be my assistant. I'm afraid you won't get much variety in this assignment, as I have recently been named as private doctor to a person high in the Central Authorities. But what your assignment lacks in variety may be made up in interest in our patient."

"Who is the patient" Victory asked.

Dr. Hei replied: "None other than Chairman Mao himself!"

Two afternoons later, Victory reported at Dr. Hei's office.

"We are going to Chairman Mao's residence," the doctor said. "I take his blood pressure every day. This is one segment of modern medicine he's addicted to — probably because it's exact, '190 over 90' and all that. He has his secretary record it every day."

"Old-style Chinese doctors depend a good deal on pulse and blood pressure, too, don't they?" asked Bright Victory.

"Right, Victory. The Chairman has an old-style doctor, too, a live-in one. They judge blood pressure by the feel of the pulse, and some are very good at it. Actually, the Chairman takes herbal medicine every day, and he's not particularly fond of the pills and capsules I prescribe. He prefers the Chinese medicine of twigs, roots and so on that is brewed like tea. He can drink that.

"Now..." Dr. Hei turned to the immediate: "You will carry my black bag. In the old days, you know, a doctor never did any physical work — wouldn't even carry his own bag. Well, this afternoon we're doing it the old-fashioned way. This black bag is your passport to enter Chairman Mao's house."

They squeezed into a motor tricycle and set out. At Chairman Mao's house the sentry on duty waved them in without examining their identity cards.

After they were shown into the great man's study, Dr. Hei

whispered: "You see what I mean, Victory? The sentry recognized me. And also my black bag, which you happened to be carrying."

The Chairman's study was quite a simple room. At least, Bright Victory reckoned that if one could see beneath the surface it would be simple. What one actually saw, however, was pile after pile of reports, books, leaflets, magazines and newspapers in disarray all over tables, chairs and floor. The shelves that lined the walls had long since given up hope of containing and restraining all the Chairman's papers, books and periodicals.

Dr. Hei explained: "This afternoon he's giving an audience to a foreign head of state. I'm often here for such occasions, in case he should suffer from stress. The bag in your hand is mostly first-aid stuff, everything from smelling salts to adrenaline."

The Chairman's private secretary stepped in. Seeing the doctor, he handed him a slip of paper written in both character and English:

DR NOKIMI UMUBO
PRIME MINISTER
REPUBLIC OF ZAMIALAND
AFRICA

"Some small nation in the middle of Africa," Dr. Hei commented to Victory. "Everybody's coming to China these days. And every head-of-state gets the red carpet treatment." Then, with a twinkle in his eye, he added: "For some the carpet gets stretched out longer than for others."

A door now opened at the far side of the study, wide enough for three people to come through together. At that point Victory had his first look at Chairman Mao, the Great Helmsman, the man who had effected more change for more people than any other one living man. He saw two nurses in the uniform of the People's Liberation Army, supporting a flabby old man.

Victory's first reaction was one of pity. He murmured to himself, *Is this the great man?*

Dr. Hei, sensing what was going on in his mind, stepped on his toe and whispered: "Don't react!"

The nurses deposited their burden on a black divan and braced him up as comfortably as they could with a half-dozen pillows. When they were finished, one of them signaled the secretary, who opened another door and ushered Dr. Umubo in. Behind him came three other Africans, one in resplendent military uniform with a great bank of ribbons on his chest.

Following them were two Chinese women in official-looking Mao jackets. "Interpreters," whispered Dr. Hei.

Dr. Umubo said in English: "Your Excellency, it is good of you to grant me and my companions an audience."

The conventionalities of the occasion were soon over, and international politics were dissected from both the African and Chinese point of view. Now and then there was a flash of wit from the Chairman that made Victory think of the many quotations he had read from the great man.

The Prime Minister of Zamialand, however, seemed to prefer personal topics to political. He enquired cordially: "And how is your health these days, Mr. Chairman?"

The Chairman's answer was the biggest surprise of the day to Bright Victory: "There comes a time when all must say goodbye. I am soon going to meet God."

Then the audience came to a close and the four Africans and two interpreters bowed themselves out. The nurses helped the Chairman to stretch out on the black divan for his daily blood-pressure check.

As Victory watched the nurses remove jacket and roll up shirt sleeve, he saw the thin arm of a very elderly person. *How thin!* he thought, and a verse from the Bible came to his mind: "How are the mighty fallen!"

On their way to a taxi stand, Dr. Hei and Bright Victory crossed a small park.

"What was your impression of the Chairman?" asked Dr. Hei, breaking into Victory's thoughts.

"Is he still Chairman?"

"He is. And he will continue to be until the minute he dies."

"And that may not be too many minutes away, medically speaking," commented Victory.

"I'd say three to six months. That's strictly between you and me. After all, he's 83 now."

Victory changed the subject: "One thing I was very surprised at."

"What's that?"

"He said he was soon going to meet God."

"He used the Christian word for God, didn't he, Victory?"

"Yes, he did. I wonder why...."

"He says that same thing to many visitors," Dr. Hei continued. "I've heard him say it a dozen times."

"Why does he say that, when he is one of the world's most renowned atheists?" asked Bright Victory.

"My guess is, there are not many atheists when the undertaker is standing at the door," Dr. Hei replied soberly.

"Excuse me, please. I've been in and out of your gate any number of times in the last few weeks and I've never stopped to pass the time of day with you...."

As Victory spoke, the deep lines in the face of the old gate-keeper softened and gradually flowed into a smile.

Bright Victory went on: "May I ask your honorable name?"

"My unworthy name is Ai. Ai Chengchong. And may I ask your honorable name, sir?"

Smiling, too, Bright Victory replied: "Lee. Bright Victory Lee. I'm a new student here at the hospital."

"Please sit down, Mr. Lee."

"Thank you," Bright Victory said, sitting down on the straight wooden bench at which the gateman waved. He continued: "There's something I've been wondering about. Maybe you could help me."

"What's that?"

"Was this a hospital before Liberation or not?"

"Oh, yes, for many years before Liberation. Why, when I was a boy...." After the old man had rambled through scenes of his childhood, Victory was finally able to pop the question he wanted answered:

"Who operated this hospital before 1949?"

"It was a Christian hospital, sir. American doctors and nurses used to pass through this gate back in those days."

"Hmm. That's interesting," remarked Victory. "Wonder why I haven't heard that before...."

"Yes, it was a Christian hospital," Old Ai said, with a faraway look in his eyes. "But today it's as if a curtain's been pulled down on the past."

"Is there any evidence left in the buildings themselves that it was a Christian hospital?" Victory asked.

"Hmm....They tore the cross down off the steeple, broke the stained-glass windows out of the chapel, and chiseled the name off the stone lintel across the top of the main entrance..."

"But could there be something nearer the ground, not as visible as what you've mentioned, that's still here?"

"Yes, sir, you're right. There is one reminder of the past left. Come with me."

Old Ai led Victory to the near corner of the main building. He got down on his knees and carefully separated some privet hedge that was overgrown with morning glory vines, then took a towel from his belt and rubbed off the moss from a stone set in the corner of the building.

"There you are," he said, as he backed away from the hole in the shrubbery.

It was Victory's turn to get down on his knees, part the

shrubbery and look. The effort was well rewarded.

Victory read aloud the characters cut into the stone:

"This cornerstone was laid
to the glory of God on
May 17, 1908
Jesus Christ Himself being
the chief cornerstone."

The old gatekeeper stood quietly while Victory read. Then he slowly shook his head and said: "That's the past, all right. But today no one knows, no one asks, no one cares."

"Victory, it's beautiful this Sunday morning. There's no church to attend. Let's take the children to the park..."

Once in the park, Virtue took Victory's arm in a way she was not accustomed to do in public; she wanted her words to be for his ear only as she said quietly: "Isn't it strange! We have to get out here in the open before we have the privacy we ought to have in our own home."

"What do you mean?" Victory demanded.

"Our house is so small and so jammed up against the neighbors that they hear everything we say."

"What makes you think that?"

"Because the neighbor next east of us came over yesterday and told me to stop telling the children 'religious myths'. I can only take it that she heard me telling them Bible stories. And I've done that *only inside the house!* She told me that if I didn't stop she would report me to the Neighborhood Street Committee."

As Bright Victory entered the main gate of the hospital, Old Ai the gateman called out: "Mr. Lee! Mr. Lee!"

Victory answered cheerfully: "Old Ai! How are you today?"

"All right, thank you, Mr. Lee... Please sit down a minute."

"Fine. Fine."

Victory sat on the front of the straight wooden bench and leaned forward.

"Something I want to tell you, Mr. Lee."

"Great. What is it?"

"In my 25 years here as gatekeeper, two other people have asked me the same question you asked about these buildings. They both turned out to be Christians. And I was just wondering..."

"And I make the third. Yes, Old Ai, I am a Christian. You guessed right."

"My wife is a Christian. I was thinking — would you like to meet some of the Christians?"

"I certainly would," said Bright Victory enthusiastically.

"I'll bring one of the men to your house next Sunday morning."

"Great! I'll look for you. Thank you, Old Ai... *Zai jian*, see you again."

"*Zai jian*, Mr. Lee."

Bright and clear on Sunday morning, Bright Victory and True Virtue heard a low, modest sound outside their front door:

"*Kai men, kai men* — open the door."

Victory quickly opened the door. There was his friend, Old Ai, with an older man whom Bright Victory recognized vaguely as having to do with hospital accounting.

"This is Old Nie," the gatekeeper introduced.

"Please come in and sit down," Bright Victory said.

The men entered but would not sit down. "We're not staying, Mr. Lee," said Old Ai. "I only wanted Old Nie to meet you and know where you live."

Old Nie spoke up: "I hear you are Christians. From where? How long have you been Christians?"

Bright Victory realized the reason for the questions; he answered them as simply as he could.

Old Nie seemed to pause for thought. Then he asked: "Could you be ready just at dark tonight?"

"We certainly will be. Shall we bring the children? They're four and two."

"It's fine with us, but it might be a little risky for you."

"We've always taken them to meetings."

"Well... good. See you later."

"Thanks for coming, both of you.... See you later."

At dusk Old Nie called softly at the Lees' front door: "*Kai men,* open the door."

Victory opened the door and invited him in. His jacket and trousers were little better than those he wore to work daily at the hospital. However, he wore a new pair of cloth shoes.

Victory and Virtue stepped out into the alley with a feeling of exhilaration — they were attending their first Christian meeting in Beijing...

The meeting was made up of prayer, testimonies, Scripture reading and a short exhortation.

"In the ten years since the beginning of the Cultural Revolution we have had no singing," Elder Nie explained. "Sometimes we hum a hymn so we will remember the tune, but we don't sing the words out loud. Singing carries farther than talking and is more noticeable. Beijing has fewer house meetings than other large cities. Maybe we here are too close to the Central Authorities."

There was real affection and concern in the believers' voices as they said good-night to the Lees: "We're so glad you could come. We'll see you again."

As they approached their own house, Victory and Virtue saw a knot of people gathered in the alley.

"I do believe those people are in front of our house!" exclaimed True Virtue.

The four in the little family slowed their pace, and Victory murmured, "Pray for me."

As they came up to the group Victory said: "Good evening" with a slight nod of acknowledgement, and started to insert the key in the door.

"Just a minute!" one of the men said. "Are you Bright Victory Lee?"

"Yes, I'm Bright Victory Lee," he answered, holding the key in his hand. "And may I know your name, please?"

"You don't need to know my name. All you need to know is that we are a delegation from the Neighborhood Street Committee. The Committee has heard that you tell your children religious myths. This comes under the head of misleading the youth of the country, which is prohibited by the constitution. The telling of religious myths must stop at once. If not, you will be turned over to the police for punishment."

Without a "Goodbye" or a "Good night" the group turned as one man and marched off down the alley. Silently Victory inserted the key in the lock, opened the door and then closed and locked it behind them.

Virtue put her head on Victory's shoulder and wept silently. Geng and Deng each grabbed their father by a knee and began to whimper.

Victory arrived home that afternoon to find Virtue and the children huddled in the kitchen. The fire was crackling away merrily and Virtue was stir-frying cabbage with bits of fat pork, a noisy procedure. At the same time she was telling Geng and Deng the story of the creation.

As Victory came in the kitchen door she was saying: "And if God is so powerful to create the sun and moon and stars and all the animals and plants and fish and birds and people, too, do you think He is powerful enough to protect us here in Beijing?"

She looked up at Victory and smiled: "It's nice and noisy

here in the kitchen, isn't it? You couldn't even tell what we were telling about from the other room, could you?"

Walking to class a few days later, Victory noticed that the radios along the street were all playing dolorous, funeral music. And when he arrived at the hospital he saw members of the staff wearing black arm bands. Old Ai met him just inside the main gate and handed him one.

"Who died?" Victory asked.

"The Chairman. Last night."

Victory went at once to see Dr. Hei. "It's the end of an era," the doctor commented solemnly. "Not just because we won't need to take the Chairman's blood pressure any more..."

At midnight that same night a loud pounding on the door awakened Bright Victory and True Virtue.

"*Kai men! Kai men!* Open the door!"

Victory got up, slipped into his trousers and went to the door asking: "Who's there?"

"The police. Open the door!"

Victory opened it to see two policemen with automatics, plus three members of the Neighborhood Street Committee whom he remembered seeing before in the lane in front of the house.

"Come in," Bright Victory said. "Who are you looking for?"

"Bright Victory Lee. Are you Bright Victory Lee?"

"Yes, I am."

"We request you, Bright Victory Lee, to come to the police station with us," the policeman said politely but firmly.

"May I ask what the charges are?" Bright Victory asked, equally polite.

"No charges. We want to ask you some questions."

"What questions? You may ask them here."

The five men whispered together for a minute or so. Finally one of the policemen said: "Our orders are to take you to the police station to answer questions there."

Five days later Bright Victory's trial was held. He was relieved when they led him to the office of the Neighborhood Street Committee, not to the office of the Garrison Commander. Somehow the surroundings did not seem so stark and threatening as Colonel Chang's military court in Shanghai. For one thing, the spectators had benches, since this was the room where neighborhood meetings were held.

Victory looked around. Sure enough, there were True Virtue, Geng and Deng on the front row. Bright Victory instinctively knew that they had been brought. And on a back seat sat Dr. Hei. *Bless him!* Victory thought. *He's running a risk to be here.*

A caustic female voice shouted: "The court will come to order!" All the people stood up. "The accused, Bright Victory Lee, will step forward!" Victory stepped forward two paces.

"The court presents City of Beijing Vice-Mayor Lei Ren, who will read the charge and question the accused."

A middle-aged woman in civilian jacket and pants stepped out of an inner office, walked to the table in the front of the room and sat down. She told the spectators to sit down then began the questioning:

"Name?"

"Bright Victory Lee."

"Age?"

"Forty."

"Address?"

"Medical School, Sixth Municipal Hospital, City of Beijing."

"Occupation?"

"Medical student."

"Bright Victory Lee, you are accused by the local Neighborhood Street Committee of corrupting the youth of China. Specifically, of corrupting your own under-age children by teaching them religious myths. You have broken a law written into the very constitution of China." After a pause, the Vice-Mayor continued: "The first witness will come forward."

The Lees' next-door neighbor-to-the-east stepped up and began: "I heard them tell about their god miraculously multiplying bread and fish. This is superstition. Such teaching corrupts the youth and is contrary to the beautiful teaching of atheism which every patriotic citizen believes in."

"Second witness."

"I am chairman of the Neighborhood Street Committee. To make sure that the reports I heard were true, I went into the house of their next-door-neighbor-to-the-west. I made a peep hole through the wall into the Lees' kitchen. With my own eyes I saw them telling a tale of how their God created the sun, moon, stars and earth...."

"Wait a minute!" the judge interrupted. "Did you *see* them tell a story or did you *hear* them tell a story?"

"There was so much noise in the kitchen, what with the frying and all, that I could not *hear* them. But I lip-read, so I *saw* them tell the story."

Victory stole a glance at Virtue; she was obviously nonplussed at this unexpected revelation.

The judge asked again: "When you say 'them', what do you mean — him or her or both of them?"

"In actuality I saw *her*, the wife, talking to the children."

"Testimony acknowledged. Sit down."

The judge glanced at some papers in her hands, then continued: "Both husband and wife are guilty of corrupting youth. However, today only the man is on trial. It is the decision of the court not to lay charges against the wife at this time. It is the magnanimity of the government not to imprison both parents at once, thus leaving the children without either parent for support."

The judge turned to Bright Victory: "It would be to your credit to acknowledge the magnanimity and compassion of the government in your case."

Out of the corner of his eye Victory looked at Virtue and the children, there on the front seat. His whole desire was to spare them as much as possible, so he fell in with the party line and said what the judge wanted him to say: "I acknowledge with gratitude to the government that I only am accused of this crime and I want to thank the judge and the Court for their compassion."

Later he was to go over and over those words in his mind, questioning whether or not he had told the truth.

"Bright Victory Lee," continued the judge, "what defense do you make for yourself?"

At that question, Bright Victory felt words welling up from deep within his being, like water from an artesian well.

"The stories I have told my children," he began, "are stories from history, as true as any account of what has happened in the history of China. I'll admit that I believe in an all-powerful, divine Being. The Constitution of our country permits belief in God. I am not the only citizen of China who believes in God. With my own two ears I heard Chairman Mao say more than once, 'I am going to meet God'. How could he say that if he did not believe there is a God? A big difference between Chairman Mao and myself, however, is that the Chairman planned to meet God after death and I have already met Him in life."

As Bright Victory talked, the people in the courtroom stood to their feet one after the other, apparently the better to hear what he was saying. When he finished speaking, it appeared for a moment that the crowd was going to break out in spontaneous applause.

Sensing the feeling in the courtroom the judge hastily

arose, gave an emphatic wave with her two hands and ordered: "Sit down! Sit down!"

The caustic female voice came on again: "The judge will now pronounce the verdict of the court."

The judge, still standing, struck the table with her gavel and shouted: "Order in the courtroom!"

Only after the gavel struck the table a third time did the whispering and talking die down. Then the judge announced: "For insulting the Constitution and for corrupting the youth of.China, Bright Victory Lee is hereby sentenced to two years of Reform through Labor in the pioneer lands of Heilongjiang on the Northeast Frontier."

The next morning True Virtue went to say goodbye to Dr. Hei before she and the children took the train to Datong.

"First thing, True Virtue," he asked, "do you have enough money for travel?"

"Yes, thank you, we have saved enough for an emergency. And when we get back to my parents we'll be all right. But there's one thing I want to ask you, Doctor. Why did the judge try to convince Victory that the government is compassionate and magnanimous? Wasn't she a dreadful hypocrite?"

"Why, no, True Virtue, not from her standpoint. She was merely being logical. She only showed herself a victim of the double-think that is built into the system. They always go to great pains to show how compassionate the government is to those it is so ruthlessly hounding to destruction."

36. The Worm Turns
Manchuria's Northeast Frontier. Autumn 1978

THE GREAT VAT of hot water bubbled and steamed. It was dish-washing time in the kitchen of Harmony Farm Commune near Baolin, the most northeasterly railway station in China, 350 miles beyond Harbin.

Not far east of Harmony Farm, China sticks its dragon snout into the ribs of the Russian bear. When snout tickles ribs, the result is not a chuckle from the bear but a growl and maybe a slap of a claw-armed paw.

But today the on-again-off-again clash between dragon and bear was not the topic of conversation. Rather, the topic was one that always sparks conversation in Chinese society — families and names.

Bright Victory began it. "My name's Lee. Bright Victory Lee," he said to the older man who stepped up to work beside him.

"Well, what d'you know! I'm a Lee, too. My given name's Little Brother. Guess we must be cousins. All Lees are related, aren't they?" The older man laughed and grabbed Victory by the hand, even though it was wet and sloppy.

Victory hesitated a moment, a wet hand not being the politest thing to shake with; when the other Lee insisted, he shook hands heartily. Instinctively, Bright Victory knew he had made a friend.

There followed a long recounting of their respective antecedents. Finally Little Brother changed the subject:

"So, you're on the washing-up detail, are you? How long've you been on?"

"Almost two years," replied Bright Victory. "Ever since I arrived at Harmony Farm Commune."

"Don't you do any field work?"

"No. You see, my major responsibility is the commune clinic..."

"So! You're a doctor, are you!" exclaimed Little Brother.

Bright Victory laughed. "Only in practice, not in name... Though people insist on calling me 'Dr. Lee'. That's a joke." He laughed again and went on scrubbing hard at a big caldron to remove burned-on food.

Again Little Brother Lee changed the subject in the way a man does who is in the habit of dominating the conversation.

"It's hot at this job, even in autumn. Summer must be terrible."

"Right. But in the winter it's the best job on the farm."

Bright Victory felt it was time for him to change the topic of conversation, so he asked: "And what was your work before you were promoted to the Northeast Frontier?"

"I was in government service. In Beijing." Something about the way he lowered his voice hinted that this was a subject better not pursued.

"Yes, this job has its benefits," commented Bright Victory, reverting to the former topic. "But it has its occupational hazards, too. The chief cook insists on keeping his butcher knives razor-sharp, for the sake of his Korean-Chinese friends who borrow them to butcher the deer they kill. Of course, the cook gets a piece of venison out of it. But then he always throws his knives into the vat. Just be careful how you fish them out."

Bright Victory's job at the clinic kept him busy.

"How did this cut happen?" he asked the four men who had carried an injured man in on a stretcher. As he listened, he bathed the damaged foot with warm water and carefully removed the piece of rough blue cloth tied around the foot to stop the bleeding.

"It's that soybean harvester," came the reply. "The

Russian one. It's so cumbersome and dangerous. Give me the American one every time!"

Victory sewed up the cut and gave a shot of tetanus anti-toxin. After sending the patient to his barracks, complete with aspirin and an antibiotic, he went to the bookshelf, found an article on "Lacerations" and settled down to read it.

Victory's elderly predecessor had just died, leaving behind some of the very textbooks that Victory had been studying in Beijing. *And* he had amassed more equipment than one might expect to find out here at the end of the earth — forceps, scissors, scalpels, needles, sutures, drugs and even a micro-scope. Bright Victory memorized as he read, and in his mind went over and over many procedures, just in case ....

"Nong, there's a verse in the Bible you need to clutch to your heart. I need to, too, here in the Northeast so far from home."

"What's that?" asked Victory's friend Nong, looking un-necessarily sceptical, Bright Victory thought.

He went on: "When I was sentenced to the coal mines, this meant a lot to me: 'All things work together for good to those who love God, to those who are the called according to his purpose.'"

Victory leaned back in the one comfortable chair in Elder Yan's house, where the Sunday afternoon meeting had just concluded. He was in a talkative mood.

"You know, Nong, on the train up here in the fall of 1976 I passed through Tangshan, and saw the destruction made by that earthquake that killed three-quarters of a million people. Weeks after the quake, most of the survivors were still living in tents and under makeshift shelters in the streets. The rail-road tracks were still being repaired, and we crept along at five miles an hour.

"Seeing the devastation reminded me of the other earth-quake ten years before that struck southwest Hebei Province so hard. I was attacked by a crazy man there and could have lost my life, but good came out of it. As a direct result of that almost-tragedy I was supplied with medicines and equipment for my clinic in the mines at Datong, and later had the chance to study medicine in Beijing.

"I've had enough formal study to know *how* to study and *what* to study. I come here as an exile to the ends of the earth and what do I find? A medical library that's exactly what I need! As of now I would not hesitate to perform a major operation, if no qualified surgeon were available."

Bright Victory paused for a moment. Nong was still listening.

"So, Nong, don't be discouraged. God is still on the throne and He will not leave us alone. Trust God and take heart."

A broad grin spread across Victory's face. He read the notice again:

"Come to Post Office to pick up parcel."

He put down the medical tome he had been reading and hurried across to the Post Office. As he had anticipated, the return address was:

"Lee
Datong Municipal Health Center
Datong, Shanxi"

Back at the clinic Bright Victory opened the parcel carefully. There they were, his wadded jacket and trousers, completely renovated, he knew, by True Virtue's loving hands, the wadding taken out and re-fluffed, then sewn back between newly-laundered outer shell and inner lining. These he had expected. But there was more: an old tea canister with press-in lid sealed with adhesive tape. Bright Victory's mouth began to water. With a scalpel he made an incision in the tape and with a screwdriver pried up the lid.

A gush of fragrance greeted his nostrils. He sat and looked

and smelled. What a beautiful sight! Green Sichuan pickles coated with ground red pepper, his favorite pickle from the time he was a boy in Chongqing! The interplay of salt, vinegar and red pepper mingled together brought tears to his eyes.

Bright Victory fished with the business end of the scalpel and brought up a small piece to taste right now. Then he replaced the press-in lid, wiped his fingers and turned to more serious business. He held the wadded jacket up to the afternoon sunlight streaming in through the window. Sure enough, a piece of paper was folded longways inside the main seam across the back!

Victory again pressed the scalpel into service and deftly slit the seam, careful not to damage the paper inside. He unfolded the piece of paper. There it was, the first uncensored letter from his wife in months!

Tears in his eyes, he spread it out flat on the table to read:

"My dearest Victory,

You were so clever to send a letter to each of us sewn into the wadding of your jacket! And how cute to write on slips of white bark. You are so original, my dear, dear Victory.

You should know that the brothers and sisters here have covenanted together to pray for your release and for your father and brother to return home. God is able to tear down barriers of Satan...." (the rest was more personal).

"Is there anything else down in the bottom of this ... dish-water?" Little Brother Lee demanded of no one in particular. "If there is I'll find it .... soon!" he went on, and swished his right hand through the water violently in a character-revealing gesture Victory had noticed before.

Suddenly he screamed: "*Aiya!*" and pulled his hand out of the vat. It was streaming with blood.

"Oh!" Victory shouted. "One of those butcher knives again!" He grabbed Little Brother's hand, examined it a moment to see if arteries had been cut, then held it high to retard the bleeding.

"Here! Hold it like this. I'll wrap these clean cloths around it, and then we'll go to the clinic."

Thirty minutes and eight stitches later the hand was bandaged and resting in a sling. Bright Victory gave the patient a shot of tetanus antitoxin and some aspirin. "You go lie down," he told him. "I'll check with you again after I get through washing up."

On the third day after the accident, Little Brother reported to Commune Leader Piao.

"How's your hand?" the Commune Leader asked.

"Not so good," replied Little Brother. "It hurts. I'd like two more days off before I go back to work."

"There's not much work to some of what you do," objected Commune Leader Piao. "Dishwashing, for instance."

"That's one thing I don't want to do."

"Why?"

"Get my hand wet."

"You're lazy, that's all!"

"What if I don't go back to dishwashing?" said Little Brother.

"That's disobeying orders. You'd be flogged."

"Well, I guess I'll have to be flogged. I'm not going back to dishwashing right now. That's final." With that, Little Brother spun around and stomped out.

Fortunately for him, he went direct to the clinic and told Victory what had happened.

"Little Brother, you sit right here and wait till I get back," ordered Victory. "With your hand in the shape it's in, the last thing you need is a flogging."

The upshot of Bright Victory's visit to Commune Leader Piao was that the dishwashing would go on as usual, with or without Little Brother's help. After some grumbling, the commune leader agreed to the compromise. And for ten days

Victory worked two hours longer each night to do Little Brother's work as well as his own.

After the ten days Victory examined the hand and told the patient: "You can do some work around the kitchen, but don't put that hand in water for another five days."

Little Brother Lee was more affected by Victory's sacrificial work than by Commune Leader Piao's threats. "How can I ever repay you, Victory?" he asked. "You saved me from a flogging!"

"No need to repay. Just doing it for you is enough payment in itself."

Little Brother did, however, make the necessary gesture of thanks. He bought twenty extra-large dried persimmons, each with its own sugar oozing to the surface and coating itself as if it had been dusted with confectioner's sugar. These he presented to Victory.

One night the two friends had just finished their dishwashing and put on their jackets. It was late autumn, and cold. As they opened the kitchen door, the wind howling down across the marshes from Siberia caught the door and flung it back at them.

"Going to be cold tonight," Victory said.

"And many a cold night after this one," Little Brother added. "Before long it'll be down to minus 25 degrees Fahrenheit again."

Once in the dormitory, Bright Victory was pulling off his shoes and relishing the prospect of bed. Then a voice called from the far side of the one clear electric bulb in the center of the room:

"Is Dr. Lee here, please?"

"I am Bright Victory Lee," answered Bright Victory. "They call me 'Dr. Lee'."

A young man in his twenties, cap in hand, appeared under the electric bulb.

"Dr. Lee," he said, "my name is Shen Wenbing and I come from Batou Village. I'm sorry to trouble you, sir, but I'm afraid my wife..." his voice quivered. He bit his lip and went on: "My wife's going to die, tonight, if something's not done for her."

Inwardly, Victory groaned. He was dead tired after a twelve-hour day. But he simply said: "Sit down. What's the problem?"

"I can't sit down, sir. I'm so nervous. I.... I'm afraid my wife's going to die."

Victory repeated his question: "What's the problem?"

"Our first baby, sir. My wife's been in labor 24 hours. She can't deliver. The midwives have done all they can, but they can't help anymore."

"How far away is your village?"

"Four miles, sir."

Victory thought to himself: *Now if I were Dr. Hei, I'd first think this through.* After a minute or more of silence, during which time the young man grew more and more fidgety, he said:

"Come with me."

Victory put his shoes on again and his warm jacket and trousers, grabbed his flashlight and the half-dozen remaining dried persimmons from Little Brother's gift, and set out for the clinic, his visitor trailing behind. There he picked up his black bag, shoved it at the young man and said:

"Hold that open for me, please."

He stuffed things into the bag until its sides bulged, half-filled another bag, and finally pulled a medical book off the shelf and looked over a section headed "Obstetrics."

"You carry the bags," Victory said finally. "I'll take the light. And chew on these persimmons as we go along ... Let's go."

As they faced the wind outside, Victory said a secret

"Thank you" to True Virtue for renovating his jacket and trousers. He was only sorry for young Shen who was not dressed as warmly as he.

They finally arrived at Batou Village. Bright Victory was surprised to find that half the houses were underground or semi underground, like those he had seen years before in Shanxi Province. They stopped before the door of such a house. Going in, it took him a couple of minutes to orient himself to the interior, lit as it was by a single pith wick burning in a saucer of rapeseed oil.

"Here is my wife, sir," the young man said, pointing to a girl lying on the *kang*, the brick bed to one side of the room.

"Is your mother here?" Bright Victory asked.

"I am the mother," said a middle-aged woman who appeared out of the shadows.

"Take a large *wok* or caldron and boil up some water, a couple of gallons or more."

"Yes, sir," the woman said, and disappeared into the darkness again.

Then Victory told the young husband: "Go to the neighbors and borrow a half-dozen rapeseed oil lamps."

Only then did he turn his attention to the young woman moaning and groaning on the bed.

"May I ask your name, please?"

"I am Meilin. And you are Doctor...?" Her voice trailed off.

"Doctor Lee." Bright Victory answered. Silently he prayed: *Lord, forgive me for lying about being a doctor.* And then to Meilin again: "I'm sorry you're having a problem. I want you just to relax and you'll be all right. First, I'm going to give you a needle to help you feel more comfortable."

"Thank you, Doctor."

Victory did the routine examination of a woman in labor, timed the frequency of contractions, checked pulse, breathing and blood pressure. Then he gave her meperidine. Before long her breathing became easier and she began to doze between contractions.

The mother came in and reported: "The water's boiling, Doctor."

"Keep it boiling," Victory said.

By this time the husband had returned with six rapeseed lamps, and Victory told him to light them. Then having oriented himself to the family situation, the house and especially the patient, he paused a moment and prayed: *Oh, Lord, show me what is the right decision to make.*"

"Is it all right with you if I operate and deliver the baby that way?" he asked the young husband.

The husband was taken aback. An operation had apparently not occurred to him. He consulted earnestly with his mother and father, and asked: "Will it hurt her?"

"No. She will be asleep. She won't feel a thing."

"Then go ahead."

That night Bright Victory performed his first operation, a Caesarean section. He handed a healthy baby boy to the astounded father. The baby weighed seven pounds, six ounces, and they named him Bright Victory after Dr. Bright Victory Lee.

Victory spent the rest of the night checking his patient as she came out from under the ether. It was as well he had something to do; he suddenly realized that this, his first major operation, had keyed him up considerably. Over and over he checked blood pressure, pulse, respiration, skin color.

Testing her alertness, he called her name from time to time, "Meilin! Meilin!"

Finally there was an answer: "Who're you?"

The family invited Victory to breakfast. The table was set out with millet gruel and great hunks of steamed bread bought on the street, Bright Victory suspected, for his benefit.

When they had sat down at the table, Father Shen said: You'll excuse us, will you, please, while we say thanks?" And he offered a Christian prayer.

"Thank you," said Victory. "You did exactly what I would do in my own home. I'm a Christian, too."

Tears flowed and there were handshakes all around as brothers in the faith discovered each other.

"You know," the mother said, "it's not surprising that God sent us a Christian doctor. Yesterday afternoon we prayed that God would send us the best doctor in the Northeast, and He did just that!"

"Thank you," Bright Victory said," but I must be honest with you and say that I am not a graduate doctor. Actually I'm a medical student."

"We're not going to worry about the formalities of degrees and that sort of thing," smiled the father. "We still say that God answered prayer and sent us the best doctor in the Northeast!"

Victory took some time to check out both mother and baby and to leave instructions for the day; it was mid-morning before he got away from the Shen home.

"I'll go with you," young Shen proposed. "You might not find your way. It's snowing outside, you know."

Sure enough, when they stepped outside Bright Victory discovered that the earth was dusted with the first snowfall of winter.

Young Shen picked up Victory's two bags plus another bag he had not seen before.

"Here are a few local apples," Mrs. Shen senior explained. "We hope you like them. Thank you again for coming and helping us."

Victory peeked into the bag. The apples were the largest and reddest he had ever seen.

It was almost noon when they arrived back at Harmony

Farm Commune, and Victory went direct to the clinic. On his desk lay a large envelope, marked — "From Little Brother Lee... Personal. To be opened by Dr. Lee only."

Turning it over, Victory discovered that the back was sealed with red ink stamped with the two characters, "Cun Ming".

Who in the world is 'Cun Ming'? Victory asked himself. He ripped open the envelope and spread the letter out on the table. It read:

"Dear Bright Victory,

At daybreak this morning I received a telegram from Deng Xiaoping ordering me to return to Beijing.

Harmony Farm was the third and last place of my rustication.

My real name is Cun Ming. My mother's name was Lee, so we are still cousins. Little Brother was my baby name.

I'll never forget your help. You saved me from a flogging
                    Your friend and cousin, Little Brother"

Victory read the letter through three times before he could take it in.

Cun Ming! he thought. *A member of the Politburo before! One of the twenty-five men who rule China — yet he was degraded to dishwasher!*

He folded the letter and slipped it into his inside jacket pocket. Then he looked at the clock. Exactly 12 noon.

Hmm! The express leaves at 12.30. If I walk fast ....

Out through the snow Bright Victory plowed again, walking fast, throwing snow in all directions. When he saw the train was still standing in the station, he broke into a run. It flashed across his mind: *Look in the soft berth car first.* And sure enough, there was Little Brother, sitting at a window.

Seeing Victory running up, Little Brother raised the window, and asked: "How was your trip last night?"

"Fine. Baby boy. Caesarean section. My first big operation."

"Congratulations!"

Just then the train whistle blasted. "And congratulations to you, ah ... erh... Little Brother."

"Just call me Little Brother." He grabbed Bright Victory by the hand, as he had that night they first met.

"Victory," he said, "the worm has turned. And I'm going to see that things change for you, too."

"No need to think of that. It was just nice working along-side you."

The train whistled again. The conductor shouted: "All aboard!"

"I'll remember you, Victory! See you again!"

"See you again," Victory answered.

The locomotive chuffed, and chuffed again. Slowly the train pulled out of the station.

Victory stood on the platform and watched black cars, black smoke and white steam as the train swung around a curve and picked up speed on the straight tracks across the snow-covered tundra of the North-east Frontier. He watched until the train was a black dot on a white horizon. Then it disappeared.

He turned his back on the station and trudged slowly through the snow back to Harmony Farm Commune.

The next morning Victory ate breakfast in the messhall by candlelight. Before the sun broke the level white horizon and rose out of Siberia to the east, he was on the way to Batou Village to check mother and child. This time he carried his own black bag.

When Victory arrived, he found Meilin contentedly nursing her baby. He gazed at the scene with almost as much satisfaction as he had experienced when he first saw True Virtue nursing Geng six years before.

"Any problems?" he asked Meilin.

"Just a little pain. Kept me awake last night."

"I'll give you something for that." Victory sat down, glad to rest after sloshing through four miles of snow.

Sitting there and listening to the Shen family talking among themselves, something suddenly struck him. He asked:

"Am I mistaken, or do I hear some Shanghai words mixed in with the Beijing dialect?"

They all laughed. Mr. Shen senior replied: "It wouldn't be surprising if you hear Shanghai words. We're all from Shanghai, even my daughter-in-law."

Victory dropped into colloquial Shanghai and said: "And you're talking to someone else from Shanghai, too!"

There was laughter all around at the sudden burst of Shanghai dialect on the Siberian border.

"What year did you come up here?" Victory asked.

"We're old-timers on the North-east Frontier," answered the father. "Came up here in the fifties. My wife and I are both music teachers by profession but we were called 'rightists'. We were ordered to leave Shanghai along with ten others from our college. Had to buy our own tickets to this wilderness, as it was then. We were told it was two years, but it has stretched out to twenty.

"We were ordered to clear the wilderness and cultivate the virgin soil. We worked at it, but almost froze to death in the attempt. As you know, nobody in Shanghai has clothing for this kind of climate. In the mercy of God they opened a primary school and put me in as teacher.

"All this time we have had our Bible, and we read it together every morning before breakfast. It's the one thing that has kept us sane all these years ..."

Once wound up, the father would have gone on and on, but Victory interrupted: "I'm sorry. I'll have to get back to the clinic now. But we'll talk later and compare notes on the mercies of the Lord."

Two weeks later Bright Victory received a telegram. It was

terse and to the point:

"Report to me
personally in Beijing
(signed) Cun Ming
Chairman
Commission on Rehabilitation"

Victory put the telegram back into its envelope and shoved it into his inside jacket pocket. As he did so, he felt another envelope in the pocket and pulled it out. It was the letter from Little Brother Lee that he had found on his desk that snowy morning.

Victory locked the clinic door behind him and went to report the news at once to Commune Leader Piao. The commune leader's reaction was cynical.

"What kind of game's this?" he asked. "Who've you got, concocting telegrams for you in Beijing?"

Victory felt the back of his neck getting red with anger. But he managed to keep the anger out of his voice as he replied: "Do you remember a telegram that came from Deng Xiaoping two weeks ago to Little Brother Lee?"

Now it was Commune Leader Piao's turn to get angry. He sputtered: "What do you know about a telegram from Deng Xiaoping?"

"I know that after getting that telegram, Little Brother Lee left at once for Beijing."

"How did you know that?"

Victory took Little Brother's letter out of its envelope, opened it out and showed it to the commune leader. His reaction was a mixture of anger and befuddlement: "What! Not *the* Cun Ming who was in the Politburo before! You're joking!"

"No, I'm not joking," Bright Victory said. He showed him the envelope. On the front was: "From Little Brother Lee.... Personal. To be opened by Dr. Lee only." And on the back of the same envelope was the seal in red ink with the characters, "Cun Ming".

The commune leader read the characters on the front. Then he turned the envelope over and looked long at the seal on the back. Slowly the blood drained from his face and he turned the color of ashes.

"Cun Ming! *The* Cun Ming! I only knew him as Little Brother Lee! And now he's back in the saddle again! Why ... why I almost had him flogged! What would happen to me now if ..."

The commune leader's voice trailed off into oblivion. Bright Victory thought he was going to collapse in a faint, but he got control of himself again and went on:

"Bright Victory! You kept me from flogging him. Why did you do that? Did ...." Piao looked at Victory suspiciously. "Did you know that Little Brother Lee was really Cun Ming of the old Politburo?"

Bright Victory felt like laughing out loud. But he controlled his laugh and reduced it to a smile. "No, Comrade Piao. Not the slightest idea. To me, Little Brother Lee was just another dishwasher."

Victory paid a final visit to the Shen family, checking Meilin's incision and little Victory's navel. Then the Shens gathered around and they prayed for each other, committing each other to the Lord.

Before Victory left, Mrs. Shen senior thrust a square box into his hands. "These are for your wife and children," she said.

"Thank you," Bright Victory said. He opened the box. Inside were twenty big red apples.

As anxious as Bright Victory was to leave the North-east Frontier and return home, he could not find it in him simply to catch the next express train to Harbin as Little Brother had done. There were patients to see for the last time, and there must be a last time of worship at the home of Elder Yan.

The elder gave his appraisal of the situation: "Things should improve for everybody now, with practical people in power instead of the doctrinaire dreamers of the past."

Victory thought for a minute, then said: "God has ultimate power. The power of man is here today, gone tomorrow. Look at Peng Dehuai, Lin Biao, Liu Shaoqi — all top-notchers, all cut down. The man who cut them down, Mao Zedong, is himself dead and gone. Those who tried to step into his shoes, The Gang of Four, are all in jail awaiting trial for high treason. How does the old saying go, "Adversity cements friends together, prosperity breaks them apart.""

"Your friendship in adversity with Little Brother Lee has turned out for your good," Elder Yan added. "For you, too, the worm has turned."

"Yes," said Bright Victory, "I'm grateful to Little Brother. But I can't forget that

'God is in the shadows
Watching o'er His own'."

PART VII

SHANGHAI
1979

37. A Family Reunion
Shanghai, Spring 1979

"THE LAST TIME I was on this wharf," Jade Moon said, "was when our family arrived from Chongqing in 1952. And now I still have all of you children plus four grandchildren, *and* your father is coming home today!"

"Yes!" Lotus Flower said, all excited. "And won't he be surprised to see Hua and Bing!"

She picked up Bing, a chunky three year old, took his finger and pointed with it at the steamer slowly bucking its way up the Huangpu River against the outgoing tide.

"See that boat, Bing? Your Grandpa is on that boat. And your Uncle Victory."

Bing dropped his pacifier on the wharf, then leaned over and looked at it.

"Hua," said Strong Hero, "look at the boat! See if you can see Grandpa!"

Hero set Hua, now five, up on his shoulders, but she was more interested in the people milling around close at hand than in anyone away out there on the river.

"I had such a hard time recognizing your father when I went to Hainan Island," remembered Jade Moon. "I could only tell him by his walk.... But later I saw beneath the lines on his face that it really was your father."

Lotus asked: "He's 66 now, isn't he? Do you think I'll recognize him after 22 years?"

"It should be better this time. Victory's with him. Just think — his rehabilitation was so slow that finally Victory had to take the orders from Beijing and go to Hainan Island in person. And he stopped by Anhui and got your brother Loyalty's papers in order ..." Tears came to Jade Moon's eyes, and a catch in her throat kept her from saying more. The others were silent.

Jade Moon cleared her throat and went on: "It's that technicality of transferring a Residence Certificate! Never mind, we'll see Loyalty and his wife in a few days." She brushed the tears away, as if she were brushing away the accumulated problems of a lifetime.

The steamer was getting closer and the black glob on deck began to resolve itself into individual people. All who could, stood at the rail; others banked up behind them. All were trying to identify familiar faces on the wharf.

"I see Bright Victory!" Lotus broke out. "But who's that old man beside him, all stooped over and with white hair?" Then she caught herself: "Oh, that's Papa!"

It seemed an age before they came down the gangplank. But finally they saw father and son making their way slowly down, Victory with rattan suitcase in one hand and a bedding bundle plus two mesh bags and a black plastic bag in the other. Noble Heart trailed behind with one hand on Victory's shoulder, the other on the gangplank guard rail.

Lotus Flower embraced her father, held him close and wept on his shoulder. A single tear slid down each of his cheeks. Then Lotus turned him loose, grabbed Victory and wept on his shoulder, too.

Noble Heart turned to Jade Moon. He took her right hand in his and said simply: "I'm glad to see your face again."

Having had her cry, Lotus was now in control of herself. She introduced: "Papa ... this is Strong Hero. And these are our children, Hua and Bing ... Victory, you haven't seen Hua and Bing either."

Victory was expressive. He hugged his mother and Lotus, shook hands warmly with Strong Hero, and lifted Hua and then Bing into his arms.

Noble Heart seemed in a daze, not quite sure what to do

next. Finally he said to Jade Moon: "We've brought some pineapples and bananas from Hainan for you."

Three days later came another special occasion. True Virtue, Geng and Deng were due by morning train from North China.

"Dr. Hei applied for back-pay for me as 'a medical student unjustly imprisoned under the Gang of Four'," Bright Victory explained to his mother. "I was paid $2,000. Otherwise we could not travel like this."

Before leaving to meet his wife and children, Victory stuck two bananas into his pockets. They were flecked with brown, just right to eat. Hero and the children went with Victory to the station. The meeting turned out to be noisier and less sad than the one on the wharf. There was, however, one minor hitch.

After introductions all around Victory pulled the two bananas out of his pocket and gave one to Geng and one to Deng.

Geng asked: "What's this for?"

"You eat it, Geng. Here, I'll peel it."

Victory peeled the banana halfway down and handed it back to her. With the peeling flopping down over her little hand she took it somewhat uncertainly.

"Go ahead," he said. "Eat it."

Geng took a bite and held it in her mouth a moment. Then she spat it out on the ground and threw the rest into the gutter.

"I don't like it," she said.

The same afternoon Victory and Hero crowded onto an electric trolley car again and went back to the station to meet Bright Loyalty and Hanah.

They paid ten cents each for a platform ticket, and stood to one side waiting to hear over the loudspeaker which track the train was coming in on.

"The trouble was," Bright Victory was explaining, "that

even though Loyalty's prison term was completed in November, 1976, he couldn't get his Residence Certificate transferred from Anhui back to Shanghai. It was only after I examined the case as a special representative of the Commission on Rehabilitation, that a telegram was sent from Beijing ordering the Anhui authorities to allow him to return to Shanghai. Fortunately he was already married by then — Hanah waited six years for him — and her name was included as well in the directive."

Just then the loudspeaker squawked: "Express from Nanjing arriving on Track 9."

Victory and Hero dashed to the gate, surrendered their platform tickets, and headed for Track 9 just as the gleaming blue-and-gold diesel-electric locomotive eased to a halt.

Hearty greetings, followed by "Let me carry this" and "I'll take that" masked the deeper feelings of the occasion. For all except Hanah. Arriving back in her native Shanghai after eight years of exile in the interior was for her a deeply emotional experience. She sobbed unashamedly.

Two trains bringing five loved ones united the Lee family for the first time in 22 years. Nature itself seemed to rejoice with them; it was unusually balmy for Shanghai in April.

While Victory and Hero had been meeting Loyalty and Hanah, the others were busy at home. They set up a borrowed table — a round one large enough for twelve people — in the rear courtyard, then pitched in to prepare the feast of welcome.

Sitting around the courtyard later, Loyalty was catching up on Shanghai news.

"I see that you and Lotus are living in The Demon's old apartment," he said to Hero. "What happened to her?"

"You remember that injury she had — broke her leg when she fell from that ladder up there?" Hero pointed to a piece of iron, still thrusting out rustily from the wall of the house.

"Right. I remember."

"Well, that same leg developed cancer of the bone. She's in the Hospital for Incurables. She's allowed out for the day now and then but she doesn't get around very well."

"And old Pastor Bao and his wife and Big Sister, and Grandfather Lee and Grandpa and Grandma Song — what's happened to all the old folks?"

"They've all passed away, Loyalty. That means that Mama and Papa are the old generation now, and you and I are the middle-aged people. Hard to imagine, isn't it? And here we have four youngsters growing up of another generation."

"Yes, and Hanah's expecting. That'll make five."

Just then there was a hustle and bustle at the doorway. Jade Moon, Virtue, Lotus and Hanah began to bring out the food from the kitchen.

First came a huge pot of rice. Then dishes of crab, shrimp, fish, oysters and pork, all done up Shanghai style with just enough vegetables and pickles mixed in each dish to add color and flavor. The table looked beautiful, with twelve bowls, twelve pairs of chopsticks, twelve tea cups, tiny saucers for soy and pepper sauce, with all the dishes of food steaming in the middle of the table and the great pot of rice over to one side on its own small table.

"Before we eat," Jade Moon said, "we should remember those who have meant so much to us in the past and whose memories mean so much to us now — old Pastor Bao and his wife, Big Sister, Grandpa and Grandma Lee, Grandpa and Grandma Song, as well as loved ones and friends in Chongqing, Hainan Island, North China, the Northeast and Anhui Province. We'll have a minute of silence as we remember them. After that, Victory will express our thanks to God for His protecting mercies and for bringing us all together again."

At the end of the minute of silence there were only four pairs of dry eyes — those of the four children. Their eyes were wide open, admiring the food in front of them and wondering why they couldn't pitch into it.

Then Bright Victory led the family in thanking God for His mercies and faithfulness, and especially for bringing the twelve together in this family reunion. At first the children closed their eyes for the prayer; this was a more understandable procedure than mere silence. But as Victory prayed long, one small eye after another opened to admire the beautiful food on the table before them.

The prayer finished and the "Amens" all said, there was much gesticulating of chopsticks as everybody urged everybody else to dig into the food — which was precisely what everybody wanted to do anyway.

After everyone had eaten to the full, they sat sipping green Chinese tea and letting their digestive processes do their destined duty. Peace, quietness, an appreciation of each other's company and the deep pleasure of a united family — this was the picture at the close of the meal.

Suddenly there was a commotion at the door. A crutch thrust itself out into the courtyard, tapped and clattered for a moment, then was followed by a heaving body, another crutch and — finally — by a young man in army uniform, very tanned and very thin.

"The Demon!" Jade Moon exclaimed under her breath.

The Demon limped out into the courtyard, not seeing at first that a dozen people were sitting around a single large table.

"Jade Moon Lee!" she exclaimed. "What's going on here? Who *are* all these people?"

"Well, you know several of them: My husband Noble Heart. Our sons, Bright Victory and Bright Loyalty. And their wives. And Lotus Flower and her husband Strong Hero ..."

The Demon was dumbfounded: "Noble Heart, I thought

you were done for on Hainan! Bright Victory, didn't you die in the coal mines? Bright Loyalty, weren't you in jail for the rest of your life?"

"Are you surprised to see us all alive?" Jade Moon asked. "Here are my daughters-in-law, Bright Victory's wife True Virtue and Bright Loyalty's wife Hanah. And Bright Victory's children, who arrived today from the North..."

"So! This is what you have to show for faith in your God!" There was no hint of cynicism in The Demon's voice but rather surprise and awe.

No one answered her. It was a very quiet moment.

Finally, The Demon went on: "This is my nephew Ding. I brought him here to show how it happened to me. My life is near its end, and he should know ..."

She turned to her nephew: "Ding, see that piece of iron sticking out of the wall up there? That's where the ladder broke and let me fall to the ground — right there at that spot — and broke my leg. Now I've got cancer of the bone. The doctor says I may live six months, maybe less ..."

The Demon twisted on her crutches and faced the Lee family:

"Since I'll soon be dead, I want to let you in on a thing or two. You never knew that Colonel Chang was my brother, did you? Well, he was — my younger brother. Don't you remember, Jade Moon, that you saw him once just after you arrived back, when he was directing morning exercises out in front of the house? He always did like to boss people around! Why didn't you guess then that he had come to visit me, his sister?"

She stopped for breath, then went on: "And that ladder, whose idea was it? And who paid for it but Colonel Chang? He didn't know it would be the death of me! And who do you think managed to have Bright Loyalty sent down to the country to Wuhu except me, to the very city where Colonel Chang was Garrison Commander? And who put Colonel

Chang on the same ship Bright Loyalty was travelling on to Wuhu except me?

"And now my brother is dead. He died an honorable but a strange death, fighting the enemy. My nephew is just back from the Vietnam Front. He'll tell you what happened." She was in tears, and motioned to the young soldier to speak.

"Good afternoon." the soldier began, very formally. "My name is Chang Ding, the nephew of Colonel Chang. I am a sergeant in the People's Liberation Army, lately assigned to the staff of Colonel Chang on the Vietnam Front.

"Colonel Chang was in charge of the offensive in the Dong Dang area. We advanced slowly, though we outnumbered the enemy two to one. Colonel Chang was angry and impatient. He used to harangue the troops and say, 'You are afraid of those little Vietnamese'.

"One night he decided he would show us what real bravery was. He picked six of us including me, and told us we were to volunteer for a dangerous mission. I could see that he was very proud and that he had pushed himself into a corner.

"We all took hand grenades and 45 automatics for close-in fighting. About midnight we crept over to the Vietnamese lines — bunkers, really, as they had a series of outposts and other bunkers behind. We crept past an outpost without being seen, then circled and came up to the rear of this bunker with a half-door and a candle burning inside. It was perfect for a hand grenade attack. We could hear a half-dozen men chatting inside.

"Colonel Chang whispered. 'I'll take care of those ... snakeheads!'

"Those were the last words he uttered on earth. He crept up twenty paces or so. I saw him silhouetted against the light from the bunker door. He drew back his arm and threw the grenade.

"At that exact instant a barrel-chested Vietnamese, big and fat like a Japanese judo wrestler, stood up in the opening above the half-door. Maybe he heard a noise outside and wanted to see what it was. Well, the grenade hit him in the middle of his chest and bounced back as if it had hit a drum.

"It landed on the ground right in front of Colonel Chang, and went off. Must have blown him into a hundred pieces.

"The rest of us belly-crawled out of there as fast as we could. Whatever happened to Colonel Chang's remains, I don't know. That was the strange death of a great soldier."

The young soldier made a half-bow and sat down stiffly. As if in deference to the dead, no one made a sound, not even the children.

During her nephew's account of her brother's death, The Demon had been sitting in a chair provided by Bright Victory. Now her crutches rattled together, then separated, and she struggled to her feet.

She cleared her throat and said: "I know what you call me — 'The Demon'. Well, that's the right name for me, because I've had a devil living in me all these years, a devil of hate ... I don't know why I've hated you and your family so much, Jade Moon, but I have. I ... I ... I wish I could live my life over again. It would be different." Her voice broke. She hesitated, then stopped.

Jade Moon stepped over and put her arm around The Demon's shoulders. The Demon turned, laid her head on Jade Moon's shoulder and wept.

Epilogue

AFTER THE LEE FAMILY REUNION IN SHANGHAI, Victory, Virtue and their children returned to Beijing where Victory took up medical studies again and graduated with an MD in the spring of 1982. He is currently a leader in the house church movement in Beijing.

Noble Heart gradually reoriented himself to life in Shanghai. By the fall of 1979 he was ready to get back to his old craft of writing. But the paths he had trodden over the past thirty years had left such marks on his soul that he did not dare enter the secular writing arena again. It was too risky for a gray-haired man. Instead he turned to writing hymns, particularly to paraphrasing Scripture.

Jade Moon's youthful training in music surged up from the subconscious and she has set many of Noble Heart's poems to old Chinese tunes. Some of these appeared in the new hymnbook called *Four Hundred Hymns*, especially published in Hong Kong for the use of the burgeoning house churches on the mainland.

Since the demise of Chairman Mao and the collapse of the Gang of Four in 1976, and particularly since the ascendancy of the pragmatists with Deng Xiaoping in 1978, the house church movement has grown by leaps and bounds. Some say that the number of Christians in China may have reached fifty million by 1984, a fifty-fold growth since the New China was founded in 1949.

Loyalty and Hanah were assigned the room left vacant by Big Sister's death shortly before the Lee family reunion. By the good offices of his old friend Mighty Tower Gou, Bright Loyalty was reinstated at the Golden Streams Weaving Factory, in time to install new looms purchased in Japan as part of the Four Modernizations Program. Hanah was placed as clerk in the Weaving Factory office.

By 1983 Strong Hero Liang had risen to Foreman at the Sunrise Starter Motor Company, and Lotus to supervisor in the clothing factory. Under the current pragmatic leadership in China, a worker's expertise in his particular field is taken into consideration in promotion; promotion is not based solely on political orthodoxy.

Both these couples are grateful to God that none of them has been assigned to jobs at a distance from Shanghai, a practice which they have seen over and over again separate husband from wife, wife from husband and parents from children.

Jade Moon retired from the Vegetable Distribution Center in 1979 at the age of 63, to take care of her three grandchildren while their parents worked. The extended family living under the same roof made this convenient. She often remarks that the present arrangement helps repay the family for the long years of separation.

In 1979 a handful of Shanghai church buildings were resurrected from their use as warehouses, theaters, factories and schools and were returned by the government to the Christians. With great rejoicing the believers gathered again in their own buildings and worshiped and sang and prayed together openly.

It was not long, however, before political emphasis trickled into the sermons and — at least for Noble Heart and Jade Moon — vitiated an otherwise spiritual message. With considerable regret the Lee family gradually withdrew from the open church operated by the government-sponsored Three-Self Patriotic Movement, and began to share fellowship only with groups meeting in private houses.

Noble Heart discovered that the pastors of the Three-Self churches were paid largely from government sources; he was not surprised that since they were beating a government drum they often beat a government tune.

But that is another story; it will have to be told some other time and place.

MORE BOOKS ABOUT CHINA FROM OMF

CHINA — THE CHURCH'S LONG MARCH
David Adeney
Covering a similar period to GOLD FEARS NO FIRE, this
book presents in a factual yet readable form the developments in
China which have affected the church, majoring on changes
since the death of Mao Zedong.
(Joint publication with Regal Books, USA)

WINDS OF CHANGE IN CHINA
Lesley Francis
A succinct introduction to modern China, written especially for
Christians thinking of working there and those who support
them.

BIOGRAPHY OF JAMES HUDSON TAYLOR
Dr & Mrs Howard Taylor
Classic biography of this pioneer missionary to China, who
founded the China Inland Mission.
(Joint publication with Hodder & Stoughton, UK)

HUDSON TAYLOR AND CHINA'S OPEN CENTURY
A J Broomhall
The six-volume definitive history, using much previously
unpublished material.
(Joint publication with Hodder & Stoughton, UK)

NEW SPRING IN CHINA
Leslie Lyall

An attempt at an honest appraisal of Communist China from a Christian point of view.
(*Joint publication with Hodder & Stoughton, UK*)

MOUNTAIN RAIN
Eileen Crossman

Biography of James O Fraser, missionary to the Lisu of Yunnan Province, written by his daughter.

J Hudson Taylor
A MAN IN CHRIST
Roger Steer

"Few men have been used to touch China for God as Hudson Taylor was ... The principles of simple lifestyle, well-reasoned obedience, confident prayer and patient endurance so clearly described in this story compel us to examine afresh what it means to be a man in Christ. I am delighted that this book is being published."

Billy Graham

"I predict that 1990 will see no book published anywhere that can do us more good than this one."

James Packer, Regent College, Vancouver